# Ethnic Community Builders

## Mexican Americans in Search of Justice and Power

*The Struggle for Citizenship Rights in San José, California*

FRANCISCO JIMÉNEZ,
ALMA M. GARCÍA,
AND RICHARD A. GARCIA

## ALTAMIRA
P R E S S

A Division of
ROWMAN & LITTLEFIELD PUBLISHERS, INC.
*Lanham • New York • Toronto • Plymouth, UK*

ALTAMIRA PRESS
A division of Rowman & Littlefield Publishers, Inc.
A wholly owned subsidary of The Rowman & Littlefield Publishing Group, Inc.
4501 Forbes Boulevard, Suite 200, Lanham, MD 20706
www.altamirapress.com

Estover Road, Plymouth PL6 7PY, United Kingdom

British Library Cataloguing in Publication Information Available

Library of Congress Cataloging-in-Publication Data

Ethnic community builders : Mexican Americans in search of justice and power : the struggle
for citizenship rights in San José, California / by Francisco Jiménez, Alma M. García, and
Richard A. Garcia.
     p. cm.
  Includes bibliographical references and index.
  ISBN-13: 978-0-7591-1100-4 (cloth : alk. paper)
  ISBN-10: 0-7591-1100-6 (cloth : alk. paper)
  ISBN-13: 978-0-7591-1101-1 (pbk. : alk. paper)
  ISBN-10: 0-7591-1101-4 (pbk. : alk. paper)
  1. Mexican Americans—California—San Jose—Politics and government. 2. Mexican
Americans—California—San Jose—Social conditions. 3. Mexican Americans—California—
San Jose—Interviews. 4. Political activists—California—San Jose—Interviews. 5.
Interviews—California—San Jose. 6. Oral history. 7. Citizenship—California—San Jose. 8.
Community life—California—San Jose. 9. San Jose (Calif.)—Ethnic relations. 10. San Jose
(Calif.)—Biography. I. Jiménez, Francisco, 1943– II. García, Alma M. III. Garcia, Richard
A., 1941–
  F869.S394E86 2007
  979.4'74004682073--dc22

                                                            2007009081

Printed in the United States of America

∞™ The paper used in this publication meets the minimum requirements of American
National Standard for Information Sciences—Permanence of Paper for Printed Library
Materials, ANSI/NISO Z39.48-1992.

# Contents

# Acknowledgments

We wish to acknowledge our debt to the many individuals who assisted us with the preparation of this work. We wish to thank the fourteen "community builders" for sharing their lives with us so candidly and for inspiring us by their commitment, struggles, and contributions to social justice. Special thanks to Don Dodson, vice provost for academic affairs, and Diane Jonte-Pace, associate provost for faculty development, for their support and encouragement; Jeff Paul, Cultural Heritage Center, San José State University, for providing us access to the library's archives and for allowing us to use parts of previous interviews with Ernestina García, Sofía Mendoza, and Adrian Vargas; Howard University Moorland-Spingarn Research Center's Ralph J. Bunche Oral History Collection for the use of an interview with Sofía Mendoza (RJB 322); Cherrie Potts for assisting us in transcribing the interviews; and Christina Dolores, Amparo Cid, and Elisa Tejeda, our Santa Clara University undergraduate research assistants, for their invaluable help, enthusiasm, and dedication to this project.

In addition, we wish to thank Santa Clara University for granting us two Presidential Research Grants to undertake this oral history project.

# Introduction

*Ethnic Community Builders: Mexican Americans in Search of Justice and Power* is an anthology of oral narratives of fourteen Mexican Americans who chose to be "community builders" in San José, California, from the 1960s through 2000, a period of social change, social tensions, and community mobilization.

These Mexican American community builders found their work central to their lives and part of their responsibility to help their community. These were individuals who sought to fulfill the promise of their individual and collective lives by building within their communities a consciousness of social justice, a desire for freedom of action and for the basic American rights inherent in citizenship. These are the stories of community builders whose activism in pursuit of social justice shaped the development of the Mexican American community of San José, California, between 1960 and 2000.

In these self-reflective testimonies, they analytically discuss the conditions, reasons, and circumstances that shaped their lives. They reflect on their childhood experiences and desires; they share their moments of triumph and pathos; above all they guide us through the labyrinth of their thoughts, emotions, and causality of their lives of commitment to themselves and their community. These life stories are not only narratives of striving for community power, reforming politics, influencing policy, rethinking their perspectives toward American culture and society, but also testimonies of their public and personal experiences living in a society that often treated them as second-class citizens. Since childhood, these Mexican American community builders became aware of themselves as somehow "different" due to their ethnicity, social class, and, in the case of women, gender. It is from within this "space of difference" in each of them that their individual searches and quest for obtaining citizenship rights both for themselves and their communities begin. Like other ethnic communities, they understood that the key to obtaining justice, power, and citizenship rights involved organizing and mobilizing their communities. They made a hopeful and firm commitment to triumph in their struggles for equality and secure a place for their Mexican American communities where the pernicious effects of discrimination and prejudice could be if not vanquished, then attenuated.

## THE SETTING: AN UNFOLDING MEXICAN AMERICAN COMMUNITY

San José, California, experienced major socio-political, cultural, and economic transformations during the forty-year period between 1960 and 2000. Key demographic changes contributed to the emergence of a network of individuals linked through intersecting sets of personal relationships and community activism within the city's Mexican immigrant and Mexican American community. These socio-economic changes led to the galvanization of a group of ethnic community builders who dedicated their lives to the pursuit of social justice.

San José's Hispanic population increased significantly during this same period. The U.S. Census only began collecting data on the Hispanic population, an umbrella category made up of all people of Latin American and Spanish origins, in 1970, making it difficult to obtain counts of Hispanics in prior decades. Census figures since 1970, however, show a dramatic growth in the city's Hispanic population. In 1970, the total number of Hispanics stood at just 55,189, but it grew to 140,000 in 1980, a 153 percent increase. By 1990, it reached 204,012, a 46 percent increase from the previous decade. The population increased by 32 percent over the next ten years, reaching 269,989 in 2000.[1] Though San José's total population has grown dramatically over the same period, the city's Hispanics make up an increasing percentage of all residents. As a proportion of San José's total population, the Hispanic population increased from 12 percent in 1970, to 22 percent in 1980, to 27 percent in 1990, and to 30 percent in 2000. Within the larger Hispanic population in San José, people of Mexican origin make up 82 percent.[2]

Constant influxes of Mexican immigrants and high birth rates among immigrants and U.S. Mexicans account for much of this demographic shift. The immigration reforms in the early 1960s led to increased immigration because of the removal of pre-existing quotas on immigration from areas outside Europe. With its proximity to Mexico, California, especially San José, became a magnet for a new wave of immigration. San José's foreign-born population increased dramatically from 1960 to 2000. By 2000, it grew to 37 percent, exceeding the national figure of 10 percent and California's foreign-born population of 26 percent.[3] Along with this population growth, the city of San José also experienced an increase in its ethnic makeup, making it one of the most ethnically and culturally diverse cities in the country. This diversity enriched the community, but it also produced tensions in politics, education, and culture. There were marked socioeconomic differences between the general, mainstream population and the Mexican community, which was concentrated primarily in the city's East Side.

## FROM THE VALLEY OF HEART'S DELIGHT TO SILICON VALLEY

San José experienced a radical transformation in its labor force and type of industrial development between 1960 and 2000. Previously known as the agricultural "Valley of Heart's Delight," the greater San José community emerged as "Silicon Valley." The fruit industry declined as the high-tech industry fueled the engine of social change and economic dynamism. The community changed from a fruit growing–based economy to a computer chip one. San José claimed the title of "the Capital of Silicon Valley," though the valley extends around a thirty-mile radius around the city. Companies such as IBM, Hewlett-Packard, Intel, Oracle, Sun, and Cisco among many others changed the social fabric of San José and its surrounding area. Silicon Valley developed into a community of professionals at the high end of the occupational ladder with service sector workers, mostly Mexican men and women, precariously clinging to its lower rungs. Just as the Valley of Heart's Delight relied on migrant and seasonal Mexican immigrants to harvest its crops, Silicon Valley employed service and assembly workers. From the late 1960s to the 1990s, a large influx of Mexican immigrants and U.S.-born Mexicans formed the laboring class in this high-tech world.

San José is situated in the geographical space of a changing agricultural economy, urban developments, and continued Mexican immigration. The rise of Silicon Valley represents a socio-economic phenomenon where history, technology, science, and people are forged in the vortex of a "Brave New World." San José is a microcosm of the emerging Californian mentality where the themes of communitarian, individualism, futuristic imagination, and historical memory meet in a postmodern assemblage of ethnic diversity, pluralist politics, technological innovation, and individualist strivings. Since the 1960s, the city has been at the juncture and rupture of two socio-economic classes: the prosperous upper and middle class of Anglo Americans, Asians, and Asian Americans connected with Silicon Valley, and the service-sector class consisting largely of Mexican immigrant and Mexican Americans, who experience high rates of poverty and lack of mobility, though there is a growing Mexican American professional and middle class. There are relatively few African Americans in the city. This makes San José different from Chicago, Houston, and Los Angeles where there exist large impoverished communities of African Americans. San José's Vietnamese population, on the other hand, has grown and continues to grow at a rapid pace. San José has the largest Vietnamese population of any city in the United States. This growth has taken place between 1980 and 2000, during which time San José's Vietnamese population increased ten times and now accounts for 9 percent of the city's population. From 1960 to 1980, Mexican Americans, rather than African Americans or Vietnamese, represented the major ethnic group struggling for a "place in the sun" in their San José community. As a result, San José has historically, and specifically from 1960 to 2000, represented an urban space of historical layering where the Mexican Americans interviewed in this study dedicated themselves to improving their community.

The Mexican American community builders interviewed for this oral history project witnessed the city's "setting" with its peak of prosperity and valley of social inequality, social injustice, and denial of citizenship rights. San José, particularly East San José, developed as a Mexican immigrant and Mexican American ethnic enclave. Specific social issues crystallized and eventually led to the development of community activism within various sectors of this ethnic community as captured in this oral history anthology. From 1960 to 2000, the Mexican American community experienced a vast array of socio-economic problems. A small but growing and increasingly vocal group of Mexican Americans developed both within East San José and the city in general. Members of this community organized around such issues as poverty, crime, educational segregation, and political representation and educational inequality.[4]

These ethnic community builders pursued many causes, but reform of the educational system for Mexican Americans became a central one. The life stories in *Ethnic Community Builders* reveal how these individuals shared a belief that access to quality education is more a right than a privilege. American history illustrates that education helps to pave the way for upward mobility, but the path has unfortunately been paved with social roadblocks for some. American history is also the story of community builders struggling to eliminate such roadblocks. Hispanics have historically had lower educational attainment levels than the total population, and the Mexican American community of San José is no exception. The percentage of high school graduates within a specific ethnic group such as Hispanics has always been a baseline for measuring the life chances when compared with the rates for the total population. The educational attainment of Hispanics increased across all levels between 1971 and 2000. Despite these increases, the gaps in attainment between Hispanics and the total population remained similar at every attainment level during this period. In 1980, 56 percent of Hispanics in the United States did not have a high school diploma in comparison to 31 percent of the general population. The percentage for Hispanics not completing high school dropped to 42 percent in 1990, but that for the total population dropped to its lowest level of 14 percent. Although there has been a steady upward swing in this rate, 49 percent of the Hispanic population still did not have a high school diploma in comparison to 20 percent of the total population in 2000. Similar rates for Mexican Americans in San José closely resemble these national trends. If the Mexican immigrant population is taken into account in these statistics, the rates of those with less than a high school diploma would increase. The majority of immigrants from Mexico arrive with fewer than twelve years of schooling because the majority of Mexico's population generally does not obtain more than a primary school education. Their U.S.-born children, with only slight exception, receive all of their schooling in the United States and are more likely than their parents to complete high school. Their rates of college attendance and college completion, however, remain low.[5]

In addition to disparities in high school graduation rates, Mexican Americans confronted many other social issues in San José. Educational segregation, political under-representation, wage inequalities, inadequate housing, and many other issues represented some, but not all, of the social issues that Mexican American community builders addressed in their crusades for social justice.

## THE HISTORICAL CONTEXT:
## SOCIAL PROTESTS AND COMMUNITY ACTIVISM

San José's Mexican American community builders included in this anthology developed a major spirit of activism within the political context of the Chicano social protest movement of the 1960s and 1970s. The rise of crusades for social justice by Mexican American community activists did not begin during the historical period covered in this anthology. These community builders inherited a legacy of movements to achieve equality for Mexican Americans in the United States from earlier historical periods.

Prior to the 1960s, Mexican Americans in communities throughout the Southwest organized around similar issues to those that San José's community activists would confront and strive to overcome. Mexican American workers in canneries, factories, mines, and agricultural fields organized unions, engaged in labor strikes, and, in general, worked for their civil rights. In cities such as Los Angeles, San Antonio, El Paso, and other major centers where they lived, Mexican Americans engaged in collective action to improve their lives and those of their children. Sometimes they were successful; other times, their obstacles proved insurmountable. In either case, the history of their struggles remains a legacy, one inherited by generations of Mexican Americans and other groups in American society who share similar struggles or maintain an empathy with such groups.

Past struggles, largely ignored until the rise of Chicano historians and social scientists, will forever form a part of the historical memory of future generations of ethnic community builders such as those included in this anthology.[6]

Mexican Americans also developed a specific style of leadership in many of the organizations that flourished prior to the '60s such as LULAC (League of United Latin American Citizens), G.I. Forum, MAPA (Mexican American Political Association), the Kennedy Clubs of 1959–1960, and the CSO (Community Service Organization). These organizations addressed the issues of social justice, citizenship, voter registration, and education. Mexican American organizations of the 1920s through the late 1950s adhered to the principles of maintaining biculturalism, gaining citizenship rights, fighting racism, registering voters, winning political elections, reforming the educational system, and addressing other community issues.[7] Although each carved out his or her own particular niche within the community, the contributors to this anthology reveal how their lives were shaped and, in some cases, even dramatically changed by the spirit of the '60s, a time when Mexican Americans throughout the Southwest became engaged in the politics of protest.[8] Influenced by the Black Nationalist movement and the legacy of pre-1965 Mexican American civil rights movements, Chicanos mobilized as students, farm workers, educators, women, and workers to confront structural inequalities in American society.[9]

Surrounded by a political climate characterized by militant activism for social justice, such as the civil rights movement, the anti–Vietnam War movement, and the women's movement, Mexican Americans challenged "the Establishment" as they mobilized communities into political activism. The Chicano Movement evolved from various struggles with specific leaders, agendas, organizational strategies, and tactics. In California, César Chávez and Dolores Huerta organized farm workers into the United Farm Workers (UFW) Union, which engaged in strikes and boycotts against the state's agribusiness. Chávez and Huerta became the soul and inspiration of the Chicano Movement and the national and international symbols of a struggle for social justice and equal rights. The urban-based Colorado Crusade for Justice, spearheaded by Rodolfo "Corky" Gonzales, mobilized Chicano communities around the issues of political self-determination and community activism. In Texas, José Angel Gutiérrez founded a third political party—the Raza Unida Party—and challenged the state's political system for its systematic exclusion of Mexican Americans. The Raza Unida Party's successful political victory in Crystal City, Texas, in 1970 became a political metaphor for the strength and tenacity of *El Movimiento*. The New Mexico land grant movement, headed by Reies López Tijerina, fought for the rights of dispossessed land grant title-holders who traced their land claims back to the war between Mexico and the United States (1846–1848). In high schools and universities throughout the Southwest, Mexican American students organized their collective efforts into a radical confrontation with an educational system that they indicted for its long-standing discriminatory policies and practices. In some form or another, all contributors to this anthology make references to these leaders and their specific protest activities. Some were influenced directly by them and joined their cause. Others recalled the Chicano Movement from a more distant position.[10]

Beginning in the early 1980s and through the 1990s, these ethnic community builders focused on the need to institutionalize their power. As the politics of protest waned, they emerged as powerbrokers and political players in San José, a city that was continuing to change politically and socially. As it changed, these individuals often adopted new forms of community mobilization and organizational strategies. Some became key players in electoral politics, entered into social and political coalitions, became heads of major community agencies or city committees, and succeeded in gaining political victories in city politics. Their activities changed San José's urban landscape, institutions, and political structures. These individuals wanted to provide their communities with new educational, cultural, and political policies for the benefit of the individuals who overwhelmingly lived in San José's Southside and East Side communities. Coming from diverse backgrounds, these community builders focused their attention and energies in making a difference in their community. They were not driven by personal and individualistic motives, but by a philosophy of virtue and commitment to social justice.

## INTERSECTING LIVES: NETWORKS OF RELATIONSHIPS

*Ethnic Community Builders* is organized by categories: Leadership and Power, Politics and Society, Education and Social Change, Culture and the Arts, and Religion

and Community. Each oral history has been placed within the category determined to be best suited for it. Each narrative stands alone, but a reading of all
fourteen will reveal that these individuals knew each other or were familiar with
each other. Their life stories reveal common experiences and interconnectedness
in time and space. This web-like network of individuals makes this collection
more than the sum of its parts. The individuals are like separate threads in an in-
tricately woven tapestry. They can stand alone as a single thread with its own richness of color and quality of texture, but when woven together they create a
beautiful tapestry of San José's Mexican American community.[11]

César Chávez and the United Farm Workers represent one of the strongest
ties that shaped these intersecting sets of personal relationships. All of these
community builders had direct or indirect contact with Chávez himself. Sal Álvarez became his close confident while Juan Olivérez attended rallies where
Chávez spoke. Adrian Vargas and his Teatro de la Gente Group performed plays
that examined the plight of the farm workers. Juan Olivérez, Rigo Chacón, Fernando Zazueta—all grew up in farm worker families and experienced the ardu-
ous life of migrant workers. Sister Gloria Loya spent many long hours
ministering to farm workers and participated in rallies for the UFW cause. Esther Medina, Sofía Mendoza, Ernestina García, and Rigo Chacón discuss how
they used Chávez and his activism as an inspiration and example for their children. Ron Gonzales considers Chávez his personal hero. So great was the impact
of his direct interaction with Chávez that Adrian Vargas needed to stop during
his interview to recover from his emotional response to our questions about his
relationship and memory of the sacrifices endured by Chávez.

The struggle to reform the educational system also brought these individuals
together. Prior to their direct participation in San José's Mexican American community, Mendoza and Alvarado engaged in various types of activism in their junior high and high school years. Mendoza identifies her "coming of age" as an
organizer when she founded a Spanish Club in her school. She recalls her anger
when she met with resistance from some of her teachers. Alvarado helped start
the Club Tapatio as a forum for Mexican American high school students to meet
and interact socially. Others came to the public arena as adults fighting for educational reforms. Mendoza and García crossed paths during many neighborhood
mobilizing committees and protests as they embarked on a struggle against prejudice and discrimination against Mexican American students, including their
own children. As a teacher, Yolanda Reynolds worked closely with students, particularly those in the Mexican American Youth Organization. Victor Garza has

been an influential presence among Mexican American students through the Enlace Program.

Incidents of police brutality against Mexican Americans, particularly youth living in East San José, led community members to establish the Community Alert
Patrol (CAP), a neighborhood group that coordinated efforts to monitor their
scanners for police calls and then try to arrive at the scene before they did. Members of CAP took pictures of those who might be arrested in order to document
subsequent police brutality. Mendoza and García worked with others to maintain
CAP as an integral part of the Mexican American community. Juan Olivérez participated in the group and, as one of the student leaders at San José State University, used CAP as an example of how students needed to establish direct
connections with community groups. Mendoza recounts working with Olivérez
to develop strategies to increase the involvement of Chicano students. His successful recruiting of Chicano students to CAP strengthened its effectiveness and
longevity as a community group. Vargas identified Olivérez as one of his role
models for the work Olivérez did as a student leader in general and his concerted
effort to bridge the gap between students and the Mexican American community.

The anti–Vietnam War movement also strengthened this web of interrela-
tionships. Mendoza, Olivérez, and Vargas recount their direct involvement in
anti-war protests. All three sharpened their community mobilization strategies
through their participation in anti-war activities such as the Chicano Moratorium held in Los Angeles in 1970 that ended when police attacked the demonstrators. Their experiences with such institutionalized violence deepened their
commitment to organize collectively to challenge police brutality.

These individuals crossed paths with each other during their attempts to create community organizations or strengthen existing ones. García's and Mendoza's role in *La Confederación de la Raza Unida* and United People Arriba
reveals their leadership skills and charismatic personalities. Both were inspired
by the "Saul Alinsky School" of community organizing that stressed grassroots
mobilization and confrontational politics.[12] Both became close friends and were
among the most recognizable and controversial community leaders in San José.
Reynolds, a reporter for Mary Andrade's *La Oferta* newspaper, wrote articles
about García's community activities and continued a friendship with her until
García's passing in 2005. Victor Garza used his experience as an active member
and local and national officer of the American G.I. Forum to establish himself as
a major player in San José politics. Garza recognized the need for Mexican Americans to institutionalize their community power and so he founded La Raza

Roundtable, an organization of Mexican American leaders from the public and private sector. La Raza Roundtable developed leadership, contributed to the development of a political power base, and helped protect the civil rights of Mexican Americans in San José. Garza gained a reputation as a coalition builder and pragmatic politician who crossed paths with almost all of the individuals in this anthology, particularly Blanca Alvarado and Ron Gonzales. Alvarado served on the San José city council and the county board of supervisors. Ron Gonzales was San José's first Latino mayor. Their political lives brought them together in the corridors of city hall and other political arenas. Both knew such community leaders as García, Mendoza, and Fernando Zazueta. Zazueta and Alvarado spearheaded the successful community campaign to establish a Mexican Heritage Plaza that has become one of San José's showcase arts and cultural centers. Rigo Chacón, San José's award-winning television newscaster for ABC affiliate San José Channel 7 News team and South Bay Bureau chief, reported on the political and civic activities of Alvarado, Gonzales, and Zazueta, who in turned participated at different levels with Chacón in his capacity as a philanthropist, including his educational scholarship program, Abrazos y Books, which has gained national recognition.

All of these community builders understood that San José's Mexican Americans, particularly those living in East San José, were largely marginalized, living in or on the brink of poverty. Many lacked adequate housing, health care, job training, and educational opportunities. Mendoza became tired of the lack of adequate health care in the East Side and organized the community into a one-issue coalition group that, through several highly public protests, won the city's support and funding to establish a neighborhood health clinic. Mendoza received the backing of García, Olivérez, and other student activists. Esther Medina is considered by the city as the most widely known and appreciated community organizer. Beginning in 1982, Medina became a pillar of the Mexican American community as executive director of the Mexican American Community Services Agency (MACSA). She transformed MACSA from a struggling agency into a powerful organization that developed critically needed programs and social services. Without exception, all of the individuals in this anthology cross paths with Medina. She started the Chicana Coalition, a group of professional women who shared a feminist vision for women's empowerment. Medina backed Alvarado's bid for election to the San José's city council. Medina as head of the powerful and influential MACSA transformed the urban landscape of East San José with its housing units, senior and youth services, after-school programs, and immigration counseling services. She clearly understood how San José was emerging as a two-tiered economy with Mexican Americans largely marginalized within Silicon Valley. Medina forged MACSA into a community organization par excellence and emerged as one of the most influential Mexican Americans in San José and the surrounding community.

Each of the activists included in this collection of oral histories worked for the betterment of San José's Mexican American community. They saw injustice and tried to right it. They faced insurmountable obstacles, but they displayed a tenacity that led them to "keep their eyes on the prize."[13] Their life struggles, hopes, disappointments, and, above all, their triumphs were shared with each other. They met, worked, and thrived during the same historical moment. They "took the path least followed" but they did not walk alone along the path of activism; they formed a network of relations and collectively "they took the [path] less traveled by / And that has made all the difference."[14]

## ORAL HISTORY: RECOVERING THE HIDDEN PAST

By using the methodology of oral history, *Ethnic Community Builders* captures the personal life journeys of individuals who shaped the development of San José during a critical period. A brief, but most certainly not exhaustive, overview of the field of oral history will provide a context for this anthology.[15] Beginning in the mid-twentieth century, oral history gained national and international prominence as a rich methodological technique. Complementing traditional historical and social science research, oral history provides a different type of historical record: the actual voices of those who made history. Oral histories, of course, existed prior to this revival, but the resurgence of oral history studies primarily focuses on individuals from marginalized groups.[16] Other studies, including *Ethnic Community Builders*, examine the lives of individuals in communities, such as San José, whose life stories have not been recorded and have been largely "hidden from history."[17]

Although oral history became more prominent in the 1960s, historian Allan Nevins was already engaged in pioneering oral history research as early as the 1940s. Nevins interviewed workers and soldiers in order to preserve their ideas, perspectives, and views of their lives in relation to their surrounding society.[18] Interestingly, in 1931, Mexican anthropologist Manuel Gamio published his classic study based on oral histories, *The Life Story of the Mexican Immigrant*.[19] Gamio's study was not widely distributed but would become influential to Mexican American scholars in the 1960s. Nevins contributed to the institutionalization of oral history research by establishing the Columbia Oral History Project. By the mid- and late 1950s, the University of California at Los Angeles and the University of California at Berkeley established their own oral history programs. In 1976, the Oral History Association was founded, providing a forum for scholars engaged in oral history projects. Oral history continues to be a major methodological research tool. The use of oral histories to document the lives of racial and ethnic groups will continue to contribute to the understanding of American society.

Over the past decade, Mexican American scholars have been turning to oral history to examine the development of Mexican American communities. Following in the classic oral history tradition of Gamio, Mexican American historians and social scientists have used oral history interviews to bring Mexicans and Mexican Americans from "out of the shadows" of history.[20] Patricia Preciado Martin's *Songs My Mother Sang to Me: An Oral History of Mexican American Women* is a collection of oral histories of women who grew up in southern Arizona in the early 1900s. Their narratives focus on the generational transmission of cultural values, hopes, and aspirations by their mothers and grandmothers.[21] Beatrice Rodriquez Owsley contributed to the research on ethnic groups and entrepreneurship by publishing the life stories of seventeen Hispanic American business owners in New Orleans. Mario T. García's approach to oral history added a new dimension to past anthologies. García crafted the life narratives of labor activist Bert Corona, educator Frances Esquibel Tywoniak, and literary critic and essayist Luis Leal into individual volumes, providing an in-depth portrait of these three individuals.[22] García's work follows in the tradition of Latin American "*testimonios*" such as those of Rigoberta Menchú and Elvira Alvarado.[23] Rosaura Sánchez takes *testimonios* to a different level by analyzing thirty *testimonios* written by *Californios* during the late 1800s.[24] Closely related to oral history "from the bottom up" are the few autobiographies of Mexican and Mexican Americans that have become part of Mexican American scholarship. The life narrative of Maria Elena Lucas is a dramatic chronicle of her life as a farm worker living in South Texas. Ramón "Tianguis" Pérez, like Lucas, records his daily life as an undocumented Mexican immigrant who makes the classic "border crossings" between Mexico and the United States.[25]

Oral histories have also represented a key source of primary data for Mexican American scholars whose works led to the further development of Mexican American Studies. Studies of specific cities such as El Paso, Los Angeles, San Diego, Santa Barbara, and Los Angeles have used oral histories as primary sources, usually integrating direct, often extensive, quotations to illustrate their analysis of the development of specific Mexican American communities.[26] In 1931, Gamio, for example, complemented his earlier publication on Mexican immigrants, in which he analyzed their oral histories using both these life stories and other more sociological data such as population statistics and employment rates, by publishing the oral histories in an anthology.[27]

Studies on San José's Mexican American communities have similarly used collections of oral histories housed in university and city archives in their studies of Mexican American communities. Ruiz's study of the coming of age of Mexican American women relies most heavily on the direct integration of oral history.[28] Zavella's study of cannery women in the Santa Clara Valley is of particular importance to *Ethnic Community Builders* for its integration of oral histories of women who lived in and worked in San José and the surrounding community.[29] Although it is not a collection of oral histories, the life narratives of these cannery women and Zavella's historical analysis of the Santa Clara Valley represent one of the few studies of San José's Mexican American community.

Stephen J. Pitti's study of Silicon Valley and San José traces the development of the Mexican American community from the 1700s to the present.[30] Pitti draws a highly nuanced portrait of San José as a place in time, space, geography, and enclave ethnic divisions and conflict. Pitti argues that it is a city that cannot be overlooked in Mexican American Studies. For his analysis of recent development in San José, Pitti relies extensively on fifty oral histories of Mexican Americans, but his work is not a collection of oral histories. In addition to other historical data, he uses these interviews of Mexican Americans to analyze the effects of racism, prejudice, and discrimination: "The Devil in Silicon Valley." *Ethnic Community Builders*, as a collection of oral histories of Mexican Americans in San José, provides a different dimension to Pitti's study by focusing on individuals who were not interviewed by Pitti and who lived, worked, and fought for civil rights for the Mexican American community in a more compressed time period (1960–2000) than Pitti's study that spans several centuries.

The life narratives of the Mexican American community activists in *Ethnic Community Builders* will assure that their life experiences will be inscribed in the historical record. Their memories about their childhoods, family, folklore, schooling, values, worldviews, and, of course, remembrances about their community building in San José come together in this anthology. Storytelling, memories, and the oral tradition make up the core of any group's legacy for future generations, and oral history anthologies preserve such a legacy by transforming the oral into the written: a legacy for future generations.

## GENESIS OF *ETHNIC COMMUNITY BUILDERS*

Several years ago, Francisco Jiménez, one of the authors of this anthology, decided to enrich his students' education by providing them with the opportunity
to learn from people in the community. He asked students in his advanced Spanish Conversation course at Santa Clara University to interview Mexican Americans in San José whose commitment to social justice had led them to become
active in various types of community organizations and activities. They taped
and transcribed these interviews. At about the same time, Jiménez and his Santa
Clara University colleague Alma M. García had lunch with Mary Andrade,
founder and editor of San José's Spanish-language newspaper, *La Oferta*. She told
them about how she had interviewed several Mexican American seniors for her
newspaper. Using her experience as a professional photographer, Mary also took
impressive portraits of these elderly men and women, most of whom have now
passed away.

Our meeting with Mary led us to discuss the need to record the lives of more
Mexican Americans who had dedicated their lives as community activists in the
San José community, but whose lives had not been collected in an oral history
anthology. We identified the years between 1960 and 2000 as an important period in San José's history and the development of its Mexican American community. We combined our firsthand knowledge of the San José community to
put a list together of those community activists that we knew had been very influential in such areas as grassroots organizations, education, politics, and the
arts.

The individuals in this anthology continue to be influential members of the
San José community. Blanca Alvarado was elected to the city council and later the
county board of supervisors. Ron Gonzales became major of San José. Victor
Garza founded La Raza Roundtable, one of the most influential political organ-
izations. Rigo Chacón developed into a major figure in broadcasting in the Bay
Area. Fernando Zazueta, a well-known attorney, spearheaded a committee that
led to the formation of the Mexican Heritage Plaza, the major cultural center of
San José. Esther Medina retired from MACSA but remains an influential figure.
Sofía Mendoza and Ernestina García became informal community consultants
called upon by local politicians to discuss present-day community issues. Adrian
Vargas founded his own production company and is a diversity consultant. Vargas and Juan Olivérez taught at local universities. Yolanda Reynolds became a
high school teacher, reporter for *La Oferta*, and a college administrator. Mary Andrade's *La Oferta* has become one on the major newspapers in San José and the

surrounding community. Rigo Chacón runs a key philanthropic organization. Sal Álvarez and Sister Gloria Loya were responsible for initiating important changes in the local churches. Sister Gloria teaches theology at the Jesuit School of Theology at Berkeley's Graduate Theological Union, and Sal Álvarez is the director of the Institute for Non-Violence, Office of Human Relations, Santa Clara County, a community organization that provides training on peace building, conflict resolution, mediation, and negotiations for civil rights and human rights advocates.

We decided to limit the number to fourteen individuals in order to be able to conduct in-depth interviews with each. After putting together a general list of questions dealing with family, childhood, education, values, and community activism, we set out to conduct the interviews. The interviews took place from 2004 to 2006. We spent two long summer afternoons with the late Ernestina García. Pictures of her children and grandchildren covered the walls in her living room. She displayed her collection of small ceramic figurines on the coffee table and bookshelf. Dressed in her Sunday best with neatly coiffed hair, Ernestina riveted us with her stories of a lifetime of struggle and community activism. Mary Andrade welcomed us to her office at the *La Oferta* newspaper. Beautiful folk art and paintings lined the hallway leading to her office. As we interviewed her, we could see on the shelves behind her several of the books she authored on the celebrations of the Day of the Dead in Mexico. When we entered the home of Yolanda Reynolds, it seemed that we had been transported to a beautiful folk art museum in New Mexico. While interviewing Esther Medina and Sofía Mendoza, we became aware of their dramatically forceful demeanor that made them such formidable community activists. In Blanca Alvarado's office of the county board of supervisors, we had a spectacular view of San José. Pictures of her children were placed next to the numerous awards and plaques she had received. Esther Medina met us at the conference room at the MACSA office building. Ron Gonzales invited us to the mayor's office, providing us with an up-close look at the center of city politics. We conducted our interview with Fernando Zazueta at his law office; he showed us an impressive photo album capturing key moments in the construction of the Mexican Heritage Plaza. Sister Gloria graciously welcomed us to her residence in San Francisco. Victor Garza, Rigo Chacón, Adrian Vargas, Juan Olivérez, and Sal Álvarez joined us at Santa Clara University for a leisurely lunch prior to our interviews, which were conducted at various locations on campus. Victor and Francisco had met at a meeting of La Raza Roundtable. All of us knew Rigo Chacón not just from watching him on television for years but from attending various community events. Adrian Vargas had taught a Chicano Theater class at Santa Clara University. During these lunches, we inevitably had to say to each of them, "That's a great story. Please remember it when we start the interview and are taping."

Each interview lasted approximately four hours. We interviewed some on two different occasions. Although the three of us took turns asking questions, we let the conversation flow as smoothly as possible, allowing each of us the opportunity to ask follow-up or additional questions as needed. As in any interview, the interviewees often introduced some topics that we had not thought of asking, and this added a richer, more textured dimension to their narratives. Our overarching goal was to allow the individuals to craft their own story while at the same time guiding the interview so that each one elicited themes that cut across all the interviews. The interviews were taped and videotaped with their permission, but we assured each that we would stop recording at whatever point they requested. The interviews were professionally transcribed. We shared in editing the transcripts, but we always tried to let the "voice" or personality of each come through in the completed version contained in this collection.

We were not surprised when most of the people became very emotional during the interviews. Their memories of grandparents and parents, whether living or not, elicited tears from them and us. Others became emotional when they recalled the injustices they had experienced as Mexican Americans. Almost all mentioned solidarity with other groups, such as African Americans and Native Americans, who have also endured social injustices and struggled to achieve their constitutional rights.

As scholars, we understood the usual role assigned to an interviewer in these circumstances, but we believed that we could not play the role of a recording instrument dispassionately taping while a human being freely and willingly poured out their very souls to us. We came to care deeply for the individuals in this collection, admiring their strength, fortitude, and commitment to social justice. We are grateful for their participation in this project and will forever admire their roles as "community builders."

From the very beginning of the project, we included undergraduate students as research assistants. We mentored them by providing them with the opportunity to engage collaboratively in our research project. Christina Dolores (Class of 2005) and Amparo Cid (Class of 2006) provided us with archival research, assisted in the development of the interview questions, analyzed demographic data, and assumed responsibility for the taping of the interviews. We wanted to take them further into the research experience and so on some occasions we allowed them to ask some of the questions. During the last stages of the project, we taught Elisa Tejeda (Class of 2007) how to do general editing.

We took turns meeting with the students shortly after each interview to discuss both the themes that had emerged from any given interview and their own response at hearing the life stories of each of these community builders. This part of the research project was particularly gratifying for us. We wanted our student research assistants to get to know these individuals and understand how each had developed a passionate commitment for social justice, a goal that forms an integral part of Santa Clara University's mission as a Catholic Jesuit institution of higher learning.

Our hope is that these life histories will provide a deeper understanding and a heightened awareness of the struggles and triumphs of Mexican Americans who made monumental and personal sacrifices for the common good and that they become a resource of inspiration for future generations. Furthermore, we trust that this work will encourage other scholars and students to use oral histories to document the lives of Mexican Americans and other ethnic groups whose commitment to social justice has made a difference in our society. We believe that a person's life narrative is his or her voice by which we can understand the process of history and the human condition. Every person is worthwhile, and through each particular one, we can examine and possibly understand the universal.

## NOTES

1. The Hispanic Population Census 2000 Brief, United States Department of Commerce, www.census.gov/prod/2001pubs/c2kbr01-3.pdf.

2. http://www.SanJoseca.gov/planning/Census/briefs/race_ethnicity.asp.

3. U.S. Census Bureau, *Coming to America: A Profile of the Nation's Foreign Born* (2000). Issued February 2002. http://www.census.gov/prod/2002pubs/cenbr01-1.pdf.

4. Stephen J. Pitti, *The Devil in Silicon Valley: Northern California, Race, and Mexican Americans* (Princeton, NJ: Princeton University Press, 2003); Glenna Matthews, *Silicon Valley, Women, and the California Dream: Gender, Class and Opposition in the 20th Century* (Stanford, CA: Stanford University Press, 2003); Kevin Starr, *Embattled Dreams: California in War and Peace, 1940* (Oxford: Oxford University Press, 2002).

5. National Center for Education Statistics, "Educational Attainment, 2000," U.S. Department of Education Office of Educational Research and Improvement, NCES

2000–010, http://nces.ed.gov/pubs2000/2000010.pdf; "Hispanics in Education," 1999 Digest of Education Statistics, Hispanic Association of Colleges and Universities (HACU), Department of Information and Analysis, August 2000, http://www.hacu.net/images/hacu/hispanics_in_education.pdf.

6. The sustained development of historical and social science works on Mexican American history is extensive. For an introduction to this literature, see Manuel G. Gonzales and Cynthia M. Gonzales, eds., *En Aquel Entonces: Readings in Mexican American History* (Bloomington: Indiana University Press, 2000); Vicki L. Ruiz and Virginia Sánchez Korrol, eds., *Latina Legacies: Identity, Biography and Community* (New York: Oxford University Press, 2005); among many others.

7. Matt S. Meier and Margo Gutiérrez, *Encyclopedia of the Mexican American Civil Rights Movement* (Westport, CT: Greenwood Press, 2000). At the end of each entry, the authors provide suggestions for further readings on specific people, organizations, and issues.

8. On the rise of the Chicano Movement, see Carlos Muñoz, Jr., *Youth, Identity, Power: The Chicano Movement* (New York: Verso, 1989); Richard Griswold del Castillo and Richard A. Garcia, *César Chávez: A Triumph of Spirit* (Norman: University of Oklahoma Press, 1995); Ernesto Chavez, *Mi Raza Primero [My People First]: Nationalism, Identity and Insurgency in the Chicano Movement in Los Angeles, 1966–1978* (Berkeley: University of California Press, 2002); Lorena Oropeza, *Raza Si! Guerra No!: Chicano Protest and Patriotism During the Vietnam War Era* (Berkeley: University of California, 2005).

9. Mario T. García, *Mexican Americans: Leadership, Ideology, and Identity, 1930–1960* (New Haven, CT: Yale University Press, 1989); Richard A. Garcia, *The Making of the Mexican-American Mind, San Antonio, Texas, 1929–1941: A Social and Intellectual History of an Ethnic Community* (College Station: Texas A and M Press, 1991).

10. See the following for specific discussions of these parts of the Chicano Movement: Sam Kushner, *Long Road to Delano* (New York: International Publishers, 1975); Christine Marin, *A Spokesman for the Mexican American Movement: Rodolfo "Corky" Gonzales and the Fight for Chicano Liberation, 1966–1972* (San Francisco: R and E Research Associates, 1977); Ignacio M. García, *United We Win: The Rise of La Raza Unida Party* (Tucson: University of Arizona Mexican American Studies and Research Center, 1989); Peter Nabokov, *Tijerina and the Courthouse Raid* (Albuquerque: University of New Mexico Press, 1969); F. Arturo Rosales, *Chicano!: The History of the Mexican American Civil Rights Movement* (Houston: Arte Publico Press, 1996).

11. Luther P. Gerlach and Virginia H. Hine, *People, Power and Change: Movements of Social Transformation* (Indianapolis: Bobbs-Merrill, 1970).

12. During the 1930s, Saul Alinsky organized the Back of the Yards neighborhood in Chicago that had been made famous by Upton Sinclair's *The Jungle*. He founded the Industrial Areas Foundation that trained organizers and assisted in the founding of community organizations around the country.

13. "Freedom Riders' Song," civil rights movement, derived from gospel song, "Gospel Plough."

14. Robert Frost, "Road Not Taken." 1916.

15. For a general overview of oral history, see Robert Parks and Alistair Thomson, eds., *The Oral History Reader* (New York: Routledge, 1998).

16. Slave narratives represent such an example. See *Slave Narratives* (New York: Penguin Putnam Library of America, 2000); Gilbert Olive, *Narrative of Sojourner Truth, a Bondswoman of Olden Time: With a History of her Labors and Correspondence Drawn from Her "Book of Life"* (New York: Oxford University Press, 1991).

17. Sheila Rowbotham, *Hidden From History: Rediscovering Women in History from the 17th Century to the Present* (New York: Pantheon Books, 1974).

18. Allan Nevins, *The Gateway to History* (Garden City, NY: Anchor Books, 1962).

19. Manuel Gamio, *The Life Story of the Mexican Immigrant* (Chicago: The University of Chicago, 1931). Gamio was the founder of modern indigenist studies and one of the first scholars to study Mexican immigration to the United States in the mid-1920s, the peak of Mexican immigration.

20. Vicki L. Ruíz, *From Out of the Shadows: Mexican Women in Twentieth-Century America* (New York: Oxford University Press, 1998). This review of the literature is not meant to be exhaustive in nature; it serves to highlight some key publications. Other scholars such as sociologist Judy Yung, Elaine H. Kim, and Eui-Young Yu have also studied ethnic communities in the United States using oral histories. See Elaine H. Kim and Eui-Young Yu, *East to America: Korean American Life Stories* (New York: The New Press, 1996); Judy Yung, *Unbound Voices: A Documentary History of Chinese Women in San Francisco* (Berkeley: University of California Press, 1999); Yen Espiritu, *Filipino Lives* (Philadelphia: Temple University Press, 1995).

21. Patricia Preciado Martin, *Songs My Mother Sang to Me: An Oral History of Mexican American Women* (Tucson: University of Arizona Press, 1992).

22. Mario T. García, *Luis Leal: An Auto/Biography* (Austin: University of Texas Press, 2000); *Memories of Chicano History: the Life and Narrative of Bert Corona* (Berkeley: University of California Press, 1994); Frances Esquibel Tywoniak and Mario T. García,

*Migrant Daughter: Coming of Age as a Mexican American Woman* (Berkeley: University of California Press, 2000).

23. Rigoberta Menchú, *I, Rigoberta Menchú: An Indian Woman in Guatemala*, edited and introduced by Elisabeth Burgos-Debray; translated by Ann Wright London (Verso: New York, 1984); Elvira Alvarado, *Don't Be Afraid Gringo*, translated and edited by Medea Benjamin (New York: Harper and Row, 1989).

24. Rosaura Sánchez, *Telling Identities: The Californio Testimonios* (Minneapolis: University of Minnesota Press, 1995). The term *Californio* refers to Mexicans who were living in California when the United States seized the area in 1846 and their descendants. The term is also used in a more restrictive sense to refer to the upper class of California Mexican landowners of the 1840s.

25. Fran Leeper Buss, ed., *Forjada Bajo el Sol [Forged under the Sun]: The Life of Maria Elena Lucas* (Lansing: University of Michigan, 1994); Ramón "Tianguis" Pérez, trans. by Dick J. Reavis, *Diary of an Undocumented Immigrant* (Houston: Arte Público Press, 1991).

26. For specific references to these and a general literature review of Mexican American Studies research, see Richard Griswold del Castillo, "History from the Margins: Chicana/o History in the 1990s," Occasional Paper No. 28 (South Bend, IN: Julian Samora Research Institute Publications and Occasional Paper Series, September 1997). For an overview of research on Mexican American women, see Teresa Cordova, "Roots and Resistance: The Emergent Writings of Twenty Years of Chicana Feminist Struggle," 175–202 in *Handbook of Hispanic Cultures in the United States: Sociology*, ed. Felix Padilla (Houston: Arte Público Press, 1994).

27. Manuel Gamio, *The Life Story of the Mexican Immigrant* (New York: Dover, 1931).

28. Vicki L. Ruiz, "'Star Struck': Acculturation, Adolescence, and Mexican American Women, 1920–1950," 109–129 in *Building with Our Hands: New Dimensions in Chicana Studies*, ed. Adela de la Torre and Beatriz Pesquera (Berkeley: University of California Press, 1993).

29. Patricia Zavella, *Women's Work and Chicano Families: Cannery Women of the Santa Clara Valley* (Ithaca, NY: Cornell University Press, 1987).

30. Stephen J. Pitti, *The Devil in Silicon Valley: Northern California, Race, and Mexican Americans* (Princeton, NJ: Princeton University Press, 2003).

**I**

# LEADERSHIP AND POWER

# Victor Garza

*Victor Garza is an active member of the American G.I. Forum, an organization*
*that was formed in Texas in 1948 by Dr. Hector García in order to provide civil*
*rights protection for Mexican American World War II veterans. He was elected to*
*many local and national American G.I. Forum offices. He founded La Raza*
*Roundtable, a San José, California, organization of Mexican American leaders, a*
*group that developed leadership, contributed to the development of a political*
*power base, and helped protect the civil rights of Mexican Americans in San José.*
*Garza was born and raised in Texas during the late 1930s to a migrant farm*
*worker family and moved to California after serving in the Navy. Throughout his*
*life, Garza has had what he refers to as "a fire inside him" that maintained his*
*passion for civil rights.*

## MEMORIES OF THE BORDERLANDS: FLAMING THE FIRE INSIDE

My dad was born in Pierdas Negras, Coahuila, in Mexico, and my mom was born
in Eagle Pass, Texas, across the border. They had seven boys and three girls. I was
born in 1937 and am the second from the oldest. We were raised in Eagle Pass,
Texas, and were migrant workers from an early age. We were also sharecroppers
in the state of Michigan and worked in the fields in Wisconsin, Minnesota, Washington, Oregon, California, New Mexico, and Arizona. We used to go to school in
October, November, December, January, February, and then in March we would
drop out of school because we had to move up north. It was very difficult for us
to compete with the regular population in school, but we managed.

Growing up along the border in Eagle Pass was great. If you don't know anything else, you think your hometown is the most beautiful town in the world. Once you start going around, you start seeing all the towns and you say my hometown is as ugly as it can be. You still have roots there that make you want to go back and be with the family, cousins, uncles, and everyone else. It was just a poor community. Ninety percent of the people in my hometown were *Mexicanos* or Mexican Americans and 10 percent were white. When I was young, all people in good positions—principals and teachers and police officers, sheriffs were white people. So 10 percent occupied all the good positions and 90 percent were the laborers who were the *Mexicanos*. That's why so many of us had to leave the area and go up north to work in the fields to find something better and a little bit better pay. That's how we were raised in that kind of environment. My hometown was a little bit different than most of the little towns. We were not segregated; we all lived together. In the little towns around us, the *Mexicanos* went to one school and white people went to another. When my brothers played football and the team would stop at a restaurant, they were not allowed to get off the bus because the restaurant would not serve *Mexicanos*. They would get the white kids to buy hamburgers, sodas, and French fries and bring them to the bus to so they could have something to eat. This was normal back in the 1950s. My brothers and I were angry. When I was in the service, in the early 1950s, I wore my Navy uniform and I would go to a restaurant and they would tell me they didn't serve Mexicans or dogs in this restaurant. Even in New Mexico and Arizona, and California, I would go into restaurants with my uniform and they wouldn't serve me. They would have a sign on the bathroom doors that said "Blacks" and one that said "Whites." Sometimes I would go into the black side and the white people would tell me that "I didn't belong there" and then I would go to the white side. Sometimes, I would go to the white side and they would tell me that I belonged up there with the blacks and then I would go with the blacks. You never knew where you belonged because they didn't have anything for brown people.

My parents were angry because when they traveled up north things were pretty bad. It would take at least three days or four days to get from Texas to Michigan, Wisconsin, Minnesota, or to Montana. They wouldn't serve coffee to my dad. When we stopped at a gasoline station, they would let you buy gasoline but they wouldn't allow you to use the bathroom. We would have to go to the bathroom out in the fields. It was terrible but it was an experience that we all went through. Our family wasn't unique; I think it was something that was happening to the whole Latino community. The Mexicans weren't segregated in Eagle Pass as they were in the surrounding towns. It used to be an old fort in the old days. Many of the Anglo soldiers married into Mexican families and then settled there. They were more into being Mexicans, Latinos. All the Fishers and Crosbys and Osburns and Johnsons—they were all Mexicans because they were the sons or grandsons or great-grandsons of those that were there many years before.

I adjusted to discrimination because I had no choice. I accepted it and moved on, but I got angry. I kept that anger inside me until I was old enough to begin to do something about it. I have carried that fire and that torch inside me for so many years that I guess that's what makes me what I am. I carry this fire—this anger—inside me. I tell people if they want to create change, they need to get angry enough to do something about it. Otherwise, we all will become habitual complainers.

We moved from Texas to California and lived in the poorest neighborhood in the area of Fresno and Sanger where my mom and my dad worked in the fields. We used to sleep in an abandoned school bus that they would rent from the people that owned the property. The old bus did not have windows or tires, but we would live inside and would cook outside. Even when I was already twenty-three or twenty-four years old my parents worked in the fields in Sanger.

I guess who I am has to do with the upbringing that my dad and mom gave me. Hard work never kills you, and being honest and thrifty can get you where you want to go. My parents were always very thrifty; my mom more so than my dad. They always managed to find money in emergencies. My parents always used to say: "*Para atrás nunca, para adelante todo lo que se pueda*" [Don't look to the past, but look forward toward the future]. My mother would never accept one penny from the government or welfare no matter what conditions we were in. She said, "We're going to do it on our own, and we have always done it alone." I think that this value embedded deeply in us. None of my brothers and sisters ever accepted government assistance. I guess being honest will always pay in the end. You work hard and you're not afraid to work—no matter what you do, it ends up rewarding you in life. I don't remember having, what you might say, a vacation. I don't ever remember even the word "vacation." When there was no work, my dad would go find a cow, buy it, kill it, and then we would sell the meat door by door. My dad would go buy a load of such things like tomatoes, onions, gravel, sand and then sell it. We were always working on Saturday and Sunday. We were always working, always trying to make that extra dollar. We were always knocking on peoples' doors and selling things.

My family members were all Catholics, but we were not very religious. I think that we all prayed. I pray every night with my family. We pray when we eat, but we are not those fanatic types of religious people. I have a brother who doesn't miss church on Sunday. He wants to be there all the times, but the rest of us aren't like that. I'd say you pray at your home, you teach your kids God's work, the Bible and the readings. I read books to my kids in Spanish and in English about God's stories. But I don't go to church every Sunday; I haven't done that since I was a teenager or in the Navy.

The macho thing? My sisters say I'm very macho. I don't consider myself to be very macho. I do wash dishes and I make up the bed. I sweep the house and I change my baby's diapers. I cook if I'm hungry and there's no food in the house, but I think a lot of that has to do more with the way my mom brought us up. We were four boys in a row and I'm the second from the oldest. In the family, the macho thing or the cultural part of it is that the oldest brother *manda* [rules] and *manda a todos* [rules everyone]. My mom and dad would never make my oldest brother wash diapers or dishes. They might put him to mop, but the things that were considered the "no-no's," they'd make me do it since I was the number two son in the family. I would go wash the diapers with a stick out here for all my little brothers. It was difficult for my mom to be doing everything while she was working alongside my dad in the fields, then come home and do everything else. I think we were brought up doing a lot more things than in other families, where the boys don't do the household chores.

## EMERGENT IDENTITIES

During those days, when I was a kid, I used to call myself Mexican American but later on, they called me Latino because Texas was known more to be Latino. I realized I was a *Tejano* [Texan] around the age of 13. I was a *Tejano*; I think that's when we were able to then afford to have boots even if it were only one pair. I have a ton of boots now, but during that time it was one pair of boots and you only used them on certain occasions because that's all you had. They were a little bit more expensive than buying us a pair of tennis shoes or a pair of shoes. We always wore Levis. We would wear a white shirt, and we would wear our *Tejano* hats. I was always proud to be a *Tejano*. When people ask me, "What are you?" I answer that "I am a *Tejano*." They say, "No, are you Mexican, are you American, or what?" And I say I am Chicano and I am Mexican American and I'm a *Tejano*. The gringos call me Latino and they also call me Hispanic.[1]

When the white people used to talk about Mexicans, I always thought they were talking about people from Mexico, but they were talking about me. It was a little bit different in my hometown because there were all these people with all these English names, but they were Mexicans, just like I was. I felt part of them and we weren't discriminated because of this. I'm sure there were other kinds of discrimination going on because white people filled up all the key positions. You didn't see a single teacher when I was growing up that was Latino in my community that was 90 percent Latino. All the teachers were white. The principal was white. The superintendents were white. The police were white. Everybody in the good positions was white. The Mexicans were there, but I didn't see them. My mother always stressed that we speak the Christian language at home and that was Spanish and we could speak English or anything else outside the home. But inside the house, she insisted that we speak Spanish all the time and we did. Our whole family speaks Spanish and some of them even studied Spanish. I didn't but they did.

You identify yourself as an American but then, you go to all these white establishments and they call you Mexican and they call you names, so it makes you think, "What am I?" Then, you begin to get angry and you begin to carry that anger and frustration with you. You carry the fire inside you. Some of us can live with it and others cannot. Other ones like me carry this anger around forever and fight to change things. I believe that I have created a lot of change, but it has never been by myself. It's always with the support of so many other people that without them I would not have ever done anything by myself. I don't believe that I could ever do anything by myself like creating social change in the community so that our people can begin to go to school without being discriminated or our people can be served at a restaurant, or if they wish to stay at a hotel or motel they can, if they wish to buy a car or buy a house they can, because before we weren't even allowed to buy a house where we wanted to live. If you did, they put you up there in little houses of carton and adobe because they didn't want you in the nice neighborhoods where you have gas and you have electricity. We didn't have gas and we didn't have electricity. I remember we didn't have water inside the house either. We had an outside toilet, and we would dig the hole every time it got full and we put another hole out there. We had a pipe and we used the pipe to be able to take a shower and carry the water inside the house so that we could have drinking water. These were the kinds of neighborhoods where I grew up with dirt floors and a little two-bedroom house. Those were our humble beginnings in life.

My wearing of boots is part of the culture of the *Tejano* and that's why I always wear boots. I don't think there's anyone in San José that has seen me wearing walking shoes in thirty-five years. They always see me with boots, always. Even if I'm wearing a tuxedo, I wear boots. I go to the White House and I wear boots. I wear a tuxedo or a suit, but I wear boots. Now that I can afford it, my clothes are tailored to fit the form of the boot. Of course, when I was a kid, we were happy to have tennis shoes or whatever we could get to keep the *piedritas* [pebbles] from getting into your feet. It's something that is embedded in you. I wear boots all the time. I'm *Tejano*.

I have always been proud of who I am and I guess that's what makes me wear a big mustache. Some things have to be telling me to look the way I do. I don't know why, but I have a feeling it has to do with pride. It has to give you pride of who you are. What does a *Mexicano* look like? A guy with a big mustache? Pancho Villa, right? Or Emiliano Zapata.[2] I have always been very proud. I have never been ashamed of who I am. I have always been proud to be a *Mexicano*, a *Tejano*, most importantly a *Tejano*. *Con sangre Mexicano porque mis padres son Mexicanos* [With Mexican blood because my parents are Mexicans]. But I'm also a proud American. I say American in the sense that I was born in this great country and I believe it belongs to me just as much as it belongs to anyone else that was born in this country. I guess that makes me fight for so much and to do so much. If you don't feel proud of who you are, I think you have a lot of things missing in your life. I had a cousin who changed his name because he didn't want to identify with his father's name. He changed his name and anglicized it. During those years many people were changing their last names to be more acceptable by the white society.

## MY MOTHER/MY HERO

My mom was my hero. I think she was the person that I admired the most in my life. My mom was tough; she endured. She was brilliant and a hard worker. My dad never went to school in his life, but my mom taught my dad how to read and write in Spanish and in English. My mom only went to school to the third grade. I remember I was going into eighth grade and she was still helping me with my homework even though she only went to third grade. She was great. Even to the day she died, she and I were very, very close. I always tell my kids to love their mother like I loved mine, in spite of the fact that I am divorced from their mother. I still wanted them to love their mother like I loved mine because I felt that she gave us everything. She helped us, molded us to be what we are. Education was her first priority. Education, education, education. My mom was the one who stressed the importance of honesty and education. I guess she had a hunger to learn, a hunger to know. My mother was a very bright woman, but she never had an opportunity for education in her life, but she always had a hunger for education. She enjoyed reading. I get a fulfillment from reading and I guess she felt the same thing. She was hungry for the education that she didn't have the opportunity to get in life. We love each other and we respect each other.

A lot of it has to do with my mom more than my dad. She united us together as a family with unity, love, and compassion. She told us not to be weak, even the women. She would tell us, "Women can't be weak; they have be strong because only the strong will survive!" Yet I think you can show a little bit of compassion, show your feelings and cry, but you can still be a *macho*. My dad was more *macho* than anything, but my mom was strong. I think that there were times when my dad would show more his weaknesses or compassion than my mom. My mom sometimes would come in just as hard as a rock; she was a very determined woman. That's what I think made her succeed in life, and that's what made her raise kids in a barrio to succeed while some of my friends are still working in the fields.

## THE EDUCATION OF VICTOR GARZA

We worked as migrant workers since I was ten years old. We would go up north, work, and then come back to go to school. Then we do this again next year and so on. Plans for the future? I guess I wanted to have a truck like all the people back home. They had big trucks so that they could load up hay or vegetables or animals and take them out and do the normal work that all the people where I lived did. That was my only dream back then. My uncles had trucks, and they would get people to help them go load it up and unload it. Even when I was in the Navy, I used to take vacations and I would go work for my uncle without pay just so I could be with him because I enjoyed being with him. I would take thirty days' vacation and spend it with him loading hay or working loading onions or whatever they were doing at that time back home. I always thought that I was going to do this the rest of my life. There were no dreams at that time. The only dream was to have a truck and be with my family working in the field and have my own big truck.

My early experiences with racism in Texas were the foundations for my life. It's true because that's what I told you earlier that it builds that fire: an anger inside you. How did I stop it? I was able to get an education and then I utilized that education to be able to fight discrimination. I just went to speak [2004] to a class at a college and I asked those kids, "How many of you have been discriminated?" They were all in their twenties and none of them had been discriminated, at least according to them. Today's discrimination is subtle and whites still discriminate against you. If you don't know what you're looking for, then you're not going to spot if you're being discriminated. I can see it easily, but that's from my years of experience and involvement. Discrimination is happening all the time; it happens every day. It happens everywhere. I have that fire—that anger—in me that got built through the years of seeing what was going on not only in my hometown but also everywhere that I traveled. I was able to use that anger here locally in San José, and I guess I started a struggle, a war, a revolution to create changes in our communities so that those that are coming behind us don't have to pay the price like I have or my parents did. I certainly don't want my kids to be discriminated. I needed to do something about it and I guess that fire inside me kept burning. Whenever I heard about issues of discrimination, I continued to build that fire and it got bigger and bigger and it's still there. It's still there.

I joined the Navy in 1955 and went back home in 1959, got married and came back to California in 1960. I worked in the fields for approximately three years in Sanger. By the time I was twenty-six I wanted to change my life. I didn't want to continue that lifestyle so I moved to Los Angeles where I found a job welding because I was a welder in the Navy. I put that skill into practice. After I had been there for about eight or seven years, I moved to San José because all my brothers and sisters were moving from Sanger to San José to go to college and to work. I was the only one that was living in Los Angeles, so I moved.

That was the best move I could have made in my life because then my younger brothers and sisters were going to college and they inspired me to go to college. My younger brothers and sisters got me to go to college. Well, if they could do it, so could I. Even though I only had an eighth-grade education—I dropped out of school when I was fourteen—and I was already thirty-four when I went back to school, I managed to come out with a 3.6 grade average in college and a 4.0 in my master's. I completed both bachelor's and master's degrees in five and a half years. I had three kids, a house, mortgage, and I worked full time or thirty hours a week. But it wasn't easy. It was a lot of work and I had to struggle because if it were easy everybody would do it.

I started to major in mechanical engineering because I used to like welding. I used to make buses, trucks, immigration buses, and armored cars. I could read the blueprints and I could construct them and make them, but I didn't know how to draw them from the beginning and I wanted to learn that. After I got into that,

I changed my mind and went into business management and then I got into politics. I decided to get my major in political science with a public administration emphasis. I continued with a minor in business management and a minor in Chicano Studies because I wanted to know more about my culture, my history, and my background. In my Chicano Studies classes, I read about the injustices in life and I got angrier and angrier.

## THE POLITICS OF PROTEST

Dr. José Carrasco was one of my mentors.[3] In 1968, he led a walkout of students from a school in San José to protest the type of education and treatment that Mexican American kids were getting in school. Dr. Carrasco also organized at least two marches that I participated in. In one, we walked from San José all the way to Sacramento to protest the type of education our kids were getting and the lack of money for bilingual programs and other services that our young people needed. It took us five days to get to Sacramento, and on the fifth day we went up the Capitol steps. At that time, Ronald Reagan was the governor. We did have State Senator Vasconcellos and other elected officials.[4] They were all there waiting for us and receiving us with open arms. They were all Democrats. What we were trying to do was for our kids. These people were there for us, and I thanked them and I still do. I still run into State Senator Alquist; he's in his 90s now.[5] His wife, Elaine, is the one who recently got elected here. I was one of her co-campaign chairs, unfortunately against a Latino that I didn't believe merited the right to serve this community. Therefore, I supported Elaine Alquist who was successful in her bid.[6] Senator Vasconcellos invited me to be one of his guests in Sacramento in August 2004 for a special function that the senate organized to honor him. He wanted me to be there and share it with him. He and I became really good friends, and I call him my *compadre* because he and I are closer than just friends.[7] We're more intimate; we have a bond that's unquestionable. Vasconcellos was always there for us, even when it was unpopular for him to be there for *Mexicanos* and Latinos. He was there with the struggle for our people so I can't help but support people like that.

At the time, Dr. Carrasco was always very involved with situations that were happening in the community. He was the organizer but always in the shadows, trying to organize to get other people to take over. Back then, I was not directly involved but I did participate, but I wasn't one of the forefront leaders. During those years, 1978 or 1977, we were boycotting Great America Amusement Park because they were going to have their grand opening but Great America was not hiring Latinos in management and supervising positions.[8] They were all the sweepers, walking around with a little broom and the pan. They weren't being put in positions they should be put in, so we were picketing them.

There were so many things like this going on at that time. At that time, the Chicano Employment Committee was a very well-known organization. They were leading a lot of these charges into these areas. There were many organizations; some of them have already disappeared, some of them are in hibernation but are still active. I was a member of the American G.I. Forum. Hispanic veterans started it in Texas in 1948. I was also the president of an organization that we called La Raza Parents of Berryessa School District. I'm one of the founding members of that organization, but the organization doesn't exist anymore. The people that continue with the struggle just dropped it. The Chicano Employment Committee was a very powerful, influential organization, but it also disappeared. We had people from MAPA [Mexican American Political Association], from the American G.I. Forum, students from MEChA [Movimiento Estudiantil Chicano de Aztlán—Chicano Student Movement of Aztlán], and others that were involved in wanting to create change. We all marched to Sacramento. We also had several professors and parents that marched with us all the way to Sacramento.

We had a lot of protests at San José State University. For example, in 1972 and 1974, I participated in a sit-in on the stairs of the president's office. I considered him to be very racist. I was one of the students who was sitting there because we wanted to have more Latinos as professors. We wanted more Latino students to be enrolled at the university. We wanted more financial aid. We wanted more housing. We wanted more counselors, and we wanted more tutoring programs. Of course, the university president was anti-all those things. So we sat there in his office and protested until he called the cops. As soon as the cops came in, we all disappeared.

I got my leadership and organizational skills from different people. For example, Dr. José Carrasco was trained by the Saul Alinsky school of leadership and organizing.[9] My younger brother, Humberto, was also trained in this school. Dr. Ramón Martínez was part of this community organizing. We also had José Villa, a strong leader who used to run MACSA [Mexican American Community Services Agency], a very powerful political organization at one time. Others activists included Joe Brito and a few others. When José Villa left MACSA and went to work at the School of Social Work at San José State, the organization MACSA didn't want to be involved politically and then it became more a service organization. There was a vacuum because MACSA used to hold what they called a Friday Forum, like the one I hold now on a monthly basis for La Raza Roundtable.

I remember going to those meetings on Fridays at 4:30 p.m. I never missed a Friday in a whole year. They had those meetings there and then all these people who supposedly were leaders would come in to discuss issues. For example, if they had a problem with the chief of police, they would bring in the chief of police. If they had a problem with the sheriff, they would bring in the sheriff. If they had a problem with the city, they brought in the city manager. They would bring all kinds of politicians to the Friday meetings. I remember just sitting there listening during all these meetings for a whole year, but I never said one word. I wanted to listen and learn and see who were the players, what cliques were there, and who were the leaders of each of the cliques. I finally decided to be vocal and then they couldn't shut me up. But I wanted to learn and I learned a lot from all those people. I learned from the best and can't help but say "Thank you" to all of them.

My mentors taught me not to fear protesting. They taught me to stand up for what I believe. They taught me to believe that I was right, and now when I do something, I do it because it's right. Fred Ross was a great leader.[10] In fact, he was one of the persons that trained César Chávez. Ross had been active in the CSO [Community Service Organization]. They brought a wealth of knowledge to organizing and we needed organizing. When we do things loosely, we don't organize. We are not successful and that's what these people brought. They trained leaders like the ones I mentioned earlier and then they trained us how go out and organize the community.

## THE MAKING OF A PRAGMATIC *POLÍTICO*

What made me want to do something about social injustices? As a child, I think it was a combination of things, but I think as a young man, I guess it was the racism and injustices that I experienced in the military service. I think I am like that Energizer rabbit from the battery commercial because my battery doesn't go out. As time goes on it energizes more. I guess the momentum continues to build, and I think one of things that has helped me a lot is that when you win a battle, it automatically energizes you so much that you have to do something else before you lose that energy. You look for other vehicles, what else to do; you deal with that issue and then you continue to energize. But you know something, when people that are around you feel that they are a part of that change, that energizes them as well. Then they also continue to do other battles. And this is what we need to do. We need to continue. It just energizes more.

My politics? I think probably a Democrat, but I don't vote consistently Democratic. I vote more for the person. And my brothers and I sit down and we talk about it. And we say, "OK, what does this candidate bring?" This is in spite of the fact that the guy is a Republican or a Democrat. We ask each other, "What has this guy done? What is his history?" We begin to look at the candidate and say, "You know what? I don't care about the party; I care about this guy. This guy has done more than this person has done." I think all my brothers and sisters are not one-party persons. They're more likely to focus on the background of an individual and then based on that background, decide how to vote. Yesterday, I was talking to this lady, who came from Fresno with a guy who is running for office in Fresno. They were here last night at this meeting where I was, and her candidate seems to be almost a shoo-in. She asked if we always endorse only Latinos. I said, "No, we have bad Latinos like we have bad white people and I support women just like I support men." We don't just give a blank check to someone because they happen to be Latino. They have to work for it. We all have to earn it, but most importantly you have to be honest with our people. I don't mind if you've never been in office and you happen to be Latino, but if you're honest and you have a reputation of being honest, I will support you. But if you're not honest and you've been in office, I say forget about Victor Garza being there in your corner and that's why I have not supported some Latinos. I guess we fluctuate depending on the issues. To me when it comes to the rights of my people, I'll fight like a wild dog and I'll grab on to you like a bulldog and I won't let you loose. Sometimes I'm conservative, but on other issues I may be very liberal. So it depends. I fluctuate depending on the issues.

I'm a disabled veteran. I had some accidents in the military service and they qualified me to receive a compensation. Knowing the history of how Mexicans, *Tejanos*, Latino, and Hispanic veterans have been treated badly, I got involved with the American G.I. Forum approximately thirty years ago. I have probably been the local commander here in San José longer than anyone else. I have been the state commander two years and I have been a national vice commander and I have been on numerous boards with veterans. There have been great injustices to our veterans, but if you look at the positive part of it, when our veterans were coming from Korea, they were able to use the military service to be able to get an education and many began to get a college education. Others, I remember, were only able to just get a skill like that of a carpenter, plumber, or electrician, but many of them decided to go to college and use their G.I. bill. Then they began to go home, like Eagle Pass, and get jobs. They became teachers, principals, and superintendents. They also became chiefs of police, members of city councils, and some were elected mayors. Many of the guys who were my age that went to Korea, or little bit older, came back and they ran the whole city in my hometown of Eagle Pass, Texas. It was a war that helped them get out of the poor community where they lived. They served their country and those who were lucky enough to come back in one piece were able to get an education to go do something for themselves and their families.

The American G.I. Forum was a vehicle for me in the sense that so many of our people faced discrimination. Hector P. García was the one who started the American G.I. Forum in Corpus Christi, Texas, in 1948. The struggles of Mexican American G.I.s got me so angry and frustrated that I had to be able to get involved and do something. I used to go and meet a lot with the secretary of Veterans Affairs in Washington, D.C., meet with the senators and congressmen and others to try to create change for our people. I tried to get money from them to give to the American G.I. Forum to develop programs so we could do more outreach for the veterans. Many of our people who are veterans are too macho and don't want to accept anything from the government. That doesn't help you. It doesn't help your family. What we needed to do was to get our people to overcome that and to tell them, "Look, you earned this, this is your entitlement, this is not welfare." You earned this by going to serve your country. You earned this by being shot at. You earned this by being wounded; therefore you are entitled to these benefits and your children are also entitled to these benefits.

The American G.I. Forum combats racism faced by those soldiers who had sacrificed themselves in World War II and those who had given the ultimate. They got killed and they were heroes in our communities and they should have been buried in the same cemeteries like the white soldiers. Felix Longoria, who was killed in action in 1944, was one of those who wasn't allowed to be buried in a white cemetery because the white people only allowed whites to be buried there. At that time, Lyndon Johnson, our congressman in Texas, who became president later on, came to the rescue of the American G.I. Forum and got Felix Longoria buried in Arlington Cemetery. When the white people found out that he was going to be buried in Arlington, they said, "Oh, no, he can't be buried here." Well, they gave him a bigger funeral in Arlington than they would have in a little cemetery in the little town. This is an example of pure racism at its best.

First and foremost, the American G.I. Forum is a veterans' organization, and as a veteran myself I felt that I could help out and learn about things that they were doing and I did. I learned a lot from some of the elders and some of the younger veterans who wanted to create changes in the organization. There's always a battle between the elders and the young ones. And a lot of it has to do, I think, with some of the older people becoming conditioned to a certain type of environment within the G.I. Forum. They don't like people coming in and changing it. They like the status quo, and some of the young people want changes. They say, "Hey, we need to do this or we need to do that and some of the older members say, "Oh, no, no, we want to stay here." So then we put it to a vote and many times we're in favor of changing while some were opposed. One of the beautiful things about the American G.I. Forum that I learned was that once a decision was made, I mean everybody gave it their best arguments, then it was placed to be voted and once it was voted on whose ever side won the other ones would get together and support that. I really learned that from the American G.I. Forum. I really like that because if I lost, I'd say, "Well, this is what they want; let's work together." If the other people won, then we'd go that way as well, and we wouldn't complain, but say, "That was the decision of the membership; now let's follow that decision."

The American G.I. Forum is helping veterans and helping our community because the American G.I. Forum focuses on helping Latino veterans, Hispanic veterans. They are focusing on civil rights that impact the Latino community. That excited me and that is what got me involved with them. I'm very much in favor of raising money for scholarships. Here in San José I have helped to raise $75,000 for scholarships. We have been giving them out every year. Our chapter alone did this and that was great, but that wasn't the only thing we did. We fought a lot of civil rights issues. We helped a lot of veterans, and I think that's what we're all about.

The American G.I. Forum is an organization that has been very instrumental in my life and in what I do today because it gave me the training that I needed for me to get involved in other organizations. The American G.I. Forum developed a name recognition for me because I believe up to now, and I'm not a hundred percent sure now, but I think I have been one of the persons that has been elected the most times to be the commander or chair of the organization then anyone else. They have a plaque, but I haven't gone to look at it to see if anybody else has more than I did in the last several years. I also served as state commander, and I helped organize state events throughout the whole state of California. I also served with a national vice commander, and I help organize a lot of activities at the national level as well.

I am still a member of LULAC, but I'm not an active member. If they need me, they call me, and I'm there. I focus on the American G.I. Forum. My time is very limited and I belong to about twenty community organizations and I chaired about half of them until about a year ago [2003]. When I retired, I began to drop some of them because I couldn't continue to come in and be involved in so many organizations. I'm dropping a lot of them off, but I'm going to stay with about four or five of them, the ones that I feel I can contribute more to, and let other leadership struggle with the other organizations. The American G.I. Forum is one organization that I will continue to be a member of and will continue to support.

One of the ones that I'm going to stay focused with and work with is one called Center for Training and Careers (CTC). I've been on their board approximately twenty-two years and they do great work. The lady who runs it has been there also about twenty-two years because I helped her get the job. The organization went from about a $200,000 program to a multimillion dollar program. The other organization is called the Enlace [Link] Program. This a program that I helped found approximately twenty-one years ago. It's a program to help graduate Latinos from Evergreen Community College. We have a tremendous success rate. Our success rate last year was about 88 percent or 90 percent. That means that of all the students that we get through Enlace, about 88 percent or 90 percent succeed and go to a four-year institution. And out of those that go to a four-year institution, if I remember correctly, hardly any don't graduate from college. Our success is admirable. We have had people from Canada, Chicago, New York, and other places come to interview us to find out what makes this program for Mexican Americans so successful and so special.

I founded La Raza Roundtable. We started with seven and we're over five hundred now [2004]. I'd love to continue to be there, but I also need to come up with a way for the organization to continue after I leave. I have told them, "Look, have other people run the meeting. I will stay and continue to be the chair but have the other ones, like co-chairs, run meetings." I will be there in the audience supporting them and then slowly begin to fade out, and by that time hopefully the organization will continue to do the work that they are doing. That's a very important organization in my life as well. Those are the ones I'm seriously thinking of keeping in traveling back and forth and supporting them. I sit on many other organizations, but I'm going to be dropping them off a little bit at a time.

## LA RAZA ROUNDTABLE: A NETWORK OF COMMUNITY BUILDERS

MACSA [Mexican American Community Services Agency] used to have a Friday Forum, but it disappeared when the leadership changed and the person who took over there didn't want to have it. So that vacuum was there. We didn't have a forum where different organizations could come in together and discuss issues that were having an impact on the community. MAPA, LULAC, American G.I. Forum, Chicano Employment Committee—all kinds of organizations were working in the community, but each one of them was doing its own little thing.

The major issues weren't being taken on because maybe only one organization will take them on and all the other ones stay out. For many, many years, about five or six years, I had people asking me to organize the La Raza Roundtable because the Friday Forum was in hibernation. I didn't want to do it because I know my people, and many times when you organize something and they get you to do something, then they disappear on you and you're left standing there by yourself. One day I said, "OK, let's do it." There were seven of us sitting there at the table. I said, "All of you have been after me to do this for a long time. So let's do it now, but I want a commitment from each and every one of you that you are going to attend every meeting we have and that you will bring one other person with you to the meetings. We're going to sit down, even if it's only us, and discuss the issues. We're going to divide the work and we're going to deal with it."

They said "OK" and so all seven of us got together and then we brought in a guest that was a potential member. Then we began to talk about it and I said, "OK, we're dealing with this issue; why don't we bring in Councilman so-and-so?" and then we brought in that councilman. Whoever had the best relationship invited the councilman. We confirmed it and we held the meeting. We let people know and then slowly the people kept coming in. We would say, "Why don't we bring in Senator Vasconcellos? And then let's bring in Congressmen Norm Mineta." We always brought someone important to our meetings, then when other people got wind of it, they began to participate. We started these meetings about thirteen or fourteen years ago.

I have always felt that I've been the same politically. Let me give you an example even if it isn't political but it is an example of involvement. When I was a kid in school, I was the guy that all the kids in my neighborhood looked at to help them out with problems, particularly fights. We used to have fights, not gangs like we have today, but we had our little cliques from the barrios. For example, we used to fight about girls. If I wanted to date a girl in another neighborhood, I couldn't because the gang out there would come and beat me up. So when something like that happened, then these guys would come to me to help them fight those guys. For some reason or another I was always in the middle. It happened in school. It happened everywhere and I was always there. Kids began to always follow me or ask me for help and I was always there for them, and I still continue to find that same trouble because I call them the underdogs. The other guys are the abusers, the bullies.

In politics, it's the same way. There are those that have and those that don't. And if you want to have something, you can't because those people up there will beat you up. And in politics I see the same thing. The politicians have all this power and the community needs certain changes. The community organizes itself and unites. If you have a little money and a lot of votes, you can influence politicians because what makes a politician is money and votes. La Raza Roundtable began to have one city councilman come and meet with us and give us a commitment. Then, we would bring in another city councilman and get a commitment. By the time we noticed it, we had four commitments from politicians. I think there were seven at one time. Then we could take up an issue and we would win. But it took time because you have to have a meeting with each one [councilman] of them separately and it takes time.

We'd have a lot of meetings before our meetings and discuss who was going to say this and who was going to say that, and who was going to take notes, or who was going to be the observer. When we all came back after the meetings, we would know what mistakes we made. These organizing meetings were always well scripted. Only those who participated in the earlier meeting were allowed to participate in the discussion with the politicians and other officials. If you didn't participate in the earlier meeting, you would not participate in the discussion with these people and that way they were forced to come in and be part of the original pre-meeting before we went into action.

The Raza Roundtable helped to organize the San José community. You'd be surprised at the composition of the organization if you attend one of our meetings. I didn't expect the Raza Roundtable to be so great. I expected it to be good, but not that great. I'm so proud of all the members and the commitment they made. We meet on Friday at 5:30 p.m. What are most people doing at 5:30 p.m.? Well, they're someplace else. They're certainly not working and doing something for the community. So you see, they have to have some strong commitment for people to attend our meetings on a Friday at 5:30 p.m. Many people have said, "Why Friday 5:30 p.m.?" I said, "Look in here, look at the room. They don't care if it's Friday at 5:30 p.m. They're here because they care, and if you care, you'll be here too." I think that the local San José community sees us as a vehicle to solve a multitude of problems. It's difficult, of course, for one organization to solve the problems of the city. Otherwise all of the members of La Raza Roundtable would be city council members and I would be mayor, but that's not so. We do make an effort to solve many problems.

## ENLACE: A STUDENT PROGRAM FOR THE FUTURE GENERATION
The idea person for the Enlace Program was a doctor named Dr. Chávez. He passed away at a very young age when he was only about forty-one years old. Dr.

Chávez was the one who started the Puente Program [Bridge Program] for high school children. We became partners with Puente; however, the leadership with Puente only focused on tutoring English. We told them that the kids needed math. It didn't do the kids any good to be successful only in English and not successful in math. If you're successful in English and in math, you can do well in the rest of the other courses. If not, you're only doing half the job.

A lot of the kids that we get in our program are failing because they don't have math and so we incorporated math into our Enlace [Link] program. We created our own organization and that's where Enlace came into play. We were Puente for a couple of years and then we transitioned into Enlace. Math and English can open the doors and you can move in any direction you want. We have incorporated science into our system because we're in Silicon Valley. Since we're in Silicon Valley, we felt that science would be a good motivator to get our students to go into Silicon Valley and get good jobs. We have done that here at Evergreen Valley College, but there have been many other groups, like African American and Asians who have created similar programs like ours. They haven't been as successful as we have and there's different reasons for that, but we are very proud of this program because I don't believe there's another, aside from Bellarmine, that can be as successful as we have been here locally with the students that are going to Evergreen Valley College who then go to Santa Clara University, the University of California at Davis, and the University of California at Santa Cruz, and some, even to Harvard.[11]

We have helped a ton of young people do that, in particularly women because more Latina women are going to college than men and many of them are single heads of household. Many of them have gone through hell in many ways, but they're beginning to put their lives together, and Enlace is a program that develops leadership skills and gets students involved.

We motivated them into leadership positions, got them involved with La Raza Roundtable, and had them meet a lot of the politicians, judges, and other people. For example, there's a judge who's working with children and families who are having problems. I asked for volunteers and I said, "I would like to see you guys up there because I normally see white students doing these kinds of things." I said, "I would like to see you involved. Go see the judge; she'd like to talk to you." Then they got involved and liked the idea of being involved with this judge. I think that's great because it motivates them to do things that they never thought they could do, like sitting in the same room with a judge. Those are the kinds of things that Enlace does.

## REFLECTIONS ON MY ACTIVISM

What kind of changes did I want to see? I wanted to see more teachers and counselors that would reflect the people that they serve. We use to call it parity. The number of Latino students who go to school happen to be a large percentage, and we wanted to have a large percentage of teachers, counselors, administrators that reflect that. I wanted the kids to be taught in bilingual classes and be able to transition them from bilingual to English only. They still say that a young person who is taught in his native language and transitions to the English language can be more successful than an Anglo American who is taking courses. I have seen some of those reports, and we felt that it was wrong in not giving them an opportunity to be taught in their native language. But not forever. The purpose is to transition them into the English language so that they can be able to perform to the best of their abilities. If you give them an English test and they're Spanish speaking, how can they do well? And then they call them "mentally retarded," and you and I know that they're not because if they were performing at their top level in their schools in Mexico, how can they be mentally retarded here, only because they cannot understand the foreign language? That was [the kind of] protests that we had in those times.

I ran for office in the '70s. In fact, I was the first Chicano ever elected to the Berryessa School District and that's an old school district.[12] I was fortunate at that time, of course, that during those years we had about 11 percent Latinos in that community. I think we had about 1.5 percent Asians, 1.5 percent blacks, and the rest were white. I managed to win handsomely, but the people loved me because I'd been involved in the community for a long time. I was involved in the church and I was involved in the school. I was also involved in different committees. I was involved in the community and they all knew me, and I went up there and they all supported me by voting for me. I got twice as many votes as the top contender that was white and yet they never had a Latino in office before. I ran for office once for the city council and I lost by about seventy-five votes. I think I would have won, but then I said, "Well, this is now the time for others and I will work and support them." And that's what I've been doing since then, just working and supporting different candidates and getting them to work with the Latino community. All I ever ask of any candidate is this: "I want you to have your office open to our community, and if you have your office open and I call you and you respond, hey, that's all I want, I don't want anything else."

## NOTES

1. *Gringo* is a term used for whites by some Mexicans/Mexican Americans.

2. Villa and Zapata were key figures of the 1910 Mexican Revolution.

3. Carrasco was a professor of social work at San José State University.

4. John B. Vasconcellos represented San José as a member of the California state assembly for thirty years and a California state senator for eight years.

5. State Senator Al Alquist began his legislative career in 1962 when he was elected to the assembly. He served there four years before winning election to the senate, where he served for thirty years. He was forced out by term limits in 1996 and passed away in 2006.

6. State Senator Elaine K. Alquist represents 13th Senate District of Santa Clara County. The district includes cities San José, Sunnyvale, Santa Clara, Mountain View, and Gilroy.

7. *Compadre* is a term usually used to refer to the godfather of a person's child. It is used here as a term of endearment for a close friend.

8. Great America is located in Santa Clara, California.

9. Saul Alinsky (1909–1972) is considered the father of community organizing. Alinsky began his organizing in Chicago and founded the Industrial Areas Foundation, which trained organizers and helped in the founding of grassroots community organizations throughout the country. He established the basis for confrontational politics.

10. Fred Ross was a community organizer, trained by Saul Alinsky, who worked in the CSO.

11. Bellarmine is an all-male, private, Jesuit college preparatory high school in San José, California.

12. This is a district adjacent to the San José Unified School District.

# 2

# Blanca Alvarado

*Before Blanca Alvarado launched her San José political career that began in 1980 when she was elected to the San José city council representing the newly created fifth district of East San José, a primarily low-income Latino neighborhood, she was involved in various community-organizing events. She was named local president of the Mexican American Political Association (MAPA); picketed Most Holy Trinity Church, demanding that the diocese hold Mass in Spanish; and headed the Northern California chapter of the Viva Carter campaign. She was elected to the Santa Clara County Board of Supervisors in March 1996, after completing Zoe Lofgren's unexpired term, and in January 1998, she served as the first Latina chairperson in the county's history. Alvarado was elected to her second term in 2000, and in 2003, she once again served as the chairperson of the board. Blanca was re-elected for her third and final term in March 2004. Blanca Alvarado represents one of the most influential political figures in San José.*

## CHILDHOOD: "I ALREADY HAD A SENSE OF SOCIAL PURPOSE AND SOCIAL JUSTICE"

I grew up in the small community of Cokedale, Colorado, where everybody knew everybody. My parents raised twelve children. My father was a coal miner, and my mother took care of raising us. My father was a seventh- or eighth-generation American-born Mexican. I have tremendous admiration and respect for my father. He was a hard-working man who cared deeply about his family. He was a very well-read man, although he had only a third-grade education. He was very knowledgeable about what was happening in current events. He was still a self-educated man. I remember that his heroes were John L. Lewis, the head of the coal miners' workers and, of course, Franklin Delano Roosevelt because we were living in the Depression era. He was also very involved in the affairs of the union, and so I consider him a role model. He always stressed how important it was for a person to be involved in civic duties. My mother was of Native American Indian stock and was a hard-working woman who devoted her life to raising twelve children.

The adage of "it takes a village to raise a child" is appropriate in describing our community. I could run into the neighbor's house or be anywhere in the camp and feel that I was safe, secure, and in a friendly environment. We had ovens where the community cooked their big loaves of bread. I still remember many of the people from my hometown, like Doña María and some of her cures. If you had a fever, she would come around and dip potato slices in vinegar and then wrap them around your head with a handkerchief. Another one was a little more unpleasant. She would make necklaces of garlic to tie around your neck as a general cure for sicknesses. I have many wonderful memories of those days. I also remember being very aware that there were many Spanish-surnamed elected officials in our county, such as the sheriff and the tax assessor. I believe that, in many ways, this environment played a role in molding my pursuing a political career.

It wasn't until many years later that I realized that although I didn't experience actual discrimination, a hierarchical system existed in our community. Only one Mexican immigrant family, for example, lived in our community. I will never forget that family. I remember Betty, one of the daughters, who was my age. The rest of the people looked down on her because she was from Mexico. I remember standing up for her because I found it unfair that the other children treated her so harshly. When I think about my childhood, I recognize that this experience showed that I already had a sense of social purpose and social justice. Another source of discrimination was that the superintendents and all of the managers of the miners considered the workers and their families lower class. They had better housing than all of us. We considered them the elite segment of the community. The coal mine company owned everything: the schools, the church, the company store, and the homes where we lived. Inequality was visible throughout the town.

In 1947, when I was about fifteen, we had to leave Colorado when the mines were closing down, and my dad had a relative in Los Angeles and he would write to my dad and tell him, "You should come to California. You're going to be able to make a lot of money in the fields. With so many in your family, you'll have more people to work in the fields than other families." My dad was the only person in the camps who had saved $2,000 to be able to move his family to California. Most of the other families went to Provo, Utah, or Pueblo, New Mexico, to find work in the mines. But my dad packed our meager belongings in a big truck and we headed west. It was a long trek across the desert, and very uncomfortable. It was very, very hot through Barstow, California, but my first glimpse of California was very awe-inspiring. I remember that I was very impressed when I saw palm trees for the first time. I knew that I was coming to glamorous California, and seeing the palm trees was something that stayed in my mind for a long time. To this day, I have a great affection for palm trees.

When we arrived in California, we went immediately to Los Angeles where we soon found a house. We lived in it for about six weeks. One of the most terrifying incidents I experienced during the short time that we lived in Los Angeles was going through Griffith Park. I was accosted by a group of *cholas* [Mexican American girl gang members]—it scared the hell out of me as you can well imagine because they were very threatening. They had beehive hairdos, and I think they had knives stuck in their hair. It was a pretty frightening experience. I don't remember how I managed to get away or if they let me get away.

Once, we came up to San José City but only intended to be here for the summer. We worked on a ranch on Quimby Road and lived in tin shacks that were common types of housing for migrant farm workers. We were expecting to go back to Los Angeles, but my father was actually offered a job as a foreman at the McClay Ranch and so we ended up staying here in San José. We lived at the McClay Ranch for about three years until we found a house in the Evergreen neighborhood of San José.

## MY SCHOOLING: "ONE SIGNIFICANT PERSON CAN MAKE ALL THE DIFFERENCE IN YOUR WORLD"

Once we settled in San José, I began attending San Jose High School. Although I only completed high school, I have taught myself most of everything that I know. I have always had an incredible interest in learning and an insatiable appetite for reading. San Jose High was a cherished experience for many reasons. Only a very small number of Latino students attended San Jose High in those days. There couldn't have been more than twenty of us at the time, and so it didn't take us long to gravitate towards each other and form our own mini-community within the school. We organized ourselves in a group with the help of a wonderful woman who used to work for Catholic Charities right there on campus. At that time, San Jose High was on the same campus as San José State University. I mention her because I have found that there are times in one's life when one significant person can make all the difference in your world. She took us under her wing and showed us that she cared about us. She helped us develop a pride in being Latinos.

We formed a club and named it the Club Tapatio [from the state of Jalisco, Mexico]. Club Tapatio was probably the first Latino ethnic social club at San Jose High. I can't imagine that there was anything like that before ours. It was kind of cool because, in addition to organizing social activities, we conducted food and clothing drives for the poor. Some of those in the group, like Bernie Zamora, had real musical talent. We organized performances and would charge an entrance fee so that we could raise money for our projects. Our Club Tapatio was a very close-knit and wonderful small group. Sometimes, when I look back on those times, I wonder what happened to Rosie and Bobby and other special childhood or high school friends who were such a very, very vital part of my life.

While I was in high school, I experienced another very important event in my life and for my future; I met José Alvarado. During the late 1940s and early 1950s, José Alvarado was a very prominent figure in this part of California. He had come from Mexico around 1920 when he was about sixteen or seventeen. His mother had sent him out of the country in order to escape from the violence of the Mexican Revolution. José Alvarado was a fascinating man who accomplished many things in his life. I would say that he was a man of heroic proportions given the times. He worked in the mines and traveled across the country but eventually settled here in San José while most of his other siblings settled in Tijuana and Los Angeles. José had a very forceful personality and didn't mince words. He was always outspoken, and this created enemies for him. He wrote a newspaper column in the *San Jose Mercury News* back in those days. He was a strong advocate for the Latino community, and his activism included his protest against the chief of police about police brutality in the Latino community. José always worked as an advocate on behalf of Latino families. He also had a very popular program on KLOK radio station, the first bilingual radio program in Northern California. He had a tremendous following in San José, Sacramento, and Fresno. He played mostly hit songs from Mexico, and people just loved his program. José was a social crusader, and he constantly exhorted the Latino community to pay attention to their lives here in the United States. He always used to say, "We're never going to get ahead if you have one foot here and one foot over in Mexico. It's important that you educate your children. It's important that you vote here in the

United States. It's important that you be involved in your community, the Latino community."

José also did something that was fairly important to help the community. Since he knew that the Latino kids didn't have a lot of outlets for recreation, he established a clubhouse for them. He set up the clubhouse in the broadcasting studio. He put up Coke machines, Ping-Pong tables, chess tables, and a jukebox so that we had a place to hang out after school. We talk about kids' after-school recreational programs now, but he thought of it a long, long time ago. My friends and I gravitated to this clubhouse, and we spent a lot of time there.

I eventually became familiar with the work that he was doing as a social advocate, as an entrepreneur, and as a radio personality. José was also an entertainment promoter who brought in some of the biggest Mexican artists from Mexico. I was not even twenty years old yet and to be in the midst of the man who brought so many famous musicians the city. I mean you name it! It was pretty remarkable. It was a very exciting and very glamorous place to be. The Mexican artists would perform in the Palomar Ballroom. Latino kids came from all over Northern California, and the lines were very long to get into the ballroom. The Palomar Ballroom was a place where the Latino community, young and old, gathered for entertainment. It was a place in our community where we took pride in our music and in our actors, singers, and performers. We had great times there. I think it was that experience at the Palomar Ballroom that planted the seed in me for the Mexican Heritage Plaza.

Eventually José and I became a twosome, a couple. When I married José in 1953, he was quite a catch. I was the envy of the town! We had built a wonderful a relationship for five years when I was a young teenager, but he was considerably older than me. José was already forty-four when I married him. Even though there was quite an age difference between us, we had a wonderful marriage and we had five very, very beautiful children who, to this day, are the source of great pride because of their own significant achievements. One of my sons, Jaime, is the executive director of a local agency, which is quite a challenging occupation. My daughter, Theresa, is the spitting image of her dad. She was the youngest of the five and the founder of the Latino Coalition. So our family's genetic political strain is being passed on.

José and I ran into some hard times about the sixth year of our marriage. He still had his radio program, but had created some enemies within the community. Some people believed that some of his remarks on his radio show were unpatriotic to the United States. When he went before the judge for his U.S. citizenship, some members of the community had found out and went there to protest. They claimed that he was a Communist and that he should not be allowed citizenship. Even though he did get his citizenship, these same people continued their efforts to undermine his popularity and his standing in the Latino community. They began an economic boycott of his program's sponsors. This boycott went on for a long time, but fortunately for José, the owner of the station supported José's work. He appreciated José for being so successful at bringing in lots of money to the station through the advertising slots purchased by businesses, but he also believed in José's causes. Eventually, as the boycott continued and José became more controversial, the station owner said, "You're going to have to just concentrate on the commercial aspects of the program or I'm just going to have to let you go." José, of course, would not compromise his values and refused to change the format of the program. The economic boycott produced so much political pressure on the radio station that José was let go.

He then went to work at KOFY, a radio station in San Francisco, but it was never the same after that. By then other prominent radio announcers had become well established in San José, and José never really regained his stature in the community. I think that affected him psychologically. It must have been very painful for him because he had great expectations that the community would come to his rally and defend him. This didn't happen and, in some ways, he was heartbroken. As time went on, that began to affect our own relationship, and we divorced in 1968.

After I divorced José, I found myself raising our children on my own and so I had to go to work. I had always worked with José during all the years before and after we were married. I ended up working for a public accountant in Palo Alto who was a wonderful man. He was very, very considerate of me. I learned good fundamental accounting skills there, using my good math ability and knowledge. This job was invaluable in refining my abilities and moving me into another field that provided financial support for my kids and myself.

## SOCIAL ACTIVIST: "A HEIGHTENED AWARENESS"

Before I divorced José, I had become very active with him in San José's East Side community when César Chávez was beginning his organizing work, particularly in the Mayfair District. José and I joined other people in the East Side and began to work with Father McDonald and César Chávez. César Chávez began to organize the Community Service Organization [CSO] that eventually led to his attending the Saul Alinsky Institute to learn more organizing skills. His success in the farm workers union movement came out of this experience. Many of San

José's community leaders refined their political skills and political awareness during this time period. I can name a lot of people in the Chicano Movement that came out of the East Side area, including Ernestina García.[1] César Chávez's activism was, of course, very crucial. We were the people that started to lay the foundation for political involvement and were responsible for helping to put in place the building blocks for the kind of political activism that is now present in San José. No one person can ever take credit for what is happening now, insofar as political activism is concerned, without acknowledging those building blocks that were formed with great difficulty back in those years. Our political activism represented a heightened awareness about the need to work towards social justice in our community.

My social activist experiences at Most Holy Trinity parish proved to be challenging and very fruitful. A large Spanish-speaking population existed near Cunningham Avenue where the Most Holy Trinity parish was located. I had been a parishioner at Guadalupe Church, but when we moved, I became a parishioner at Most Holy Trinity. We soon began to advocate for a Spanish-language Mass and of course they said, "No way. You can't have a Spanish-language Mass." But we were not going to take a "no" for an answer, and so we organized ourselves and even went up to the archbishop in San Francisco to picket. We made a lot of noise and, eventually, they conceded and we finally got our Sunday morning, eight o'-clock Spanish-language Mass. Then we said, "Well, we're going to do a little bit more. We're going to organize a breakfast every Sunday." We called ourselves, "*Los Amigos de* Most Holy Trinity" [Friends of Most Holy Trinity]. This group reminded me of my childhood upbringing in Colorado where a community of families met to worship on Sundays and also engaged in social activism and organized social gatherings. To this day, my kids will say that those were some of the happiest memories for them. They never even protested about going to Mass because it was fun and it was meaningful. It was wonderful because it bonded members of our community. These kinds of community activities produced leaders who succeeded in influencing the church and working to improve the educational system. It was just a natural setting for us to continue evolving towards an activism that recognized the value of us, as Latinos, in determining our own destiny.

This activism became a real lightning rod for other types of social activism. Community activism was spreading throughout the Latino community. For example, when Danny Treviño was killed, the entire community, led by our clergy, mobilized to protest his killing and police brutality in San José. Although we were only a small group, we became a forceful presence in the community.

After working in Palo Alto, I had a short stint at a social services agency as an eligibility worker. Since I was on welfare at the time, my eligibility worker said, "OK, there's a new opening the state has made available. You should apply for it. It will give you chance to work with other welfare families having been a welfare recipient yourself. The experience that you bring and the empathy that you bring will be very helpful." So I did and it was great because I got to help many families. All of a sudden, in 1966, when Ronald Reagan became governor of California and the so-called welfare reform took place, it was chaotic for those of us who were eligibility workers. You could spend days and days and days and hours and hours not knowing what the welfare regulations were and literally not being able to help people. It was a very frustrating time.

It was about that time that I was recruited by the Opportunities Industrial Council [OIC], now known as the Center for Employment and Training [CET]. The establishment of OIC grew out of a tremendous amount of community activism. Antonio Soto [community activist] was at the helm. It was also the hub for training people for better jobs. I was a counselor although I had never been trained to be a counselor. I started working with the head of the electronics-training unit. This unit was the best of all of the OIC units because the electronics industry was beginning to flourish in San José and the surrounding area.

When I talked to trainees, I learned to empathize with their life situation. I tried to inspire them to develop a sense of purpose and self-confidence. We were training a lot of students and finding job placements for them. Later, I was transferred to the Market Street office to do job development, and we ran into a lot of problems there because by then the recession had hit. We were having a very difficult time, but in the process of my work at OIC, I was greatly inspired by one particular OIC member. He was a great orator and, in the traditional African American style of oratory, a very inspiring man. He would mesmerize the staff, students, and trainees. In some ways, we were like a cult at OIC. There was such closeness, such dedication, and such devotion to the cause that any attempt to deviate from the primary mission was frowned upon. Our job was to provide our trainees with the necessary skills to get them out into the workforce.

Internal problems, however, eventually developed in OIC. It became a little bit unhealthy for me. When I applied to be a manager, I was told very clearly that only males could be managers in the organization. I remember them saying, "No way, Blanca! You'll never be a manager here." Women experienced discrimination because they would not be hired or promoted to certain jobs. It was a very discriminatory practice that began to create serious polarization within the ranks.

The women were the teachers and the clerks, but there was no opportunity to advance within the organization, no matter how hard you tried, and no matter how much you produced. Rumblings among the women soon developed, and over a period of two years, the discontent continued to grow, but the managers refused to acknowledge that discrimination existed. As more supervisors became aware that the rumblings were deepening and that friction was increasing, members of the board began to raise concerns about it. Ernie Abatia, who was a key figure in the farm worker movement, was a member of the board of OIC. He began to raise this issue, but very little was done to address our concerns.

## BREAKING INTO POLITICS

I was the chapter chair for the San José Mexican American Political Association [MAPA]. Some San José politicians became aware of my work in MAPA. Mayor Janet Gray Hayes appointed me to serve on the Bicentennial Commission, which was celebrating the 200th birthday of the city of San José. This appointment was key to the mayor, who later appointed me to sit on a newly formed citizens review committee. The committee would explore the forms of municipal government across the country so that we could then present a proposal to the San José city council regarding the election of our council representatives. At that time the council was elected at large and the only Latino to sit on the city council—Al Garza—had been appointed. I spent two years working on the charter review committee, and at the end of that review, we presented a proposal to the city council recommending that the city council be elected by district. It was monumental. It was historical. The council approved the recommendation, took it to the ballot, voters voted on it, and it passed, but by a very, very short margin, but it passed nonetheless.

It was 1978 and voters were saying things like, "Yes, we need to have districted elections for the city council." And so I said, "OK, we've got a district now!" We've been fighting and talking about a district for East San José for a long time. Now what are we as the leaders in MAPA going to do? We began to ask various people if they wanted to run for election, but nobody was interested. A city council member earned about $400 a month, which was a great incentive, but you really had to have a lot of fire in the belly to run for office. I had worked on several political campaigns for local and state Latino candidates, including José Vasquez's campaign in the early 1970s when he ran for the city council. Many of the candidates for whom I campaigned never won, but I got a lot of practice in electoral politics. Those of us active in MAPA learned a lot about how politics worked.

When we couldn't find anybody that was willing to run for the city council position, people began to ask me. "Well, why don't you do it, Blanca?" I said, "No, I
can't do it. I can't do it. I can't do it. This isn't what I want to do." I believed that
running for office was very intimidating and candidates who run and those who
are elected take on an enormous responsibility. As time went on, we found ourselves wondering, "What's going to happen here? We, as Latinos have aspired for
this political opportunity for such a long time, and yet we can't find anybody
who wants to do it."

Then, one day, a young, handsome-looking man came to me and said, "You
know, Al Garza suggested that I come and talk to you. I'm running for the city
council from the fifth district." I looked at him and I was polite and attentive, but
as soon as he walked out the door, I called some of my friends and said, "You
know what? We can't stand by and let a person who has never lived in the district
win the election!" He probably considered the fifth district as the easiest district
to win in because of the low voter participation among Latinos living in this district. He probably was thinking that he could take advantage of such a district
that had low-income residents who were not very familiar with the voting
process. I thought to myself, "This is ridiculous! We cannot just stand by and let
this happen. Of course he has a right to run, but we've got to get our candidate."
So I began to reflect on it and thought, "Well, I've been in the district for thirty
years and I have strong ties to the community. So maybe I should do it. Maybe I
should run." And I did run.

It was one of the best decisions I ever made in my life. That campaign of 1980
was so invigorating and so exciting. I found it thrilling that we were able to put
together an organization of volunteers to run the campaign. We were able to get
broad support from stakeholders in the community, and we just had a ball! The
election was just powerful. Five candidates ran in the election, but some tension
and hostility developed among the candidates and within the community that
carried over to the 1982 election. As I remember, I won 68 percent of the vote.
We got a taste of victory, and to this day, those of us who were in that campaign
remember it with tremendous pride and emotion. What a monumental under-
taking that was, but what a huge victory we pulled off when I won the election.

I took the oath of office in January of 1981, but because there were ten brand
new districts, the re-elections had to be staggered. The odd-numbered districts,
like five, would have to run for re-election the following year. Since I was installed
in 1981, I had to go back for re-election in 1982. I said, "I just got elected. I can't
imagine that the public isn't going to support my re-election." It just made sense

to me that having only been in office one year that my constituents would not have unreasonable expectations of my productivity during that year, so I didn't really pay enough serious attention to the primary. The woman that ran in 1980, Juanita Duarte, put in a lot of her own money and ran a very aggressive, anti-Blanca campaign. While the 1980 election campaign had been so powerful and so positive and so energized, this was entirely the opposite. I was devastated by the time that the primary ended. I could not believe that I came in second and Juanita came in first. It was one of the most slanderous primary campaigns one can imagine. It was vile. It was truly vile. I was accused of embezzlement and some other really horrendous, ugly things. But because I didn't think anybody could possibly believe it, I campaigned, but I didn't defend myself or make any effort to set the record straight. I was reeling from the shock of it all.

I was still on the council of course, but my supporters began to put things in perspective and they said, "You know Blanca, we've worked too hard for this. We can't afford to lose this seat. She's a Latina and the community may believe that her heart is in the right place, but you can't give up." So one of my kids told me, "Mom, you have to go and see that movie *Rocky*." I did and I came out of the theater and said to myself, "OK. I'm going to come out swinging this time." I really was so refreshed in my outlook after having staggered from the first initial almost-knockout blow. Soon, I was ready to go out there and campaign. We pulled ourselves together and had a tremendous second part of the election. I remember a quote that came out in the media from one community hearing out at Overfelt High School where my opponent and I were debating: "Alvarado tells opponent it takes more than a big mouth to get things done at city hall." That quote was everywhere: "It takes more than a big mouth." I said that because at that meeting she was truly outrageous and had some of people she had "planted" in the audience come up and make presentations like, "Here's proof that you've been embezzling from the city. And here is proof that you've been doing it." It was slanderous. Nonetheless, we got through that second election and won again with high marks in the November election. That was really the start of my political career in San José.

Looking back, I realize that I was really a political novice. I knew a lot about the community, but it was a very difficult time. Getting elected is probably the easiest part. Once you're in office, what you have to balance is not only the needs of the district, which oftentimes leads to conflict among constituencies, but those of the other nine council districts and the mayor. I found that sometimes their responsibilities and needs were very different from mine. The needs of my district were probably the harshest because it was a very low-income community within the city of San José. The first four years were spent trying to put together a political agenda because there were so many issues, so many problems. Where do you start? I found it very difficult to know where to begin.

I knew that we had many problems in the East Side: drug use, police brutality, substandard housing, unemployment, poverty, and teenage pregnancy. Every social ill imaginable was concentrated in the fifth district. One serious problem involved the cruising on Story Road. It was really terrible. We had thousands of cruisers coming to Story Road from as far away as Sacramento, Fresno, and Salinas. San José was considered the cruising capital of the world. It was a disaster because thousands of cars were cruising up and down Story Road. Families living along Story Road couldn't get in or out of their driveways and were subjected to noise until two, three, four o'clock in the morning. Oftentimes, emergency vehicles couldn't get through. The worst thing for me was that so many of our youth were getting involved in cruising as a pastime. The environment was pretty highly charged with drug use, and it was common to see ten-, eleven-, twelve-year-olds getting involved in the cruising scene.

Ironically, I had been a supporter of cruising as a cultural phenomenon! Sometimes it can be a good thing. I have found that those involved in cruising take pride in their beautiful cars. It is a cultural thing, but I had to weigh that against the needs of the community. Talk about conflicting needs in the district! I decided to take on the problem of cruising head on. Believe me, I was pilloried for it, especially by the car clubs and even by our own chief of police who did not support my initial efforts to deal with the cruising problem. The night that we were going to discuss it with the city council, the chief of police said, "No, it's not a good idea. We can't do this." So the city council rejected my proposal at that time.

I then began to work with the city attorney. Story Road, where the cruising was taking place, is a public street, and there are limitations to what you can do on streets. Since everybody has the right to have access to the entire street, I began to look at legal options available to me in dealing with the cruising. The first thing that I had to do was go to the private property owners along the strip and see if they would be willing to post "No Parking" signs. The merchants were having a terrible time with the litter and with the noise associated with the cruising. Once the property owners agreed and those signs were posted, then the police department had the legal means by which they could try to move them out. After doing much research, I came up with the idea of creating a "No Cruising" zone. The law permits this under special circumstances. With the help of my attorney, I was able to establish a "No Cruising" zone on Story Road. That didn't completely eliminate the problem, but it lessened it. A "No Cruising" zone meant that the police could enforce the law if the cars were blocking the parking lots. The law also prohibited cars from driving slowly along Story Road. In other words, cars couldn't cruise down the street. This area is now a very thriving neighborhood business district. The people that lived along Story and King were just so grateful, and to this day, they say that this was one of the most important things that happened during my tenure on the city council.

It's now wonderful to drive along Story Road and see all the development that has taken place over the years. The problem with the cruising helped me because it gave me the political experience to set the stage for the kind of development projects that were eventually carried out on Story Road and other parts of San José's East Side. These projects took me, and those working with me, about eight years to complete.

After addressing the cruising issue, I then turned my attention to another extraordinarily serious problem: the horrific slum housing on Story Road. Some of the tenants living in these properties contacted me to complain loudly. They were living in substandard housing and no matter how many times they called the landlord, there was never any resolution to their problem. They had leaking roofs, vermin, and everything else that made their living conditions uninhabitable. I was challenged with this major problem because, while we had no jurisdiction except through code enforcement, the property owners ignored the code enforcement citations that they received. An apartment unit located on the frontage of Story Road had become a drug haven. It was so bad that it was disgusting. It just turned your stomach when you saw these living conditions. The first thing that I did was to establish a neighborhood community center near that location. As a community center, police would have to make regular rounds to enforce various city codes and maintain order. Eventually, one of the landlords committed suicide because he was under such tremendous pressure. The media had focused on his units, describing their horrible conditions. The public interest law firm had taken on this particular landlord, and we had our code enforcement and legal people going after him, too. He couldn't take the pressure so he committed suicide.

Soon after this, I began to explore the possibility of acquiring all of the housing units in order to create a completely new neighborhood. I realized that this was a daunting task that was going to take millions of dollars to accomplish. I didn't know if the city council would be willing to make that kind of an investment.

Alex Sánchez, who was our housing director at the time, and I put our heads together. He said, "This is how we can do it. We can do it if the city will purchase these lands." We agreed that some of the apartment buildings should be completely demolished, but others suggested that they be renovated. As a result, we identified which ones would be torn down and which ones would be remodeled. We presented a proposal to the city council that asked for about twenty million dollars to carry out this plan. I had no idea if the council would be supportive, but by then the local newspaper published an exposé of the terrible housing conditions, putting a tremendous amount of pressure on the city council. Eventually, the council approved the twenty million and we immediately began our plans to implement our project by creating a Neighborhood Task Force composed of residents from that area.

We spent a whole year coming up with the design for the new community housing units. I think I can say that all those involved believed that their work on this task force was a fabulous experience. We built a park and completely remodeled the school playground that was located next door to the beautiful new housing units. This area is now completely different from how it was when I first took office. When I look back on the things that I accomplished when I was on the city council, I think that this neighborhood renewal project has got to be the most amazing success story.

I then turned my attention to another project: the establishment of a cultural plaza. I first got the idea of the plaza because I knew that San José didn't really have a place where people could come together to share and enjoy our Mexican culture through organized community activities, through which we would both preserve and pass on our culture and share it with other communities in San José. Then Mayor Tom McEnery was very supportive of this project from the very beginning. We had come up with the idea that San José would become a city of ethnic gardens. We had the Japanese Friendship Gardens and the Chinese Overfelt Gardens. Then we said, "You know we ought to have other ethnic gardens. We should have a Mexican garden." The city said, "Oh, great idea." Tom was very supportive, and I have to give him a lot of credit for being there with me in those early years. As we began to plan and to talk about what we wanted, we formed a task force. Task forces are great because they come up with great visions and great ideas, but the problem is how to implement these ideas and visions.

We soon started the search for a site for the cultural center. I had always liked the idea of building the center next door to San José's Guadalupe Church because of its significance in the city's history. I had been to San Antonio, Texas, and I saw what they did at their Avenida de Guadalupe. I said, "God, this is cool! They've got the community plaza, a theatre, and a church." I wanted to see San José's Mexican culture center develop into a place where many types of activities such as the celebration of special holidays like the Cinco de Mayo could take place. So I thought, "We should try to get something near Guadalupe Church." Our site committee eventually selected a place on Alum Rock Avenue. This location actually had much more significance than the site next to the Guadalupe Church. César Chávez had organized one of his biggest and most successful grape boycotts at a Safeway store located near this site.

Although the proposal for the plaza had been accepted, some difficult problems developed. At times, I felt that the city council was not going to fund it. Back in the mid-'80s, Mayor Susan Hammer said, "We can't afford it. What you have planned is too expensive. We cannot afford it." She also said, "We can afford to build some of the proposed buildings, but we can't afford building everything like the theatre." We answered by saying, "No. We are sold to this entire design and all its specific components. There is no way we will take anything less than what we have here." It was a real big struggle. Nobody has the faintest idea of the political struggles we went through in getting it done, but it's done now and that's what matters.

In 1994, when I was completing my term on the city council, Zoe Lofgren, a member of Santa Clara County board of supervisors, ran and won the election for Congress. Her election created a vacancy on the board of supervisors. They say timing is everything in life. I just happened to have completed my term on the San José city council when Zoe decided to run for Congress. I was appointed to fill her position for the remaining two years of her term. I was installed in 1995 and then had to run for election in 1996 and I won. I did not have any opposition when I ran in 2000 and 2004. I'm now at the end of my third term as a supervisor. I'll be out of office in December of 2008.

My work as a county supervisor has been very meaningful for me. The work at the county is very complex. It deals with the real life-and-death needs of people. It has been a blessing for me to be here. My previous work on the San José city council as an elected official gave me a great deal of experiences to understand how to work with local communities and government. I would say that coming to the board is the culmination of a very successful political career and an opportunity to really address issues that affect Latino communities.

I am proud of the many wonderful services provided by the county. We have a policy in this county that nobody will be turned away from medical services regardless of their ability to pay. There are many people who receive top-quality medical services. This state is known for having the best public hospitals and clinics. Latino families are the majority who use these medical services. I am really proud to have been a part of working to improve these services.

I am also proud of our county's welfare service. I was head of the county committee that dealt with the needs of children, seniors, and families. We were able to improve the systems so that they could best respond to the needs of Latino families. Our Latino families are the ones most in need of assistance in the county welfare system. It's sad to say this but that is the truth.

Another issue I have addressed on the board of supervisors deals with the conditions in our jails. Most of the inmates in our jails are Latinos. Many of them are suffering from use of drugs, other types of substance abuse and general medical problems. Our county provides a very humane environment for these inmates during their time in jail when they are paying their debt to society. Surveys show that medical care provided in our jails is the best of all California jails.

I am also concerned that 67 percent of the detainees in juvenile homes are Latino. We are working very hard to provide them with a better learning environment with the hope that they will be able to straighten out their lives so that, once they are released, they won't find themselves back in juvenile hall. My hope has always been that we provide educational opportunities for these youth. My hope is that they can finish school so that they can be able to improve their lives when they are released into society. We have put a lot of money into juvenile detention reform, and I take great pride in that because I was the one that initiated these reforms. I think it's going to be seen as a success.

I have also devoted a great deal of my time working on the First Five Commission that addresses the needs of Latino families. The First Five Commission is unique because it has a very different approach to how we utilize First Five dollars in dealing with children zero to five years old and their families. We conducted an exhaustive survey to determine the areas in the county that are at highest risks for family poverty, child abuse, sexual abuse, physical abuse, and domestic violence. We now have a very good profile of where these very high-risk families are located, and we are targeting our services directly at them. Nobody else in California is doing what we're doing. In fact, our model is now getting so much attention those other counties in California want to do what we're doing. I believe that this is a significant achievement.

As I said earlier, my working as a county supervisor has tremendous meaning for me. I am able to help provide opportunities for underserved communities in ways that often times are immeasurable. It's a fascinating place, and I would strongly encourage anybody who has any interest in pursuing electoral office to become civically engaged. Everyone should volunteer and be invested in their community. Young people should volunteer for different projects in their community and learn how the different layers of government systems work. I spent almost thirty years on community activism before I was elected to my first position so don't expect that public office will be handed to you on a silver platter. You've got to work for it, right from the get-go, as I did when I was a student at San José High, throughout my middle years, and now throughout my senior years. You've got to give to the community if you really want to run for office. You've got to prove your credentials or pay your dues, as they say. That's the best bit of advice that I can give anybody.

**NOTE**

1. See interview with Ernestina García in this anthology.

# 3

# Ron Gonzales

*Ron Gonzales served as mayor of San José, California, from 1998 to 2006. He was the first Hispanic mayor of San José since California became a U.S. state in 1850. Prior to becoming mayor, he served in local government, first on the city council of Sunnyvale, California, including two terms as mayor, and then as a member of the Santa Clara County board of supervisors for eight years (1989–1996). During his administration, Gonzales worked to improve the city's schools, improve social services for youth and families, and control gang-related activities. He initiated programs to attract and retain teachers through a teacher-homebuyer program. Gonzales has played a pivotal role in civic activities. He started the Role Model Program, a grassroots initiative that recruits adult role models to visit local middle schools. Gonzales grew up in the Santa Clara Valley and graduated from the University of California, Santa Cruz and the Mayors Leadership Program at Harvard University's Kennedy School of Government. Prior to his election as mayor of San José, Gonzales was an executive at Hewlett-Packard.*

## PARENTS: PILLARS OF TRADITIONAL VALUES

My parents are natives of Arizona. My mom was born in Tucson, and my father was born in a small copper mining town called Morenci. Their childhoods were difficult because they were raised during the Great Depression in the U.S. Those were very hard economic times, particularly for families of minority background. My father was raised by his relatives because his father abandoned the family during that time. His family came from the state of Sonora, in the northern part of Mexico. His brothers and sisters were separated and distributed across family lines. My mother was in a very similar situation. Her father abandoned her family so she and her siblings were also raised by family members. The manner in which I was raised goes back to my parents' roots, in terms of their experience of being raised in a unique family setting. The strong sense of family that they really wanted to provide for their five children really resonated with my brothers and sisters. My parents' goal was to make sure that their children's lives were better than their own lives.

My father went into the Navy in WWII and was stationed out of San Francisco. It was his first experience outside of Arizona, his first experience seeing the ocean and the San Francisco Bay Area, and he fell in love with it. After WWII he went back to Arizona, married my mother, and my older brother was born in Tucson. He went back into the Navy during the Korean War and was stationed outside of San Francisco. My mother and my brother lived in what is now known as Hunter's Point or Bay View area of San Francisco, where I was born. At the time, those projects were military housing and housing for the naval shipyard workers. After the Korean War, my father got a job driving trucks out of the San Francisco airport. It was a good job that paid well and had good benefits for those times. He took his G.I. loan and bought a home in Sunnyvale in 1954 for about $18,000. His relatives thought he was nuts because he was going out to the country. I was raised in what would have been classified as a white, middle-class neighborhood. My father continued to be a truck driver, and my mother worked seasonal jobs at the local canneries. Many moms worked during those times because the family needed extra money to pay for school clothes, bills, and so forth.

My mom is the female tiger, very protective of her cubs and very, very supportive of my father. She gave up a lot of things. It is a tremendous sacrifice to be the mother or wife of a person in politics. I think it's too big of a sacrifice these days. But it is what it is. It can be a very difficult life for family members and spouses. Mom still lives in that house in Sunnyvale. I can't get her out of there. She loves all of her children and grandchildren, and she is just a wonderful human being.

## FATHER: SELF-EDUCATED, COMPASSIONATE, AND DEVOTED PARENT

My dad, like many men of his generation, didn't have the educational opportunity because of the economic situation. He graduated from eighth grade, but never had the opportunity to go to high school. He really felt that was something that was taken from him, that he never had that opportunity. He knew that his lack of formal education limited his job opportunities. My mother found herself in a similar situation and so they both valued education tremendously. The lack of educational opportunities that characterized that generation that came out of the Depression was reflected in the state of mood in California at that time. For example, school bonds and school taxes always got passed because that generation knew that if their kids were going to have better lives, they needed to have an education. The University of California and the California State University systems, which were built by Governor Pat Brown, were heavily supported by the voters of California. The whole state realized, probably more so than now, the importance of education in terms of building a first-class state.

My father was, in many respects, a self-educated man. His knowledge of things always amazed me. He would read everything from history and fiction to *National Geographic* magazines. Oftentimes people would be glowing after they met him because he had that kind of impact. I would ask them, "What do you think his degree is in?" And they would say, "History or psychology or political science." And they were always amazed when I would tell them he never attended high school. I think that speaks to the concept that there are many ways to learn in society. And my father valued them all. He was a person that had an innate ability to make a personal connection with you as an individual. People always liked that about him.

I have so many stories about my father. One of my favorite stories is from 1988, when I had a yearlong, very grueling campaign running for the board of supervisors. By that time, my father had retired but he walked a precinct a day for almost a year. He was dedicated and determined to my getting elected. About six or eight months after I got elected and was in office, my secretary came in and said, "We have a constituent who is very angry. All of our staff are out in the field right now. Could you handle the call?" I said, "Sure. No problem." I talked to the gentleman and figured out the situation and then he said, "Well, you know I voted for you because of your father." I said, "Well, I've had a lot of people tell me that. But what was unique about my dad for you?" He says, "Well, he came and knocked on my door and he answered all my questions. He was so proud of you. I just figured I had to vote for you because your dad was so proud of you. Then he talked to my wife and my wife kept him at the door for half an hour." I said, "Yeah, that's my dad." The gentleman said, "She [his wife] fell in love with him. When he left, it started to rain and she felt so bad that your dad was out walking the precinct in the rain, she got the car out of the garage and drove him around our precinct." That's the kind of impact my dad would have on people. He was very unique.

His political involvement started with his involvement with the Catholic Church. He went through a period where he had to find his relationship with his faith. He wasn't raised in a real active Catholic family. But at a particular time in his life he felt he needed something and something was missing, so he got very involved with the Catholic Church, which led to being involved with the Bracero Program, the last guest worker program this nation had.[1] He would visit the migrant camps and take them food and just be there as a friend. One thing led to another and he got really involved. His involvement was pretty widespread.

My dad would drive an hour to get to work every morning, and I remember him literally racing into the house, showering, and inhaling his dinner because he had to get to some meeting. This routine went on for a little while, and I was curious, thinking, "Where does he go? What's he doing?" So one day I asked him if I could go with him to one of his meetings. He said, "Oh, sure." There were times I would go with him to school board meetings, and other times I'd go with him to migrant camps. It was a very moving and eye-opening experience for me because I had no idea what was going on outside of my neighborhood. I distinctly remember going to the farm worker camps and seeing the wear and tear on the people working in the fields in the sun. Their skin was almost like leather, and every one of them looked ten to fifteen years older than they were. I remember looking at their mud-caked hands. But you could feel their love for anybody who would come and visit them and talk to them because there wasn't the kind of communication we have now. There were no cell phones. They were away from their families. The reason my dad and others from the church went was to try to provide a sense of community for them. My dad would be so emotionally drained when he'd come out of the camps because it was such a moving experience for him. He would be pretty quiet coming home. I think he was trying to process everything he'd seen and heard and dealing with his frustration. He was very careful about trying to stay positive.

With regard to political issues, there were conversations—if you consider a conversation listening to him rant and rave about certain things. It was more of a lecture than a conversation. He was very opinionated. The conversations tended to be around Democratic and Republican politics, such as who was in the White House, which was Nixon for years. He obviously didn't have high regard for Nixon. As far as the local scene, the issues that meant the most to him are the ones that mean the most to me because they mean the most to our community, such as education.

But the issues my father was concerned about varied. There were some years where he'd be mad at his own union. There were times during the farm workers' strike that the Teamsters were working with the "bad guys" so to speak, and he was really upset about that. He wanted to quit the Teamsters, but he worked in a union shop so he couldn't. Then Jimmy Hoffa disappeared and eventually Fitzsimmons took over, and my father didn't have much regard for Fitzsimmons.[2] The day Fitzsimmons accepted an invitation to have lunch with Nixon at the White House, my dad came home the maddest I've ever seen him. My dad said, "No Teamster in his right mind would ever lunch with a Republican in the White House!"

My father was cofounder of *La Confederación de la Raza Unida,* an organization that he and Jack Ybarra put together.[3] It was probably the first and last best organization around. I never knew whether the numbers that he passed around were accurate, but they would say something like fifty different organizations constituted *La Confederación de la Raza Unida.* These organizations dealt with various issues, ranging from education to health, and it was an excellent idea at the time. All these groups had been working in their specific area, but there was no involvement that brought them together until *La Confederación.* Nowadays, things are different. You don't have many people outside walking around with a picket sign. You have people on the city council who are open to hearing from you. It was a very important tool to have in that era.

I participated with my father in the last day of the great march from Delano to Sacramento while I was still in high school. It was an unusual experience for me because it was the first time that I participated in an actual march. There were anti–farm worker protesters on the sidewalks, and as people were walking down the street, they were yelling things at us. I don't think it ever got to any kind of violence, but it was clear they weren't happy about us marching into Sacramento. My dad warned me about it because that can leave an impression on you, going through that for the first time. But for me it was more of a positive experience to be in that kind of visible demonstration.

## CHILDHOOD MEMORIES: BASIS FOR POLITICAL PRIORITIES

My childhood was a happy one. There's a poem that says, "Everything I know, I learned in kindergarten." Well, everything I base my life on, the older I get and the more I think about it, I learned in my neighborhood, in the home my parents provided. I learned things like the importance of safety, having activities in neighborhoods, and having homes where people can live.

Oftentimes I go out to cut a ribbon in a new housing community and I tell the audience that one of the reasons I feel so strongly about a city's responsibility to build affordable housing is because of my childhood. I lived in the same home, in the same neighborhood, in the same community from the time I entered kindergarten until the time I graduated from high school. I had the same friends and the same teachers that my brothers and sisters had, so there was less fooling around. The teachers knew my parents and my brothers and sisters, and it was pretty much true of all my friends. That's pretty uncommon nowadays because of the lack of affordability of housing. The strong sense of making sure that people feel good and proud and safe in their neighborhoods comes from the fact that I felt that way about my neighborhood. Pretty much everything I do in this job and what I try to do as a public-sector leader is based around making sure that we do everything that we can to provide that kind of environment for all children, no matter what race they are, no matter what income neighborhood they live in. That's really been my guiding light.

The community I lived in was primarily a white community, although we did have different ethnic groups in our neighborhood. As I got older, new groups came in, particularly Filipino Americans and Samoans. We had an interesting Southeast Asia/Pacific Islander community in our neighborhood, so there was a good amount of diversity, particularly when I got into high school. I went to Sunnyvale High School, which is no longer open, and it was probably the most diverse in terms of its population in the Sunnyvale area. We had virtually every ethnic group you could imagine: African American students, Latino students, Asian students. It was a community that got along pretty well. I don't remember much racial strife at all in high school. I was active in high school, probably more active in sports than in getting good grades. But I made up for it later when I was in college. I didn't get involved in politics in high school because it didn't attract me at that point. It was a very different time. Politics in high school in the 1960s meant organizing car washes and that kind of stuff.

I started my college career at De Anza Community College, which was a very good option for me. Our community colleges are still the tops in the nation. It was good for me because it was something I could afford. My parents were still very much blue-collar workers. They didn't have the financial resources to provide for me to go to any other school. Plus I felt that a community college provided me with the opportunity to learn without having to pay a lot for making mistakes. My experience at De Anza Community College was excellent. I felt that the classes I took there were as good as the ones I would later take at UC Santa

Cruz. The teachers were interested in me as a student, and it was a very welcoming campus.

## COLLEGE: A FOCUS ON LEARNING

In terms of my politics, college was the antithesis of high school. I got very involved in student government although I was not yet on the student council. My brother, Bob, who preceded me at De Anza, was very involved with the multicultural program. I went to some meetings and became involved in the student group and ran for student council during my second year. It's one of the few political campaigns I can't remember a thing about, so it must have been fairly easy. It was a positive experience but very difficult in relation to other things going on in the world at the time. Student council was very split because of the special interest groups who were on the council at the time. Many students were against the war in Vietnam. In spite of that, we were able to bring ourselves together around issues that were specific to the campus. All in all, it was a positive experience in terms of student leadership. We would interact with student organizations from other college campuses at a rally or a farm workers picket or that sort of thing.

I was also involved with the Latino student organization on campus and served as its president for one year. I was very involved with the Hispanic student movement at that time. Two primary things were going on in politics while I was in college. The farm workers' union strike was very active in the late '60s and early '70s. Our student organization would attend tent rallies and support picket lines at Safeway stores or wherever the union was boycotting at that particular time. The year I was president, we organized a community event that raised a substantial amount of money for scholarships for high school students to come to De Anza. That was something we were proud of. We worked with the college administration to look at affirmative action, for example, and I think we were successful in that regard. But I'd also have to say that the administration of the community college at that time was very open to diversity, and to issues that our group was raising. I felt that we laid a good foundation, which De Anza built upon over the years.

But our first job was being students and we did a really good job of remembering that at De Anza. Our graduation and transfer rates were a little higher than other campuses because we focused on education, and in our spare time, we were involved in the community. The other thing is that the community college student tends to be in transition and between going to classes and working and studying, there wasn't a whole lot of time to get involved in different issues.

When I was looking to transfer from the community college to a four-year school, I received a scholarship from the Ford Foundation based on my academic performance and my student involvement. That scholarship really provided me with the financial flexibility to consider going to a UC campus. I transferred in 1971, when all the big campuses were very active. I spent some time at UC Berkeley and visited some other UC campuses and I thought to myself, "If I come up here, I'm never going to be in a classroom." My goal was to get a degree, and I felt that if I went to campuses where there was so much activity, I would get easily distracted and not focus on my studies. So when I transferred from De Anza to UC Santa Cruz, I really stepped back from the political involvement. I successfully completed my degree in four years and graduated in 1973. My UC Santa Cruz and De Anza experiences were very positive in different ways.

My parents were always very good about not providing a specific road map. They said, "This is the state of California. You've got incredible opportunity. You can go anywhere you want." They never said, "We'd like to see you be a doctor or lawyer." But they always emphasized the college education.

One of the things that I find interesting about Latinos is that we want to do things that make our parents proud. I distinctly remember thinking, "Well, my buddies are going into the trades. They're going to carpentry school, plumbing school and making a ton of money. They're driving new cars and I have to go to college and barely make it month to month. I'm driving a beat-up old car . . ." If I had taken the short-sighted view, I would have done what they did. I'm not downgrading them at all. They've done very well for themselves. But I just felt that there was another opportunity for me. My parents felt that education was very, very important. As a consequence, four of five of us in the family have degrees. The second thing was—I've said this a number of times—that my father really emphasized the importance of every one of us as a community, as a nation. He set as a goal in our lives to find some way to improve the lives of others. I remember that phrase because it was general enough to do in a lot of different ways. You can lead a Boy Scout troop. You can be a professor. You can be a doctor. You can be an advocate. I'm glad to say that my brothers and sisters have found in their own ways, like I have, a way to do that.

## POLITICAL CAREER:
## "FIND SOME WAY TO IMPROVE THE LIVES OF OTHERS"

People now take for granted how open government is. At that time white Americans were really struggling with the question of "Do we let these folks into the system? Are we going to keep them out?" I think most of them wanted to just keep us out. There were a few leaders who wanted to include everyone, but they were in the minority. The first time I thought something needed to be changed was at a school board meeting where my dad was lobbying on behalf of a solution. The school board wasn't paying attention to him. Instead, they were talking amongst themselves and giggling with each other. I thought they were being very disrespectful to other speakers, and I thought, "This is not how democracy is supposed to work." That's when I really began to think, "Well, maybe we need to have different types of folks up there." Whether as a school board or a city council or corporate board of directors or whatever, change needed to take place, and I thought to myself, "Oh! Now I know why my dad's doing this." Before I'd hear my dad talking about all these things, but this was really the first time where I thought, "This has got to change." I got involved and this led from one thing to another, and before I knew it I was sitting on the city council.

My political role models at the time were César Chávez, Bobby Kennedy, Dr. Martin Luther King, and of course, John Kennedy. JFK might have been the first person to light the candle as someone who talked about public service and our responsibilities as U.S. citizens to do something for our country. He did it in such a way that was passionate and memorable, saying, "Don't ask what your country can do for you, but ask what you can do for your country." Interestingly enough, they were all men of nonviolent methods, which was a signal to our entire country. For me, the best way to improve the lives of others was to enter the political leadership area, public service.

I've talked to a lot of elected officials over these twenty-four years of public service, and it's surprising how many of us started the same way. I got started because I was concerned about an issue in my neighborhood, in my city. That concern grew, and before I knew it, I was asked to sit on this committee and then encouraged to run for Sunnyvale city council in 1977 with no prior elected experience. I served on the planning commission, which was the usual route at that time throughout the county to establish name recognition and then run for council. What had happened in Sunnyvale was that like a lot of communities in the '60s and '70s, the downtown area had fallen by the wayside, a victim of the regional shopping malls, like Valley Fair and Vallco. As a consequence, businesses really fell off and for years it had been in a state of decline. The city fathers at that time decided to basically raze the downtown and put in its own shopping mall. I felt that some type of redevelopment was necessary but destroying the Main Street area and putting in a shopping mall was not the answer. I got involved with that issue, which led to me serving on and chairing a general plan review committee for downtown. That was a real interesting experience because we had about fifty people and all of them owned property. Today, almost every one of them would have a conflict of interest. Some owned businesses and some owned homes, and the homeowners didn't want what the businesspeople wanted. It was a very difficult political process to manage, but we did reach consensus on the plan. It was really a neighborhood issue that had citywide implications.

In 1977, I ran for city council as an underdog and almost won. When we went back and looked at all the precinct breakouts, what was encouraging for me was that I came close citywide. In order to get on the Sunnyvale city council in those days, you had to get votes from the central part of the city and the south part of the city. When I looked at the polling results for those precincts particularly, I knew I did well in North Sunnyvale, which was kind of my 'hood. But when I looked at those other areas and saw that I did well, that was encouraging. So I decided to stay involved in local politics there. In 1979, I was elected without opposition, and some would say that I chased everybody away because they were concerned that I had come so close the last time. When I won in Sunnyvale, my dad was jumping out of his shoes. My whole family was very proud, and it was a happy time for all of us. It was a tremendous educational experience because you work to get to office and then say, "OK. I'm here. What am I going to do? How does this place really work?" Joining that city council was a great way for me to start my political service because it was a very progressive city council and probably the most intelligent group of elected officials I've ever worked with. We had an environment where we could hotly debate a number of issues but those hot discussions always stayed in the council chambers. Once we left those chambers we were friends and able to talk about anything. Unfortunately, that's not an environment you find these days in politics. I served eight years on the Sunnyvale city council and was then chosen by the city council to be its manager for two years.

## TRANSITION FROM SUNNYVALE TO SAN JOSÉ: "GOING FROM SINGLE A BASEBALL TO THE PROS"

Running for mayor of San José is the same as going from single A baseball to the pros. This is big time. Running for mayor of this city is overwhelming. I don't remember ever being as physically or mentally exhausted as I was when my campaign was done in November of 1998. I had a full-time job at Hewlett Packard and was running for mayor of what was at that time the eleventh-largest city in the country. It is all-encompassing and tremendously grueling, and that's the way it should be because the big city has a lot of needs. You want someone who is going to be able to do this job 24/7. I think back to that election year and compare it to what's going on now, and I don't think there's anything that comes close to what we had to go through in 1998. But on the other hand, it prepared me to come into this office and do this job for eight years. The fact that I had served in Sunnyvale and served on the board of supervisors gave me name recognition. The fact that I came from the private sector helped a great deal. I didn't have the common résumé for someone running for office. I didn't come from a rich family, so it wasn't being handed to me. I wasn't born with a silver spoon in my mouth. I had many hurdles to overcome and being Latino was certainly one of them. I was very proud of the fact that this city looked at my résumé and my accomplishments and said, "We're going to give this guy a shot at it." It was a very close election, and I'm grateful the voters gave me the opportunity to do this job.

The one thing that has always helped me is that I view myself as first, being a mayor and second, of Latino background. Maybe I see issues through a different set of lenses than other people. Whether you're talking to the Latino, Asian, African American community, or even the white community, our issues are always the same when it comes to local government. They're not Democratic or Republican issues. We want city services at the same level that everyone else gets them throughout the community. One of the things that I worked on with my colleagues in Sunnyvale was the strong feeling that the community on the northern part of town didn't get the same respect and attention as other parts of the community. A lot of that was perception. But in politics, perception is reality and in some cases it was for sure. I worked actively with my colleagues on the city council when it came to spending on city parks and other city services, to make sure that we were cognizant of that feeling. Whether it's real or not, we felt the need to address it. We made sure we made our investments in different neighborhoods and made sure that people knew about it. My view has always been that I come into any political office, particularly this one, with preconceived notions. On the other hand, I will come into an organization and see if they're right or wrong. Walking precincts and being involved in this community for many years, I felt that many of the complaints that I heard were real. Some complaints were that neighborhoods had not gotten the same level of service, like some got new libraries and some didn't. Some had different levels of police and fire protection and attention to streets, the basic things that you want. As I say, the kinds of things that you survey from your driveway. When you go out and pick up the morning newspaper, you look around. Is the street clean? Is the park safe? Is the library open when your kids want to go there? That was my agenda for hopefully eight years as mayor.

## POLITICAL LEGACY: RESPONSIVE TO COMMUNITY NEEDS

The Role Model Program has a very special place in my heart. It is one of many things that I'm so proud of. As I walk away from politics in the next couple of months, I look back over twenty-three years of elected public service and the Role Model Program stands out as something that I hope will live on for many, many years. The Role Model Program had its birth in a classroom in Sunnyvale in 1987. I was mayor of Sunnyvale at the time, which was a part-time job. So I worked at a full-time job at Hewlett Packard and did political stuff in the evening. I was invited to come out to a classroom of fourth or fifth graders of primarily Latino students, and the teacher was very excited to have me there. The teacher said, "We have a very special guest with us today. He's going to talk to us about what it's like to run a city. He's the mayor of Sunnyvale, our city." Well, something very strange happened. The students didn't believe her. I went through this five-minute "Yes, I am" "No, you're not." So finally I reached into my pocket and pulled out my business card that was the proof and the students said "OK." As I was driving back to work that afternoon, I thought, "What was that all about?" So I talked to some educators that spend a lot of time with children and they said that part of the explanation was that children begin to set their own limitations at a very early age. What those kids were telling me was that a person with a name like Gonzales or López or Sánchez can't be the mayor. That's not possible because they don't see people on the news with those names. I said, "Wow, that's powerful. We've got to do something about it because they probably don't see people with those names being doctors or teachers or lawyers or scientists or astronauts." I said, "We've got to do something about this. We've got people who are doing these jobs in our community that can help our children get these blinders off their eyes and see all the possibilities that they have in this great country."

Over several years we developed this program, which was formally organized in 1989. We've had role models from every different career visiting middle school and elementary school classrooms, talking about the importance of education. They talk about their careers, why they chose to be a police officer or a teacher, and what they had to do to get there. They have about 150 role models every year providing services to thousands of students here in San José and Santa Clara County. That program is something I'm so proud of. To this day I find young people that will come up to me and say, "I remember you. You visited my class-room and you talked about education." It's really very rewarding to do that. The role models get a lot of personal satisfaction, too. In fact, most of them say, "I learned more from the students than I could ever provide to them." That is prob-ably true of any teacher's position.

Our educational initiatives here go back to everything I learned in my neigh-borhood and my family. When I first ran for mayor in 1998, I made improving public education my number one priority. The press jumped all over me, saying, "That's impossible. Schools don't report to you. You don't choose the school board and superintendent. You have no governance authority over them." Well, I don't choose the transit board either, but if I told you I'm not going to pay at-tention to transit, are you going to accept that as mayor of the biggest city in the county? I don't think so. Education is the most important thing that a commu-nity can provide, alongside public safety. I said, "You don't have to have gover-nance authority. You've just got to be willing to be a partner." In 1999, we began to talk to the education community, and that's what led to our teacher home-buying program and many of the other initiatives. We have after-school home-work centers, our Smart Start preschool education program, and all kinds of things. The teacher home-buying program has now assisted over 530 public school teachers in buying their first home in San José, one of the toughest hous-ing markets in the country. We're so proud of that because it has helped our school districts attract quality teachers and, more importantly, retain them. I think we've only lost a couple from the teaching ranks with that program. It's worked very effectively, and I think that we've ended the debate as to whether or not a mayor or a city council has a role in public education. Many of our educa-tion initiatives are used now as national models for implementation in other communities.

If you just drive around, you can see communities where schools aren't per-forming up to the level they would like to perform. You can see neighborhoods that are neglected in terms of sidewalk repairs and street repairs and street light-ing. You can see parks that are not maintained, or not even built. You see kids playing in the street because there is no playground nearby. You can see that there's not a branch library within walking distance. You see a lot of police cars and a lot of graffiti and litter. You ask yourself, "Would I want to live here?" And if the answer is no, then that's your first assignment. That's why we came up with the Strong Neighborhoods Initiative. How do we move an entire city organiza-tion, not a department, but how do we move the entire organization to be more responsive to everyone in the community? How do we put all the resources that we have in this incredible government in the hands of the people? That's what the Strong Neighborhoods Initiative is all about. It's as important in my heart as the Role Model Program. The great part about the selection process is that it's done by the neighborhoods themselves. They choose their leadership and form their NAC, Neighborhood Advisory Councils. They choose their chairpersons, their committee leaders, and so forth. Simply put, it's a process where they define their community. What are our assets? What are the things we'd like to improve on? How do we work with city hall to deal with the issues? They developed a list of their top ten priorities, which we worked on with them. It's a process that empowers them to take control of their neighborhood and say, "We're tired of waiting for everyone else to respond. We're going to do it ourselves. We're going to work with the city to do it." I think it's a program that has a lasting legacy for the city that will carry on. Once community leaders see that their actions have led to a better neighborhood, others will follow. It's going to be a very powerful era for government, to have those groups make their presentations to the city council and say, "I was very skeptical when this all started. I didn't imagine you guys would listen to us. But my mind has changed. I really feel like part of this community." That is worth twenty-four years of very long meetings, very boring meetings sometimes. That's the payoff.

I don't know that community organizations are as influential as they once were. I think a lot of it has to do with the fact that those organizations came into existence because we needed a voice in our community. That voice didn't exist within institutions, on a city council, a school board, a county board of supervisors, or any of the government organizations. But with change comes progress: Now we have people of different ethnic groups within the Latino community on city council. You've got the mayor, Latino council members, Latinos on the board of supervisors. What happens now is that whether you're a parent group or neighborhood association, you go to those individuals. You don't necessarily need to go to a community organization. I'm not sure what that means for these organizations in the future. Maybe they'll focus more on statewide and national issues. There are times when their advocacy is needed on different issues, but when you've got a city council like ours, there's very little debate about what the issues are. Maybe there is more debate on how to resolve them. Back in the '60s it was a matter of convincing the nation, the state, or city that your issues were their issues. That's why you needed organizations. But now it's a very different time.

## REFLECTIONS ON POLITICS: "ALL GREAT IDEAS START IN CITIES"

When we look at opportunities for political elections, we sometimes oversimplify things. The media has always oversimplified the Latino community and tried to pigeonhole us as primarily Democrats. As we continue to grow as a community and achieve things we've been working on, we find that the diversity of opinion is immense. It is an overgeneralized issue to think that we're going to be a voting block and then be a swing voting block. A lot of people look back to Arnold Schwarzenegger's election as governor of California and say, "Why did he get so much support from the Hispanic community?" There are a multitude of answers. It may have been that they felt the state wasn't responding to their child's need for education, so they voted for him. It may be that they felt that they'd get more leadership. I think there were a variety of issues that were attractive. Maybe some of them liked his movies. I don't know! They were probably the same reasons that a lot of white voters voted for him.

When I was on the board of supervisors, NAFTA was being debated and the national media was searching for answers and at that time had very little experience dealing with the Hispanic community.[4] They are much more experienced now. They asked, "Well, Mr. Supervisor, where do you think the Latino community is on the issue of NAFTA?" I said, "Well, they're all over the map! If you're a union member, you probably hate it. If you're a small business owner that exports to Central America or Mexico or South America, you probably love it. And the rest of us are probably in-between, not knowing what the heck we think, just like the general American population. We're questioning whether this thing is going to work or not." I try not to fall into the trap of stereotyping our community. We're diverse, and I like the fact that we're everywhere on the issues because you have a greater impact.

Our community is made up of first generation, third-generation, twentieth-generation immigrants. I don't know that we're all that unified on immigration. I've heard first-time immigrants say, "Hey, I went through the process. Everyone should go through the process." The process should be improved, and the INS should be done away with. I think the INS should be re-engineered because they make the process way too damn long. The total opposite point of view is complete forgiveness. I think it's a very broad range and my guess is that like many political issues, you've got 10 percent of the population up here and 10 percent over here and the other 80 percent is trying to figure out a reasonable solution. It's a tough one.

We mayors think all great ideas start in cities, and they probably do. I haven't seen a great idea ever start at a state capital or in the nation's capital. In fact, most of them usually go there and die. I have some pretty strong opinions about those levels of government, although obviously they have an appropriate role. We, as voters, look to leadership at the state and federal level. The one thing that has been the most disappointing to me over the years, watching all these gubernatorial races and presidential campaigns, is how focused they've become on issues that don't really matter to us, either as Latinos or as a nation. They tend to be focused around the media's questions. Can you remember Bush or Kerry's position on cities during the last presidential election?[5] They were never asked. These people campaigned for two years, and you never know what their urban agenda is. "What are you going to do for housing? What are you going to do for transportation? Air quality? The environment?" No. We're worried about whether they smoked marijuana in college or their military record. These issues take over with the hysteria of the media and blogs and all this stuff. It's become a circus rather than an election, and it's very disappointing.

I remember watching the great debates between Nixon and Kennedy on a black-and-white TV as a child.[6] I was just fascinated! The only thing I remember was that Nixon looked like he just came out of a washing machine! He looked horrible! It was quite an experience. I think back to all the things I've seen on TV, and it's been an incredible fifty-five years of progress and conflict. To go from those great debates to what I see now, I'm thinking, "Where did it go wrong? Where did so much information become a bad thing?" I'm hoping that someday whether you're running for president or for governor, you're going to say, "Under your administration, what are you going to do that will help the neighborhoods and our nation's cities?" No one asks that question.

Another important issue is that schools are so challenged to teach the curriculum and to teach to the tests that I'm not sure that our children are learning about the values of this country. Sometimes I think immigrant parents know more than their children know. Their parents came here because they believed this was the land of opportunity. They came here because they knew that the chances here were greater than where they were coming from and wanted their children to have better lives. But I'm not sure that's being translated to the children. There's this sense of inheritance that I see with a lot of young people, that so much of it is owed to them. The only thing this country owes you is an equal opportunity. No matter what background you come from, that's what is owed to you by the Constitution. You have the responsibility to carry out the duties as a citizen. I am really concerned that we're not spending time in our schools talking about those things.

## REFLECTION ON VALUES: COMMUNITY, FAITH, OPPORTUNITY, RESPONSIBILITY, HARD WORK

All my values I learned in my neighborhood and my family. I have been thinking about this a lot in the last six months as I complete my term as mayor. I have been thinking about the values of community, faith, opportunity, responsibility, which, unfortunately, I'm not sure that our children are being taught them. This is a country of opportunity, but it's also a country of responsibility. These opportunities are out there, if you take the responsibility to work hard and get an education. I'm more and more convinced that the golden ring is there for our children, more so than any other time in our community's history. It's described to each of us in different ways, which is the way it should be. But it will be a question of whether we get our children to reach out and grab it. That's one of our biggest challenges right now.

I also really value hard work, which I learned from my parents and many others. I am probably working as hard on my last day here as I did the first day. I really believe that's important to do. I go back to what my father told each and every one of us, which was to take each job you're given, and work as hard and do the best you possibly can and good things will come your way. I really believe that. It's never failed me yet. I always have been blessed to have a job and a career that makes me want to jump out of bed to go to work in the morning.

I was raised a Catholic. I didn't like Latin Mass or the High Mass because they were always a little bit longer! I was the kid in the pew that got pinched by Mom or Dad. But as a young man, I got away from my faith and the Church. My wife, Giselle, and I have been practicing Catholics for several years now. We attend St. Joseph's Cathedral Mass on Sunday because we live downtown and that's our church. I find that it gives me a spiritual opportunity and a sense of community. We're really getting into the church's community and knowing individuals in the church. It is a refreshing experience for us because it's a whole new set of people to interact with. It is hard to be able to talk with folks about something other than politics when you're mayor of the city. It comes up every once in a while, but it's more about their children and other kinds of things. Faith is a very personal thing, and for me, it's been very much of a strengthening opportunity.

Despite everything I've said, the glass is still half full. This is still the best country in the world. It's got to be. Everyone wants to come here! They're getting here by plane, boat, and foot continuously. I think that the optimism in our country comes from the new generations, from people who don't come here with a sense of entitlement. They're here because they want something better. They're going to work hard for it, and I think our children can learn a lot from people who emigrate here because they have no other experience. If I had my way, every high school student would be sent for six months to another country. Any country. I don't care. Many have no clue or appreciation about what is provided to them. Again, it goes back to this sense of entitlement that our children are raised with. My optimism comes from talking with a lot with young people. I know that they're ambitious and goal oriented. I just hope that they're the right goals and the right ambitions for the common good.

## NOTES

1. The Bracero Program was a program for bringing Mexican workers into the United States. In July 1942, President Franklin D. Roosevelt and Manuel Avila Camacho entered into a bilateral agreement that permitted the entry of Mexican farm workers into the United States to work in the agricultural fields of the Southwest.

2. James "Jimmy" Hoffa was a American labor leader who presumably had ties to the Mafia. As the president of the International Brotherhood of Teamsters from the mid-1950s to the mid-1960s, Hoffa wielded considerable influence. He disappeared in 1975 under mysterious circumstances.

3. *La Confederación de la Raza Unida* was a political coalition of sixty-seven Chicano organizations that was formed to protest the Fiesta de las Rosas in 1969. Chicanos protested this parade because of the stereotypes of Mexicans depicted in some of its floats.

4. The North American Free Trade Agreement (NAFTA) began on January 1, 1994. This agreement removes most barriers to trade and investment among the United States, Canada, and Mexico. Under NAFTA, all nontariff barriers to agricultural trade between the United States and Mexico were eliminated.

5. Refers to 2004 presidential election between incumbent George W. Bush and John Kerry, the Democratic senator from Massachusetts.

6. On September 26, 1960, seventy million U.S. viewers tuned in to watch Senator John Kennedy of Massachusetts and Vice President Richard Nixon in the first-ever televised presidential debate.

# II

# POLITICS AND SOCIETY

# Esther Medina

*Esther Medina, long-time resident of San José, has an illustrious record of commu-*
*nity activism. She made a transition from a businesswoman to become a public ser-*
*vant, including working in San José's Anti-Poverty Agency and the Commission on*
*the Status of Women for Santa Clara County, California. Beginning in 1982, Med-*
*ina became a pillar of the Mexican American community as executive director of the*
*Mexican American Community Services Agency (MACSA) in San José, California.*
*She transformed MACSA into a powerful organization with an operating budget of*
*over $7 million. She retired from MACSA in 2003. Esther's influence expands to all*
*areas of Silicon Valley community life and provides input to elected officials and*
*leaders of industry on various issues such as the development of affordable housing,*
*improvements in public transportation, and initiatives for better and equitable*
*wages. The* San Jose Mercury News *named her one of the one hundred most influ-*
*ential people in Silicon Valley, and Santa Clara University awarded her an honorary*
*doctorate in 1999 for public service.*

## FROM REVOLUTION TO ORCHARDS: A FAMILY'S SAGA

I was born in Ventura, California. At the time, my family was picking lemons in
a little *ranchito* [little ranch] near Santa Paula. When I was about five, my family
settled in San José, California, and I've been here ever since. I am the youngest of
eight children of Mexican farm workers.

Although all of us kids were born in the United States, both of my parents
were born in Mexico. They were both from Zacatecas, and they knew each other

since they were children. They always talked a lot about their life in Mexico. It was a tiny, little town where everybody knew everybody. They would tell us about the big celebrations in their town, particularly those that were centered on the Church and Mexican holidays. My father was a farmer, but he was also involved in politics. He told us that he would come in from the fields, bathe, and then go to community meetings. He was involved in the Mexican Revolution of 1910 and so was my mother, but in her own way. When my father was off in the revolution, my mother would organize the women in the community, taking them to the nearby mountains to hide in caves. She knew that the enemy would come, rape the women, and take them away.

Towards the end of the revolution, my father was very tired of the conflicts and decided that he wanted to raise his kids in a more serene environment, a more peaceful place, and that's why he came to the United States. My father didn't talk very much about going back to Mexico. I think he had been through a real bad experience with the revolution and all the killings. He didn't want to see or experience violence again, but after my parents came to this country, they always referred to themselves as Mexican. They felt that way until the day they died.

They came to New Mexico, then traveled to Arizona and arrived in Ventura, California. They worked there for a while, but didn't settle there. My family had migrated throughout the whole state, but we didn't settle anywhere really until we came to San José. We finally settled in San José because one of my older brothers got married and settled in San José. Since we were a very close family, we also settled in San José where we all began to do farm work.

My parents, my father especially, was very active in the community. He started the *Comisión Honorífica Mexicana*, celebrating the *Fiestas Patrias* [Mexican national celebrations]. As a little girl I picked up things from my father, such as the importance of community activism. My father started the *Fiestas Patrias* after he talked to other men who were also very interested in preserving Mexican culture. That's how they added more members to the group, and then they decided to start putting on the celebrations in San José. They had few members when they first started, but their organization eventually increased in numbers. I don't know how they did it exactly, but they got permission to have a parade. They developed a program with poems, speeches, dancing, and other kinds of entertainment. A grand ball took place in the evening. They organized the whole thing, and it was a huge event in the community, but, of course, only Latinos attended.

My father was still organizing the *Fiestas Patrias* when I was in high school. When I got older, I participated in the *Fiestas*, but I would cringe because he often wanted me to get up on a stage and recite poems in Spanish. My sisters and I would try to get out of it. He always put me on a float in the parade, and I hated it. It was so hot, and I'd break out in rash from the heat. I'm allergic to the sun and it was misery, but yet we had to participate. We were all expected to be involved.

My father was also involved in other community organizations. I can't remember which ones. He was really into joining community organizations because he wanted to get things done to improve the community and promote Mexican culture. He wanted all Mexican kids to have knowledge of the culture and to preserve it. That was his main goal as I was growing up, and I always agreed with this. My mother didn't go to meetings. She would read the Spanish newspaper to my father to keep him informed about what was going on. This is why when I was a little kid and started school, I could read Spanish. I would sit with her when she was reading to him, and so I learned to read Spanish but I couldn't read English.

When we were growing up, we only spoke Spanish, and, in fact, my parents had a rule that in our house we would only speak Spanish. I don't know if this was so that they could understand us because sometimes we could speak English. I think it was mostly so we wouldn't forget our language and our culture. You would think that we were living in Mexico the way we celebrated every Mexican holiday, like *El Día de los Muertos* [the Day of the Dead].[1] Both of my parents wanted us kids to have knowledge of the culture and to preserve it. That was their main goal.

My father used to invite poor families whose cars had broken down to our house and we'd feed them. We just shared whatever we had with those in need. My mother and father believed that a person had a responsibility to help others. Even though we didn't have much, my father always shared what little we did have with those in need. My parents did not agree with the attitude that "well, somebody else will do it." It had to be done, and they believed that they needed to do it. They both had organizing skills and were highly respected by San José's Mexican community.

My father was passionate about social justice. He was angered by the way the farm workers were treated. I know he participated in some kind of a farm workers strike around 1939. He felt it was unjust that farm workers, like my family, would get kicked out of their houses. The farm owner provided little shacks for people to live in. We had to buy stuff from his store because other markets were far away and we didn't have cars. Sometimes, by the time you got paid, you had to use all your paycheck to pay what you owed the store. My father and some of the men decided they were going to go on strike. They did and they lost. The farm owner threw us out of the shacks, and we ended up living in a tent city. My father felt very bad about this, but I think that he would have done it all over again. He felt it was so unfair that we were being treated this way. He also thought that what we were getting paid was unfair. I think we got ten cents an hour and they were striking for thirteen cents an hour. Sometimes my father would hear people say, "If you farm workers don't like it here, you should go back to Mexico." He encountered many people who felt that way, except my father was very fair skinned and had light eyes and so a lot of the people thought he was white. I think that his other friends had it worse than he did because some of the farm workers would actually talk about him, thinking that he was white and didn't understand Spanish. They'd say, "*Mire ese viejito, ese viejo gringo*" [Look at that old man, that old American man]. He'd let them talk and then he'd talk back to them in Spanish and they'd be all upset and embarrassed. But I think he had it a little easier because he looked white.

All these experiences made me more Mexican because I saw things that weren't fair for us and it didn't make us very comfortable, especially in school. I didn't feel very American. I'll give you an example. One year we had a really good year picking prunes and my father got enough money together to try to buy a house in Willow Glen, but they wouldn't sell it to him. He was very disappointed. My father explained to me that they wouldn't sell us the house because: "*Es porque somos Mexicanos*" [It's because we are Mexican]. When my father talked about problems, like not being able to buy the house, my mother would also get upset. I think the whole family did. When I would hear things like this, it just made me angry. I wanted people to be able buy a house wherever they could afford it. I would wish that I could make things fair for us, for Latinos.

Those are the injustices that I was angry about. I think my father taught me to have a fierce loyalty to Mexicans and to try to fix situations that weren't fair. He provided me with an example of how we should try to make things better. My mother also had a very strong sense of fairness. When she would talk about black people, she'd talk about them "*con cariño*" [with affection]. She was a very kind person, but she was also a very strong woman.

## EDUCATION AND THE NOT-SO-HIDDEN INJURIES OF PREJUDICE

When we first came to San José we lived right downtown, right by where the House of Pizza used to be. There are some old Victorian houses there, and we lived in a little house in the back. We were still living there during World War II when my brothers went to the war. My father was devastated when my brothers went off to war. He didn't want them to go. My entire family didn't want them to go, but of course they had to go. My father thought it was unfair that his sons were fighting off in Europe while we, Latinos, were treated so unfairly here in the United States. I remember he was very sad when they went. When my brother, who had been stationed in Germany, came home, he told my father about the Holocaust and I remember my father crying. I wasn't supposed to be listening but, as usual, I was. My brother was describing what they found in the camps, and I remember my father being shocked and my brother being angry. He asked my brother, "How could people do that to each other?" During the time we lived in downtown San José, I went up to about the third grade and then we moved to *el rancho* [the ranch], a place out towards Willow Glen,[2] which was nothing but orchards. We lived there until I was in about the eighth grade, and then we moved back to San José, over to the East Side. There was a real mixture of people in San José's East Side. There were some Italian families who had lived there for a long time, but, of course, there were many Latinos. The East Side was kind of a little pocket of Latinos, but we went to school with kids from different ethnic backgrounds, but everybody was just as poor as we were. We continued working in the fields. We would go out to the ranches and pick fruit all over Santa Clara County. My mother never worked in the fields. That was one thing my father was very, very adamant about. She was not to work in the fields because, since there were eight of us, she had a lot of work to do at home. She always worked very hard to keep the family together. Even though we had problems, I don't remember hearing my parents discussing their life here in the United States and the problems they were having. They kept these things to themselves.

When I started school, I had a very difficult time. It took me a long time to learn the English language and, in general, to feel comfortable. There were positives and negatives in my school experience. My parents put me and my brother in Catholic school for a while, but he and I hated Catholic school. I don't think that my brother and I lasted even a year. I experienced discrimination in Catholic school, including from the nuns. It was a terrible experience for me. They favored some kids over others, and they were very blatant about their favoritism. It was just so cliquey. The nuns were so difficult and so strict. They'd hit you in the head with this little clicker that they had. They didn't give us Latinos a break even though we had a problem with speaking English. The nuns didn't try to help us out. My parents sacrificed to send us to Catholic school because they thought that we'd get a better education, but it was a disaster. I was very happy to leave this Catholic school.

Like in Catholic school, I experienced a lot of discrimination in grammar school in Willow Glen. My family lived on the wrong side of the tracks. We lived over near the berry camps and prune orchards, but we had to go to school with kids from white families who were better off than we were. There was a lot of discrimination. We, the Latino kids, would be lined up in the hall to have our hair and feet checked by the teachers to see if they were cleaned. We stood in line for hours while the other kids would go to recess. They would come back to the classroom and laugh at us because we were in the line. My teacher used to play this game. I was maybe in the third or fourth grade. She would divide the class into two groups and line each group on opposite sides of the classroom. She would then say, "The side with the cleanest and the neatest students gets to go to recess and the other side doesn't." And of course all the Chicanitos had walked about a mile or even many miles to school. They never thought to send a bus after us. Our braids would be falling apart and we'd be all sweaty. So, of course, we never got to go to recess. The white kids that ended up on our side of the room would be very angry with us and call us names. They would call us names like "you dirty Mexicans." It was a really terrible experience.

My high school counselors didn't talk to me about college; they never even mentioned college to me. They suggested my being a hairdresser, beautician, or things like that, and I did end up going to beauty school. It really bothered me that there was a difference in the way we, all Latinos, were being treated by the teachers and the counselors. I thought that, for some reason, I was the only one that noticed and was upset over these things. I noticed that the teachers discouraged brown kids and black kids from going to college, but encouraged white kids to go to college and made sure white kids took the right classes to prepare them for college. They would put us in any class they felt they should put us in. Actually, I didn't go to college because there wasn't enough money, so after finishing high school, I went to beauty school. Then I opened my own hair salon, as well as a restaurant and liquor store. At one point, I had about sixty people working for me. I always knew that women and Latinos were just as smart, and maybe smarter, than whites. I think this is why I wanted to improve our situation and create better conditions for our Latino community. Maybe it's about showing people that we are just as good as anybody else. I talked to my friends about this situation, but they just thought I was too intense all the time. I'd tell them, "You know, I just notice those things. I've always noticed those things." I cared about things that they didn't care about, but I kept pushing.

When I was in high school, there was nothing in our schoolbooks that I could relate to. Not at all! Not at all! Not even in my California history book. At home

I was learning that, as Mexicans, we were good and smart people and had a great culture. My parents talked about our heritage and taught us to appreciate it and made sure we preserved our culture. People used to tell my mother that I was smart, and I think that's why she wanted me to use my intelligence to better myself. School was a different world; Mexicans were mostly looked down on by the teachers and white students.

I often wondered why these injustices were happening. I asked myself, for example, "Why do Latinos have the worst teachers?" I saw a big difference in the quality of teachers. I saw our teachers as kind of like the rejects. I wondered why the school was such a mess and nobody seemed to care or worry about it. My parents were somewhat aware of the situation, but as I said, because they didn't speak English there was little they could do about it, even though the people in the community considered them to be leaders.

## CREATING A SPACE: THE LATIN AMERICAN CLUB

After attending Roosevelt High School, I was in the first class to start and graduate from the new San Jose High on Julian Street. This high school was great. I was very active. There were a lot of clubs with different groups of kids, but it was still kind of cliquish. There was a club for the guys who were the jocks and one for the kids who were outstanding in their schoolwork. There was another club that was for the girls, but mostly white girls were members of it. I kind of admired them because they were the most popular girls, and when they asked me to join their club, I really thought about it, but then I thought, "I really don't like them." I guess I just wanted to be asked. I looked up to these kids, but then I started to notice that they were really snobby and mean to other kids. I didn't like the way they acted. They kind of looked down on other people, like Latinos. So then when they asked me, I decided not to join. I then decided to form my own club and I did. I thought, "Well, you know the Mexican kids don't have anything." This is why I started a Latin American Club. I started talking to other Latinos at the school, and they really liked the idea. I wanted the Latin American Club to include kids from other Latin American countries and so I called us Latin Americans. I felt that this term encompassed more people and it kind of made everybody comfortable. Soon we had a pretty big club. We also had a few white kids that wanted to be with us, so we let them join and they just loved it. They liked to hang out with us. I don't think the teachers liked it. In fact, we had a hard time finding a teacher who would be our sponsor, but eventually we found a teacher that spoke Spanish and agreed to be our advisor; he was very good to us.

He was always very encouraging and helpful. I think that he had lived in Mexico at one time or Central America somewhere because he knew how to speak Spanish and he really liked our culture and liked us kids.

The Latin American Club sponsored celebrations of Mexican holidays, but, of course, the white kids didn't know what these celebrations meant. We went ahead and had our own Mexican celebrations, which teachers and some of the other kids thought were weird. The club was something that was very important to me. I guess I wanted to show everyone at school that Latinos were just as good as others and maybe even better than everyone else. My parents knew that I had started this club, and they were very proud. They thought it was great that I was doing this and always encouraged me to do things like organize activities. I'm not sure my parents knew that one of the reasons why I organized the club was that I felt a lot of anger from all the discrimination I had experienced in school. Ever since I was very young I decided that I could either do something negative or something positive with my anger and my energy. I decided to concentrate on using my energy to do positive things, like starting the Latin American Club.

When I refer to myself I say Mexican American. My parents call themselves Mexicans and told us that we would always be Mexican. The distinction between the two is that we were kind of in between two cultures. We could be very Mexican and Mexican American. When I say "very Mexican," I mean that we could embrace our culture, our holidays, our food, our language, our music, everything. Everything in my life was "very Mexican,," but I began to be more exposed to American culture. I started listening to the music that was popular at that time like Johnny Ray and Nat King Cole and others. It was difficult at times. It was like one world was over here and the other world was over there, but somehow I was more comfortable in the Mexican one.

## THE EMERGENCE OF A COMMUNITY ACTIVIST: "I THINK I WAS JUST BORN DIFFERENT"

I was involved in the Latino community by the time I was in high school. I spent a lot of time on the East Side with Father McDonald. Someone donated a barrack, and he had some families help him put it on this piece of land where the Mayfair Community Center is now located. He would say Mass there, and all the families in the community would attend.

I got recruited to organize youth activities for this center. I think it was strange because I usually am the one that prefers to sit in the corner and be silent. I sometimes feel like I don't want people to look at me, to notice that I'm there, but it seems I always end up having do to all the work and become president or vice president of some group or organization. I guess I am very reserved and very shy. But ever since I was a kid, I always ended up running things for some reason, which is inconsistent with my personality, and I've never come to terms with that. I did agree to be involved with the youth group. The priest picked me out and asked me to organize an activity, and when I finished with that project, he asked me to organize another one. Then I began having ideas of my own about doing things, and that's how I got more involved. I'd organize basketball games, boxing matches. I even organized a fashion show. The kids liked these programs, which surprised me because they were really rough kids. Sometimes, I'd be in the middle of them and breaking up fights. I would just think of things for them to do. Sometimes, I'd get day-old donuts donated for them. I'd just get donations and had them hang out there. I figured at least they won't be fighting if they hang out at the center and I kept them entertained and fed.

My parents encouraged me to get involved in the center, particularly because these activities were connected to the Church. They'd give me a bad time about my getting involved in other things because they were very protective, but when I was doing things for the Church, they were OK with it. But sometimes my father would object. I was just born different. Perhaps I was just too smart for my own good. My brothers got to do all kinds of things, but my sisters didn't. I wouldn't accept that I couldn't do what my brothers did, and I always asked why. So my father and I would have these little debates. He sometimes had a hard time dealing with me and yet he was very proud that I started the Latin American Club, so there was a kind of dilemma. My mother quietly encouraged me. She was on my side always; she always stood up for me.

Father McDonald was a different type of priest from what I had ever known. The Latino community loved him. He spoke Spanish and would come to your house and knock on the door when you didn't expect him. He'd come in and have coffee and talk to you. Sometimes he would pray with us in our own homes. He was always there for people. If they were sick, he'd visit them in the hospital. If they were in jail, he'd go visit them. He used to have a rinky-dink bus, but he would still go out and bring farm workers in from the fields to go to church. He even had a little altar in a station wagon so that he could go out in the fields and say Mass. He was really an activist kind of priest, and I think that's why he got moved away from here. I don't remember what year it was, but the Latino community was really devastated by his leaving. He was assigned to someplace else, San Francisco, I believe. The hall next to the church was named McDonald Hall.

No one was loved by our community as much as he was. I learned from him that as a community activist you must keep going even if you're tired. He would get himself so tired that he would doze off when he was meeting with somebody because he had been up all night. He just cared so much for the community. He was a real role model for me.

After I graduated from high school, I ended up going to beauty school and then working in some salons. I married a hairstylist, and later, we opened our own shop. We then decided that we were going to buy a restaurant and after that a liquor store. I didn't know any women who owned businesses at that time. When my husband and I had our businesses, I was the one that actually ran them. My husband was the public relations person because he was great at that, but I've always been very shy and reserved. I'd handle the books, but people who came in to talk to us about some aspect of the business would always talk to him. I ended up doing the business deal, but they started out dealing with him. I think it was because I was a woman.

My husband and I were making really good money, but somehow that didn't feel right to me. Even though our businesses were very successful, I always felt that something was missing in my life. I had always wanted to do something that would really help people. Then, when I was thirty-five, I got divorced. I decided that my divorce could be the end of something or the beginning of something else. I knew I'd make a lot less money, but I was determined to do something I felt passionate about. I decided to work in the community so that I could help others.

I've always been concerned about equal rights for women, so, back in 1973 or 1974, my first nonprofit position was investigating sex-discrimination complaints for the county executive in Santa Clara County. There was a lot of preparation involved such as searching through files and just plain grunt work, but I kept on going. Women would file a complaint, and I had to go investigate it and somehow negotiate a resolution. It turned out that I was very good at it. I'd win 98 percent of my cases.

I then was recruited to work for an antipoverty agency to run the women's program. It was a tiny program that only had a $20,000 budget and a few Center for Employment Training Agency (CETA) positions at that time. I decided to make the program a really big thing. I submitted proposals for funding everywhere I could think of, and eventually, I received funding for some of them. I started the first employment and training program for women. In eleven months after I was there, the budget increased from $20,000 to about $400,000. We opened a halfway house for women who had been released from institutions. They would finish their sentence in this program. We'd get them back together with their kids, teach them parenting skills, and get them into an employment-training program. It became one of the biggest divisions of the agency. I was in charge of all the twenty programs, and I eventually worked my way up to deputy director of CETA.

## MACSA: A CASE STUDY OF INSTITUTION BUILDING

I eventually went on to other jobs in the nonprofit sector, and then, in 1983, the Mexican American Community Services Agency [MACSA] recruited me. I had already been on the MACSA board. So I took the job and I was shocked! There were only two people working there, and the place looked abandoned and quite shabby. I found myself working until midnight for days and days. The agency was in dire straits and was about to be closed down by United Way. I ended up begging the United Way for $27,000 to keep the doors open for myself and a staff of two people for the next three months. Then I spent six months just cleaning up the mess that had been left. There were unpaid bills and about thirteen lawsuits against the agency from creditors and disgruntled ex-employees. During this period, I was also writing grant proposals and working to get people to trust MACSA once again. Someone on our board of directors wanted to change the name because it was so tarnished. I said, "No, we are going to keep the name, but we will change the reputation."

When policy makers took a chance on MACSA by giving us funding, we made sure to deliver what was promised in an efficient and professional manner. When your word becomes as certain as a written contract, you are respected and your credibility opens many doors. We succeeded through very hard work and good decision-making skills. From there, we started building programs, and even when things were tough, MACSA continued to grow. Today our budget for programs is seven million dollars and for building projects it's thirty-five million dollars. MACSA has a staff of 120 people.

MACSA kept growing and growing. I was trying to open an Adult Bay Health Center, but I couldn't find a building. I then asked myself, "Why can't we build our own building?" I started submitting proposals, and then I got a large loan from the state health authority to put up a building that would house the health center. In addition, MACSA has always placed an emphasis on putting together programs for our young people. Although we started many of these kinds of programs, I decided we needed to build a youth center and so we did. The lot was too big, and we had to decide what we were going to do with the extra space in the back. I knew that there was a great need for housing. We always listened to what the community told us, and they said that they needed housing, especially housing for the elderly. As a result, we built housing and then we bought some more land and built more. We also decided that there was a great need for first-time home-buyer housing, which is being built down a few blocks from here. We're also working on our third senior-housing project, expanding our youth center and building another one in a nearby town, and purchasing and remodeling an intervention center for high-risk youths. The center deals with the elderly with mental or physical challenges, a youth center with a computer lab, tutoring, after-school homework clubs, sports leagues, and a charter-schools program.

I would say that the MACSA Male Responsibility Project is one of the programs that I consider to be most successful and most innovative. In fact, we debated whether or not to implement it because we didn't know if it was going to work. The program focused on antipregnancy prevention with boys instead of girls. Counseling represented an important part of the program. We felt that maybe Latino boys had the same negative attitude about counseling that some of the older Latinos did, but we thought we didn't have anything to lose so we tried it. It was a huge success. The young men were craving somebody to talk to, particularly other males. We thought, "Well, it's easier for men to talk to men," and so we hired males to do the counseling and this was also a huge success. We received an award from Hillary Clinton for our successful efforts.

I thought that MACSA could be the focal point for the entire Latino community. I wanted to make MACSA a model agency, like the Latin American Club when I was a kid. I always understood that women were just as smart as men, and maybe smarter at times. This inspires me to work to create better conditions in our community. That's probably one of the things that motivates me.

I thought that I could even get MACSA to a point where it could be self-sufficient. Since I had kind of a business background by accident, I started thinking that maybe someday MACSA would become self-sufficient and not be at the mercy of the city, the county, and the state all the time, although MACSA still gets a lot of money from these funding sources. I never did make MACSA totally self-sufficient, but there are some programs that are creating income.

MACSA has made a difference in the lives of Latinos in San José because of the services that we have provided and the fact that those services were designed by listening to the Latino community identify their problems and needs to us. In this way we were able to understand their problems and develop programs to address their needs. I think that we proved that we could run MACSA as a business and make it a model agency. I hope MACSA lasts forever and ever and that it keeps growing and meeting the community's needs.

## THE CHICANA COALITION: WOMEN ORGANIZING WOMEN

In the early 1970s, I started the Chicana Coalition. I had been involved with a women's organization called MANA, but I wanted a local group here in San José.[3] I started this group like I started the Latin American Club. I recruited women who were department heads of various agencies and community leaders into this group. One of the women was the affirmative action officer for the city of San José. Another worked as an administrator in one of the school districts. I brought together very ambitious and successful women. We were really tight and supportive of each other. We tried to push women into political office. The membership of the Chicana Coalition kept growing. I kept talking to women, and if they thought it was a good idea, they talked to some more women about the group. This is how the Chicana Coalition got larger. We had young Chicana students come and watch us at our meetings so they could learn about leadership.

The Chicana Coalition dealt with a variety of key community issues, such as the lack of hiring Latino police officers. We were involved with the San José police and the lawsuit filed against them. We joined with others in the Latino community who wanted more Latinos on the police force. Members of the Chicana Coalition were also members of city committees such as the one dealing with affirmative action.

## MY LIFE, MY ACTIVISM, AND MY COMMUNITY

I think that my desire to correct injustices comes from all the things that I saw and experienced when I was a child. It also comes from my parents who believed in the importance of changing things that weren't right. I never got a chance to go to college, but I decided that I would either feel sorry for myself or try to do something important with my life. I thought, "I want to see how much I can do even though I don't have a college degree." This is why I was shocked—totally shocked!—when Santa Clara University gave me an honorary doctorate for service in 1999. If my parents had been alive when I received this honorary doctorate, they would have been so proud. All my family was there—my brothers and sisters and my husband. They were all very proud of me.

I believe we Latinos should preserve many parts of our Mexican culture. Some of those traditional values that we should retain include the importance of the family and staying together and working things out. We need to be responsible for our kids, teaching them respect and hard work. I think many of us wanted to give them what we didn't have when we were growing up and now they expect things without working. This is why I think we need to make sure that we pass on a work ethic to our children. It really makes me sad when I work with gangs, like the *Norteño/Sureño* gangs.[4] My father really believed in brotherhood, not in gangs. The way these kids hate each other is just devastating. Many of our values are being lost, and we have to make sure we recover and preserve them.

Of course I'm biased, but I think that everybody should go into social work. I can't think of anything that you can do that would bring you as much satisfaction. I didn't leave my job as a social worker because I didn't like it. I left it because it was time for me to leave. It feels really good to be able to do something that makes a difference for your community. I think it is possible to make money, but there's always a way that you can help your community. We all have a responsibility, especially to our people, to Latinos.

## NOTES

1. *Día de los Muertos* [Day of the Dead] is a Latin American celebration that takes place on November 1. People visit the graves of their family and friends, bringing flowers and food to celebrate their lives. Celebrants believe that the souls of the dead return and are all around them. Families remember the departed by telling stories about them.

2. Neighborhood in west San José that eventually became an affluent area with few Mexicans.

3. MANA stands for the Mexican American National Association, named when it was originally founded in 1974 by Mexican American women. In January 1994, members voted to become MANA, A National Latina Organization, to reflect the growing diversity of its membership. Today, MANA is the largest national pan-Latina membership organization.

4. Mexican gangs that have crossed over the border from Mexico and are mainly concentrated in California. Each gang represents a specific area of Mexico: north and south.

# 5

# Sofía Mendoza

*Sofía Mendoza was born in Fillmore, California, in the early 1930s, and her family eventually made their home in San José. Her father was a labor organizer throughout the 1930s and served as her role model for her life as a community activist. Mendoza became one of the most recognized community activists in San José. She founded United People Arriba, an umbrella group that brought together grassroots community organizations. The organization mobilized around education, health care, police brutality, and immigration. Mendoza was instrumental in establishing the first major health clinic in East San José. She participated in protest marches in California and Washington, D.C., and joined solidarity delegations to Nicaragua, Vietnam, and El Salvador to show support for international liberation movements.*

## THE ORGANIZERS' DAUGHTER

I was born in 1934 in a little town called Fillmore in Ventura County, California. My father's name was Tiburcio, you know, like Tiburcio Vásquez.[1] My mother's name was Margarita. My father used to tell me that his father had owned some land in Mexico but much of it had been stolen. His father had to fight to get his land back, and this made my dad a rebellious kind of person.

The reason I was born in Fillmore was because my father was a labor organizer there during the 1930s. He went to Fillmore to organize citrus fruit and avocado pickers in the largest ranch in California. Even though these farm workers had never had a union, they went on strike soon after my father started working with them. Their strike only lasted six months because they didn't get enough financial support. My father told me it was one of the California strikes that lasted for the longest time. My mother was pregnant with me at the time, and I was born while they were still organizing in Fillmore.

In about 1939, my father went to Arizona to organize the copper miners near Phoenix. The workers organized themselves into the Miners Smelting Workers union, and my father became one of its officers. My mother was also very active; she worked with the families of the strikers. My mother was always involved in supporting the families of the people that my dad was organizing. When World War II broke out during the strike, the mining company had to settle because they needed the copper for the war. So you see, I grew up in a family that was very involved in community activism.

When I was growing up, my parents always told me I was Mexican. I've been through American and Spanish surnames. I've called myself Latino, Mexican American, and Mexican. I'm told I'm all of these things. When someone asks me what I am, I still struggle to find an answer. When someone asks me this question in Spanish, I say outright that I am *Mexicana*. When I went to Mexico I told people that I was a Mexican: "*Soy Mexicana*" [I am Mexican], but people would answer, "*No eres Mexicana*" [You are not Mexican]. This shocked me. It absolutely shocked me. It really hurt me that I didn't know who I was and what I should call myself. It makes a big difference in how you feel about yourself. The reason I bring this up is because using different names causes divisions. If you talk to people from New Mexico, they consider themselves to be different from *Tejanos* [Texans]. *Tejanos* consider themselves different from us in California. We can be very divided over names, and this is never a good thing.

Ever since I can remember, I knew farm workers faced a lot of discrimination. I had no idea that *Mexicanos* couldn't live in certain neighborhoods. I used to hear people always tell us, "Oh, why don't you guys get organized? You people never get organized." We have a very long history of organizing around a lot of issues, but our history has not been fully written. We don't get credit for what we have done. My father expected that one of his children would follow in his footsteps as an organizer. He was expecting one of my brothers to become an organizer, but it just turned out to be me. He was very surprised that a girl would become an organizer, but he wasn't surprised that I would become one! I was the oldest in the family and had a lot of responsibility for my brothers and sisters. They said I was bossy and pushy. I got a lot of experience from being the oldest, and when my dad saw that I was doing a good job, he said, "Good for you. You're going to go up against nothing but men because they are the ones that run everything, but you're going to get away with it because you're a woman and they have to respect you." And you know what? He was right! When I was working in the community, I would just sit there and men would be respectful because I was a woman! I took advantage of this because it was a very good organizing tactic. As I was growing up, I was expected to help people. My dad always said, "If you want something, you can get it, but you've got to work for it." I was just very fortunate to be the daughter of a labor organizer.

My father has been the greatest influence in my life; he was an excellent role model for me. He was a very caring, wise person, and I learned a lot of good lessons from him. I believe I got my wisdom from my father. I always wanted to be like my dad because he always wanted to put an end to injustices. When I was very young, my father used to tell me that we are born into this life with a purpose: to help one another. This is why I have always felt a responsibility to help other people, especially those less fortunate.

## ROOTS OF COMMUNITY ACTIVISM

We came to San José from Arizona because most of my family on my mother's side was living in San José. We settled in Campbell and were one of the few Mexican families living there.[2] I remember Campbell when it was a township and then a city. It was a very little town way out in the middle of a lot of orchards. This whole place was an agricultural valley. There were a lot of Japanese families in the area because they were the ones growing the strawberries. I went to Campbell Grammar School. I had very few Mexican classmates, and that has had a great impact on me.

My first organizing effort took place when I was a freshman at Campbell High School. My school had a math, a French, and a German club but didn't have a Spanish club. I came home one day and complained to my dad and he said, "You know what you've got to do." He taught me how to circulate petitions, get signatures, talk to the students, and approach the teachers to gain their support for starting the club. My father was very proud of me when I told him that my organizing had succeeded and our high school finally had a Spanish Club. That was my first organizing effort that I did by myself, but I had been involved in a lot of work with my family. It was just expected of me. We always had a lot of discussions at home about justice and injustice. We talked about the way people should live and be treated by others.

I met my husband just after I got out of high school. He and his parents were visiting here from Westminster, California. He told me that he had gone to a segregated school. I didn't believe him because I went to Campbell School where there were Anglos and Mexicans. I had all the opportunity that everybody else had there. I thought that's the way it was for everybody, but he told me that this was not true. He said they used to put Mexicans in the bus and take them over to another school where all of the teachers were Mexican. The teachers and administrators did not have degrees and were not qualified. I found this hard to believe. I said, "That doesn't happen. It might happen to blacks in the South, but it doesn't happen to Mexican people in California." Years later, I found a book in the library titled *North From Mexico* by Carey McWilliams, and it described the Westminster desegregation case.[3] I couldn't believe it. My husband had been absolutely right about his school. The Westminster case involved a businessman who got fed up with his daughter being sent to a segregated school. He took the case to court and won. When the schools were desegregated, my husband couldn't compete with the other students and he failed the ninth grade. He had a very difficult time adjusting to the new school system, but he always said that it was best that the schools desegregated.

I went to San José State University. Once I got there, I remember going for days and days without seeing another brown face on the campus. I was the only one in most of my classes. I don't know how many of us were going to San José State, but I know there were very few. I almost completed my third year, but I didn't finish. I got married and I had a child. I always said I would finish my last year, but I didn't do it.

My experience was different than most Latino kids when I started organizing. They didn't have enough counselors in schools. Students didn't get much information about college. Teachers and counselors have to start talking to students about college when they're very young. Students, even young ones, need to understand it's not impossible to go to the university even if their parents don't have the money or because the parents haven't been to college. Proposition 13 did away with a lot of the counselors.[4] Someone has to direct students to prepare them for college. By the time they're in their senior year and they want to go to college, it's too late. The Chicano community had to face a sad situation: More than 50 percent of Latino students were dropping out before they finished high school.[5] It was a tragedy! I served on the state's Hispanic Advisory Council to study the dropout rate. Everyone should have a chance to go to college whether their parents are farm workers or executives. Children are our future but the situation looked very bleak in those days, and it really hasn't changed that much today. I have dedicated my life working to improve education and will continue to do so as long as I am able.

Education is the most important thing in a human being's life. Without a good education you can't be secure in life. Long ago, I decided to dedicate myself to helping children get an education. Students were complaining about being expelled for minor violations. The school was sending students to juvenile homes without dealing directly with their parents. I heard that teachers and students had been involved in fistfights. Students were not given books because they were told they probably wouldn't take care of them. I knew I couldn't rely on the PTA to help solve these problems because it is a conventional organization that only represents students who are doing well in school. When I started to help the parents, the PTA gave us the strongest resistance. They didn't want to listen to us or believe that the school had problems. Only about nine or ten parents actually went to PTA meetings. When we called a meeting of the Mexican parents and students, we had over three hundred. This is what I call a real PTA. I asked an attorney who was a friend of mine to defend the students who had been arrested and we won the case.

After this incident, I started visiting other Mexican parents to ask them how their kids were being treated at school. I documented everything they told me about the junior high school. The parents and the children signed what I wrote down on paper. This is how I began organizing the parents. Saul Alinsky taught his organizers to schedule home visits before calling for a community meeting.[6] My father used this same tactic when he was organizing farm workers. My dad always told me, "If you're going to organize people, you've got to do it one person at a time. You visit one person, get them to talk to another person, and then that person talks to someone else. You can't call a big meeting and expect everybody to come." I also learned this strategy from César Chávez. He used to say, "You've got to organize one person at a time."

About five hundred parents and students attended a meeting with the school administrators to discuss this situation. We had a list of demands. We told the administrators that our students had the right to change their schools if they were experiencing discrimination. We made them understand that as taxpayers we were the ones who paid their salary and so they had to treat our children with a lot more respect. We won this battle too.

My strategy was to continue working with parents and helping them to mobilize around other issues. I also encouraged the students to organize themselves. I used to tell the students, "Don't say anything to anybody about your activities. You're going to do it the right way if you want to avoid getting yourselves into trouble." We decided that we needed to form and organize committees if we wanted to solve future problems. The parents and students organized several committees to help them work with the administration in an effort to make sure that all these unfair practices were really eliminated. They even had a discipline committee for dealing with violation of specific rules. We formed committees of parents, teachers, guidance counselors, the superintendent of schools, and others who had something to do with the students. One issue we worked on was the use of police to patrol the school grounds. We went to the chief of police and asked him to remove all the policemen. After we put a lot of pressure on him, the police finally stopped patrolling the schools.

The students learned so much from their organizing. It was really wonderful. The children learned that people could make changes in the system. They learned they have every right to make changes without winding up in juvenile hall for being labeled as troublemakers. They did something meaningful and not just for themselves, but for other people. I still see some of these students, and they tell me that these were some of the best days of their lives because they did something so meaningful: They made a difference.

During this time, Dr. Ernesto Galarza and I had a lot of discussions about education.[7] He had a passion for fairness and justice for all people no matter who they were. He wanted to make sure that everybody got what was rightfully theirs. Dr. Galarza and I shared the view that education was the most important thing in a human being's life. We would talk and get frustrated about the problems with our educational system. We raised all kinds of questions. Why is education denied to so many children? Why is it that the children grow up not feeling intelligent and not feeling loved? We used to sit there and fantasize about what would be a perfect system of education. He used to talk to me even more when he started writing children's books. He used to tell me, "It doesn't cost the teacher anything to start the class every day by telling children that they are intelligent." This will help them believe that they are intelligent. It will make them eager to learn and believe that they can go to college. But it just doesn't happen. We would sit there and fantasize about what a perfect day in school would be like for a little child. We hoped that someday our dream would come through.

## MOBILIZING THE EAST SIDE

Our success at Roosevelt High School taught us that we had real power in our community to bring about change. I said to myself, "If we can make important changes at Roosevelt, then we can create change anywhere else." We turned our mobilization efforts to another very serious community issue: the relationship between our community and the police. The community was fed up with the San José Police Department's treatment of Chicanos. The chief of police had been in office for forty-two years, and personally I thought he should have retired long before we started protesting. The Police Officers Association played a key role in running the department. You could go to a city council meeting and they were sitting in the meeting controlling the people on the city council! I mean they ran this town and I couldn't believe what I was seeing. Every time the police were accused of a killing, we would go to the city council, but they'd just sit there. They didn't understand why we were complaining and why we wanted an investigation, and so they wouldn't do anything.

When I used to walk door-to-door organizing people, I saw cops kicking doors down in the East Side. I saw it with my own eyes. I saw policemen stopping people for traffic infractions at gunpoint! I saw this with my own eyes, and nobody can say that I didn't see it. I saw it because I was out in the streets a lot. During some of the marches and demonstrations, the police were really brutal. The community responded with a march down to city hall. The newspaper estimated that about 2,000 people participated. We were asked for a civilian review board. In 1972, Mayor Norman Mineta appointed a committee on police policies and procedures.[8] The Ad Hoc Police Department Administrative Policies and Procedures Committee reviewed the police policies and procedures manual. We wanted to see what rules the police department had in place such as the ones about the police use of firearms. Chief of Police Joseph McNamara changed some things, but he did it because he was pressured by the community to do it. I always like to give credit to the community.

We mobilized an organization of citizens to monitor the police. We called ourselves the Community Alert Patrol, and we set up our base station at Our Lady of Guadalupe Church in San José. We had a lot of equipment, including radio scanners to monitor police calls so we could drive to the place where the police had been dispatched. People used their own cars to follow the police. The Community Alert Patrol operated on Fridays and Saturdays. We had two-way radios that would connect the base station to the cars. We used cameras and tape recorders to document these incidents. Our goal was to be ready to record any type of police discrimination and brutality. When we received a police call, we would jump in our cars and sometimes we would get there before the police arrived. We would take pictures of the people before and after the cops got there so we could have documentation of any police brutality. People would use these pictures to help their cases in court. We had to go that far to stop the police brutality that was going on in East San José. I was extremely bothered because not only were they killing our young men in Vietnam, they were also killing them here in the streets of San José.

We organized a committee on public safety to deal with police brutality cases. We had a lot of marches to city hall, and we got a lot of publicity. The whole Chicano community was fed up with the police. We just had it. We had reached our limit. The police had guns, mace, and billy clubs. They were always ready to attack us. It seemed as if nobody could stop what the police were doing here in San José. They could do whatever they wanted. We didn't give up. Our organizing increased; nobody could stop us. We mobilized 2,000 people to march down the street to city hall to protest police brutality.

We kept working with our Community Alert Patrol. It was dangerous because we would be out at night and we never knew what might happen. We would be out to until two or three in the morning. We made sure to train the people before they went out on patrol. We would brief them on our rules. They were not to interfere when the police were making an arrest even if they were beating somebody. Our job was to document any incidents of police brutality with pictures and tape recordings. We would take down the name of the policeman, the badge number, and the car number. Our patrol would also find witnesses to write down what they told us.

The Community Alert Patrol changed how the police treated us. Bu it took a lot of mobilizing. Many community people became part of the Community Alert Patrol. We had over 1,000 people going out into the San José community, particularly into the East Side. A lot of students from San José State were very involved in the Community Alert Patrol. We couldn't separate one community struggle from another. We were supporting the students by trying to help them get new ethnic studies programs and more funds for the student loan program. The students always were involved in the community. We were all involved with the war in Vietnam. Everything was affecting all of us. Not only were we making changes, but we were also very interested in developing leadership among young people. Many these young men and women who were active back then are now leaders in our community.

While I was helping to mobilize the community to end police brutality, I helped organize the community to challenge the way members of the San José's city council were elected. At that time, five people sat on the city council and they were elected at-large. They all came from affluent communities. They didn't care how many East Siders got killed. They wouldn't listen to us. We believed that we could bring about change only if we changed the election system for the San José city council. We set out to end at-large elections. We didn't know whether we were going to succeed because we knew it would not be an easy job; it would be big challenge. We had to get signatures for a petition to change the election process, but I don't remember the percentage of the voters we needed to get an initiative on the ballot. We attempted three times and the third time we did win, and as a result, San José was divided into ten council districts including one from the East Side. We turned San José on its head, and let me tell you, if people ever say that Chicanos don't know about politics, I will answer, "Man, we do know how to work the system left and right."

## PROTESTING AGAINST THE VIETNAM WAR: THE CHICANO MORATORIUM[10]

The '60s were a time of activism all over the United States, including, of course, our community in San José. We had also become aware of what was going on with blacks in the South and their civil rights movement. The Chicano community started becoming more aware of what was going on within its neighborhoods. We had to deal with many issues, and one was the war in Vietnam. A lot of young Chicano men, many of whom were students, were fighting and dying in Vietnam. I would hear people and politicians say, "If you can't use them, send them to the war." Those young Chicanos who weren't going to school were being drafted and sent to Vietnam. This is why we protested against Vietnam. Students at San José State organized a protest when Dow Chemical Company was recruiting on campus. Dow Chemical was making napalm for the army's use in Vietnam. When they tried to keep those army recruiters from coming onto campus, students said, "We don't want them coming here to recruit any of our students so they can go drop napalm in Vietnam. Stay away from here." It really bothered me to see the pictures of Vietnamese children with their skin all burnt as a result of the napalm. The students organized a big demonstration. We got tear-gassed during this demonstration. The police turned the water hoses on us. It was really a bad situation. But you know, the wonderful thing was that we were all protesting together.

The Chicano Anti-Vietnam Moratorium was a nightmare—a terrible nightmare—to see the police attack all of us demonstrators. I was so afraid when I was at the moratorium. I was terrified, but I felt that I had to do what I was doing. We had to make everyone aware of the situation in Vietnam. It makes me cry when I think about it. It's just something that bothers me about a human life being lost. I felt that I had to be at the Chicano Moratorium to protest against Vietnam. We all have our time when we're going to die, and I always tell myself maybe this is the way that I'm going to go. I would feel better dying for a cause than any other way. I always tell myself that as long as I have a breath of life in me, I have to fight against injustices.

I met Rosalio Muñoz when students walked out of San José's Roosevelt Junior High School in 1967 and 1968.[10] The students decided that they were not going to go to school that day. They did not cross into the school grounds, but they stayed outside and picketed all day long. Rosalio heard about the walkout, and soon after he talked to me and he helped organize a walkout in East Los Angeles. This took place in March 1968. Their walkout got more attention than ours because ours was really spontaneous. A group of Brown Berets helped us here in San José, too. Sal Candelaria and other kids belonged to the Brown Berets, but I think that the Brown Berets in Los Angeles were a little bit more sophisticated than the Brown Berets here in San José. The kids that were the Brown Berets were also in other organizations like United People Arriba, the organization I helped start.

Education and the war in Vietnam were two of the issues that contributed to the growth of the *Movimiento*.[11] I worked with Chicano students from other states in the Southwest who shared their opposition to the war in Vietnam. I had never seen such massive organizing as that for the Chicano Moratorium. It was the kind of organizing that we didn't get credit for but we still did it. We said over and over again: "Enough is enough! Enough is enough! When is the war going to stop?" We came together and mobilized. The result was the Chicano Moratorium. I haven't gotten so emotional thinking about the Chicano Moratorium and the Vietnam War until now during this interview.[12]

## CONFRONTING COMMUNITY ISSUES: MOBILIZATION AND ORGANIZATION

The organizing tactics of Saul Alinsky influenced how I mobilized the San José community. When I started organizing, I had a plan about how to get many community people involved. I organized many house meetings, but only after I, and others, did a lot of planning. We would put together a leaflet calling for a house meeting to discuss an issue. Each section of the East Side community was experiencing specific problems, and as organizers we had to know how to get people to work together. This was a difficult task back then because many people were afraid because they were undocumented immigrants. Others were afraid that their welfare money would be taken away if the welfare authorities found out they had been "rabble-rousing." People had many other reasons to be afraid. We wanted our leaflets to bring people to the house meetings. We were careful to focus on a specific message such as "You have a right to lights on your streets" or "You have a right to public transportation in your district." We were also concerned with many of the Vista volunteers that were being sent to San José to do community organizing. Many lacked organizing experience, so we brought them to our meetings and trained them how to organize.

After having many meetings in peoples' homes, we put together our first community meeting. A couple of hundred people attended. People were interested in many issues such as education, medical services, transportation, and housing. Police brutality was another main issue because the police were killing people. Many of the people who attended the meeting did not want to organize around that issue because they were afraid of what might happen if the police found out that they were involved in the protests. Actually, I was afraid too!

We decided to form an organization and agreed that it had to be a multi-issue organization because not everybody was interested in organizing around the same thing. We didn't want to lose anybody. Some people, for example, were disgusted because cars were hitting children because there were not enough traffic lights. This affected all groups, not just Mexicans. This is why we wanted to start an organization that was not limited to one ethnic group. We wanted one that would represent the entire community, and so we called ourselves "United People Arriba"—United People Upward. Two-thirds of this name is in English and the last third is in Spanish. We liked the term "United People" because it got the idea across that people from different ethnic backgrounds were coming together in San José to work for social change. Blacks, Mexicans, Puerto Ricans, and whites were working together in one organization. Our organization's name of United People Arriba also showed everyone that we developed a sense of solidarity within the group. I learned that agencies wouldn't give you funds if you want your organization to stay independent like United People Arriba. So our group relied completely on fund-raisers and donations. I taught the members of United People Arriba to write a petition and mobilize the community. Members went before the city council, presented their petition, and eventually, the city put up more traffic lights.

We were also concerned with the lack of adequate health care on the East Side. People were complaining that there were only nineteen doctors working in East San José. Our community lacked enough doctors. That was just unbelievable. A group of students from universities in the San José area and some people from the community got together to organize a protest. We went to the board of supervisors and demanded that they put a branch of the Valley Medical Center in

East San José because most of the people that attended the county hospital did not live in the surrounding area and most did not have cars to get to Valley Medical.

This is why United People Arriba demanded a clinic. This led to a big fight. A local newspaper reported that we had mobbed a city representative. This was not true. No one mobbed him. This is what happened. He went to the bathroom and we followed him. We stood on both sides of the bathroom door, holding up our posters demanding the clinic. He had to pass by us when he walked out. We yelled at him because he did not want the clinic in East San José. That's all we did and the newspaper referred to us as a mob. The city representative was one of the owners of a hardware store, so we decided to put a picket line in front his store. We picketed for months and months.

The board of supervisors thought they would settle this issue by setting up direct rides to Valley Medical for people living in the East Side. The county chartered a big Greyhound bus. It made stops all over the East Side. This arrangement took place during the winter. I felt that the board wanted to sabotage our plans for a community center, so we fought back and organized a community boycott of the bus. I went with others to all the bus stops and told the people not to ride the bus. We gave rides to Valley Medical to those who joined the boycott and needed medical attention. When we arrived at the center, we asked people who were waiting for the bus to join the boycott and, if they agreed, we gave them a ride back to the East Side. Starting a community clinic was crucial; we had to organize this boycott. The newspaper published photos of an empty bus going back and forth from the East Side to Valley Medical Center.

United People Arriba was very successful. We kept getting more and more people involved. After three years, we finally got the clinic even though we started out with one little room. The board thought that our clinic wouldn't last. They didn't know how determined and strong we were as a community. They give us a little office in the basement of Alexian Brothers Hospital. Since it wasn't easy to find our office, we would go outside of the hospital to tell patients where the clinic was located. It felt great when we could finally see people from the East Side waiting for a doctor at the clinic we had set up.

I'm glad to see that we had an impact on the availability of medical services to East San José. It feels good to see our East Valley Health Center because we organized the community to get it. I can see the results of our organizing and our protests, and this is really very rewarding. It was a wonderful time for all the people, like Ernestina García, who marched, screamed, and picketed.[13] We made a big difference. I learned that we would always have to struggle on a daily basis and work around the system to bring about change for the community.

The clinic celebrated its twentieth anniversary in 1988, and I was the keynote speaker. It was so nice that a lot of students, patients, and politicians also spoke. They made me feel sort of important. I thought about the time when we protested to start the clinic and some people hated me. They treated me as though I was a really a "bad guy." People who were working for the city and county government really hated all of us because we were fighting so hard to get our clinic. Some of those on the board of supervisors and doctors who were at the celebration were making me feel important that day, but I still remember when I was their enemy. When I walked into the clinic, they had my picture and all the newspaper articles about the marches pinned on the bulletin board. It was a wonderful celebration, and some of the kids from my son's dance group performed. In my speech I told everyone how important it was to always remember community struggles, like the one we had in starting the clinic.

Let me tell you about a more recent community problem. About 1998, Mayor Tom McEnery and the city wanted to put up a stupid statue of Thomas Fallon.[14] I joined the Chicano community in protests to putting up his statue in downtown San José. I found out about it after the cement work for the foundation had been finished for the statue. I was so mad because the law says that you have to have public hearings before a statue can be put up in a public place. They never had one single public hearing. The city turned to private funds for the Fallon statute, but that still didn't mean it could be put on a public street. We complained and told them, "You're not going to put that statue there, no matter what." The Chicano community won this struggle; we stopped that statue from being put in the park. They kept it in storage until just last year.[15] So you see, my dad was right when he told me protests could bring change if you organize. This is why I am very proud of the work that we did. I really am. I know that we can easily win any issue, but we've got to get ourselves together and organize.

These are examples of the community issues I have worked on over the years. I've learned that you have to be careful how you organize. You have to study the specific issue before you organize a protest or confrontation. After that, it's a matter of being persistent and not giving up. I learned never to give up, no matter what. The music and the theater groups like the Teatro Campesino[16] became an important part of the *Movimiento*. People were more likely to attend a rally or a demonstration if organizers included cultural activities like music and plays. When I look back, I see that we really were very sophisticated in organizing the

Chicano community. Before you can organize, you have to show the community that there is a real need to work on a specific issue. I have never seen anything like the protests back then, and I know that we can keep on organizing in the future.

## MARCHING FOR JUSTICE:
## THE ROAD TO WASHINGTON AND SACRAMENTO

I helped organize a group from San José to the 1963 Poor People's March in Washington, D.C. We worked together to raise money for the trip. There was just no way that we couldn't be part of that movement. I mean, a human being is a human being, no matter where he's at or no matter what color he is. I think we have a responsibility for each other. I just feel it. That's the way that I was brought up. I will always believe that I have a responsibility for others. Even if the situation is dangerous, I will try to change it.

While I was raising funds for this trip, I began receiving letters from the American Nazi Party. A mailing list was stolen from the Peace Center, and my name was on it since I did some work with the center. Soon after this, a hate group called the Minutemen sent letters to almost all the people on the list. These letters contained all kinds of threats, such as "Look out because the next time you start your car, it might blow up. Be careful when you bring your milk in from your doorstep because it might have arsenic in it. Be careful when you're walking down the street because a gun might be aimed at your neck." They called us all welfare bums and said that we belonged in concentration camps. I was also getting very scary anonymous phone calls. My husband always worked swing shift, and one night a man called and told me he knew when my husband got home from work and that I should be careful when I was alone. In one call he said, "If I don't get you, I'm going to get your children." The calls got worse until one time he asked, "What do you prefer? A knife or a gun?" I didn't let any of these threats stop me from my organizing. I knew that they wanted me to stop organizing, but I wasn't going to stop. I kept on. I was very afraid, but I had to do what I did.

While I was on the march in Washington, I kept hearing about Black Power and I eventually believed in what the organization stood for. Black Power reverberated with Brown Power and so I supported the Poor People's March. I knew I was going to learn something by being there. I worked with people from the Black Panther Party but from a distance, not too close because the Black Panthers that were here in California were different than those in the South. The experiences of blacks in the South are different because they have had to put up with more discrimination. It's similar to my husband's experience. He went to a segregated school, but I didn't and so his experiences were different from mine. I learned that when you try organizing a community, you have to know about the different kinds of experiences that people have had if you are going to be successful.

In 1967, I joined a march from San José to Sacramento.[17] Ronald Reagan was governor then. One time, when he came to San José, we got a phone call that he wanted to talk to some community organizers. We were told to wait by the telephone at six o'clock in the morning, that they would call us and tell us where he would meet us. He wasn't willing to announce ahead of time where he was going to be. They finally called and told us where to meet Reagan, but when we got there he was actually in another building. I was so mad about their having us run around. When we got there, the room was already full of community leaders. Black and brown people filled the room, and there was a desk in front where Reagan was going to sit. I sat right next to the door, and I put my feet across the entrance. When Reagan came into the room, I said, "You've got to jump over my feet because I'm not going to move." I sat right there and I didn't move. I made him jump over my feet.

I snuck one of the reporters from the *East Side Sun* into the meeting. I wanted a reporter to be there with me to record whatever happened. A young man—Chicano or Mexican—who was a Republican, was screening everybody who came in to meet with Reagan. Since I knew him, he allowed me to bring in the reporter, but he didn't know he was a reporter. People stood up when they asked Reagan questions. They spoke to him in a very polite way. I was sitting there and I was just so mad at everybody. I was thinking to myself, "How can these community leaders show him such respect?" I waited while everybody asked their questions. When it was time for me to ask a question, I didn't stand up. I just sat right there and said, "I want to know why you're taking men out of the prisons and putting them out in the fields to break the farm workers' strike." Reagan then asked, "What is your name?" I said, "I asked you a question. Just answer me. Why are you making strike breakers out of all of these prisoners?" Then he shouted, "What is your name?" I mean he's yelling at me. He was madder than heck. He had a pencil in his hand while I repeated my question over and over again. He wasn't going to back down, and I wasn't going to back down either. Finally, he took the pencil, snapped it, and threw it on the desk. I waited as part of it went flying. I stood up and I said calmly, "My name is Sofía Mendoza." I repeated it about four or five times, and then I said, "And don't you ever forget my name and now answer my question." The reporter took pictures the whole time and some of them came out in the paper!

As I said earlier, we marched to Sacramento, and when we reached the steps of the capitol, we asked for Reagan to come out and address the crowd. Someone from his staff told us said that he wasn't going to come out. "How can he call himself the people's governor?" I thought. There were a lot of people there that day. As I was addressing the crowd, I noticed that Reagan finally came out. I looked over at him and said, "You wait until I finish." I kept addressing the crowd and then, when I finished, I started walking past him and he said, "Hello, Sofía Mendoza." He had not forgotten my name!

## INTERNATIONAL SOLIDARITY

You can read about and understand something intellectually about different countries like Nicaragua, but when you're actually there in the country, it's very different. I knew that the American government had a hand in the conflict in Nicaragua. I heard the bombing for myself when I went to Nicaragua. I learned that twenty-five farm workers had been killed. I knew that the U.S. was giving money to help the Contras.[18] I was deeply affected when I heard about the killings. I had read about the problems in Nicaragua, but it was only when I was there that I really understood what was happening.

I also visited El Salvador and Vietnam, and I discovered that these countries were having problems similar to Nicaragua's. I can't understand why the United States was spending so much money in both of these countries. It wasn't fair. It wasn't right. When I talked to people in El Salvador, they told me they just wanted to survive. That's all they wanted. They wanted to be able to eat, raise their children, and be safe. They didn't want anything else. They didn't want anything that we have. I had a similar experience when I visited Vietnam.

I went to the Soviet Union just a few days after the coup in Chile.[19] My husband and I were delegates to the World Congress of Peace Forces. He attended as a union representative, and I went as a community organizer. A lot of Vietnamese people were at the Congress, and they sat together and asked us, "Do you know who we are? Do you think that there's a difference between us?" And one person said, "Look, I'm from North Vietnam," and another said, "I'm from South Vietnam." They told us that they were the same people and explained what was happening in Vietnam. They said that they didn't cause the division of their country into North and South. The U.S. caused it. I found it amazing that they asked us about César Chávez and the farm workers in California. They were very aware of what was going on over here and they cared.

## A HOPEFUL MESSAGE FOR SOCIAL CHANGE

My children have always been involved in political activities and demonstrations. I used to take my little ones—even when they weren't in school yet—to community meetings with a little bag of cookies and color crayons. They would sit there during the meeting. Before my son was in school, he could name the people who were on the city council and board of supervisors because he had been going with me to those meetings. We used to push them in strollers to demonstrations. I felt that this experience would eventually help them educate people about community organizing.

I think it's wonderful for a family to be involved together and to do really meaningful kinds of organizing. I think it's what really held and bound my family so tightly together. My children are still involved. I feel very proud that my children have been shop stewards and union members. That means that they're providing leadership for the other workers to make sure that they get justice. They're still involved to this very day.

I have always wanted to make sure that my children learned about their Mexican culture. I started sending them to Mexico when they were about fifteen. They would get out of school on Friday and on Saturday they were already in Mexico, where they studied music and folkloric dance. I thought that this would be a good way to help them learn about their culture. My oldest son is involved in music and plays different instruments.

It's important to teach my children to be proud of their Mexican heritage. Our culture is so rich, but I just get so angry when we're treated like we're invisible in this country. This has to change; we have to be more appreciated for all our cultural contributions to the United States. My dad always said, "You can have many things, and they can take everything away from you. But the only thing they can't take away from you is your culture." While I was growing up, my father taught me that our culture was ignored in the United States, and I really listened to what he said. I grew up feeling cheated because I knew that Mexican culture was not appreciated here.

My husband passed away in December 2004; we would have been married fifty years. We had a wonderful marriage and had wonderful children. I would do it all over again. I always believed that community organizing starts at home. I've been an organizer all my life, and this affected our lives at home. We were so involved in so many important community activities that my husband and I never had any time to fight or argue. We just didn't. If something happened between us that made us angry, we knew that it was trivial in comparison with everything else that was going on in the community. He and I regretted that sometimes people accept what they have and the way they are treated. People don't always fight for their rights. My husband and I always fought for justice.

Sometimes I wish I had limited myself to one or two community issues instead of working on so many at one time, but considering what was happening during the '60s, I had to be involved in many issues: education, police brutality, the Vietnam War, etc. I believe I contributed to solving some of these problems. I would leave my house at seven in the morning, and I wouldn't come home until four o'clock in the morning. It was tough. I was a whirlwind. I was everywhere. But I wouldn't change anything in my life. I would do the same thing over again. I've been touched by a lot of people, and I've had a very rewarding life. I wouldn't change anything.

The message that I would give our Mexican American young people is that they should get up every day, look at themselves in the mirror, and say, "I am a very intelligent person. I have a purpose for being here on this earth. Enough is enough. I'm going to make things better." I would tell them that they should never be satisfied with what they have. I always tell young people that every day, they've got to try and make the world a better place. If they were to tell me everything is just fine now, I would say, "No, it's got to be better. When you reach one goal, you have to go on to another one." I hope that young people are never satisfied with society but always say to themselves, "I'm going to make my community and the world better."

I'm absolutely not a religious person. My faith is in mankind. I believe in people. I think we're all born with a purpose and that's to serve each other, to help each other because we can do it. I know that people do care, but sometimes I think some people don't try to help others because they feel that they won't be able to make changes. But we can. Even if it's just going up and showing a little bit of compassion by saying, "I can tell that you're hurting. Is there anything I can do?"

I hope I don't sound hopeless because I am not. I feel very desperate that we need to improve our world. I have a great passion for change. I think change is a wonderful thing, but change is also very scary. Even though I've struggled for change all my life, it still scares me because it causes so much uncertainty. You don't know what all the consequences of change will be. We will always need to work for change and justice. When I was working in the community struggles in San José, César Chávez started organizing the farm workers. I knew César very well. He had a great influence on me. He wanted to make sure that there was justice for everybody. This is the message I want to give to young people today. We can't be satisfied with what we have. We should always try to make the world better. Always. Always.

## NOTES

1. Tiburcio Vásquez (August 11, 1839–March 19, 1875) was a Mexican bandit who was active in California from as early as 1857 to his last capture in 1874. During the 1960s, Chicano activists turned Vásquez into a "Robin Hood" figure.

2. At the time, Campbell was a small middle-class community west of downtown San José.

3. Carey McWilliams, *North From Mexico: The Spanish-Speaking People of the United States* (Philadelphia: Lippincott, 1949).

4. In 1978, California passed Proposition 13 as a result of a "taxpayer revolt." The measure placed a cap on property taxes and made it difficult for the state to make future tax increases. Proposition 13 led to major educational cutbacks such as funding for counselors.

5. The U.S. Census Bureau reports that in 2000, 49 percent of all U.S.-born Mexican did not graduate from high school in comparison to 20 percent of the total population. National Center for Education Statistics, "Educational Attainment, 2000," U.S. Department of Education Office of Educational Research and Improvement NCES 2000–010.

6. Saul Alinsky (1909–1972) is considered the father of community organizing. Alinsky began his organizing in Chicago and founded the Industrial Areas Foundation, which trained organizers and helped in the founding of grassroots community organizations throughout the country. He established the basis for confrontational politics.

7. Dr. Ernesto Galarza, a longtime resident of San José was an educator and social activist. His autobiography, *Barrio Boy*, is a classic. He wrote extensively on California agribusiness and farm workers including *Merchants of Labor: The Mexican Bracero Story; An Account of the Managed Migration of Mexican Farm Workers in California, 1942–1960* (Charlotte, CA: McNally and Loftin, 1964).

8. Elected in 1971, Norman Mineta became the fifty-ninth mayor of San José, becoming the first Asian American mayor of a major U.S. city.

9. Chicano activists organized a major protest against the Vietnam War. Over 30,000 demonstrators gathered in East Los Angeles on August 29, 1970. Police attacked the demonstrators. Ruben Salazar, a noted journalist, was killed under suspicious circumstances that afternoon when police fired rubber bullets into a bar where Salazar was sitting. See F. Arturo Rosales, ed., *Chicano!: The History of the Mexican American Civil Rights Movement* (Houston, TX: Arte Público Press, 1997).

10. Rosalio Muñoz was the co-organizer of the Chicano Anti-Vietnam War Moratorium.

11. During the 1960s and 1970s, Chicano activists referred to their social protest movement as "*El Movimiento*"—The Movement.

12. Interview with Sofía Mendoza took place in 2005.

13. See interview with Ernestina García in this anthology.

14. In 1846, Thomas Fallon (1825–1885) joined the Bear Flag Revolt, named himself captain of a troop of volunteers, and captured the Mexican town of San José. He raised the American flag over the town's administrative building. He became the tenth mayor of San José in 1859.

15. In 2002, the Fallon statue was brought to San José from the Oakland warehouse where it had been stored since the early 1980s. It was placed near a freeway ramp in downtown San José.

16. Theater group founded by Luis Valdez during the Chicano Movement. Plays were originally performed in the fields for farm workers, particularly during boycotts and strikes.

17. Thousands marched to Sacramento to protest against a tuition increase for the University of California proposed by Governor Ronald Reagan. A broad coalition of groups joined together, including the United Farm Workers.

18. The Contras were a paramilitary group that fought, with financial support by the Reagan administration, to overthrow the Sandinista government of Nicaragua.

19. In 1972, the democratically elected president, Salvador Allende, was overthrown in a military coup that was heavily subsidized by the U.S. government. Allende committed suicide while defending the presidential palace.

# 6

# Ernestina García

*Ernestina García spent over forty years fighting for justice and civil rights for the Mexican American community. Born and raised in Arizona in the early 1930s, García was the daughter of Mexican migrant workers who eventually settled in Union City. Her life changed when she became aware of the discrimination against students at her daughter's high school. She turned to organizing other parents and then took on other social problems prevalent in Chicano communities. García founded the* Confederación de la Raza Unida, *a grassroots organization that fought against discrimination and racism in education, housing, and politics. She was a fiery community leader who was dauntless in her crusade for justice and equality. Her husband, Antonio S. García, died in 1996. They had five children, two of whom have passed away. García was a well-known community activist who thrived on fighting city hall when the rights of Mexican Americans were at stake. Ernestina García passed away in 2005.*

## MY PARENTS: "BEAUTIFUL MEMORIES"

My father was from Sinaloa, Mexico. He joined *la Revolución* [the Mexican Revolution] because the rich were getting richer and the poor were getting poorer. The rich were taking the land away from the poor. The *peones* [peasants] lived like slaves. After years of fighting, Mexico was in chaos because everybody was fighting everybody else and they didn't even know who they were fighting! "*Se agarraban por nada*" [They fought with one another for no reason]. Mexico was full of hate.

My mother was from Sonora, and she met and married my father in Mexico. My parents came to the United States because life was getting too miserable in Mexico. My father always told us how difficult it was in Mexico because of the poverty. They wanted their children to have a better life. They came to the United States with their three children: two boys and a girl. They were born in Mexico, but the rest of my brothers and sisters were born in the United States. My paternal grandmother was a midwife, and she helped my mother during childbirth. When people got sick in the *rancho* [ranch], they went to her because there weren't any doctors in the ranch. I was born *en un rancho* [on a ranch] between Phoenix and Glendale, Arizona. We lived there because my father brought my mother and the family to Arizona from Mexico.

I have some beautiful memories of my mother and father, but especially my father. My father was the sweetest man. He was very quiet and had his own way of doing things. He taught all of us so much about life. My father showed me how to act in a group of people, and this helped me later in my life when I was organizing the community. He taught me to listen to people and to stand up for my opinions. I can still hear him tell me: "*No te dejes de nadie*" [Don't let anyone take advantage of you]. "*Nunca se dejen que nadie los pisotee*" [Never let anyone trample on you]. "*Somos Mexicanos* [We are Mexicans] and God brought us in this world for a purpose *y Dios sabe* [and God knows] what this purpose is. We don't question. We don't say, 'Why am I here? Why are you here? Why are things the way they are?' You don't question God because he brought us in this world because he loves us. There's a reason he wants us to be here, so do the best you can while you're here. Do it to help others. Don't just do it for yourself because if you do it for yourself, you're going to end up with nothing anyway."

My father also gave us advice on how to deal with people from different backgrounds. He used to tell us, "We are Mexicans, but, when we go to Phoenix, you will go into the *tienda* [store] where we will shop. *Es de Chinos*" [It belongs to Chinese people]. He'd ask, "Do you ever see any *negros* [African Americans] around there? Never. Do you see any *indios* [Native Americans]? *Nunca* [Never]. *Porque los indios estaban en la reservación* [Because the Native Americans were on the reservation] *y los negros* [the blacks] were not allowed to come to town." If they did come into the town, I never saw them. I didn't know what a *negro* was until we came to Oakland!

My father also explained why Mexicans were not rich. I used to ask him, "*Pero, Papá, ¿por qué es que mi mamá tiene que lavar* [but, Father, why is it that mom has to go wash] the Anglos' clothes while the American ladies are out there in the yard playing cards?" He'd say, "Let the rich people play cards all they want. It's none of your business. *Usted no más oiga, mire, y no diga nada. No le importa por qué*" [You just listen, watch, and do not say anything. It's none of your business]. I used to tell him, "*Pero no me gusta cómo ellas están sentadas ahí muy agustos, jugando cartas, y mi mamá y hermana están lavándoles la ropa*" [But I don't like the way they are sitting there, very comfortable, playing cards, and my mother and sister are washing their clothes]. He'd say, "*Cállese la boca* [be quiet] because this is the way everybody has to live." This is how I learned that we the poor had to cater to the rich because you had to survive. At the same time, it seemed like my father and mother wanted so bad to have the best for their children. *Todos los Mexicanos en ese rancho* [All the Mexicans on that ranch] wanted to have the best, and I would look at how the rich people across the street lived and think we can't live like them. But I always thought it was good because we were happy.

My father was very proud of being Mexican, and he always referred to himself as a *Mexicano*. At that time, I also called myself *Mexicana*. When we moved to California from Arizona, some of the people would say, "*Allí vienen los pochos*" [Here come the *pochos*].[1] I didn't like this. Later on, I started calling myself Mexican American because I was born and lived in the United States.

My parents never became American citizens. My father paid attention to politics in Mexico and in the United States. My parents used to visit their family in Mexico, and I went with them a few times. I thought the people over there were beautiful because they treat us so differently from the people here in the United States. However, even though they treated us better in Mexico, I never really thought that I would want to live there. I would get angry because they would say, "*Allá viene la gringa*" [here comes the *gringa*[2]]. I couldn't take that, and I'd say, "*A mí no me llamen gringa* [Don't call me a *gringa*] because I'm not. *Soy Mexicana*" [I am Mexican]. They would reply, "*Usted no nació aquí* [You were not born here]. *Usted nació en Estados Unidos*" [You were born in the United States]. I'd tell them, "*Pues sí, pero* [Well, yes, but] that's not my fault." I talked them into understanding that I was like them. "*Todos somos iguales*" [We are all the same]. My father never instilled in us that we were *Americanos* [Americans]. He used to instill in us that we were *Mexicanos*. He always told us, "*Nacieron aquí pero son Mexicanos*" [You were born here in the United States, but you are Mexican].

## RELIGION: A SEPARATE REALITY

We couldn't go to church in Arizona. I'll tell you why. We were Catholics but when we went to the church in Phoenix, they told us "*Vayanse al subterranio*" [Go to the basement]. *Mexicanos* would have Mass downstairs and whites would have Mass upstairs. My dad said, "We're not going downstairs. We're going home. We're all God's children and we're not going downstairs so you can keep your Mass and you can keep your church. We're never coming back to this church again." We went home, and the only time we went to church was when there were baptisms or weddings.

We used to pray *en el rancho* [on the ranch]. My grandmother raised my dad and his sisters as Catholics so my dad was used to praying. Since we didn't go to the church because it wanted us to pray in the basement, my father taught us our prayers. My parents instilled in us that there was no other religion than Catholicism. When I think about it now, I see that even the Church was racist. But as I tell my kids, it's not the Church because the church is a building. It's not the religion that is to blame but the people who run it who are sometimes racist because that is how they were raised. They were brought into this world thinking that they are better than the others. It's bad to be a racist or a sexist. Religion helped me to overcome some of the hate that I had against the way we were treated when we were kids because we were Mexicans. My father and mother taught us that everyone is God's child. They used to say, "When Jesus came to earth, they did what they did to him and he took it. Who are we to complain?" They also used to tell us, "If somebody hits you on the right cheek, turn around and let them hit you on the left one." I used to say, "They're not going to hit me. No way!" I dare that white person to come and hit me on one cheek and then try to hit me on the other one. I dared them! My dad would say, "*No. Así no se habla* [No. Don't say things like that]. You forgive, you forget and then you forgive, you forget again. *Somos iguales*" [We are all equal]. I'd answer, "*Pues si nosotros Mexicanos somos iguales ¿por qué cuando andamos allá con otros que no son Mexicanos no dicen que somos iguales?* [Well, if Mexicans are equal with everyone else, why is it that when we are with others who are not Mexicans, they don't tell us we are equal to them?] *Ellos dicen que nosotros no somos nada*" [They tell us we are nothing]. He would say, "*Cuando eso pase, no se deje* [When this happens, don't take it]. *Usted dígales que usted es igual que ellos*" [You tell them you are equal to them]. He wanted all of us to be proud of who we were: *Mexicanos*. He always instilled this pride in me.

Our Lady of Guadalupe was very important to me as I was growing.[3] My parents always taught all of us that she is *la madre de Dios* [God's mother]. Although we all believe in God and Jesus, there is a difference because other religions don't believe in the Virgin. My belief in Our Lady changed as I grew older, but I still have faith in her. I don't practice my religion in a church. When I visit a church for other reasons, I like to see that the church has a statue or picture of the *Virgen*. Some of the Catholic churches don't have her picture or statue. They had one here in Saint John's when my husband and I first registered in the little chapel, but then, as time went by, they changed priests and the new priests took down the statue of the *Virgen*. When the change happened, we went and asked the priest, "Can we have a Mass in Spanish?" He said, "If you collect about twenty signatures of people who want to have a Mass in Spanish, then I'll have it for you." I organized some of my neighbors and we stood on the steps of the church and asked people who were coming out of Mass to sign the petition. We collected a lot more than twenty signatures, and we took the petitions to him. We were shocked when he said that he only would count the signatures from parishioners. Many people went to Mass there but were not actually registered in the parish. I think this was so because parishioners had to pay dues and they couldn't afford them. A lot of people who heard about our petition drive came over to help us and signed the petition. *Me dio un coraje* [This infuriated me]. It seemed as if I were back in Arizona, so I told him, "You know what? You're a racist." *¡Y se enojó el padre! Y dijo* [And the priest got mad at me and said], "You can't talk to me this way." I said, "You are a racist because first you said one thing about the signature and then you said another. You didn't keep your word, and I think it was because you don't want us to have a Mass in Spanish. You are a racist and you can keep your Mass." I did what my father would have wanted me to do; I told the community that we would not give one more cent to this church. Mexicans had been paying the church to rent the hall for dances. I told the priest, "You're not going to get a penny from us."

## GROWING UP *MEXICANA*

As far as I can remember, Arizona was always a very bad place to live because of the segregation. I still ask myself, "Why did these people do this to us?" My dad was a *ranchero* [ranch hand], and my mom and oldest sister washed clothes for the lady my dad worked for. I used to go with my sister to the *ranchero's* [rancher's] house and I used to think, "Why do these people live like this? They're rich people, but why are they so mean *con los Mexicanos* [to Mexicans]?" It hurts me when I think about it because we were forced to go to school in a bus that was only for *Mexicanos*. We couldn't ride the same bus as the Anglo kids because we were Mexicans. Our bus would come to all the *ranchos* and pick us up. Another bus picked up the *gringos* across the street.

We used to migrate to California to work in the fields and then return to Arizona. Life was rough over there in California because we were picking cotton and that is one of the worst jobs. We had to carry the sacks filled with cotton. If you don't have long sleeves, you scratch your arms. That's how poor people like us worked, but we were happy. I remember the bad things about living near some of the Anglos over there. Many of them were racists. I used to call them *gente maldita* [those damned people].

## EDUCATION AND RACISM

I attended Washington School in Arizona. We had a dilapidated faucet, and across from the second fence we could see the other school that was for the Anglo kids. Their school had shiny faucets, and we could see the children running to drink water and then running to play. On our side, you had to hold the faucet handle until the water would finally come out and sometimes it would take a long time. We had to wait. Other times, the water would squirt up and it was hard to drink it. I used to think, "Why, why do they do this to us?" Christmas time was the only time we were able to go across that second fence into the Anglo school because they used to take all the children into the auditorium to see Santa Claus. They would sit us in the back of the room. The white kids were sitting in the front of the room. All the *Mexicano* kids were scared of *Santo Claus*. I didn't know who he was. He was passing popcorn in a bowl to all of us. I would sit there and look at the white kids with their shiny, patent leather shoes and see them all dressed very pretty. Then, I'd look at my shoes and at their shoes and think, "*¿Por qué tengo esos zapatos? ¿Por qué?*" [Why do I have these kinds of shoes?] I felt ashamed and didn't want anybody to see my shoes because they had holes in the bottom. In the middle of the stage, there was a Christmas tree with presents underneath it. A little girl that looked like Shirley Temple jumped out of a big box and started tap-dancing. She was the *hija del ranchero* [the rancher's daughter]. I look back now and think, "What kind of message was being sent to us, *los Mexicanos?*" It was a very bad message because we all knew that one of us would never be selected to jump out of the box and dance. After Santa Claus left the auditorium, they took us to the cafeteria in the Anglo school. I don't know why but we had to eat the food. I couldn't eat anything because I couldn't stand that food; it was Anglo food. I just wanted to leave the auditorium and go home. I also used to think, "If it's Christmas, where are the *Tres Reyes* [Three Kings]?"[4] When I was growing up, we never had a Christmas tree or a picture of *Santo Claus* in our home. We had *Los Tres Reyes. En el rancho* [at the ranch], three men would dress up like the Three Kings and we would all gather around, sing songs, and eat tamales.

Years later, when we came to California, we learned that the staff from the schools were going around our neighborhood picking up *Mexicanos* and forcing them to go to school. Schools received money for each student enrolled. That was their way of keeping us in school. They didn't really care about us. They only wanted Mexicans in their schools in order to show that their schools cared about students from all races, especially the *Mexicanos*. I didn't know this is what they were doing because I was just a kid. I learned this later in my life and I still wonder, "Why were these people so mean to us?" My dad tried to explain all this to me, "*La razón que no quieren al Mexicano es porque el Mexicano le puede quitar los calcetines al gringo*" [The reason that they do not like Mexicans is because Mexicans can take the Americans' socks off]. He would say, "*El Mexicano puede quitarle los calcetines sin quitarle los zapatos*" [Mexicans can take off their socks without taking off their shoes]. I used to say, "I'm going to try that!"

## CALIFORNIA BOUND: EVOLVING IDENTITIES

In about 1937, we moved to the San José area. My dad had bought an old car, and we drove the whole way from Arizona. The tires were all worn out *pero nos venimos* [but we came] because my dad didn't want to live in Arizona anymore and our family was growing. When we moved over here in that little car, my dad said, "That's it. We're not going back because it's getting rougher to survive in Arizona." We came to the hills here in San José. A Portuguese man owned the land, but he wasn't around. My dad made a stove out of oil drums he cleaned, and my mom would make coffee and those big Sonora tortillas. From San José we moved to Decoto.[5] I liked our new home there. Everybody knew everybody; you could leave your door open. You could sleep outside if you wanted to because everybody was somebody's *comadre* or *compadre*.[6] We all loved each other and got along very well. When I was growing up, I didn't really think much about what my life would be like. I never said, "I'm going to grow up and become somebody big or important." Something like this never entered my head. I didn't really make plans or said to myself, "I'm going to do this or I'm going to do that." I just thought that I was going to survive and live the best life I could with all my family and friends. I thought that I would learn how to get along with everyone but *nada de que a subir alto* [nothing about rising to the top]. We all went to school just to learn and try to survive. We were all living the same. We were all poor.

## LIFE IN THE CANNERIES

My dad kept working and saving money. When I graduated from the eighth grade, I went to high school, but only for two months. The following year I went another two months and that was it. I didn't go to college, and I didn't finish high school. The cannery in Hayward needed people so I went to work there and they didn't even ask to see my ID. I didn't have to tell them how old I was. I was about fourteen. The cannery owners also used to bring *los sailors* [the sailors] to work in the cannery because they needed help and there was hardly any help at all. This was in 1943 and 1944, during the Second World War. I told them I was eighteen so that they would hire me. I worked from six in the morning to six in *la tarde* [the evening]. Sometimes, I would work until ten o'clock at night to earn more money. I was working quite a few hours. *Toda la familia trabajaba* [The whole family worked]. This was just like when we all worked in the fields and we all put our monies together. Whenever any one of us got paid, we would give the money to my dad and he saved it. That's how my dad managed to buy us a home. When we moved to our new house, there were thirteen of us in the family. We really were a big family. I stayed in my parents' home until I was around twenty-three. I kept working at the cannery, but I also did seasonal work in the fields.

I was about the same age as my coworkers at the cannery. I'd either take the bus or get a ride with the sister of a friend of mine. I used to like working in the cannery, but it was hard work for a fourteen-year-old girl. I was cutting peaches on the machines, sorting *asparragos* [asparagus] for canning. The apricots *venían por el* [came on the conveyor] belt. *Gente hay mala por dondequiera* [Bad people are everywhere]. *Las foreladies se creían muy grandes* [The foreladies thought very highly of themselves]. They'd come up behind us, pinch us in the back, and tell us to hurry up! Many times, *me acuerdo que había mucha gente que se volteaban y* [I remember that many people would turn around and] threaten to hit the foreladies because they were so mean. Most of the foreladies were *Portuguesas* [Portuguese] or *Italianas* [Italian]. My coworkers were all Mexicans or *puertorriqueñas* [Puerto Ricans]. The Hunts owned the cannery. They were *güeros Americanos* [white Americans].

The girls at the cannery would talk about what they wanted to do with their lives. We could talk about everything. We talked about how we were going to grow up, get married, and have children. We were going to have a beautiful life. Some said they were going to become *secretarias* [secretaries]. In those days, being a secretary was a big thing; it was like being a movie star! *Pero nunca oías que* [But you would never hear] something like, "I'm going to go into a profession." *No, no se oía* [No, you would not hear] any of that. That's because we lived in poverty and so we didn't dream big. We tried to survive, and we were happy surviving from day to day. I used to believe that one day, I would not be as poor as

I was, but then I realized that no matter what happened *Diosito* [God] is going to make sure I survive. *Mañana es otro día y Dios sabe lo que hace* [Tomorrow is another day, and God knows what he is doing]. I still say that. Our parents and the Catholic Church taught us that we're supposed to think this way, and we did grow up thinking that way. I didn't think, "Oh, I'm going to be somebody real important."

We never had any labor problems like walkouts at the cannery because we were all too busy and wanting to work, get our paycheck, and enjoy the money *que agarrábamos* [that we received]. They paid us by the hour, and some of it was piecework. The salary was around seventy-five cents an hour. If you got a dollar, you were doing pretty good. We didn't even know who ran the union and yet they used to take some of our money, *fíjate* [imagine that]. Who was the union? Why do we have to pay dues to the union? We didn't know! The ones who used to take our money from the union *eran todos italianos* [were all Italians]. My thoughts always went back to segregation and the way we were treated because we were *Mexicanos* or because we had a different color skin.

### PARENTS PRO-*ESTUDIANTIL*: TAKING ON THE EDUCATIONAL "SYSTEM"

Before we moved here to Milpitas, my kids were in Catholic school in Oakland. When we moved here, they had to go to public school because there was no Catholic school in the neighborhood. I was giving catechism in my home because there was none over there at Saint John's Church. I wanted the kids to learn about their religion and their culture like the *Virgen de Guadalupe.*

One day, when she was still in high school, my daughter came home and said, "You know what they're doing at school? Some teachers are making some Mexican kids pick up papers with a stick during the time they're supposed to be in the classroom." I said, "You're kidding." "No," she says, "the teacher told a couple of boys to go pick up papers because they couldn't speak English." I knew I had to do something. I said, "All right, I'm going to find out what's going on, so let me know what time students are out there picking up the trash." I went to school and I saw them. One student told me that he lived a few blocks from the school, so I went right over to his house and told his mother what was going on at the school. *Hicimos un barullo que no te imaginas* [You can't even imagine the racket that we made]. I went to the people's homes to try to talk to the parents of those students who were being forced to pick up papers. I didn't know all of them. I would also go in the car to talk to people. We soon started getting together as a group and called ourselves Parents Pro-*Estudiantil*, meaning "Parents for Students." We all agreed on this name for our organization. We had some *Mexicanos* in our group who caused a little friction because they didn't want Parents Pro-*Estudiantil* to become too "radical." But we all agreed that we wanted this organization to be there to help Chicano students and be ready to help out in any way if something happened at the school.

Pro-*Estudiantil* didn't have regular elections. We asked one of the parents to be the president and his role was to run the meetings. The whole group discussed all the issues and agreed on what we were going to do. We asked for help from other community people because we wanted to make sure that we knew what other things were going on in the community. Pro-*Estudiantil* relied a lot on a lawyer from the legal aid society. She advised when we were trying to become an incorporated group. Members of the legal aid would attend our meeting to advise us how to deal with the school district issue in order to avoid lawsuits.

We also decided to talk to some people that were involved in some Chicano community organization from San José and let them know what was going on at our school. I thought it was a good idea to ask for help from Chicano organizations that were already established. MAPA was a political group that helped organize Chicanos to do away with discrimination and try to do better things for *la raza*, like getting people to register and vote.[7] I hoped that they would support our group because MAPA was already helping students set up Chicano Student Unions in the schools. These student unions would help Chicanos when they ran into trouble at their schools. I had heard very little about the G.I. Forum. The only reason I heard about it was because the guy who was running the G.I. Forum at that time was very tuned in with the system. I also knew that MACSA[8] was also helping Chicano students. Their work-study program for students at the different high schools taught Chicano students about the Chicano Movement. The Movement was already going on, but it wasn't until about 1969 when it became strong here in San José, and this is why our group, Parents Pro-*Estudiantil*, got so much support in pressuring the school to stop making *Mexicano* students pick up trash because they couldn't speak English.

Our group also got the Elkettes out of our school. We found out that they had a chapter of the Elks Club that met at our school. The wives of the Elks called themselves the Elkettes. We wanted to know why this club was using the school for their meetings. I had heard that these women didn't like Mexicans. I told a friend of mine, Mrs. Vásquez, "*Vamos a la junta de las* Elkettes" [Let's go to the meeting of the Elkettes]. They asked me, "*¿Y qué vamos a hacer?*" [And what are we going to do?] I told them that I wanted to tell the Elkettes that we wanted to join them. We

went and you should have seen it! It looked like a bomb was thrown on those people. *Entramos yo y la Señora Vásquez* [Mrs. Vásquez and I went in] and there was
nothing but white women, and they turned around and stopped their meeting.
They said, "What are you doing here?" I said, "We came to your meeting." *Dijo* [She
said], "Who invited you?" I told her, "We heard that you were having a meeting and
we'd like to join you." She said we couldn't join them, and I asked, "Why can't we?"
She responded, "Because we don't accept Mexicans, we don't accept Chinese, we
don't take Japanese, and we don't accept blacks. You have to be from our race."
Then la Señora Vásquez said, "You can't bar us from here because our husbands are
Elks so we want to be Elkettes." *¡Cómo que eran Elks nuestros esposos!* [How could
our husbands be Elks!] *¡No eran!* [Of course they weren't!] *Y dijeron* [And they
said], "Well, you can't. You can't be members." We came home, got on the phone,
called the school district, and said, "We want to be on your agenda for the next
meeting." We got on their agenda and *cuando fuimos allá* [when we went over
there], we told them these women were discriminating against us, but I was sure
that *ya tenían todo el chisme* [they already knew the whole story]. We said, "These
women can't use the schools." We became angrier, and I said, "We all pay our taxes."
I have been paying taxes in Milpitas since 1966! Another parent told them, "You
can't allow the Elkettes to use this school if they're racist." We won and the Elkettes
could no longer use the school.

Parents Pro-*Estudiantil* also challenged the school yearbook, which was run by
little adult supervision. If a student didn't turn in a picture for the yearbook, the
yearbook staff left an empty space next to the student's name. When a Mexican
kid didn't turn in a picture, they put a picture of a sleeping *Mexicano con un big-*
*otón y con un sombrero* [a Mexican with a large mustache wearing a Mexican hat].
Instead of just putting the student's name, they put "Pancho Villa" with the cap-
tion "Sleeping again" *y el nombre del muchachito* [and the name of the boy]. Mrs.
Mercado called me and said, "Señora García, *quiero que venga para acá, le voy a*
*enseñar lo que trajo mi muchacho a la casa*" [I want you to come over here; I am
going to show you what my boy brought home]. I looked at the yearbook and
said, "Oh, no, this has to change."

Our organization made a big *barullo* [racket] because we wanted the sponsors
of the yearbook fired. We brought in Chicanos from several organizations from
San José to support us. I knew that we needed to get a whole group of people on
our side. Chicanos from different community organizations from San José came
to the meetings of Parents *Pro-Estudiantil*. I knew that having other organizations know about our issues would help us deal with other issues, and then we

could help them out if they needed us in San José. I wanted all of us to know what was happening all over this valley.

## "TODOS JUNTOS": LA CONFEDERACIÓN DE LA RAZA UNIDA[9]

My husband, Tony, worked as a longshoreman, so he had lots of experience with unions. He went to all the union meetings and so he knew all about how union meetings were run. I didn't know beans about these kinds of meetings. When I started going to MAPA meetings with him, I began to learn about running meetings and taking action as a group.

San José had been celebrating *Fiesta de las Rosas* [Festival of the Roses] Parade since the early 1900s.[10] The confederation really got going during the 1969 *Fiesta* celebration. Our group, Parents Pro-*Estudiantil* had been meeting to discuss how to deal with this year's parade. We met with other groups in San José and other different places. We joined the meetings that different Chicano groups were calling all over San José. That's when all the *Confederación de la Raza Unida* [Confederation of the United Latino People] formed itself to become one body and elected our first president. Chicanos saw *Fiesta de las Rosas* parade as a celebration honoring Spain and the conquistadors who came to Mexico. The *Fiesta* was a real insult to Chicanos. It was a disgrace. It was like we didn't exist. The word got out through word of mouth, "There's going to be a *Fiesta de las Rosas*." *Nosotros—los Mexicanos—nos juntamos* [we—Mexicans—got together] from all over, from one end of Palo Alto to the end of Gilroy. We knew a guy who worked for the city who told us to be careful when we started protesting. He told us that the city was getting prepared by having the police ready. My husband said, "You know we're going to go, but we're going to leave the kids home. If something happens, that way it's just us adults." We went, and it was the worst thing I've ever seen in my whole life.

We watched the parade and saw Lorne Greene, who was the star of the TV show *Bonanza,* pass on a float in front of us. Right behind him, *venía un Mexicano* [a Mexican followed] wearing *huaraches* [sandals], the *sarape* [a Mexican shawl], and a *sombrero.* He was riding a donkey and waving to the crowd. The people were all clapping, and we thought, "See? This is how the parade shows the *Mexicanos.*" The parade people knew that something was going to happen because all kinds of police came from all over on horses, on foot, and on motorcycles. They started pushing people off the streets and hitting Chicanos with their batons. When we saw that more police were coming, we all started running away from there. Everybody started yelling to each other, "Let's meet over at the corner." We met at a field where the Center of Performing Arts is now. You know who was with us? Ron Gonzales's father—el Señor Bob Gonzales.[11] He gave a big speech there, saying, "We're going to go to the Guadalupe Church on the East Side. We'll meet over there. Everybody get together and let's all meet over there." I thought it was so beautiful because after seeing what the police did to us, we stayed *unidos* [united] to help our people.

When we got to the park, everybody was asking, "What group are you with? Who are you representing?" And this is how the *Confederación* grew. We knew that we had to get ourselves organized. We decided to get some legal aid lawyers to support us and help our people who got arrested.

Our protest united us, and *Confederación* started working on other issues. We went to the San José school board and asked them to pass a resolution to protest the Frito Bandito commercial that Frito Lay Company was using on commercials and on signs all over the city. The Bandito showed a Mexican with a big mustache and wearing a big sombrero. It was disgusting. We also asked the district to give the schools a holiday for the Cinco de Mayo. We wanted the 16th of September, but this holiday was too close to the beginning of the school year. The Cinco de Mayo would be a little better because students were still in school and then we could organize a big celebration. We asked for a day for Chicanos: "Martin Luther King has a day. Why can't we have a day for our own celebration?" We took some blacks with us too. They had been participating in the *Confederación*, and they thought that it was a good idea that they go with us to show that we were all working together. Some of us from the *Confederación* used to go to their NAACP meetings. By the end of our meeting, the school approved our plans for a Cinco de Mayo celebration.

The *Confederación* also organized a protest against the San José Public Library. We heard from some Chicano students that the library had some very racist books. We went over there and looked at them. I have some here that I never gave back to the library. You should see how bad those books were!

The *Confederación* was also involved with these issues, but not all of us had formal education or degrees. We had something bigger. We taught them that you don't mistreat people and that we're all equal. We taught them that we were going to send our children to school, but we expected them to not discriminate against our children. They had this idea that *Mexicanos* went along with whatever the teachers or the district told them. In their eyes, we were supposed to be quiet and not make noise about issues. They didn't want us to rock the boat. It was about that time that Che Guevara and Fidel Castro were going strong and

Chicanos were going to visit Cuba. We saw all the discrimination and other problems in our Chicano communities and we shouted, "That's it." The words were *ya basta!* [that's enough!]. We were up to our ears with discrimination and we organized so that it wouldn't happen anymore. People thought I was too outspoken. I learned that you can make a lot of changes if you want to, but you always have to use power wisely.

More and more people started coming to our *Confederación's* monthly meetings. They came from different communities all around San José and reported the problems they had in their towns. We talked about what we should do and how we were going to support each other. So when there was something going on in Gilroy, we'd pack up and go all the way to Gilroy. If there was something going on in Mountain View, we'd pack up and go support the ones in Mountain View. This is how we ran the *Confederación*. It was an organization to support each other. I have always liked the name *Confederación de la Raza Unida* because "confederation" means a group of people. *Raza Unida* because we were all *raza* and *unida*, because we were all united as a people, as Chicanos. We were all *Mexicanos* and we were all fighting for one cause.

The *Confederación* was also involved in picketing the courtroom of Judge Chargin from San José.[12] He said some very bad things at the courtroom against *Mexicanos, diciendo que éramos animales* [saying we were animals]. We were picketing on one side of the superior court, and some members from the G.I. Forum got mad because they wanted to be the first ones to picket. I heard one of them say, "We were supposed to be here first. Why did you come along?" That was nonsense. We needed to be all together. We all used to use the word *carnalismo,* but Chicano students and the Brown Berets used the term more than we [*Confederación*] did.[13] We felt the same way. Chicanos from all organizations and places had to stay together as a group. If we want to get things done, the older people like me would support the students. We had to help each other. If the students needed our help, we were there to help them. When they marched to Sacramento, we marched with them. If a group from the *Confederación* protested at city hall, someone from the *Confederación* always went along.

The problems we faced as Chicanos were, like we used to say in the '60s, "pretty heavy." Members from the *Confederación* helped organize San José's Community Alert Patrol that followed the police on Friday and Saturday nights as they went out on calls. The Patrol was on the lookout to document incidents of police brutality. It was a dangerous time. It became part of the *Confederación's* efforts, but Chicano students were more active in it. The people in it were not only *Mexicanos* but also professors and people from the community who wanted to stop the police brutality. My husband and I continued working on the Patrol because this police harassment had to stop. I told everyone that we had to unite as a community.

We always had to deal with discrimination at the schools. Chicano students kept having trouble with the schools. My daughter got expelled from the high school. She was ready to get her diploma, but they wouldn't give it to her because she passed out leaflets about the Chicano Moratorium that was going to take place in Los Angeles.[14] We had to take them to court and sue the school district to get the diploma from them. When they learned they were getting sued, they called me right away and said that I could come over and get my daughter's diploma. The school did *todas esas cosas* [all those things] *porque eran Mexicanos* [because they were Mexican].

I think that *El Movimiento* was the best thing that could have happened be-cause it developed confidence in a lot of Chicanos by encouraging them to be-come active in community issues. It motivated Chicanos to try to better themselves but also their conditions and that of others. *Se abrieron muchas puer-tas* [A lot of doors opened] through our protests. We picketed over at the Uni-versity of Santa Clara in the 1980s. Chicano students had organized a group called MEChA El Frente.[15] Some of us, like Sofía Mendoza were on their board.[16] We used to go to their meetings and help the students learn how to deal with racism at their school. The students were demanding that the university hire more Latino professors. The students used to tell us that the only Latinos they saw on campus were the ones cleaning and picking up the garbage cans. They also wanted more professors to teach classes dealing with Mexican Americans. The *Movimiento* was the greatest thing that could have happened to make so many changes. Our voices were being heard loud and clear even thought dis-crimination was still present.

Around 1968, the *Confederación* decided to protest against the city of San José when construction started on the Center for the Performing Arts. We wanted the city to hire more *Mexicanos* to work on the construction. All of us were also up-set because we wanted more housing and not another auditorium. Many new people joined the *Confederación* when they heard that we were going to have a protest. Some Chicano priests supported us too, like Antonio Soto. There were about a thousand people at the protest. As we're picketing at the site, the foreman and his construction workers came to the fence and started yelling dirty stuff at all the picketers. The police came and started arresting protesters, including some of the priests. While I was walking on the picket line, I said to the others, "Why do only our people—*Mexicanos*—get arrested? Those construction workers are also yelling. All of us are yelling. The people from inside the building are yelling at the *Mexicanos*. All of us are yelling so why are only the *Mexicanos* getting arrested?" The protest got bigger and bigger. Some of the *Mexicanos* who were working in offices for the city would come and picket with us during their lunch hour. As more people joined the picket lines, the noise got louder and louder. Then the police chief came to the line and a member of the *Confederación* told him, "You're going to have to do something here because we're not leaving. This isn't right. Our people are getting arrested but what about the rest?" The police chief looked around and saw that the workers were yelling just as much as we were, and he said, "All right. One of them will get arrested, but one of you will to have do it with a citizen's arrest." I said, "What are you talking about? You make the arrest." The police chief told me that he would be right behind me when I made the citizen's arrest. *Yo donde en mi vida, andar en esas cosas* [When in my life was I ever mixed up in that stuff]. I had to go all the way in through the gate, all the way *donde estaba el mero jefe* [where the construction boss was] with the police following me. I had to touch him on the arm and say, "Citizen's arrest. You're under arrest for instigating a riot." The man got mad and said, "Instigating a riot? That's ridiculous." I told him, "You instigated a riot out there with us Mexicans." I felt so small and scared because I had never done anything like that. I thought, "Am I arresting a *gringo*? Oh, my God!" They put him in the same tank where they put the Mexicans they had just arrested. I still laugh and joke about that day when I arrested a *gringo*.

My goal as president of the *Confederación* was to deal with the discrimination that existed against Chicanos and keep our community informed about all the issues. I thought that if protest was done in the right way, we didn't have to use or cause violence. The *Confederación* always supported the farm workers' movement, and I wanted to make sure that we always did. We were also trying to better the situation in the cities so that when the farm workers left the fields, they would have work in the cities and have better jobs. As president of the *Confederación*, I thought, "If I can do something to make things better, I'm going to do it."

My father taught me that I need to practice what I preach and not to open my mouth until I have to. So I'm opening my mouth now to protest. If we can learn to treat each other *como humanos* [like human beings] and even if we can't stand each other, we need to try to overcome this and learn how to respect each other. While I was president, I met with Corky Gonzales and Reies Tijerina when they came to San José.[17] All of us agreed that what had to be done was try to get our own community together and then figure out how we could get the rest of *la raza* together. I didn't think that creating one big organization of Chicanos would work because then we wouldn't be able to focus on our own local problems so we kept our organizations separate.

## "MAKING MEN CHANGE": *MUJERES DE AZTLÁN*

When I became president of the *Confederación* in 1976 or 1977, most of the men had to work full time to support their families. Tony, my husband, said, "*Mira* [Look], you want to get involved, get involved. I'll support you. I'll work and support the family. You get involved, but stay out of jail. Whatever you do, don't go to jail. I'm not going to get you out, I tell you that." I knew he was just joking with me.

Some of the men in the *Confederación* did not support me for president of the organization because I was a woman. They believed that if a woman became president, the organization was bound to fail. For example, one of them said to me, "Whenever a man has a tool that's really working and then the tool is no good anymore, then what do you do? You pass it on and a woman will finish ruining everything. *Se acaba*" [It's over]. I said, "*Oh ¿sí?* [Oh, really?] *¿Eso es lo que pasa?*" [Is that what happens?] He says, "Yeah, *eso es lo que pasa* [That's what happens]. Women won't be able to run the *Confederación*." And I said, "All right. Let me tell you something. It's going to work as long as I want it to work. And when I don't want it to work, I'm going to walk out of it. You're going to see that." He was one of those big machos.

About that time, women from different organizations decided to get together and meet every Friday. We met and decided to call our organization *Mujeres de Aztlán*[18] [Women of Aztlán]. Some men didn't like it and called us all kinds of names. We broke their male bubble. They claimed, and even some of the women agreed, "Oh, you women must be those *lesbianas* [lesbians]; that's why you want to be by yourselves over there." We'd say, "Call us whatever you want to call us, but we're not going to go along with what you think. You men are *puro hablar* [all talk]."

Chicano men didn't like the idea of our *Mujeres* group because they feared that more and more women would start speaking up at meetings. We probably were too outspoken, and they had never been around women who spoke up. It was hard for them to see women as leaders. Their wives were at home since they never brought them to meetings. Then our *Mujeres de Aztlán* came along, and the men felt threatened. They thought we were going to take something away from them. We weren't taking anything away from anybody because there was nothing to take in the first place! They thought that women were to be seen but not heard. I used to think, "This has to change."

I realized that the men just weren't discriminating against us. They were scared by the new role women were taking. They thought women were supposed to be seen but not heard, but we weren't going to keep quiet. I was one of first members of the *Confederación*, and then I became a trustee, a treasurer, a vice president, then president. I watched and learned how men ran the meetings and I memorized everything they did at the meetings. I learned how to play the game. The *Mujeres de Aztlán* made men change; they couldn't hold us back.

The women's liberation was going on strong when we started *Mujeres de Aztlán*, and Anglo women used to come to our meetings and ask us to join them. We always said no because we first had to get ourselves together as Chicanas. If we joined the women's lib,[19] that's doing away with what we thought because we have our husbands, our children, and our fathers who are also men. We can't join the women's lib if it's going against the men because their philosophy was that women had to be against men. We said, "No. We're not against men. That's not what we're about. We're about working together as a team and doing things together, so we can't join you because if we do it's going against the men. All of us want to work with our men. We want them to treat us as equals. We're not going against our own *raza*. If we do, what do we become? We can't. I won't."

### "MY PASSION: MAKE THE WORLD A BETTER ONE"

Our women aren't getting involved in community issues as much I would like to see. If you get the women together to ask, "What do we want for the future? How can we make a better future, not just for ourselves but for others?" That's the direction that I would like to see for young women and men. Adults have to take the reins and say, "Let's do it this way." I've learned that the young people today want guidance and respect, and we have to give them the respect. Organizations like *Confederación* are here to fight for social justice.

My husband used to joke with me and say, "You know what's wrong with you, Ernestina? You eat movement, you sleep movement, you think movement. That's all you have in your mind." You should have seen me at night, especially when I was president; I'd get up and look out my bedroom window and ask God, "*Por favor* [Please] enlighten me. Tell me what to do. I'm not quite sure why I have this passion deep inside of me to keep on working for our community." I guess I feel this passion for justice because of the way that my father and my mother taught me. They put in our heads and in our hearts to love others because we are all humans and are all equal. Charity starts at home. First of all, you have to love your-self and love the human being that you are in order for you to love another per-son. If you want to make things better in this world for yourself and for your family and for others, then you'd better go out and do it, but do it without vio-lence. Do it the right way. We used to tell the students, "After you go through that door and leave school, go out to the barrio and help those who need it. Don't go through that door and then we don't see you again because if you do, then you lose an opportunity to help your community."

I want people to remember me as someone who wanted to see our *gente* [peo-ple] and all races loving each other and caring for each other as human beings. See where I live here in Milpitas. I'm surrounded with all different races. Some Indian people live across the street and a Filipino family lives next door and a Chinese family lives next door to them. There are also white families and some from the Middle East. My community is just like the United Nations. We can learn more if we live in a diverse community. We all have to help each other and work together. I want people to think of me as someone who wanted to help make the world a better one.

## NOTES

1. *Pocho* literally means short or small. It is a pejorative term used especially by Mexicans for Chicanos to point out that they have lost their Mexican culture through Americanization.

2. Gringo/gringa is a mildly pejorative Mexican term for an Anglo American.

3. The *Virgen de Guadalupe* is the Virgin Mary depicted as a mestiza—a person of mixed European and Indian blood. According to the sixteenth-century oral tradition, the Virgin appeared on the hill of Tepeyac to an Indian named Juan Diego in December 1531. To prove that she was the Virgin Mary, she changed a bouquet of roses that Juan Diego had gathered in his cloak into her image as a dark-skinned Virgin. She is considered the patron of the Americas.

4. Latin Americans usually celebrate and exchange gifts on January 6 as the day when the Three Kings visited the newborn Jesus. This custom is changing; many Latin Americans and Mexican Americans celebrate both Christmas and the Day of the Three Kings.

5. Decoto, California, was a small community located near what is now Union City that was incorporated in 1959, combining the communities of Alvarado, Decoto, and New Haven.

6. *Comadre* or co-mother is the title by which a godmother and mother of her godchild address each other. *Compadre* or co-father is the title by which a godfather and father of his godchild address each other. *Compadrazgo*, co-parenthood, is a religious-ritual-kinship system that establishes a three-way relationship between godparents, godchild, and the godchild's parents. Godparents are most frequently used for a child's baptism.

7. MAPA, the Mexican American Political Association, was established in 1959 in Fresno, California, as a challenge to the two-party American political structure. MAPA functions as a nonpartisan pressure organization.

8. MACSA, the Mexican American Community Services Agency, was established in San José, California, in 1964, when a group of community activists joined together to address key issues facing the growing Latino community, including discrimination, racism, poverty, police brutality, and educational inequality.

9. The *Confederación* was an umbrella organization of about sixty-seven Chicano organizations from the larger San José area.

10. Started in 1926, San José's *Fiesta de las Rosas* was considered one of the city's highlights, drawing large crowds of mostly Anglo Americans. Common throughout the Southwest, such cultural parades have been criticized for perpetuating negative stereotypes of Latinos and reinforcing a "fantasy heritage" of the contributions of Spaniards and ignoring the growing Latino communities in California. Parades such as these functioned to minimize the discrimination and racism that clouded relations between Anglo Americans and Latinos.

11. Ron Gonzales was elected mayor of San José in 1998, becoming the first Hispanic mayor of San José. He was re-elected in 2002.

12. Gerald S. Chargin, Judge of the County of Santa Clara, California, Juvenile Court, became infamous among the Chicano Community after a vicious outburst during a trial in September 1969. Chargin referred to Chicanos as animals that should be locked up in prison. Despite community efforts to remove him from the bench, Chargin served until his retirement several years later.

13. *Carnalismo*, term closely related to "brotherhood" but not used in formal Spanish, was used by Chicano activists in the 1960s to refer to an ethnic kinship based on a collective consciousness created out of common experiences. It signified a spiritual, unifying ideology for the Chicano Movement.

14. Chicano activists organized a major protest against the Vietnam War. Over 30,000 demonstrators gathered in East Los Angeles on August 29, 1970. Police attacked the

demonstrators. Ruben Salazar, a noted journalist, was killed under suspicious circumstances that afternoon when police fired rubber bullets into a bar where Salazar was sitting. See F. Arturo Rosales, *Chicano!: The History of the Mexican American Civil Rights Movement* (Houston: Arte Público Press, 1997).

15. The acronym, MEChA, stands for Movimiento Estudiantil Chicano de Aztlán [the Chicano Student Movement of Aztlán]. The word means "spark" in Spanish and was adopted by Chicano students as the name of their organization to symbolize their commitment to igniting social change for Chicanos during the 1960s.

16. See interview with Sofía Mendoza in this anthology.

17. Rodolfo "Corky" Gonzales headed the Colorado-based Crusade for Justice, a nationalist Chicano urban civil rights and culture movement, and became one of the central leaders of the Chicano Movement. Reies López Tijerina, another Chicano activist, founded the Alianza Federal de Mercedes that spearheaded the land grants recovery movement for New Mexicans who lost their lands beginning in 1848. Like Gonzales, Tijerina became one of the major leaders of the Chicano Movement.

18. Aztlán is the name for the historical and mythical place of origin of the Aztecs. Chicano activists referred to the Southwest as Aztlán. It became a metaphor for a Chicano sovereign homeland outside of the reach of Anglo Americans and the United States in general.

19. The women's movement was often referred to as "women's lib," a term that many feminists saw as an attempt to trivialize women's issues.

# III

# EDUCATION AND SOCIAL CHANGE

# Fernando Rochin Zazueta

*Fernando Rochin Zazueta emigrated from Mexico to the United States and as a child worked alongside his family in the fields throughout California's Central Valley and Santa Clara County. He holds a degree in business from San José State University and a law degree from University of California School of Law, where he founded the La Raza Law Students organization. He helped write the law requiring certification of court interpreters in the State of California and has been an active member of the La Raza National Lawyers Association. In the late 1970s, he was appointed chair of the Community Advisory Council of the San José Unified School District for the alleviation of ethnic and racial isolation of students. He is the cofounder of San José's Mexican Heritage Corporation, which created the Mexican Heritage Plaza, a cultural nexus that celebrates the city's Mexican cultural and artistic heritage. As a successful lawyer in San José, he has been actively involved in various civic and community organizations, including the Rotary Club and the American G.I. Forum.*

## CHILDHOOD: A "BRIDGE BETWEEN TWO WORLDS"

I was born in Culiacán, Sinaloa, Mexico, and was the youngest of the children that my mother had with my father, Alberto Zazueta Gil. But it turns out that my father had more than one family. When my mother, Antonieta, found that out, she decided she wasn't going to stay in Culiacán any longer. She had a sister, my aunt Juanita, who had married a Spaniard, Tío Agustín, and lived in Anaheim, California. Aunt Juanita had always asked my mom and her younger sister to join her there, so my mom went north to Mexicali and basically just walked across the border with me in her arms. My aunt Juanita was on the San Ysidro side and drove them to Anaheim. My mom, my brother Robert, my sister Lillian, and I were living with my aunt Juanita and my tío [uncle] Agustin, who was a barber. With time, my mom needed to get on with her life and so she started picking different crops, like *chicharros* [peas] and green beans. She went from Santa Maria and then to Fresno and later to Santa Clara County, following the migrant route. My mom ultimately met a truck driver named Francisco Castro Miramontes, who was from Zacatecas but had settled in the Delano area. He and my mom began to live together and got married. He was willing to take my brother and sister in because they were older, but I was a baby and I cried a lot. My aunt Aurora, my mom's younger sister, had, by that time, married my uncle Tomás, and so she said, "You know, we could take care of little Fernandito. We don't have any children, so we can do that." We were a migrant family as well. I was raised by my uncle Tomás and my aunt Aurora from the time I was about two and a half, to the time he died of a cerebral hemorrhage, when I was fourteen. But by that time I was pretty much "launched" as they say!

I grew up in the San Joaquin and Santa Clara valleys because more crops were harvested here. We kept coming back to Santa Clara because there were even more jobs here. My uncle eventually became a labor contractor because, although he only had three years of schooling in Jalisco, Mexico, he was smart enough to figure out that farmers needed somebody like him to gather up workers to harvest the crops that needed to be picked, such as cherries, pears, tomatoes, apricots, and prunes. Those were the main local crops in the area.

We also lived in Delano, Huron, Dos Palos, Colbus, Selma, Tracy, San José, and Gilroy. Those are the towns I remember the most. We lived in the outskirts of these towns, usually in farm labor camps, in Army surplus tents. We picked grapes and figs in Fresno and cotton in Dos Palos and garlic in Gilroy. We harvested broccoli in the wintertime and had to wear raincoats and rain slickers because it's wet when they cut it so that it would be really fresh. We harvested tomatoes in Tracy, a small town in the Central Valley, and I had to walk from the dirt road to the asphalt pavement to catch the school bus. We also lived in a ranch located in what is now De Anza College, but at that time a wealthy local family owned it.[1]

In Dos Palos, we lived out in this old house that used to be a dairy on a dirt road. My family and I also lived in what is now the Block Fruit Company. There used to be a big plum orchard with a big barn. The workers would ask me to go with them to a drugstore across the El Camino to buy their supplies. They needed somebody who spoke English and Spanish and I was that guy. The pharmacist liked that idea so much that he would pay me five dollars, which was considered a lot of money back then, to serve as an interpreter for his customers. I was the bridge between the Spanish-speaking world and the English-speaking world for them. This experience gave me a lot of self-confidence that may explain why I was able to continue my efforts to improve my life beyond working in the fields. Many of the farm workers would say to me, "You don't want to be doing this when you're our age. You better stay in school and learn something and do something with yourself. We're here because we didn't do that."

I was fourteen when my uncle passed away. It was then that I stopped following different harvests and stayed in San José. We had bought a little flat-roofed, two-bedroom house on the other side of where the Mexican Heritage Plaza is now.[2] A skating rink, a dairy, and a drive-in were located on the street behind our house. Sometimes we went underneath the fence surrounding the drive-in, unhooked one of the speakers, and turned it on and then watched the drive-in movies. We were on the bank of a creek, Arroyo de la Plata, where there is now a very large housing project. This was right after the World War II. That became a kind of market and the Esparza Brothers had a meat market, so I got a job working at their store. I cleaned the meat cases and did other small odd jobs. I've always worked, particularly after my uncle died.

## MY EDUCATION: "LEAVING THE SPANISH-SPEAKING WORLD BEHIND ME"

Whenever we got to a new campsite, my uncle Tom always asked the farmer, "Where is the nearest school? I want my boy to go to school." He would take me in his pickup and find the school and say, "*Ándale, váyase a la escuela*" [Go on, go to school]. Somehow or other I found my way back to the bus that took me back to the ranch. I don't know how that worked. I can't remember how I made it home from school. I was in what they called *Cinco Puntas* or Five Points between Huron and Coalinga. I remember coming home to this camp that we lived at which was about a mile away from the asphalt road. All the kids had to walk from the camp to the road, and the bus would pick us up, take us to school, and bring us back. I remember saying to my uncle, "The teacher says I shouldn't speak Spanish in school." And he said, "That's right. We're sending you to learn English. Just don't speak English at home and you'll be fine." So for me there was never confusion. In school, I always spoke English, and at home I always spoke Spanish. I always heard Spanish at home because the radio was always tuned to the Spanish-language stations. My uncle subscribed to *La Opinión* newspaper. I remember reading the cartoons *Fantasma* [Phantom] and *Pato Pascual* [Donald Duck] and *El Ratón Miguelito* [Mickey Mouse] in this paper. I never confused the two languages, and that's really been helpful to me because I now have a niche in the legal community. I'm a bilingual lawyer, and people come to see me because of that. The English-speaking community looks to me because I can deal with the Spanish-speaking community.

When I first started practicing law, I was asked by one of the senior partners in this law firm, "What was one of the most rewarding experiences that you had in school? And what do you think were some of the most negative experiences?" I said, "Well, I think they both happened in this one school." I went into history class, and I don't think I'd been there a week and he gave an exam. The teacher says, "Fernando, you don't have to take this exam. You just got here, so we won't expect you to take the exam." I said, "Do you mind if I take it just to see where I am in your class?" The teacher said, "Sure." I took the exam, and I got the highest grade in the class. The teacher then says, "You know, class, I don't know where this young man has been, but he got the highest grade in the class. So let's give him a hand." I will always remember this experience as one of the high marks of my education because I went into this class being a new kid and then did really well on this test.

Another time, the school said I had a choice for electives, so I asked, "Can I take another English class?" The school counselor said, "Why do you want an English class? You've already taken an English class." I told them, "Well, I keep moving around and I don't know English grammar terminology, like the subjunctive." I said, "I'd like to take an extra class in English." I took a class with Mrs. Hamilton, and she had us write a story, an extemporaneous writing assignment. I handed it in and she said, "Young man, can you stay after class?" I said, "Okay," and then she said, "Where did you copy this?" I said, "What?" She said again, "Where did you copy this?" I told her, "I didn't copy that." She told me, "Yes, you did. Don't lie to me. I know how kids write, and you didn't write this." I told her again, "I wrote it." I was so embarrassed that she accused me of copying the assignment when I hadn't. She says, "I don't believe you, and if you don't tell me the truth, I'm going to have you expelled from my class." I said, "Give me a piece of paper and I'll write some more." So I sat down and I wrote some more and I said, "Here." She read it and said, "Get the hell out of here." I was really hurt by that. I felt that I had been unfairly treated and that she had assumed something just because of my ethnicity.

I didn't know what I might want to do with my life. Nobody ever said, "Why don't you become a lawyer? Or why don't you go on to graduate school?" I was so unaware that I'd never heard of Stanford and I didn't know about the University of California or Santa Clara University. A counselor at Roosevelt Junior High School was the one who said to me, "You know, I think you ought to get into the university curriculum at San Jose High." I didn't know what a university curriculum was, but she explained it to me. If it hadn't been for that counselor, maybe I would not have taken college prep courses and therefore I wouldn't have gotten into college. When I got to San Jose High School, I had to take algebra, chemistry, and French. They wouldn't let me take Spanish because I already spoke it. I challenged this policy later on in my life. This is how the high school started you off because otherwise I would have gone into mechanics, carpentry, woodworking, and electrical shop.

I credit that counselor with getting me into a university curriculum. I also credit the people at the high school level for making sure that all graduating students from high school could go to San José State. It's a feeder school, and it worked out great because later I went to San José State. However, when I graduated from high school, I thought I was through with school. That summer after graduation I went to Delano where my mom lived and helped her. My friend and I would work harvesting hay but only up until ten in the morning because it was too hot to work any later. One went on to the military service, another one went to Bakersfield Junior College, and another went to live in Fresno. I asked myself, "What am I going to do?" I came back to San José State and said, "Well, here I am." Just like I'd been doing all these years, in all these camps and going to all these places, I said, "Here I am." The people at the admissions office told me that I was too late to register for that semester but told me that I could attend as a part-time student. I only took two classes for six units. It was probably a good thing because I would have been overwhelmed by the full fifteen-unit load. It was a nice way to get into the college system. I graduated in five years instead of four. I started at San José State in 1957 and graduated in 1962.

When I left to go to college, it was only down the street from where I lived. My aunt lived on Norwalk Avenue and San José State was on Seventh Street, and State was just a bus ride away. But to me it was a world away because when I started at San José State, I left farm work and a Spanish-speaking world behind me. Everything was left behind when I went to college. I never had any Mexican or Latino teachers at college.

I never viewed myself as a minority until I got to college and realized that I had to answer questions about my self-identification. I found out that my answer would put me into a specific category or compartment with others who identified the same way I did. I didn't know too much about other ethnic groups in the United States. I didn't know about the Japanese internment until some of my buddies that were Japanese told me that their parents had been shipped out to Manzanar.[3] I didn't know much about the experiences of blacks until I went to San José State and some of my friends who were from Alabama told me what life was like over there.

## LAW SCHOOL AND SOCIAL CHANGE: "APPROACHING THE ESTABLISHED ORDER"

I graduated from college in 1962, and I got married in 1964. I went back to college in 1966, and it seemed as if everyone was sitting around smoking pot and feeling really mellow. I was shocked. Before I left, students would organize a beer bust and play rock and roll. I was not aware of the changes taking place among college students. I never really identified with the new student identity. It wasn't until I went to law school in 1972 that I really identified more with some of these changes like what César Chávez was doing. That's not to say I didn't do local community activities in between because I did. But the change had been more in the society than it had been in me. I had changed internally, but society in general had changed externally.

There were occasions at San José State where students would be protesting for some purpose. I knew about the free speech movement, for example with Mario Savio at Berkeley.[4] They were taking on the establishment, and I was more interested in figuring out how I could become a part of it. I've always been impressed by those who seem to have everything going for them, and then come back and work with the poor and disadvantaged people. I find that to be an interesting and altruistic thing to do. I think of myself as running as fast as I can to succeed and to do better financially than where I came from. I'm passing them as they're coming one way and I'm going another way. I remembered being moved by a friend of mine who was a law student. He was dedicating himself to working with the different law programs that had been created to help the needy and abused women. I said, "Thank God for people like you who are willing to do that." I remember getting emotional about that because I was struggling so that I could leave that milieu and he was willing to come into it. Perhaps he knew he could always return, whereas I wanted to leave it because I didn't want to be there. I said, "Look, not everyone can become a lawyer that deals with issues related to poverty. We cannot all be public defenders. Some of us might choose to work in the district attorney's office because the DA office is the one that determines whether there's enough evidence to warrant a charge or not. And so we need to be on all sides. We need to be in corporate law. We need to be in every part of this society, just as we are already in every part of this society. And as lawyers, we need to do the same." Some had a very definite and genuine passion to go into a particular type of law. People are always motivated by different causes.

I was older than most of the students in law school, and I was more settled because I had a wife and two children and owned a duplex. I felt I was part of an established order already. I also felt we were beginning to assert ourselves as an ethnic group. By this time, Dolores Huerta and César Chávez had reached a sufficient level of acceptance as spokespersons for a particular segment of our population, with whom I identified. I grew up as a farm worker, and I hoped I could help in the ways that I was familiar with, which was approaching it from the established order and seeing if I could work with them. That's why, for example, a judge would come and ask me, "Can you help me with this problem?" Perhaps if he saw me as overtly radical, they wouldn't have asked. I wasn't picketing in front of Safeway like some of my colleagues, but I was trying to rectify some of the ills that I came in contact with and believed I could help make changes.

## LEGAL JUSTICE: CREATION OF AN INTEGRATED PROGRAM

I helped start the La Raza Law Student Association at the University of California at Davis. Our objective was to serve as a kind of a depot for incoming Raza law students, both men and women, because our class had 50 percent women and 50 percent men, which was unusual. We were probably the largest Latino class they had, something like forty out of five hundred students. I always felt that I wanted to help Latinos in some way. I had an experience with court interpreters. They asked me in law school if I was bilingual, and when I said yes, they said, "Would you mind coming to court and helping us out? We're having a problem." I took my law books and my dictionary and went to court. The first thing I saw was an interpreter who was supposed to be helping a Latino kid. I signaled to the judge and I said, "Your interpreter is a Filipino." He says, "What? He said he was Latino." I said, "No. If you asked him that, I'm sure he misunderstood you. He's Filipino." The judge said, "Well, does he speak Spanish?" I said, "Not from what I've heard. He's speaking Tagalog because I understand a few words in Tagalog." The judge called him over and he said, "Do you speak Spanish?" The guy said, "No, sir." The judge says, "No Spanish at all?" The guy responded, "No, sir. My name is a Filipino name." I asked the judge how this interpreter had been selected. The judge says,

"Well, we asked if anybody knew anybody that spoke Spanish." The courts did not have any organized way of selecting interpreters or making sure that they were qualified to serve as interpreters. I said, "Your Honor, would you like to have a source of interpreters at least that might be of some help to you and that are familiar with court terms?" He said, "Sure!" So I started an interpreter program at UC Davis Law School.

UC Davis is one of the few law schools that had a student-run law review. The students selected the topics for each issue. As a result of the strength in numbers in the law students association for Latinos, Asians, and Blacks, we succeeded in setting up an issue that focused on the theme of immigration and nationality. The law review is usually the purview of the higher-achieving students, the ones who do really well in their classes and get invited to write on a particular subject. They can also volunteer to participate if they qualify. Although we were instrumental in selecting the special issue, a lot of our La Raza law students who signed up to write articles on it one by one peeled away and I was the only one left. I felt a certain degree of pride in staying and writing my piece.[5] My topic was "An Attorney's Guide to the Use of Court Interpreters." I did the research about what other states and the federal government were doing regarding court interpreters. I concluded at the end of my piece that we should find a way to certify court interpreters to make sure they get trained, evaluated, and have at least certain minimum qualifications of competency in their particular field. As a result of starting that court interpreter program, I was asked by a state agency to work with them in setting up laws that would address this need for interpreters. I was invited to work with Dr. Anderson and the Judicial Council and that's how I got involved in helping Senator Alex García write a bill that called for certification of court interpreters.[6] The interpreter program is now an industry, and people make a living teaching how to become an interpreter. It doesn't just help the Spanish-speaking population, but anybody who has a language obstacle.

Law school opened my eyes to the potential for change that law allows a person to have by working, as I did, with various legislators and by becoming involved in the political process. You understand what can be done and what should be done. Law school is what changed my direction in life. I was active in Latino groups here, like the San Juan Development Corporation, which helped build some affordable housing in San Juan Bautista Center, off of Monterey Road. It's so hard to do when you're just one individual, trying to do one little thing at a time. However, with the law, you can affect the entire state. That's why it's so critical for involvement as voters. I've always said, "So long as we don't exercise the franchise of voting, we'll always be given as little as possible. In order to get more, you have to earn it, you have to work for it, and you have to demand it."

## COMMUNITY ACTIVISM: BUILDING NETWORKS FOR SOCIAL CHANGE

I came back to San José and interviewed with the district attorney's office and the public defender's office. I was told by the district attorney's office, "I don't know why you bothered to interview. You didn't qualify and you're not qualified but thank you very much for coming." The public defender's office told me, "Gee, you're the best-qualified guy we've had," which gives you an idea of what life was like back then. There was still a lot of tension between the Latino community and the Anglo community. I found that to be true when I went to Salinas and found a much more polarized community. I went to the DA's office and asked if they had any Spanish-speaking lawyers, and they said, "No, we don't need them." I said, "Well, do you have any Spanish-speaking merchants that get robbed? Or Spanish-speaking women that get accosted or complain to you about domestic violence?" They said, "Well, if that happens we'll just ask if any of our staff is bilingual." They didn't have a very good grasp at that time of tension between Latinos and Anglos that I'd say evolved from the time Mexico lost the war with the U.S. I find that is more prevalent in those areas where there were a lot of Mexicans during that period when Mexico lost its northern territories. I think we felt a lot more discrimination at that time than if we had grown up in New Jersey or Massachusetts, for example. There we'd be seen as more "exotic," but down here we were seen as a problem.

Not long after I came here to San José, I was involved with the La Raza Lawyers Association. La Raza Law Students Association had been an offshoot of the La Raza Lawyers Association started by Mario Obledo, Cruz Reynoso, and Luis García, a judge up in San Francisco. They also worked with MALDEF [Mexican American and Legal Defense Fund] and CRLA [California Rural Legal Assistance].[7] These were real pioneers because they did so much for Latinos through the legal system. I came in and was a beneficiary of what they had accomplished. Since I was familiar with the La Raza Law Students Association, I joined the La Raza Lawyers Association. I went to a conference they held in San Francisco and was voted in as treasurer for the state organization. I served for two years and got to know all the different lawyers up and down the state who were graduating from law schools, entering practices, and going into different governmental agencies. One of the main goals of the association was to provide a directory of Latino lawyers. Now we had an organization that provided us with a network.

I helped start the group called Friends of PACT [People Acting in Community Together].[8] We wanted to get money from among our various constituents. We were business people from all walks of life: professionals, dentists, lawyers, and teachers. We would contribute a certain amount of money and go to a fund-raising event and say, "We're here on behalf of the Friends of PACT." It was nothing more than a gathering so we could identify as a group and get the money to give to a campaign. We would give money with the idea that politicians would respond positively to our interests or our requests for action, whether it was to put in a streetlight or provide for affirmative action in the businesses that were invited to bid at the airport, for example.

## MEDIATING DESEGREGATION

In 1979, I was appointed chair of the Community Advisory Council of the San José Unified School District. At the time, there was a lawsuit brought by some Latino parents because they felt that their kids were being shortchanged in the school district.[9] The parents said different schools like San Jose High School and Lincoln were segregated because they were primarily Latino and, in addition, they weren't being properly funded. Through their lawsuit, the parents wanted to figure out a way to alleviate the imbalance of students in the various schools. The schools didn't have enough laboratory equipment or sports equipment, and they felt that their kids were not getting the right support for their education. These are primarily inner-city schools. That's when the idea started of bussing kids and altering the percentages of students in the schools to make it a little bit more even. That way, all the students received the same sort of level of support for their education. In 1984, the Ninth Circuit Court of Appeals ruled in favor of the parents who had sued the San José Unified School District for discriminatory practices.[10] The newspaper headlines were a vindication of what the Latino community had been saying: "You need to stop looking at kids in a vacuum. You've got to look at them and fund their education the way we always had up until now." Later, the courts upheld Proposition 13 and tax structures continued to favor long-time homeowners, not Latinos and others that were recent homeowners.[11] Once you took away that source of funding, people from the wealthier areas were able to find ways to continue to fund their schools, but people from the poorer areas had no way to fund their schools and so resources to support their children's academic achievement plummeted. The support that they received was quite a bit less. The fact that plaintiffs were vindicated as a result of winning their segregation case meant that the school district had to fix the problem. They tried fixing it, but I think the fixing of it was just as unfair because when you start bussing kids into these schools, you're waking them up at five or six in the morning to get to school by seven in the morning. It was tough on the kids on both sides, whether it was the Latino kids coming into the Anglo neighborhood or the Anglo kids going to the Latino neighborhood. Nobody was happy. We've been raised with the idea that you ought to be able to walk to your school, and that was taken away from both sides by the implementation of the desegregation plan.

My job as the chairman was to facilitate discussions between the parents, who sometimes didn't speak English, and the other parents and school district administrators. As a result of that lawsuit, the school district had to create this committee for the desegregation of the school district. While I was on the committee, the courts had already ruled against the parents but they kept appealing and appealing. I met with some of the parents and introduced myself saying, "I'll be working here in a more neutral sense, trying to make sure they hear you. But we also have to hear the views of those who oppose this particular approach to addressing this problem." Our committee would make recommendations to the school district concerning what they would say to the judge. The school district had to approve what the committee had done. We did a lot of documenting of the approaches and the different issues that had been discussed. Then we came up with recommendations about why we supported a particular viewpoint.

During the time I was on the committee, I would have liked to see more funding for the schools. Money makes the difference between what you have and what you don't have. If you have enough money, you can buy enough lab equipment and books. You can hire enough custodians and teachers who are dedicated and have proper teaching credentials. With enough money you can do all this. But if you start cutting back on all of those areas, you start cutting back on the quality of the education available to that particular student in that school. I would like to have seen more money coming to those schools because no parent is going to say, "I want to get my kid up at five o'clock in the morning to ship them ten miles south of here" without some reason.[12] That school located ten miles south is better equipped, has better teachers, nicer surroundings. It has everything that parents would want for their children. However, if you provide these things to Latino children in their communities, their parents won't want to have them bussed.

## THE MEXICAN HERITAGE PLAZA:
## "A LATINO FRIENDLY ENVIRONMENT FOR CULTURAL ACTIVITIES"

The idea for a cultural heritage center started in 1986 when Mayor Tom McEnery gave his State of the City report. He said, "I envision a time when we can have places for our various ethnic communities, much like we have with the Japanese Friendship Gardens. We would like to see a Filipino Friendship Garden, a Mexican Friendship Garden, and others celebrating our various ethnic communities."[13] Addressing Blanca Alvarado, who was on the city council, McEnery said, "Blanca, maybe you can look to see if there's some interest in your community for that."[14] She convened a meeting at the Mayfair district, next to the Church of Guadalupe in late 1986 or the beginning of 1987. She invited a lot of people, including myself, to this meeting. Blanca presented the idea about establishing a community garden. There were a lot of positive responses, but some of those present raised the question regarding its location. Some people who were representing specific neighborhoods said, "Not in my backyard!" Nobody wanted such a garden because it would create so much traffic that it would pose hazards for neighborhood kids and create noise disturbances, particularly at night. Nobody wanted to have it in their particular neighborhood, but they liked the idea. I was asked if I would consider being the interim chairman of a committee to study the feasibility of a community garden. We hadn't called it anything yet. It was just community gardens. I said, "No, I don't think I want to be interim chairman. Things tend to turn into long-term obligation." Sure enough, I spent fifteen years as the chair of that organization. At that time, we were thinking of a place that could have gazebos and have a plaza where bands could play on stage. We wanted a place where young people could congregate and socialize. People on the committee presented different ideas. "What if we plant some trees that are part of the area's culture like pear, cherry, apricot, and prune trees? We could plant rows of tomatoes and onions and garlic and things." Then one person said, "Who's going to trim all these? Who's going to prune them? Who's going to spray them? Who's going to pick them? Who's going to water them?" So the committee decided against this idea and decided to focus on building a bandstand. At one time, we thought about putting the stand on rollers so that it could be moved around and put in different parts of the plaza.

The question about the plaza's location became a major issue. We all asked, "Where would we put such a place?" We looked around and had some ideas about potential sites and looked over some vacant lots. The city presented us with a plan. City officials told us that if we agreed to put it at the southeastern corner of King Road and Alum Rock Avenue, the city would provide us with some funding. The city also told us that they would help us deal with the process involving eminent domain, that the city would knock down some buildings and so we could build a proper center. The city wanted and needed a couple things. They wanted to eliminate some of the urban blight that was developing in that area, including a Safeway store that had been turned into a job center. At first, we thought, "Well, let's just convert the job center and make it into the plaza itself." This was our idea, but the city said, "Well no, we'd like to make the plaza larger."

The city exercised eminent domain to evict the homeowners whose property was located on the site. One owner was particularly upset and got community support against this cultural center. I said, "The city is going to give you more than those dumps are worth! What's the problem with that?" He said, "No, man, this is my livelihood. I expect to retire here." I said, "Well, you may be able to retire sooner." We paid him a lot more for his property, even more than the comparable properties were worth, but the idea was to pay him and move him out. He was actually renting some houses to two or three families even though the houses were built for one family. The city told each of the families, "We will pay you five years of rent if you go to another place. Or we can just give you the money all at once and you do what you want." So quite a few people bought houses in Arizona. They'd been doing nothing more than renting in what was below-standard housing and now they could afford to own their own home. The use of eminent domain usually results in negative attitudes within the community who doesn't think that it's really an economic benefit. But the city wanted to locate the center in that location not only to eliminate or diminish urban blight but also to stimulate more economic growth. And that's in fact what happened.

We saw the Mexican Heritage Plaza as a place that we—the Latino community—would be able to call our own, a place where we could have exhibits of art and dance and music. It wasn't a guarantee that it would be built there because a lot of the community, particularly those who were better off economically, felt that it should be built in downtown. They said, "If you're going to build a cultural center that highlights the Mexican contributions to this country, it ought to be downtown where everybody will see it and you'll have a lot of people come." But the cost of land in downtown was too expensive, even at eminent domain prices. In addition, the community had never had a center like this and we wanted it to be a place in their own neighborhood where they could have all kinds of cultural activities. Many people who lived in this area didn't go to downtown for many things, particularly cultural events. The city wanted to start a program called "Entrances into the City." There would be entrances to San José from the east, from the south, from the north, and from the west. People entering San José would get the feeling that they were entering a specific, special place called San José. The Mexican Heritage Plaza would be part of the community and also help in developing the neighborhood.

We finally incorporated the Mexican Heritage Corporation in 1988. I wanted to call it "America's Mexican Heritage," but this was too long and it got voted down. I wanted the message to be, "This isn't just *our* Mexican heritage. It's America's Mexican heritage." That meaning is lost when you don't put that modifier in front of it. I wanted people to understand that this was America's Mexican heritage. A lot of people don't understand how much of Spanish has come into the American psyche and English language.

We formed a new committee to plan the center specifically for this purpose so as not to have any "baggage" from the previous committee. We didn't have any of the negatives that other organizations might bring with them, not the least of which were people in committees who didn't want to give up positions. They're there forever and ever, and we didn't want to have such a situation. They didn't say what their objections were, but you can imagine that you were talking about either taking away some of the funding that might otherwise have gone to them, or that you might become in some way an organization that might eclipse them as a force within the community. As a matter of fact, when we learned that we were going to get funded, we had a meeting at the Mother Olsen's Inn. A lot of people showed up from different organizations, like G.I. Forum, MACSA, and other groups. They're all in the audience and I'm in front with some other people in the city, trying to explain our plan and some guy calls out, "Who the f___ appointed you chief Chicano?" I said, "Nobody, man. This is what we're trying to avoid. We're just telling you here's what we're going to do. If you can't help us, don't get in the way. All we want to do is build something that's going to help our community have a place where we can have art exhibits, theatrical presentations, community events, and cultural celebrations." We didn't have such a center in San José. We couldn't get into the Montgomery Theater and we couldn't use the Museum of Art because they already had scheduled events for the next five years. I said, "These places are not very receptive, Latino-friendly environments for cultural activities." The people on our board of directors worked toward that goal. Over time, the other community organizations could see that we weren't taking anything from any of the community groups. We were providing a better venue for cultural activities than we had ever had in the past, so that helped assuage some of those concerns.

From the time we got incorporated, we always scrambled to organize fundraising events for our activities. We knew that we needed to raise three million dollars before the city would ever bother with us. We talked to fund-raisers who said, "Three million in your community? I don't think so. The YMCA is ramping up for something on the East Side and the Boy Scouts are also trying to raise money." Nobody gave us any encouragement except for a man from the Spanish-speaking Unity Council. He told us that we could do it. He agreed that the plaza was a great idea. He advised us to sit down and write letters to different people and tell them what we were trying to do. Housing and Urban Development (HUD) gave us a million dollars. We eventually raised the three million, and the city was forced to take notice because that was the condition they had set up. We got the three million and said, "Now what?" They had promised to contribute nine million toward this cultural center if we were able to come up with this three million. Well, that nine became twelve and twelve became eighteen. The center wound up costing the city thirty-one million and our three million never increased! But the city owns it, including the three million we contributed. It became much more expensive when we added the theater. When we started off, we had this idea of a plaza where we could gather and have musical events on a minor scale. A city councilman suggested that we put a tower in the plaza to serve as a signpost for the people coming to the plaza.

We'd been renting a place out on Park Avenue near the Police Athletic League for a dollar a year, along with other arts groups. It was a building that was slated for demolition. We were discussing ideas for fund-raising activities. We just weren't succeeding with our events. Our net profits were very low. Then, Dr. Pete Carrillo, from the East Side Union School District, said to us, "Look, Tucson sponsors a yearly mariachi festival." He'd been inviting us to go down there for two or three years. His nephews were part of a mariachi group that would play down there. He told us, "It's wonderful. You ought to go."

We thought about trying out this idea. Dr. Carrillo told us, "Look, if you're willing to do this, I'll help you organize a mariachi festival here in San José." The city said, "All right. Tell you what. We'll pay for a certain number of people to go to Tucson, stay overnight, see what's done, and come back and see if it's feasible." I agreed and we all went to Tucson, along with the redevelopment director and a representative from the mayor's office and myself. We went to Tucson and attended this event. We were impressed that the event drew such a large audience, just like a professional athletic event. It was wonderful and the music was terrific. I said, "We can do this here in San José!" We patterned ourselves after Tucson and organized mariachi lessons and *folklórico* [folkloric] dance lessons and other events for the students. We also put on an international mariachi conference. Later on, we had the fair in the park so that the people who couldn't afford to go to the mariachi concerts would still have a chance to hear all these wonderful mariachis. That's how we started. We went to Tucson in April 1992, and we put on our mariachi festival in July of 1992. The city gave us some money to front-load the event, and it was a big success. We had wonderful mariachis come from all over, like Mariachi Vargas and Mariachi Cobre and others.

With the success our first mariachi festival, we began the planning for the following year's festival. The second festival was just as successful as the first. We've continued this event every year. I think the impact that the festival has had on the community is hard to measure because even though they respond positively to it, the numbers that attend are not as large as we would like to see, given the numbers of Latinos in our community. Our goal has never been to address just the middle-class community. Our goal is to bring our cultural programs to our people from all economic walks of life. The problem is that it's expensive to do that. You've got to have high-ticketed events that will produce more than they cost, so that you can then put on low-cost or free events.

Let me address what I hope is the impact that the Mexican Heritage Plaza has had on our community. When I was a child, I didn't grow up feeling pride in our people, our language, and our customs. Now that I'm older, I can go back and realize the beauty that I'm an heir to. I'd like to have young children not wait until they're old to find out that there is beauty in their culture and who they are. I'd like them to feel good about themselves so that they have an improved self-esteem when they're young. In doing so, it allows them to reach their potential more readily than if they were missing that sense of self-esteem. Otherwise, they may feel that they cannot achieve their goals or dreams. I want them to feel good about themselves. I get emotional about this. It is a wonderful thing for me to get a chance to participate in the center because it has given me a chance to open up doors for children. That's ultimately my personal objective: that the parents, who feel good about who they are, bring their children, who will in turn feel good about themselves. Ultimately, if the parents feel good about themselves, they'll bring their kids. If the kids then see that their parents are taking pride in who they are, then the kids will respond accordingly. That has been the most rewarding aspect of my involvement with the Mexican Heritage Plaza. I have dedicated fifteen years of my life to this project, and I'm sure I've put in several thousand hours of time.

We selected September 9, 1999, as the date of my inaugural speech for the opening of the Mexican Heritage Plaza for a couple of reasons, not the least of which was the numerology of the 9999. That date is also when California joined the union. We fly five flags: Spain, Mexico, U.S., San José, and California. We are recognizing that it's a heritage that we as a nation have, and it stems from those three interwoven countries. When we had our ground breaking, I referred to the new cosmic race, *la raza cósmica*, which was to be a combination of all the good that was in each of the world's tribes.[15] This union of peoples would produce a new cosmic race in this new world. You would have the white tribe, red tribe, yellow tribe, and black tribe uniting as this *raza cósmica* and producing this new brown race of people with all the good qualities of the different races. For our ground breaking, we had a Spanish flamenco guitarist and dancer, along with a Vietnamese priest, a Sioux, and a Yoruba. Then, the Mexican mariachis came out and sang. These groups represented the *raza cósmica*.

## COMMITMENT TO ACTION:
## "CERTAIN THINGS NEED TO BE DONE AND SO I DO THEM"

I think that I have been a bridge between our community and the general community. That's true for almost any other educated Latino or Latina whom I know. We know two worlds, and we are comfortable in both. My clients try to obtain some sort of compensation that they probably would not get because so many of my clients speak only Spanish. Not exclusively, but a large number of my clients don't speak English well at all. So I'm that bridge; I'm that person who knows the law over here and knows this community over there. That's how I continue to feel like I'm helping. I get paid well for what I do, but at the same time there's a psychological reward of feeling good above the financial one. We can be the most useful when we use our talents that we have as individuals. I know that I can deal with the general community for the benefit of my Latino community. I know that if people talk to me and feel that I am a contributing member to whatever organization or group I'm with, then they extend that and think more positively about Latinos generally. People make their perceptions about general stereotypes according to their experiences with individuals. If it's a negative experience, then it's a negative stereotype that they would have about Latinos generally. I think that's why a lot of us do what we do because we want to put a good foot forward. I don't say that we do this consciously or that I'm always thinking of myself in a particular role. But I do have a sense of responsibility, a sense of making sure that I am helping my community.

Our Latino community faces many problems. One issue in our community is trying to resolve the crisis in our kids' education. Many kids drop out and don't go through with their educational goals. In time, they're going to wind up being a burden to us, rather than the ones that will carry us forward into the future. If this were a problem within the Anglo community, they'd be up in arms trying to figure out what to do about it. But because it's not, the government doesn't pay as much attention to it, although they should because they're going to need them as workers just as much as we're going to need them as workers.

My core values have developed over my entire life. You learn values and they resonate with you. I feel, for example, that certain things need to be done and so I do them, like making a contribution to the church. I could say no to that, but on the other hand, I feel like I've been fortunate and if I can help, I'm happy to do that. I've been known to say, "I'm happy to be paying taxes because I'm happy to be able to pay taxes. I'm happy to have earned enough money that makes it possible for me to be able to pay taxes." People say, "You're crazy. I don't want the government to have anything." I say, "Well, who do you think is going to take care of all these problems that we have, and fix all these roads if we don't pay our taxes?" So it's an interesting paradox that we have a lot of freedoms and some people take those freedoms for granted. For my part, I always feel like I've been very fortunate to have come here to this country.

I was in my second year of law school and I decided to take my mom, my sister, and my wife down to Mexico during the Christmas holidays. We got to Mexicali and we parked our car in our friend's garage and then got on the train and headed down the Pacific coast and entered Sinaloa. At one point I asked my sister, "Where's Mom?" and she said, "I think I saw her heading toward the back of the train." So I walked to the back and she's in the caboose, holding onto the railing with her tears flowing as we're passing shacks covered with tarpaper and cardboard and old boards. I asked in Spanish, "Why are you crying?" And she says, "This is why I left Mexico behind, to take you away from this." At that moment, I fully understood what it meant to her that I had achieved her dream of getting her children out of poverty and away from all the problems that she was facing. Her dream was to bring us to the United States and watch her family blossom the way we did. Her dream was for her children to get an education, own their own home, and succeed in life. What is the American Dream? It is that a migrant farm kid that harvested crops, like I did, becomes successful. To me that is certainly the reason for thinking that an American Dream exists and it can be achieved. There's no guarantee that you're going to achieve it, but the fact is that it's possible, and available to anyone, regardless of ethnicity, regardless of economic status.

When I was recognized as one of a hundred people that had an impact on the shaping of the Silicon Valley, I didn't think they knew what they were talking about! In my acceptance speech, I said, "Thank you very much for this award. I don't think I did anything out of the ordinary for this, but it's certainly nice to receive it." You don't do it because you're looking for acknowledgment or recognition. You do something because it's something that you want to do, that's driving you, and that you've dedicated yourself to. If in the process, there's some sort of recognition by your community or by your peers or by your city, hey, it's great! It means somebody took notice of it and perhaps others will be encouraged to do something similar.

How would I like to be remembered? I suppose I would want to be remembered as someone who achieved the American Dream because of hard work and good luck, someone who gave something back to the community because he felt that the community had given him a lot.

## NOTES

1. De Anza College is located in Cupertino, California, which was not in existence at the time that Fernando Zazueta was growing up. The location was considered a rural one, filled with orchards.

2. This location is in East San José. Zazueta became one of the community leaders that worked together with Blanca Alvarado and others to establish San José's Mexican Heritage Plaza, which was completed in 1999. See interview with Blanca Alvarado in this anthology.

3. Manzanar War Relocation Center, located in eastern California's Owens Valley, was one of ten camps where Japanese American citizens and resident Japanese aliens were interned during World War II.

4. Mario Savio was one of the major leaders of the University of California at Berkeley's Free Speech Movement. He is most famous for mobilizing a student demonstration in front of Berkeley's Sproul Plaza on December 3, 1964.

5. Zazueta is referring to his article, "Attorney's Guide to the Use of Court Interpreters with an English and Spanish Glossary of Criminal Law Terms," *University of California at Davis Law Review*, 8, 1975.

6. In 1976, Senator Alex García wrote Senate Bill 420. The bill passed and became a law regarding the use of interpreters in judicial and administration hearings.

7. MALDEF, founded in 1968, is an organization dedicated to using the legal system to protect the civil rights of American citizens of Mexican descent. It has filed and won many lawsuits dealing with such issues as segregation in schools and employment, police brutality, at-large elections, and gerrymandering. CRLA, founded in 1966,

provides free legal service to poverty-level clients, particularly farm workers, and focuses on class-action suits.

8. Founded in 1985, People Acting in Community Together is a national interfaith, grassroots organization that empowers everyday people to create a more just community by providing leadership training and experience to community members of many different ethnic, religious, and socio-economic backgrounds.

9. This action began in 1971 when plaintiffs filed a class action on behalf of all Spanish-surnamed students enrolled in the San José Unified School District and their parents: *Diaz v. San José Unified School District*. The complaint alleged that defendants were operating an unconstitutionally segregated public school system. Parents won the case in 1984, and the city was forced to implement a desegregation policy.

10. The 1931 case, *Alvarez v. Lemon Grove School District*, in California represents an earlier lawsuit by Mexicans and Mexican immigrants that successfully challenged segregation. Others challenges to segregation followed, including *Mendez v. Westminster School District of Orange County, California*. Sofía Mendoza's interview in this anthology discusses the Mendez case because her husband attended Westminster School.

11. In 1992, *Nordlinger v. Hahn* challenged Proposition 13, claiming it violated the Equal Protection Clause of the Fourteenth Amendment. The County Superior Court of Los Angeles dismissed the complaint without leave to amend, and the State Court of Appeal affirmed this decision.

12. Latino students were concentrated in the northern sector of the San José School District while the Anglo students were in the southern sector. The desegregation plan called for Latino students to be bused to the southern sector in order to achieve a racial balance.

13. Tom McEnery was mayor of San José, California, from 1983 until 1990.

14. See interview with Blanca Alvarado in this anthology.

15. Jose Vasconcelos, the noted early twentieth-century Mexican philosopher, coined the phrase *la raza cósmica* [cosmic race] to refer to his view that Latin Americans needed to replace the idea of racial and ethnic differences with a philosophy that stressed a common humanity because they shared ancestral roots with Europeans, Asians, Native Americans, and blacks.

# 8

# Juan Olivérez

*Juan Olivérez was born in Fresno, California, in 1946. Son of a Puerto Rican father and Mexican American mother, he worked in the fields in the Salinas Valley until the age of twenty-one. In spite of economic obstacles, he managed to graduate from Hartnell Community College, San José State University, and the University of California, Berkeley where he completed his M.A. and Ph.D. in sociology. He was an important leader in student demonstrations at San José State University during the 1970s. He began his teaching career at SJSU as an adjunct lecturer and taught at Hartnell Community College for nearly twenty-five years. During that time, he was involved in local politics, serving in various offices, including president of the League of United Latin American Citizens and the Salinas city council. Currently he is an adjunct faculty member at California State University, Monterey Bay, where he teaches history and politics.*

### "MY PARENTS TAUGHT US TO WORK HARD, TO DO OUR BEST, AND TO STAY OUT OF TROUBLE"

My mom was born in Texas and my father was born in Puerto Rico. Texas was really where they both met because of what historians call *el enganche* [the hookup]. My dad was working for the railroad at the time, and farmers went down into Texas to recruit people to work in the fields. That's where my dad met my mom. They got married about a year later and had a child a year after that.

I once interviewed my mom and found out that working outside the home was one of the things she missed after she got married. Once she got married to my dad and after having the first child, she didn't get to work in the fields. They actually brought my uncle from Puerto Rico to baby-sit. But then my dad decided he'd rather have my mom at home and my uncle working because my uncle was about twenty-one years old at the time. My dad thought the man should go to work. Well, my mom didn't like that. She'd rather have him baby-sitting so she could work because she really liked working in the field. She liked doing something, being out of the house and contributing in some way, even though she became a very traditional mom. In that interview, I learned a lot; she was not the person I thought she was. She told me her real dreams and the way she saw the world.

My grandparents lived just on the other side of the U.S.-Mexican border, either in Coahuila or Chihuahua. After the Mexican Revolution, they moved north to get some land, but it didn't work out because a lot of the land in the north wasn't good for farming. So then they came back to the United States. During the interview, I found out something about *guayule*.[1] I thought my mom made the word up. Then I saw an article in the *Salinas Californian* on *guayule* and how people actually tried to grow this thing. They tried to cultivate these plants so they could make some money. Salinas has lots of marshy land that is supposed to be ideal for this plant. So she talked about how her dad would grow *guayule*. He was literally a peasant, working off the land, trying to get as much as he could and taking it into town to sell. That was how he made a living. He didn't want the girls to work, but he didn't want them to go to school either.

I found out something later from my mom about her dad that really upset me. She was talking about education and said, "One of the things that really bothered me about my dad is that he did not value education. I told him, 'Send my brother to school.'" There were six sisters and one brother. "At least send him to school," she begged him. "He needs an education." I got to know him eventually when he lived in Salinas. He lived to be in his mid-eighties. When I look at his children and the fact that they didn't get an education and the kind of life and problems they had, I think about the advice that my mom was trying to give her dad about the value of education. Maybe even though I didn't realize it, she made sure we got to school and we did well.

I think getting up in the morning was something my mom knew she had to do and she did it because there was a purpose in it, whether it was sending us to school or sending us to work. I remember when we used to work in the field, and we had to do what they called "day haul" where you just go out and look for a job that particular day. She'd get up at four o'clock in the morning to make breakfast and we'd leave about five or six. I really admired my mom a lot.

My parents taught us to work hard, to do our best, and to stay out of trouble. These were their traditional values. And even though they suffered pain and racism, they never talked about it. I learned about racism when I was young, but I didn't know the word for it. I just learned about it from experience. It wasn't something that my parents taught me. I didn't accept racism. I fought it as much as I could, even when I was a little kid. I'd get really angry when I saw racism. I was the first one to graduate from high school, although I was the eighth child. What's interesting is that even though my older brother—who just passed away a couple of years ago—didn't graduate, I graduated and then my sister and my brother graduated. It's kind of like breaking the mold. Once you break the mold, it's not so damn hard.

We left Nyssa, Oregon, in 1954 right about the end of the Korean War when my brothers were starting to come back home from the service. We moved to Salinas and sharecropped strawberries from 1954 until my father passed away. I was still working in the fields when I started school. My parents were like immigrants in the sense that their first language was Spanish and their culture was very different. My dad told me, "Remember, the United States took over Puerto Rico from Spain in 1898." He was born in 1898 and became a citizen not by his will, but by the will of the U.S. government in 1917. We knew that and therefore, to us, he was an American. And my mom was born in the United States, so she was also an American. My family and I never really thought of ourselves as immigrants. As an academic, I can relate to a lot of the things sociologically, like the fact that we went from a Spanish-speaking world to an English-speaking one. Chicanos, *Mexicanos*, and *Puertorriqueños* have suffered in this country, but neither was ever a part of my identity. We always thought of ourselves as American and we deserved citizenship rights, even though we knew we weren't getting them. A lot of us were blinded because we thought we had those rights and if we didn't succeed, it was because we're lazy or *pendejos* [stupid] or not studying hard enough or we haven't figured out the system or we haven't figured out the game. Now some of us say, "Wait, no. That's racism and sexism and ageism." There's a lot more going on there than meets the eye. But when we were kids the answer to "Why are you not succeeding?" was "It's because we are not capable, or lazy."

## CHILDHOOD MEMORIES: LEARNING TO COPE IN SCHOOL

This is how I recall my first day of school. I was between six and seven years old. I have a picture of myself when I was about seven or eight, and I think "What a cute little kid!" Then I think, "How come if you're such a cute little kid, people beat you up for no good reason?" I remember my first day of school. I stood alone by a tree because I was new to school. English is not my first language, although I did learn English pretty fast. But at the time, I don't know how much English I spoke. My brothers could speak English, but it wasn't the language we spoke at home. Anyway, I remember vividly that I was standing by this tree and all of a sudden five or six kids came over and asked, "Are you a Mexican?" And then they jumped me. I started crying and went to a teacher to complain. She said, "Aw, kids will be kids." I got really upset. My brothers were boxers; one of them was a Golden Glove champ. They taught me how to box and so I decided, "You know what? Maybe I'm going to fight some of these damn kids." So I did. I went and I grabbed each one of them.

I wanted to attend school, even with all the negative stuff that I experienced. When I would do well my teachers would never say, "Oh, Johnny's doing well." However, they would point out that how well all the *gabachitos* [Anglo kids] did. In classes, I usually helped the other kids in school, but nobody praised me. None of the teachers praised me. I remember in the sixth grade I was doing really well but the teacher didn't like me because I had a bit of an attitude since I was not happy with the way that he taught. So he kicked me up to a higher class. The next day the kids told me that the teacher said that I was not going to be the star in that higher-level class, instead of saying, "Hey, look at Johnny. He's doing well. We're going to reward him by putting him up in the next class." I was always experiencing that kind of negative stuff.

The first school I went to was in Nyssa, Oregon, which is near the border of California, Idaho, and Oregon. I was about six years old when we moved there. In 1952, my three brothers were drafted into the Korean War. This was very difficult for my father. That was also a very difficult time for me as a kid because my older brothers were gone, and my other brothers weren't really old enough to do a lot of work. They were fourteen, fifteen and sixteen years old, which put a lot of pressure on them and they ran away. Later, maybe because of my sociological training, I started putting some of the pieces together. I began to see where some of my anger came from and why I moved towards the Chicano movement. One of my older brothers suspects that my dad tried real hard to keep them out of the war by moving a lot. But somehow the Army caught up with them. They actually tried to put them in jail, but my brothers said, "No, we'll go. We're not trying to avoid the Army." It was just my dad trying to keep his kids from going to war.

I lived in towns where there was a lot of racism. Idaho was very racist at the time. In the camps everybody was Mexican, and so it was only when you left and went to school that you experienced a lot of this racism. It was the same in Salinas, which has a lot of people who came from the South, like Mississippi, Arkansas, and Oklahoma. Many of these people came to California as a result of the dustbowl and brought their racism with them. They didn't like blacks or Mexicans or Asians. They didn't like different people. The teachers would always try to tell me to turn the other cheek. And even though I was raised a good Christian, at the same time I thought, "But wait a minute. How come the *gabachitos* get to fight? They're supposed to be assertive and not supposed to take any crap?" I learned that approach and it served me well when I went to the university in terms of my student activism.

When I was about seven years old, we had a lot of *Mexicanos, braceros* living in the camp with us.[2] The *braceros* would tell us, "*Hey, una peseta si tú le ganas a él*" [a quarter if you beat him]. At first, I would fight for that quarter because I could buy a lot of stuff with a quarter back in 1952. I'd say, "I think I can beat that damn kid up anyway, so *órale pues*" [come on]. We would take our shirts off because the kids were tearing them! We thought we were boxers, like the boxer Ratón Macías back in the early 1950s.[3]

So even though I got in fights every day, I don't think my parents or my older brothers ever found out. They said they had a hard life, and they thought mine was a charmed life. I thought to myself that my life wasn't so charmed. I got beat up every day. I got in fights every day. Once I was with some kids and we're all Chicanos, playing around. All of a sudden they claimed they were *Mexicanos* and said I was different. They started arguing with me about something and three minutes later I'm on the ground and they're hitting me with boards. Those are the conflicts that I experienced as a child in terms of the distinctions that we made between Chicanos and *Mexicanos*, which I always thought were artificial. That's why I jumped on the Chicano movement pretty easily.

## "I THOUGHT EDUCATION WOULD GIVE ME SOME KIND OF FREEDOM"

Even through I had negative experiences in elementary school, I still loved school. I loved the learning. I didn't love the social part of it or the teachers because many of them were never any good. It was as if I had blinders on and what mattered to me was learning and the fact that eventually I wanted a high school diploma and a college degree. I thought education would give me some kind of freedom. The high school that I attended was on San José's East Side. It wasn't predominantly Chicano at that time, and there were probably fewer Chicanos then than there were *gabachos*. I graduated about 150th out of 450 in high school, so I was in the top third of my class, which is not very good. But I worked hard and was very serious about my education. I participated in sports my senior year. I didn't play soccer because I thought that was a Mexican thing and I was Chicano. I wanted to play baseball, but I couldn't because I didn't have good eyesight. The only thing I could do was run track, which I did in both high school and college. I actually had thoughts of going to the Olympics since I had earned athletic letters from Berkeley and San José State. I knew I would never succeed at Berkeley if I had to run unless they would tutor me. I wished Berkeley had let me in, but they wouldn't unless I was going to run, and I knew that if I ran, I couldn't pass without tutoring.

Even though I was a good student in high school, I wasn't that great. My family members were farm workers, and I would sometimes miss thirty days of school a semester. But when I was at school, I got As and Bs. It was not hard for me, perhaps because I was a little older than the other students. However, even though I didn't go to high school until I was seventeen, I never felt older than the other kids. I always thought they were my peers. When we lived in Oregon, Idaho, and Arizona, we went to school for a month or so or didn't go at all. I went to the same school once we moved to Salinas, but I still missed a lot of school. That's when I felt that having missed so much school would haunt me in my high school years and even my junior college years because I graduated with a 2.1 G.P.A.

Between 1963 and 1965, when I went to high school, I tried as hard as I could to be anglicized. I tried to learn English and do well in school, participate in sports, and just be assimilated into the mainstream culture. I found that it wasn't really working. I tried to associate with *gabachitos* [whites] and relate to them. For example, when I was in junior high, one of my favorite ball players was Orlando Cepeda because he was Puerto Rican. I told this kid, "Hey, my favorite ball player is Orlando Cepeda of the San Francisco Giants." That *gabachito* told me, "You like that chocolate bar?" And I said, "Chocolate bar? What do you mean chocolate bar?" He said, "You know. He's a nigger." I said, "What? No. He's Puerto Rican." If you look at old pictures of Orlando Cepeda, he actually looks pretty light. But if you look at him now, like when he was elected to the Hall of Fame, he looks like a black Latino. Puerto Ricans make a lot of distinctions, mulatto, *cuateron* [has one quarter African blood]. I learned to make these distinctions in terms of blood from my dad. We'd see some black Puerto Ricans and some that were lighter and some that were even blonde and blue-eyed, but they were all Puerto Rican.

Listening to the music of Bob Dylan and the Beatles had a big influence on me because up until that time I was trying to assimilate into Anglo culture. The Beatles marked the beginning of the counterculture of the 1960s, and over time, I thought, "Wait a minute. We're a counterculture. Chicanos are a counterculture. We're going against economic and political exploitation." I found myself beginning to learn some of those words and apply them, little by little, to my own experience. By the time I finished high school, I started to see myself as a poor person. Even though I didn't have the word "class" in my vocabulary, I began to identify with my economic class. And even though I didn't have the word "race" in my vocabulary, I was realizing that Chicanos were defined as a racially different people.

## COLLEGE: AN UNEXPECTED EXPERIENCE

When I started thinking about college, I didn't have anyone from high school that encouraged me to even consider college. I knew that if I wanted to go to college, I had to do something different. I couldn't talk to my friends because many of them did not graduate and the ones who did graduate, most didn't even think about going to college. Some kids went into construction because they had a construction program in high school, but these were not kids that were a part of my circle at all. We all had very little in common. I always found it interesting that I didn't have a circle of friends. We went to school together at the same time, and we'd talk about girls and guys and cars, but not about school.

When I started junior college, my father had passed away and my mom didn't talk about school, but she was happy and proud of me and she was certainly supportive. I felt a lot of support from my family as a whole but particularly from my uncle and my mom. I felt blessed that I always got support from my family. The fact is that those who really love us will always be there with us. That's how I feel about my education. In retrospect, I did what I believed and I was lucky enough that in the end, I really did get a lot of support. They did not ridicule me. They pretty much said, "Hey, that's Johnny!" and they accepted me. I've always felt that was part of our culture.

## IDENTITY: MY SHIFTING SELVES

Although Chicanos are socially and economically diverse, we are still one people, one *raza*. We all have the same indigenous roots from Mexico. The *gabachos* [whites] pretty much see us as being all the same. We don't all look alike. We can be *güero* [blond] and be from Mexico. We can be *güero* and be from Texas. American society has created stereotypes of Chicanos, and this has caused divisions among us. For example, the other day I heard one *Mexicano* on the radio criticizing another *Mexicano* by saying, "*Mexicanos* are terrible." He was making a distinction between those Mexicans who are *ciudadanos* [citizens] and those who are not. Distinctions exist but we are all same people. Some of us don't speak English as well as others and some of us don't speak Spanish very well. In the 1950s, schools forced Chicanos to speak English only. I changed my name from Juan to Johnny, and I tried really hard to only speak English. Those of us who tried to speak only English also tried to be better than the *gabachito* and correct their English. I used to correct *gabachitos* when they used slang. I told them, "No, you can't say 'ain't.'" I was like the English-language police.

I considered myself a *Mexicano* but was influenced by mainstream American culture. For example, in the late 1950s, Ricky Nelson was my favorite singer. I liked watching the Nelsons on television. Ricky's father wore a suit or a sweater and a tie all the time, even for lunch. Sometimes, Ricky and his brother also wore ties, like their father, when they ate dinner at home. My sister used to say, "Daddy, *siempre debes usar una corbata*" [You should always wear a tie]. When Ricky Nelson went off to college, he became my role model. I wanted to go to college too. But I knew I would always be different from Ricky and his family.

Before I started college in 1967, I had been working in the fields. I worked really hard. I usually worked ten, twelve, or even fourteen hours every day. I always gave my mom most of my paycheck, but the summer before I started college, she let me keep the last check. So I had $150 to buy clothes for college.

In 1968, right after Martin Luther King Jr. died, I started to become aware of what some students were calling "Mexican American liberation." I still wasn't really active with the students at San José State, but that spring the Mexican American group bought some members of the Brown Berets to campus.[4] That was the first time I really started to think about the Mexican American movement. I was also starting to refer to myself as a "Chicano." The Chicano Commencement protests at San José State took place at the end of the spring semester of 1968. After that the term "Chicano" became part of my language, and the concept, part of my identity. My mom sometimes used "Chicano" when she was referring to Mexicans who were born in the U.S. However, even though she had been born in the U.S., she didn't call herself a Chicana. I'm not sure why. As I said before, my dad was Puerto Rican, but he never raised us to identify as Puerto Ricans. Both of my parents tried to raise us to be Americans. It was actually sort of confusing.

My mom used the word *Americanos* and *gabachos* for Anglos. Even though people say that the word *gabacho* is a pejorative term, to me it just means white people. The word *gringo* [white] was never a part of our vernacular although we did hear it. When my brothers came back from the war, they were very American. They always called themselves Americans even though they had called themselves Mexicans before they went to Korea. My brother was a decorated hero and had a Purple Heart and Silver Stars. He threw away all his medals when he realized that even with these medals he still had trouble finding a job because he was Mexican. My brothers were in a Mexican world dealing with *gabachos* but trying as hard as they could to be American and teach me to be American, too. They wanted all of us in the family to consider ourselves American. After they came back from the service, they used the G.I. bill to go to college. So I tried to be American.

When I became active in the Chicano Movement, I knew I was American but as a Chicano I started to focus on Chicano *liberación* [liberation]. I started reading books about colonization. I believed that we Chicanos had to work to de-colonize ourselves. We needed to fight for our independence and community control and self-determination.

## MY RADICALIZATION: "GETTING TURNED ON TO PROTESTS"

The war in Vietnam really concerned me. One of the first protests I experienced involved the Dow Chemical demonstrations.[5] I saw the cops tear gas students. Even professors were protesting. Even though I was just watching, I was getting turned on to protests. I was upset about what was going on in Vietnam, but I didn't have a clear idea of what to do. One day, I was having a conversation with a student and for some reason I realized I was getting very angry while I was explaining why I was against the war. Then this hippie-looking guy came up and said, "If you are so concerned, what are you doing to end the war?" At the time, I couldn't think of what I was doing to stop the war. I had been involved in some activities and I was starting to go to meetings, but at that moment it just struck me that I was not prepared to protest, at least not yet as I would find out later.

Almost at the same time that the demonstrations against Dow Chemical were taking place on campus, the Chicano students were protesting at the treatment they were experiencing. The university was showing a film about the plight of black students. Chicanos protested that they were not being represented in this film. The film didn't examine the segregation and racism Chicanos were experiencing at San José State. That was the first time I saw the Chicanos protesting. I wanted to be a part of it, but I didn't know how, so I just observed.

Chicanos represented a very small part of the entire student body. Armando and Danny Hernández created a group called Student Initiative (SI). The Chicano students from SI created a university program for high school students. It allowed twenty-five Chicano students to enter the university through special admission. Someone called me to see if I want to become a recruiter and I was told that they might be able to pay me. I had been working at Lockheed to help pay my tuition, but I decided to quit my job at Lockheed to become a recruiter. I was already unhappy with Lockheed because I knew it was very heavily involved providing materials for the war in Vietnam. A friend of mine, Juan Antú, and I started recruiting high school students from several San José school districts. I had never thought about participating in these types of student organizations. Making demands of the university and protesting for Chicano rights now became a part of me, an exciting part of my life.

Later on, Chicano students started making specific demands on the university. We wanted more financial aid for Chicano students because most Chicanos couldn't afford the tuition. We also demanded money for a Chicano Studies Department and more research money for Chicano professors. We pushed the university in many different ways because we wanted to bring about institutional change. Our demands were really grandiose and much larger than I envisioned at the time. Only later did I get a real sense of what we as Chicano students were demanding and how significant these protests were in our Chicano history.

One of the most important experiences of my life was my undergraduate years at the university. I was involved in all kinds of student activism. I helped create other student organizations. In my first year, I thought that college was just a really great place. I was growing very, very fast in terms of my politics. I wanted to learn as much as I could so that I could work for social change. I worked very hard to succeed in my classes. I knew that Chicano students in SI were involved in all kinds of protests and I admired this. The name SI was eventually changed to the Mexican-American Student Confederation [MASC]. MASC developed a specific ideology. The group wanted to convince Chicano students to stay in school so that they could go back into their communities and try to improve conditions. The group was involved in other struggles. They held a vigil to support the Mexican students who were protesting the 1968 Olympics held in Mexico City. The Mexican police broke up their demonstrations and killed many of them. MASC supported the United Farm Workers by picketing Safeway because the store was selling non-union lettuce. Chicano students were really making demands and protesting, and I wanted to be a part of this.

I was really impressed with the Chicano student leaders. I attended meetings but I was on the outside, just listening. I was very humble or shy, which may come from being a farm worker and coming from very humble roots. I wasn't going to go right out and say, "I can be a leader." I eventually grew into the role of a student leader.

In 1968, I joined the Chicanos who went into the college president's office to protest and it changed my life forever. I had just come out of the library with a friend and all of a sudden two Chicanas came up to us and said, "Hey, there's going to be a protest at the president's office and we need some people." I said, "Really? I've never seen the president of a college, even of a junior college." I had read about the president and how he was against the students who protested against Dow Chemical. So I went with them and I sat down in the president's office. The Chicanos took the demands to him. I sat there and watched the Chicano student leaders who represented MASC talking to the president as if they were equals. I never saw Chicanos talk to the administration that way because we were too scared of them. As a farm worker, we never talked that way to the *gabachos*, ever. We were afraid even of the *mayordomos, que eran Chicanos también* [overseers, who were also Chicanos]. That changed my life forever because after that, I believed I could talk to anyone in authority. This experience gave me a voice. It wasn't that I never said anything, but I never felt comfortable doing it. I always felt like I shouldn't say anything.

Within months after that protest in the president's office, I was speaking to crowds of 25,000 in anti-war demonstrations and even organizing the Chicano Liberation Days in '69, '70 and '71. I was looking at a crowd of 15,000 Chicanitos from all the schools in Santa Clara County and thinking, "How come when we're little kids, they make us feel ugly and we want to look like them, like Anglos?" I said, "Those kids are the most beautiful kids in the world." I realized how beautiful they were and I said, "How come we try so hard to be like them?" It almost made me cry because I thought, "All these years we're trying so hard to be like them. And then you look at 15,000 of them and you feel like, God, the most beautiful people on the planet earth." I'm saying, "They're better looking than anybody else!" This is what I'm talking about when I say that I believed in Chicano cultural nationalism. I believed we needed a sense of identity that was opposed to all those that made us feel unimportant.

I spoke at many anti-war rallies. I talked about the number of Chicanos dying in the war and the fact that we suffer the most and get the least in terms of benefits. I also asked, "Why are we fighting a war against those people over there? We should be fighting the war here in our country against racism and discrimination and lack of participation." It was really holding this country to the standards and the values that they'd been teaching us all those years, and taking that seriously in terms of equality and justice. While we were organizing, we were talking to a lot of young guys who had come from the war and were saying, "Oh, my God! I went and fought." They had no clue what they were fighting for.

## NATIONALISM AND COALITION BUILDING

The Chicano student group was really a Third World Coalition. We were nationalists. I read a lot of literature about protest movements and the role of coalitions. I believed that we could make a real difference if we banded together as Chicano, black, Asian, and Native American students. That was the kind of coalition we formed on campus. Again, at first I was just a participant, but at some point I got passionate about it and eventually became the leader.

But the real leader was Juan Antú because he was the guy our coalition ran for student body president.[6] He was really intelligent, personable, and articulate. He was a tall, good-looking guy. We were working on trying to create a coalition that could help him get elected president but at the same time we said, "Hey, wait a minute. We should be running some of our people—Chicanos—for office." We too were learning how to manipulate the system to get more of our group elected. For example, we ran a couple students that had Anglo surnames, like Sue Helmer, who was a Chicana, and Vernon Robinson, who was as Chicano as they come. There was even an Asian whose last name was Lee, so we thought, "Well, they don't know that Lee is *gabacho* or Asian, right?" We sat down and thought of what students could get more votes because *gabacho* students would think they were also *gabachos*. We would have meetings and decide which of us had names that would get the *gabacho* vote. We would have a good time saying, "Hey, that would be a perfect name!" But what we were really learning was how to create a really diverse coalition. We also supported general community issues like the UFW and the grape boycott. We created a climate in which Chicanos, Asians, Native Americans, gays, women, and other groups began to flex their muscles, work together, and bring about change.

We also started to organize against the Vietnam War. MASC had a few demonstrations, but I wasn't really that active with them at first. But soon, I was developing my leadership skills and my perspective on the war. When the U.S. invaded Cambodia in 1970, Chicanos joined in the protests. One of your brothers helped us with the pamphlets we put out against the war.[7] It really helps when academics are doing that kind of work with us. I was able to distribute 50,000 flyers out into the Chicano community near the college and on the East Side. I believe in coalitions, but I also believe that sometimes you have to talk to your own community and you can't rely on *gabachos* and other groups working in our communities.

Chicanos were not being racist when we were fighting for our piece of the pie, our liberation, and our self-determination. That's what I was learning from Tijerina, Gonzales, and Gutiérrez.[8] We had meetings when we were trying to form the La Raza Unida Party here in California in the early '70s.[9] I was attending meetings in Hayward, Fresno, Oakland, San Francisco, and other places where Chicanos were becoming active in *El Movimiento*. We were trying to say, "We need to form our own organizations and elect our own people."

## THE ACTIVIST SOCIOLOGIST:
## "I USED SOCIOLOGY TO STUDY *EL MOVIMIENTO*"

I took a lot of sociology classes at San José State, and I learned how to be very critical of social science studies on Chicanos. I wondered why social scientists were referring to Chicanos as Spanish Americans. I read one study of Chicanos in a small town in New Mexico. How could social scientists generalize about Chicanos from one study? How could *gabachos* not see the methodological problems with making generalizations from that? Yet, some of my professors didn't understand why this sociological study had problems. They told me, "You are going too far with this Chicano thing. We're not all racist. Some of us have done some really good research." I'm not saying they didn't try or that their hearts weren't in the right place. It's not about intent. I thought this sociology study was really terrible. I realized then I wanted to do research on Chicanos that didn't create stereotypes or generalizations.

Knowing that so many studies about Chicanos had created stereotypes, I decided I wanted to write about the development of Chicanos in California from 1830 to 1860 for a history term paper. I went to Stanford and Berkeley and spent hours at the Bancroft Library. I went to museums here in Santa Clara County and read anything I could find on all kinds of topics related to California history, like the life of Tiburcio Vázquez.[10] I spent the whole semester writing this paper, and when I finished it, I said, "My paper is not about the development of Chicanos in California. It's about our decline." The professor gives me a B+ and told me, "You were too angry when you wrote this paper and couldn't be objective." I felt so bad that I grabbed the paper and threw it at his feet and walked away. I thought to myself, "I did the very best job I ever have done on a research paper." I worked

very hard to make sure it was well written. Then, when this same professor found
out that I was teaching at State the next semester, he says, "Did I hear that you're
teaching here?" I said, "Yeah." He says, "You haven't lived long enough yet to be a
teacher. You've got to work first." And I thought to myself, "I've worked all of my
entire life! What are you talking about?" I worked in the fields that whole summer until the last weekend before leaving Salinas to start college. When I read
about day haul laborers in my college history, I'd think, "That's what I did." We
would look for work every day, and if we were lucky, we would work for months
with one guy. Workers had to push each other so that they could get on the truck
and work for the day. So I was shocked and really angry when that professor told
me that I had to work before I could teach. How could that *vato* [guy] tell me that
I hadn't worked? What he meant was I hadn't taught long enough or I didn't have
a Ph.D. But I thought if a *gabachito* had been given that same teaching position,
he would have probably been told, "Good for you, congratulations, and now go
on and get your Ph.D." That professor didn't succeed in discouraging me from
wanting to become a sociologist and do research on Chicanos. During my last
years at the university, I wrote a lot about politics for my classes. I wrote about
the Movement and our protests. I used sociology to study *El Movimiento*. I
helped write pamphlets about Chicanos that we used for our protests and to educate other Chicano students and the Chicano community.

## MASS MOBILIZATIONS:
## "I WANTED TO CREATE INSTITUTIONAL CHANGE"

I once heard that César Chávez appointed four vice presidents to his United
Farm Workers organization. So when I was elected student body president, I appointed four other people. I appointed a woman because I wanted a woman to
be a high-ranking officer in the organization. I wanted to equalize the genders
within the organization. I got her involved with a lot of Chicano activities. For
example, I said, "You work on the *Semana Chicana*." When I thought *Semana
Chicana*, I thought Chicano Week, right? But it became *Semana de las Chicanas*
[Chicanas' Week]. I said, "In Spanish, *Semana Chicana* means a week about Chicanos: men and women!" In Spanish, you have to say "Chicana" because the word
"semana" is feminine in Spanish grammar. But I wasn't upset with that because
my ex-wife participated in it and so did these other women. I thought it was a really good idea to have a week to study women's issues.

   I believe that what I've done and what other people have done is to create an
environment where these things could happen. I was what is called a "true be-

liever," and I believed in the rhetoric of equality, justice, liberation, and self-determination.[11] I tried to bring about these ideals. I would listen to Chicano student activists who had already been involved in *El Movimiento* when I came around. I was honest and said to the other Chicano students, "Here's what we're going to do" and then I would see if I had convinced enough people to do what I wanted them to do. If we could do things to outsmart those in power, then we won the day.

I wanted Chicanos to be represented in everything but I also wanted them to try to create opportunities for others. I wanted them to do what people had talked about in MASC, which was, "Go back to your community. Get back to your community. Work for your community. Sacrifice for your community." I always knew you could do both. I wasn't sacrificing myself, and I didn't get arrested or into trouble at the university. And yet, I was protesting and organizing people in a way that the system would allow and still make a difference. I thought sometimes people felt like if you didn't get in trouble, then it wasn't real, it wasn't authentic. I wanted to create institutional change for Chicanos.

I believe we were effective. I think that at some point the goals became too grandiose. We wanted so much more than what was possible, but that's only because we didn't know the system that well. I keep talking about coming from the fields to the university and certainly I was going to school and taking classes, but still I didn't feel part of the university. What was so exciting to me about the Movement was that we were saying, "We want the institution to change. We want the university to change to meet our goals and our values." It really struck me that we were demanding that the system change and that we were liberating ourselves. I think we were liberating ourselves from colonization. We didn't want someone else defining what it means to be a Chicano or what it means to be an American. We wanted to define ourselves as being both.

I was influenced by the black student movement, black civil rights movement, and the African movement in Africa. I really believed that those movements influenced Chicanos, but we were not going to copy them. We learned concepts like liberation, self-determination, and identity in our own cultural way. Our protests were always compared to those by blacks or the SDS group.[12] We [Chicano student leaders] had read a little bit of Marx and so we started saying that we were against the ruling capitalist class. We knew that we couldn't discuss this with the Chicano community. We were handing out pamphlets and trying to get more Chicanos to go to a meeting or a walkout. Anglo students wanted to organize a demonstration because Robert Kennedy had just been killed the weekend before.

I attended a long meeting that lasted until four or five in the morning where people like me said, "Let's have the protest anyway!" But then we said, "Wait a minute. How's the media going to portray us and how are other Chicanos going to handle this?" What they said was, "We'll do the protest in honor of Robert Kennedy," because Chicanos are very much into the Kennedys. I thought, "Why? The hell with the *gabachos*." But they were a little smarter than that and they realized that our community looked up to Kennedy mostly because he supported Chávez and the farm workers. So we joined the protest.

One of my biggest projects was organizing Chicano Liberation Day. It was September of 1969 and by this time I was on the student council. That was the summer when my leadership got bigger. Corky Gonzales had called for the Liberation Day in the Plan de Aztlán.[13] Gonzales declared September 16, Mexican Independence Day, as Chicano Liberation Day. He wanted Chicanos all over the United States to have walkouts from all the schools in the country to protest the educational system. I had read an article in 1960 that said Chicanos were dropping out of high school at a rate of at least 50 percent. This percentage had changed by 1969. So I'm thinking, "This is one thing I could really fight for!" This is where I met Ernestina García.[14] We organized a walkout outside of their school. That's the first one I organized. It was for high school and college students. We even asked Stanford and a bunch of other schools to come and join us. We used a lot of students at the university but had to get some community people to work with the police because they had buses full of cops waiting to arrest us if we made trouble.

## CONSEQUENCE OF PROTESTING: EXPOSURE TO VIOLENCE

I went to the Chicano Moratorium in 1969 with my wife and a couple of guys.[15] They were going to have Tijerina, Gutiérrez, and Chávez, who were our icons, so we said, "All of them in one place? ¡Órale, vámonos!" [Well, let's go!] We went to LA. I had just been in a car accident so I had a cane and I could barely walk. Although I did hear that there might be problems with the police, I didn't really believe it. My wife and I were sitting down in the park, and there's music playing and people walking around the park. We're kind of groovin', as they say back then! We're waiting for the speakers and all of a sudden we see people running and then we see tear gas. Now we're going to try to run, but we see a fence because it's a baseball park. We're going, "Oh, my God." We see cops hitting people, and we're getting scared because they're just running out of the way and yet they're getting clobbered. I'm thinking, "How am I going to get out of here? I can't jump over that fence. My wife couldn't jump over the fence. She's kind of small too." But somehow the people knocked the fence down and we were able to run over it. Now we were on Whittier Boulevard, right in the middle of the Chicano community. We're knocking on doors because now the cops are coming from the other side too. They're trying to get us on both sides, and they didn't want us to run out of the park. Later, we learned that they were supposedly trying to catch somebody, but I don't believe that. I certainly never believed that. Honest to God, we were scared because we didn't know what was going to happen to us. Although I'd seen violence, this was the first time where I was in the middle of it and I was potentially a victim.

There were a couple of times when we had demonstrations on campus where I thought of being a martyr. We talked about bombing a building, but when I got up at five in the morning and I decided I wasn't going. Some kid blew half his hand off and I said, "Look, I will actively walk out of the classes," which I did. A lot of people did walk out of their classes because of me, but I said, "I will not blow up buildings and I will not hurt other people." That was just something that I decided for myself.

I believed in nonviolence. It was something that I developed from listening to Joan Baez's songs, reading a little bit of Gandhi, and later hearing Martin Luther King and some of these other people talk about nonviolence. I could understand why some people were violent. But I felt that in our country we could be nonviolent and I felt that there was no alternative. I think if you read Gandhi correctly, you find that he didn't think there was an alternative and that's why he did it. People think he did it because he didn't believe in violence, but actually, he didn't believe that you could win with violence.

Even though in 1969 we did not experience the revolution that many of us thought was just around the corner, we nevertheless changed the United States profoundly.

## EDUCATIONAL ACTIVISM: STUDENTS CHANGING THE WORLD

After I graduated from college, I really wanted to get a job in Salinas. I went to the unemployment office and said, "Look, I just graduated with a degree in political science and I'm looking for a job." They asked me about my work experience. I replied, "Field work. But I don't want to do field work. I want something else. I want an office job." Then, later on, Jose Villa from San José State said, "We need someone to teach an Introduction to Chicano Studies class."[16] So this is how I started teaching at State. I didn't know anything more than what my teachers had done in their classes. Before this offer, I was going to get a credential to be a high school teacher, but then I got into a master's program. I had just graduated and was starting to teach before I even had my master's degree. I taught Introduction to Chicano Studies, Race Relations, and Political Sociology. While I was teaching these courses, I was also working on my master's degree in sociology at State. I had almost finished when I got an offer at Foothill College and De Anza College to teach full time in sociology and Chicano studies. I had already applied to the Ph.D. program in sociology at Berkeley, so I didn't accept these offers. In retrospect, I could have been making a lot of money, but I went to Berkeley for ten years instead. I worked and taught at several community colleges during these years.

I thought, "Wherever I'm teaching, if that's what I want to do, then that's the college for me. If I care about students, which I do, and I care about what I'm doing, then that's what matters to me most." Many faculty didn't want me to be on college committees due to my politics. One year, I had actually been appointed to several committees and they wanted me out of there, so I said, "To hell with this. I'm trying to make a difference, trying to help students. I can't do this being on these committees." I got involved in local politics because I was a committed college teacher.

One of the things I wanted to do when I became a teacher was talk about the truth and what's really going on in everyday life. I wanted to inspire and encourage students. I wanted them to believe in themselves. I knew that because I was young, students would challenge me in class. I opened the door for them to do that, whereas most professors wouldn't let you talk that much. I encouraged dialogue in my classes. I welcomed them to question what I said and to come up with new ideas. I wanted students to go out and change the world.

## NOTES

1. *Guayule* is a shrub native to the southwestern United States and northern Mexico that can be used as an alternate source of latex that is also hypoallergenic. This plant saw a brief and intense amount of agricultural research during World War II when Japan cut off America's Malaysian latex resources. The war ended before large-scale farming of the *guayule* plant began because it was cheaper to import tree-derived latex than to crush the shrubs for a smaller amount of latex.

2. *Bracero*, a Spanish word derived from *brazo* [arm], is used when referring to a day laborer. The term is usually associated with the Bracero Program (1942 until 1964 with

some breaks) between Mexico and the United States in which Mexicans were brought into the U.S. to work as temporary agricultural or railway workers.

3. Raúl "Ratón" Macías was one of Televisa's first boxing stars. With television in its infancy around the world, Macías was one of Mexico's popular fighters of the time, and many of his fights were shown live on Televisa during the 1950s. He had a large following among Mexicans in the United States.

4. The Brown Berets, founded in 1967 in Los Angeles, was a Chicano organization that advocated confrontational, often violent, political tactics.

5. Dow Chemical Company's best-known product became napalm, and its use as a weapon in Vietnam triggered widespread student protests during the 1960s. When Dow Chemical went on campuses to recruit college students, sit-ins and protests against the company were organized throughout the United States.

6. Juan Antú was a Chicano student leader at San José State University in the late 1960s.

7. Olivérez is making reference to Mario T. García who was teaching at San José State during this time and is the brother of Alma M. García who, along with Francisco Jiménez, was interviewing Olivérez for this anthology.

8. Reies López Tijerina, Corky Gonzales, and José Angel Gutiérrez were all leaders during the 1960s Chicano Protest Movement.

9. La Raza Unida Party (LRUP) was founded by Chicanos in Crystal City, Texas, in 1970, as an alternative to the Republican and Democratic parties. By 1972, LRUP had chapters throughout the United States and had its first national convention in El Paso, Texas, in 1972.

10. Tiburcio Vásquez (1835–1875) was considered a sort of "Robin Hood" after he was accused of killing an Anglo constable in California and fled to the mountains where he gained legendary status among Mexicans. He was captured, tried, and hanged in San José, California, in 1875 and is buried in the Santa Clara Catholic Cemetery.

11. The "true believer syndrome" is sometimes used broadly in the sense of Eric Hoffer's general study of fanaticism in *The True Believer* (1951). The true believer syndrome is usually used within the context of anti-establishment activities. See Eric Hoffer, *The True Believer: Thoughts on the Nature of Mass Movements* (New York: Harper and Row, 1951).

12. The Students for a Democratic Society (SDS), a radical student organization founded in 1960, called for students to join in a movement to establish "participatory democracy." It was not until later in the decade, with the growth of the anti–Vietnam

War movement, that the organization became well known. SDS demonstrations against the war drew thousands of protesters. In 1968, SDS sponsored a protest at Columbia University that was ended by the arrest of more than seven hundred protesters. In that same year, increasingly divided by factional disputes, the organization collapsed, leaving behind a small faction, known as the Weathermen, who advocated violent revolutionary action.

13. Rodolfo "Corky" Gonzales, one of the major leaders in the Chicano Movement, issued the *Plan Espiritual de Aztlán* [Spiritual Plan of Aztlán] in 1969 during the first Chicano Youth Liberation Conference held in Denver, Colorado. The Plan called for Chicanos to work together and organize a new political party based on Chicano nationalism.

14. See interview with Ernestina García in this anthology.

15. Chicano activists organized a major protest against the Vietnam War. Over 30,000 demonstrators gathered in East Los Angeles on August 29, 1970. Police attacked the demonstrators. Ruben Salazar, a noted journalist, was killed under suspicious circumstances that afternoon when police fired rubber bullets into a bar where Salazar was sitting.

16. José Villa was a professor at San José State University.

# 9

# Yolanda Reynolds

*Maria de la Luz Yolanda Gallegos y Espinosa de Reynolds was born in 1934 in Del Norte, Colorado. She attended school at Mt. St. Scholastica Academy in Atchison, Kansas. The family left the ranch in Colorado and moved to the village of Santa Cruz, New Mexico. After working first for her father in a department store, then a bank, she and her brothers established their own retail business. She then attended the University of New Mexico and later finished her B.A. and M.A. at San José State University in San José, California. After spending years in education as a teacher and counselor, she became an administrator at Evergreen Community College. She was the founder and first president of the Shasta/Hachett Neighborhood Association and later became a news writer for the Spanish/English weekly newspaper* La Oferta *in San José. She covered issues related to San José's Latino community. She and her husband are retired, but she remains active in community activities and is a co-host of a local radio talk show.*

## CHILDHOOD AND PARENTS

My family was very proud of its heritage and we all felt very good about whom we were. We settled in a very difficult part of the world, but we survived. My family believed in the importance of education and hard work. We were all expected to work hard. All of us believed that family was very important. I grew up on a ranch, but my father was not a farmer. My grandfather owned a lot of ranches in New Mexico, but he lost most of them during the Great Depression. He became the manager of a very nice store in town. I have such sentiment towards many

Jewish people because the man my father worked for was Jewish and when some European Americans came and said, "We will not trade in that store if you make Modesto the manager," the owner of that business said, "Well, you can just go to stores in Denver or Pueblo, I don't care. He's good and he's going to be my manager." I will never forget this. Later my brother and I started a store and we got huge extensions of credit to start our business and they were all Jewish families.

My father once met a man who worked for the big company International Harvester. He thought my father was very bright and decided they would groom him to be an executive with International Harvester. I have photos of my father when they sent him to the university. The company found a home for him to stay in so he would learn all the social graces. Not that my family didn't have social graces but just so that he'd understand the broader community's mannerisms. The company sent him to Chicago and, later, to South America. Even though there was a lot of discrimination, my father had a great personality and incredible wit. They would always ask him to be the master of ceremonies at the Rotary Club's social events. He had a way of telling people right to their face, "You are a bigot" in such a way that they would just take it. I don't have that skill.

Since my father was in business, my mother would have to go to functions with him. I remember an incident when I was a very young girl. Mom and Dad were going to a dance sponsored by the Chamber of Commerce. When they arrived some people told them that they couldn't go to the dance and that they should go to a dance in another part of town. One of my father's friends happened to be Jewish, and he was ready to fight because he was so mad. My father said, "I'm going to this dance, and if I don't get into this dance, this is the last time you're going to have this function here in this town." So they admitted Mom and Dad to the dance. The men who told my father this were very embarrassed and then came over and wanted to dance with my mother and she just told them "No." She didn't care who they were, that was not something she was going to do. She was always like that. My mother was very independent, and she didn't have to feel that she had to impress anybody else. She was very modest in her way. She was very kind to people, but she was not going to try to belong to the club. My mother and father were very special people.

We would always call ourselves Spanish. We spoke in Spanish, but we would also say we were *Mexicanos.* We also spoke English because my parents knew that it was important that their children know how to speak English. My father always talked about the rest of the country as the States. That part of southern Colorado didn't become a part of the United States until about 1912, so it was very recent.

It was really exciting to go to school and find out that most of our food came from Native Americans and all our famous Spanish explorers were following the trails that the Indians had already established. They had established commercial paths a long time ago.

## RELIGION: TRADITION AND LEGENDS

Religion played a very important role in our family. We were very traditional Catholics. We always prayed together and said the rosary together. In fact, I remember one of my brothers couldn't understand a part of one prayer. We would say out loud, "*Ruega por nosotros*" [Pray for us], and he thought that we were saying *borregas por nosotros* [sheep for us]. He would ask my parents, "What do we want all those sheep for?" We always had Holy Water in our house and went to church every Sunday. One of the first things that anybody asked in terms of dating patterns was "Is your friend a Catholic or not?" This was especially true if you were to get married. It was bad news if you didn't marry somebody who was Catholic and preferably someone who was Hispanic. Since there was so much discrimination, my family thought it would be better if their children married other Hispanics. My mother felt that others would not be able to understand what it was like to be Hispanic and experience discrimination. If a European American married someone who was Hispanic, they would feel the pressure from their own community that they might have married beneath them. I began to question some of that advice because I saw Catholics whom I thought behaved very poorly compared to some of my friends who were not Catholic. I had great difficulty accepting the fact that I was placing myself in a state of mortal sin by having a friend who was not a Catholic. I began to question that belief at a rather young age, and it continued throughout my life.

Our pastor was a priest from Spain. He was the pastor of our parish for most of my young life. He loved Palestrina, the classical religious music.[1] He really wanted to put an end to the old songs that the people had held onto for generations. I was very offended by that because I thought he was denigrating the fact that the faith had survived all those years from the absence of priests because of the *penitentes*. I don't know a lot about them because it's a men's organization. I have a nephew who just got his degree with honors from University of New Mexico and he is a *penitente*, which really shocked me. They get together to pray and perform certain rituals. It was always a big deal among the young people to peek in the windows to see the *penitentes* because they used to whip themselves and do other kinds of penances. I don't think their ceremonies were any different than most other men's organizations except these were always directed towards their patron saint. Each saint had a little chapel and somebody from the organization would maintain it.

Chimayó is a place in New Mexico that people believe is sacred.[2] It's an old story, but the Native Americans considered that place sacred. The people will take the soil and either put it in a glass of water and drink it or rub on their bodies. You'll see people at the shrine who are crippled and walking with crutches or canes. There are photographs on a wall inside the shrine of people who believe that they were cured by making the visit there. I think it's losing a little bit of its tradition because they put a big parking lot behind the chapel. The surroundings there are just beautiful. When I was dating my husband, we would ride over there. It was so mystical and so beautiful. I remember a moonlit night when the light was really bright and there was this stream behind the church, sort of like a little valley, and there were a few sheep down there. It was just gorgeous. It has lost some of its beauty to accommodate all the tourists who go there.

I used to walk all the way from my home, which was about a six-mile walk, to see the processions on Good Friday. People would walk from Los Alamos, Santa Fe, and Albuquerque to come to the shrine. The police have to direct traffic so people don't get hurt. I decided to make that pilgrimage because it's so beautiful. They have five or six masses on Sunday, and every one of them is packed with people of all ages, from the very young to the very old. Everybody takes communion, and you just feel that the people really believe in the miracle. I think it is beautiful that people have such a strong faith that helps them deal with all their problems. There's a real sense of community among the people. In many respects, I feel that I'm not a churchgoing person anymore, but I feel that there should be justice and honesty. I feel all the things that people say they get from religion are still a part of my life.

## MY SCHOOLING: A DIVERSITY OF EXPERIENCES

Where I grew up in southern Colorado, you could not get into the first grade if you had any Spanish accent in your English. When I was a five-year-old, I went to the steps of school and the teacher was standing there and she said "You're not going to the first grade." I said, "I am going to the first grade." I remember putting my hands on my hips and arguing with her. I didn't want to tell her who my father was. I finally had to tell her who he was because I knew there were a lot of other children who weren't as privileged as I. They'd put all the *Hispano* children into a special class. Their rationale was that they did not speak English. I said, "I speak English." Very shortly after I was in the first grade, the teacher wanted to put me in the second grade. I thought she still wanted to get rid of me, so I wouldn't go. It wasn't until I started to teach that I realized that probably I could have gone to the second grade and that she was using me to help other students learn. She thought I could have gone on, but I didn't trust her and that's the real tragedy when there's prejudice and discrimination. You lose your ability to judge whether you're being pushed aside because you have a nasty personality or because of your ethnicity. My mother was a very strong woman. If she could talk to me now, she would tell me, like my husband does now, that all that discrimination that my family and I went through forced us to live like in a fortress. You always knew you could come home and there was somebody there for you.

When I was in the seventh grade, I didn't have many friends and they tended to be other people who were rejected by the "in" crowds at schools. A friend of mine once called me a "dirty Mexican." This is what people called us when they wanted to make fun of us. We happened to be in the restroom when she said that to me. She was supposedly my best friend. I just hauled off and hit her, and she went flying across into the stall door and into the toilet. I came home and told Mamá, "I could have killed her." My mother said, "I think you need to go away to school." So my mother sent me away to the same school she had attended: an academy in Kansas run by Benedictine nuns. This was a very good experience for me because I found there could be other kinds of prejudices. I went to school with the daughters of the then treasurer of Mexico and the owners of an airline in Mexico. I saw that the nuns just fawned over the very wealthy girls and I was just this little girl from Colorado. The nuns favored these rich girls, and that was a very important lesson for me to learn. This is how I realized that there are all kinds of prejudice.

I was married at the time I attended San José State in the late 1960s. Having experienced prejudice in southern Colorado and southern New Mexico where there were fewer Latinos, I remember coming here to San José and feeling, "It's so nice there's no prejudice and discrimination here." This changed one day when I was walking down the street by myself and I heard this little voice say, "Dirty jap, dirty jap!" I looked all around and the child was shouting at me because he thought I was Japanese. I talked to one of my husband's colleagues and asked, "Why do people not like Japanese?" I didn't know too much about how the Japanese were interned during World War II. I thought, "Here was this little boy, years after the end of the war, and he was still shouting bad things at me because he thought I was Japanese."

When my children were very young, I was very busy going to school and so I really didn't get involved in politics during those times. I'd read the paper and I was aware of these things, but I did not get involved. My husband really encouraged me to work, and this is how I eventually developed my own curriculum in school, which is now the basis for Mexican American Studies. Though my family was here many generations in what is the United States, people would ask me who I was, where I was from, and as a young person I always wondered "Who am I? What's my history?" There was no place to look for answers.

## TEACHING: TOWARD AN INCLUSIVE CURRICULUM

I had such a bad experience going to school that I did not think very highly of teachers. It was nothing I aspired to be. The reason I became a teacher was because my husband encouraged me. Before I was going to the university, one of the things people would ask me was who I was and where was I from. One of the reasons was to find out who I was. So when I went to the university I decided I had to study Spanish literature, Southwestern history, Latin American history, anthropology, and archaeology in the quest to find out who I was.

When I married, we came out here to California to live and I enrolled at San José State University. At that time there was the big social movement—the Chicano Movement—and my husband said, "You know, you have the experience, you should get involved. You should go teach." I went to see somebody I had read about in the paper who was the principal at San Jose High School. He wanted to hire me, but he had no money left and he said, "Well, we really need you." He called another principal and that afternoon I was hired.

This was in 1969 and, at that time, we did not have a Mexican American Studies program or anything like that. I was with the San José Unified School District. Four of us worked together to develop the curriculum in Mexican American Studies for the district. When I began teaching, I realized the need to offer the courses on Mexican American history and culture to Latino students. Without this, I believed that they would feel excluded.

I remember having a big disagreement with a consultant who didn't want to include Native American history in the curriculum. I said, "You can't separate it; it's a part of our life. Many of our foods, many of the ways we do things, we learned from the Native American people." I thought she was just totally wrong. I remember being so angry that Native American history was not being included in the curriculum because although the adobe is used in Spain, the Spanish modified a lot of it based on the practices of Native Americans. We also talked about the conquistadors and the pioneers who all used the roadways and the train routes that the Indians had been using before the Spaniards came to California. The Spaniards were basically coming to an inhabited area. Our new curriculum included material on the culture and literature from Spain. There are still people who are angry and want to turn their back on Spain and our Spanish heritage, but that is a part of who Mexican Americans are. Spain gave us our language and religion. Certainly a lot of our food is different from food in Spain. We really eat what was the Native American food. The Spaniards introduced them to larger animals, cows and other things, but beans, tomatoes, and corn are all products that the Native American used.

I worked with others on the curriculum for our Mexican American Studies program. We developed objectives and questions for the teachers so that they would know what was important in the curriculum at every grade level, up to high school. We included studies of our literature, food, music, history, anthropology, and archaeology. I always stressed the study of folklore, especially since, at that time, scholars at Berkeley were conducting a lot of research in this area. My uncle was Juan Rael from Stanford.[3] He collected and studied the *cuentos* that had been passed down orally from generation to generation in Latino families. He came every year and collected *cuentos*.[4] I love those *cuentos*. The core of that program eventually became the core of Mexican American Studies at San José State University.

I think our innovation to include a curriculum on Mexican American Studies was well received back then or it wouldn't have survived that long. The students seemed to like it. Sometimes schools try to make this a totally separate curriculum for Mexican American students. This is both good and bad because other people don't become aware of that history. There are two sides to every coin on the issue of whether you make it a separate studies or if it is integrated. I feel it's very important to do both but then focus on integrating it because, in my own experience, I was always asking myself, "Who am I? What am I?" I needed to know my history, and finding out gave me a lot of pride. I knew things that other people didn't know. I was the first person in the high school to teach the Mexican American Studies class. At the time, there were no textbooks, so everything came out of my own resources. I had to loan the students my books for them to do research. Teaching is an art and I can't brag about anything I did, other than struggle, but I survived that first year.

## ADVOCATE FOR EDUCATION AND EQUALITY

I couldn't attribute the changes in the Latino students to just the introduction of Mexican American history and culture into curriculum because there were a lot of other factors. The students' involvement in the MAYO club was one of these.[5] One of the biggest issues in the late 1960s was the lack of access to education. More and more Chicano students began to enroll in colleges due to an increase in scholarships such as Cal Grants.[6] I remember talking to my students about going on to college and they just sort of looked at me as if they were thinking, "What are you talking about?" A lot of people in our community would talk to kids about going to college. We would tell them to go to school, and they were saying, "¿Con qué, con qué?" [With what, with what?] I knew people who were counselors at the college. One day, I happened to meet a Latino counselor at a nearby city college, so I invited him come talk to my students. I knew that his visit would encourage the students and tell them all about financial aid and how to apply for it and for scholarships. I wanted to make sure that I did everything possible to encourage Latino students to go to college. You could see the smiles on the children's faces when this counselor talked to them. It was as if a light bulb turned on in their heads because they knew that they could get money that did not have to be paid back. They began to think, "Yeah, I can go to school."

I also told students to talk about college with their parents. Latina students experienced added pressure about going on to college. Their parents, particularly their fathers, did not necessarily want their daughters to go on to college. I didn't try to convince the fathers myself because some of those macho Chicanos saw me as an "uppity" woman. I would get a male teacher to try and talk to them about how important it was that their daughters go to college and become independent. I always worked with male teachers whom I thought would be able to talk to the parents about these issues. I suggested that they tell the parents that going to college did not necessarily mean that their daughters would never marry or never have children, but it was a way to help them. If her husband ever got sick, she would have a way to provide for her children. I don't recall having as much objection from mothers as I did from fathers, which was interesting. I guess it's partly because even though the mother really rules in the *Hispano* [Hispanic] home, out in public, men want to give the impression that they rule. I didn't treat women—Latinas—differently from anybody else. I would try and figure out how to help make them enthusiastic about studying. I would ask them what were their favorite activities and then I would tie those interests into some kind of education or training.

During those times a lot of people were saying that the problem wasn't the school system but that young Latinos and Latinas just were not studying hard and didn't want to buy into the American Dream. I didn't notice that attitude among the students because we had a very active MAYO club, which was kind of the social club. The kids were all trying to achieve, and they went on to community college or Berkeley or some other institution. The MAYO club was very, very good because it was a place for the Latino students to feel welcomed in a school where they were definitely a minority. The kids were feeling sort of isolated and didn't want to participate in sports or other school activities. Another Latino teacher, who taught Spanish, had been the club's adviser and was really good with the students. When I started teaching, I became the new adviser for Latino students. I was out almost every weekend, many times at night, working with the students on different projects. It was very difficult because I had two young sons and my husband was in the midst of his career. Often I wouldn't get to bed before two o'clock in the morning and had to be up early to teach a class.

I had my whole family work with MAYO. My two little boys and I washed cars and sold candy at all the dances with the kids of the MAYO club. A lot of the Latino kids didn't feel comfortable at the school functions, especially at Willow Glen High School because it was so predominately non-Hispanic. I convinced the school to give MAYO the concession to sell food at all the school events. We would sell the Cokes and the candy, but I was very strict with them. They could split a half a candy bar, but they couldn't have a whole one so they wouldn't eat up all the profits. We used the profits to hand out scholarships at the end of the year. I hoped that this project would get them involved with school and give them more and more confidence.

Our MAYO club also sponsored one really big event that we called People Day. We called it "People Day" because there were a lot of Italians, Jews, Asians, especially Japanese American, Mexican, Irish, and Germans at our school. We started People Day because we wanted to recognize everyone's ancestry. I got permission from the principal so that parents could bring in food to the event. We prepared three times more the amount of food than on normal days and we still ran out of food. That was really exciting. We brought in speakers to make presentations at the school's general assembly and then the teachers would have the speakers come into the classrooms to talk to students in a smaller group. This event took a lot of effort and a little money. It was worth it. I was disappointed when the school stopped having People Day.

The students in MAYO were the kind of people that you could ask to do something and they did it well. That told me they were going to be successful persons in life. One time, I told students to remember to bring pencils and paper to school. One student, a really smart one, didn't bring these supplies to school and so I finally went to visit this boy's family. I was so surprised. There was no place for this boy to study. I thought, "I'll never, ever again demand that students bring their own pencils and paper." I decided to always have a paper and pencil in my classroom to give to students if they needed them. If I were to be a consultant for the school system again, I would say that in order to better things for Latino students, we really have to go visit their homes on the East Side and let them and their parents know that we're concerned. I remember having to go to homes where the kids would tell their parents, "Oh, they ran out of textbooks." I would have to tell the parents that their children were doing something wrong because they weren't bringing their schoolbooks home so that they could study. I didn't want to insult the parents. I used to tell them that their children were really smart, but they weren't doing their homework. This made them feel proud and comfortable speaking with me. I wanted them to trust me. I also made sure that I would ask them if they preferred to speak Spanish. I also made sure to tell them that they could contact me anytime they needed help with their kids.

The Chicano Movement began in the late 1960s. Students began to pay attention to all kinds of social issues. Luis Valdez and his Teatro Campesino performed here in San José, and since he grew up here, it was even more exciting.[7] César Chávez was organizing at that time. The first time I went to a big gathering, I don't remember who was speaking, but San José State's stadium was packed with students. The children were as quiet as I was. It was a very moving experience to see that a person could stand up and say, "I'm proud to be Mexican" or "I'm proud to be Latino" or whatever you felt that you were. At that meeting they were just telling people, "Let's organize, sí se puede"[8] [It can be done] and "Yes, you can go to school." I remember they had some big sessions where all the universities would come around and try to recruit students. Affirmative action was a big thing, and they were looking for students, trying to show that they were institutions of good will.

One of the biggest problems facing all Latinos was the lack of money and not having anybody else in their family who had gone on to school. They didn't know that they could succeed. Very few people had encouraged them, and they thought that education was out of their reach. As I told you, some of the children were really poor and I would become very upset when I visited their homes and saw their poor living conditions. Latino students have always faced many problems. Money was a real obstacle. Most of the school counselors didn't take the time to explain all the requirements to the Latino students, particularly those requirements that they needed to go to college. They really didn't have people—role models—to encourage them.

When I made the move to Evergreen Community College, I started out as a counselor. At the time I made this transition, the schools were already suffering from lack of funding. I later became an assistant dean at Evergreen. I had responsibility for the English division of the college, and it really grew a lot under my administration. Some of the people that had previously worked with me developing the curriculum in high schools were now teachers at Evergreen. So they were basically using the curriculum on Mexican American Studies that we had created, but they expanded it even further and were getting the students to do more research. They advanced what we started out with, and it grew enormously in subsequent years. The climate for the students was good.

One of the things that I most wanted for the students was for them to learn the importance of persistence and determination. With those two things and with, what I would say, average intelligence, a person can go a long way. I would just like it if they were able to gain more confidence in themselves. I didn't want my students to ever think that I gave them something or anything like that. I wanted them to feel that they did it on their own and I helped them. I always wanted to have my students understand that there's no question that education is important in many ways, not only because of a job, but for their own families. It's important for their community. They need to learn how to read the newspaper, how to speak up for themselves and not be afraid.

## "I'VE GOT TO START WRITING": *LA OFERTA*

At about the time I left my job at the community college and was recovering from a major illness, I came to the realization that city policies and the city council were making questionable decisions that were affecting neighborhoods and the children. I was still involved in the San José Unified School District and persuaded them to invite the city council to one of their meetings. I told one of the council members that my neighborhood was being neglected and she said, "We'll have a meeting at your house and I'll come." I asked, "If only three people come, will it make any difference?" and she said, "No." I only knew one person because I had always been working and going to school and my husband was frequently out of state with his work. I was still walking around the neighborhood with a cane, and I said to the one neighbor I knew, "Please give these flyers to a few people and tell them we're going to meet with a member of the San José city council here at my house." We had forty people show up here at the house. We sat around talking about what we liked about our neighborhood, what concerned us, and many other issues. We had really good discussions and asked the councilperson to promise us to come back to another one of our meetings and report to us what progress has been made. At the next meeting we had seventy-five people, then 150 people. Eventually I ended up forming a neighborhood association because the politicians started using me like a ward-boss.

When San José decided to go ahead with plans for a new convention center, a lot of people were being displaced downtown to make room for it. I also became more aware of how the community in East San José was totally neglected.

I looked at the newspapers and saw that they were not doing a good job covering issues regarding Latinos. I was really upset and so I thought, "I've got to start writing," and so I started writing for a Spanish-language newspaper called *La Oferta*.[9] It was amazing that the editor, Mary Andrade, was trying to do absolutely everything to run the newspaper and she almost ruined her health. I decided I wanted to help. I'm not a writer. I don't like to write and it's not something I wanted to do, but I was so upset about how the newspapers were manipulating the community, saying certain things without telling the whole truth. I started to write for *La Oferta* under a pseudonym and I used my middle name "Maria Gallegos" and so I wrote Maria G. Reynolds. After Mary read some of my first short articles, she said, "Yolanda, you know so much about the community, I want you to write a whole article." I was so thrilled that she had the nerve to do that because I did say a lot of controversial things.

The city council was discussing a couple of items that I and other Latinos were opposing. They were discussing the question of tearing down the last Spanish-language theater in downtown San José. Then the city wanted to set up the Fallon statue in a downtown park. The *San Jose Mercury News* published an article about Thomas Fallon saying that he was a great man.[10] Many people in the Latino community were very outspoken and began to oppose the construction of the statue. In the meantime, I was writing articles for *La Oferta* to oppose the statue. Things got worse with all the protests, and Tom McEnery decided that he was going to reach out to the Latino community to settle the issue and stop the protests. He called the Latino media, including Mary from *La Oferta*, and asked her to come to a meeting. Mary said, "Yolanda Reynolds will go to the meeting." About two to three minutes later, she got a telephone call from the mayor's office: "You are invited, but Yolanda is not invited." I told Mary, "Do you want me to go there?" And she said, "Yes." I said, "Are you the owner of the paper?" She said, "Yes," so I said, "Well, then I'm going." They said I couldn't go and that I was going to be banned. I was feeling really proud about standing up to the government and the mayor. That was pretty exciting, but it was also very tense. All the newspapers were coming and we were getting telephone calls from the *Los Angeles Times* and from the *San Francisco Chronicle* because that was a really big effort to squelch freedom of the press. I was invited to another meeting, and one of the editors of the *Mercury News* pulled me aside and asked me, "What are you doing with these people?" And I said, "What do you mean 'these people'? What do you think? This is my community as well, so why shouldn't I be able to do this sort of thing?" I was so mad.

This debate over the Fallon statue happened at the same time that the city's redevelopment policy was starting to affect downtown San José and the East Side. The city's use of eminent domain allowed it to take control or ownership of a person's property so that the city can build something like a road. The city also determines what they are going to pay you for it. City hall was telling us that the property they wanted in the East Side was what they called "blighted property." We said, "Yes, of course it's blighted if the city never sweeps the streets, if the police never come around, if people are parking their cars on their front lawns because the city builds inadequate housing without garages." If city hall doesn't provide services for our community in the East Side, then the neighborhood is what they call "blighted." The city had a plan to tear down all the houses near Julian Street. The only thing that was going to stop them was that Highway 280 ran across there. The city did not reimburse the people who were displaced, and many of them disappeared; they left the community. I thought the community was falling apart. I wrote my articles in English because I wanted people to not be fearful to go to city hall and speak out and to realize that their communities were vulnerable. I'd go to meetings over on the East Side, and I would see that developers were very excited because they realized how much profit they could make if they could redevelop the East Side. I could see the dollar signs in their eyes. I knew that our Latino community was in real trouble.

I wrote my newspaper articles so that people who read my articles would use them to fight city hall. I'm proud because what little I contributed helped more people be aware of what was happening. Almost a third of the city of San José is now in redevelopment. It really started in the late '50s and later, in the '60s. The Latino community protested when the city started to build the Center of Performing Arts in downtown San José. This was all before my time, but Ernestina García told me that she and others were protesting because the construction company was not hiring Latinos to work on that construction project.[11]

I have always felt very strongly about a lot of issues facing the Latino community in San José. I was concerned about the quality of our schools because of my career, so I went to a lot of community meetings. We were all trying to fix the problems with our schools. I also care about the people who have very little advantages and need homes. A Latino *Mercury News* writer once told me, "Yolanda, you're so biased." I said, "Let's talk about bias, what topics do you choose to write about, who do you choose to interview, let's just go right down the line." About three or four weeks later, the guy called me up and he said some other Latino writers had come to San José and that he discussed the whole thing that I had told him. He said, "I have to tell you something, they all agreed with you, Yolanda." I thanked him for letting me know that. When you have a heated discussion, you never know what effect you are going to have on somebody. I don't like it when anybody speaks for me as a Latina. Ask me and I'll tell you what I think, but I'm not going to tell you what everybody else thinks.

## REFLECTIONS ON LIFE

I'm American, but I still always consider myself Latina. I always will because I have my culture, my music, and the art you see in my house. These are things I relate to. They are a part of me. I always try to make my sons understand our history and culture because I'm very proud of it. I will always try to bring these things to everyone's attention and try to do something to end prejudice and discrimination.

I tend to consider myself "liberal," a bad word in certain circles. I really support public education. I think there's a real need for places like Santa Clara University.[12] I think you have to have private schools to keep the public schools honest. We have an agreement among ourselves as a democracy, and this is something that was very important to my family at the time the Americans were coming and they were deciding whether to return to Mexico or stay here. We have our U.S. Constitution. It gives us rights, but we have responsibilities. We pay taxes for hospitals and the government provides us with free public education.

I want all of us to be able to do the best we can, and I have to say that in spite of all the problems this country has, it is a good country. We need to keep our ideals. I have never even thought in terms of goals. Things have happened and I've seized the opportunity, like writing, for which I did receive a number of honors. I was so irritated about something that I decided to write. And again when I went to teach, I felt that there was a real need for somebody like myself to go and do what little I could do. I'm just sort of driven by it. I'm very much a self-motivator, and it just seems so obvious to me that if I want something to happen, I'm just going to have to get in there and try and do it myself. I always gave my students this advice: "You must try because then you have no one to blame but yourself and so you can't really complain about it." I think that everyone should make the effort to do whatever they need to do to bring about social change.

## NOTES

1. Giovanni Pierluigi de Palestrina created Palestrina liturgical music in the mid-sixteenth century. He is most famous for his Improperia for Holy Week.

2. The church in Chimayó, located in northern New Mexico, is the most visited site in New Mexico. According to legend, a friar found a crucifix buried in a nearby hill and after bringing it to the church, it continued to disappear only to be found in the same location. A chapel was built and miraculous healings followed. Dirt from a nearby pit is known for its curative powers. During Holy Week, thousands of people make a pilgrimage to this site.

3. Juan B. Rael, folklorist, author of *Cuentos Españoles de Colorado y Nuevo Mexico* (New York: Arno Press, 1977) and *The Source and Diffusion of the Mexican Shepherds' Plays* (Guadalajara, Mexico: Gráfica, 1965).

4. Folk tales.

5. MAYO (Mexican American Youth Organization) was founded in 1967 in San Antonio, Texas, by José Angel Gutiérrez, Mario Compean, and other Chicanos. MAYO brought college and high school students together in a activist organization to work for civil rights and educational reform. From 1967 to 1969, MAYO played a leading role in the student walkouts.

6. Cal Grant awards are state-funded monetary grants given to students to help pay for college expenses. The awards do not have to be paid back.

7. Luis Valdez founded the Teatro Campesino, the most successful Chicano theatre, in 1967 and produced one-act plays to support the farm workers' cause. The Teatro became a vehicle for consciousness-raising for Chicanos.

8. The phrase *Sí se puede* became the rally cry for the Chicano Movement, particularly César Chávez and the farm workers' movement.

9. *La Oferta* newspaper was founded in San José by Mary and Frank Andrade. See interview in this anthology.

10. In 1846, Thomas Fallon (1825–1885) joined the Bear Flag Revolt, named himself captain of a troop of volunteers, and captured the Mexican town of San José. He raised the American flag over the town's administrative building. He became the tenth mayor

of San José in 1859. Mexican Americans protested erecting a statue to Fallon, as they considered him a symbol of American imperialism and repression of the Mexican population.

11. Ernestina García was one of the community activists who was very involved in this issue. See interview with her in this anthology.

12. Santa Clara University, founded in 1857, is the oldest institution of higher education in the State of California. It is a Jesuit Catholic university.

# IV

# CULTURE AND THE ARTS

# Adrian Vargas

*Adrian Vargas, born in El Paso, Texas, has been active in the Latino artistic and cultural movement for more than thirty years as a theater director, playwright, actor, musician, and producer. For ten years he directed San José's former Teatro de la Gente and was cofounder of El Centro Cultural de la Gente, the South Bay's first Chicano/Latino cultural center during the 1970s. He received his B.A. in theater arts from San José State and a Master of Fine Arts in directing and playwriting from the University of California at Davis. During his artistic career, he has been involved in various theater group productions, including the San Jose Multicultural Artists Guild, Teatro Visión, City Lights Theatre Company, and Teatro Nacional de Aztlán (TENAZ). He served as artistic director of Teatro Familia Aztlán, a resident theater company at the Mexican Heritage Plaza, and as a member of the board of directors of the San José Multicultural Artists Guild and as a member of the board of directors of the Mexican Heritage Plaza. He has received numerous awards, including the California Arts Council Director's Award for lifetime contributions to the arts for the people of California. Currently he is the artistic director of Casa Vargas Productions, a Latino multicultural arts organization, and an adjunct faculty in theater arts at Evergreen Community College, Santa Clara University, and Escuela Popular.*

## PARENTS: LEGACY OF CREATIVITY AND SACRIFICE

My father was born in Mexico City, and my mother was born in Camargo, Chihuahua. My mother was a painter in Juárez. While she was in school, she went to an art school and learned how to paint. She's a great painter. She's evolved over the course of years into a folk artist. To make ends meet, she made original greeting cards and sold them for $60 a dozen. When I was in high school, she would put up a table and start drawing. When she painted birthday cards, she would draw something related to a person's birthday. I always saw her drawing. I know that I inherited my own creativity from her. I found out about eight to ten years ago that when she was twelve and lived in Casas Grandes, she organized a little theater group that would do performances in the barn in town. They would get a *carreta* [cart] downtown, pass out flyers, and charge a nickel for people to come see the play. I didn't know all that so it was just amazing for me to find out she did that when she was a child. So I definitely got a lot of the creative spirit from her.

In the 1950s, my mother, a young female worker and with children, crossed the border to work at the Farah pants factory in El Paso, Texas. I went there once or twice. She didn't tell us much about her job. We just knew she was gone early in the morning and came back late at night. I understood later that companies like the Farah Manufacturing Company were basically sweatshops that used immigrant women to exploit their economic situation and make their profit. A lot of the *mujeres* [women] were *Mexicanas.* Later on in college, I found out that as a result of their exploitation, the Mexican women factory workers organized a major strike and a national boycott developed against Farah.[1] Years later, when I was involved with Chicano theater, I was asked to write some music for a film documentary on that Farah pants strike and the struggle. It's been used in a couple of other visual pieces like *Viva La Causa,* a video by Benito Martínez. So it was nice to be able to get even with Farah years later. My mother got a kick out of that.

When we moved to Tijuana, my mother was working in San Diego as a hotel maid at the King's Inn. She continued to work the whole time that we lived in San Diego. Then we moved from San Diego to Mountain View, California, and she worked in a nursing home as an aide. Eventually, she got a job as an electronics assembler and was hired at Hewlett-Packard. She worked there until she retired.

I was very close to both of my parents, even though in Juárez I didn't see my father that much until we all were reunited in Tijuana. I have good memories of both of them. My parents always referred to themselves as *Mexicanos.* My father never became a U.S. citizen. My mother became a U.S. citizen after my father passed away in 1991. My parents would complain about situations in Mexican politics, but they wouldn't necessarily talk to us about it. When I started to getting involved with the Chicano Movement, they supported my ideas and me. They were becoming aware of all that was taking place. Even though they were not directly involved in any activism, they understood and supported what I was doing. My mother gave a sense of half hope and half faith. She used to take us to church every Sunday, and most of the time her prayers were strong. She believed that *milagros* [miracles] could occur to those that prayed. She taught us to always keep a strong religious belief no matter what difficulties we were facing. She would tell us to have faith and hope. My father instilled in me a sense of pride because he was very proud to be *Mexicano*. My parents wanted us to keep speaking Spanish, so we spoke nothing but Spanish at home when we were talking to them. They would get upset when we would speak English amongst ourselves because they'd think we were hiding something from them. When we lived in Mexico City, my father had a little furniture business with one of my mom's uncles. They put their money together and were selling furniture in Juárez. The business didn't go that well since a lot of people in Juárez would cross the border to buy their furniture because it was more modern looking. My parents didn't talk much about hopes and dreams for our future. We were always hoping and praying that we'd see our dad soon when we were kids because he was out as a salesman. He was selling calculators, not the electronic ones but the old machines. While we were living in Juárez, my father was primarily a traveling salesman, a kind of urban migrant. He was looking for work and trying to sell things to make a living. There was a time when we didn't see him that much and I remember that it was really exciting to see him when he came home.

When we moved to Tijuana, he found work at the Sands Hotel in San Diego as a busboy and dishwasher. From the time I was fourteen, my father played a small part in my life because of his own situation. After my father left the hospital, he still had back problems and couldn't do certain kinds of work. Eventually he sued the company, Beckman Industries, and won around $10,000 to $15,000 and this paid for some of the doctor's bills. During that period of time there was a lot of instability and financial problems in our family. When we moved up here to Silicon Valley, he worked as a janitor. Then he became an assembler. He started taking classes at Foothill College and learned how to be a draftsman and worked as one for about ten years before he retired. It was a really varied work experience for my parents. In the end, they both worked for Hewlett-Packard in Palo Alto until they retired.

## STRADDLING TWO CULTURES

I was born in El Paso, Texas, but raised in Juárez, Mexico. It was common for Mexican women to give birth to their kids on the U.S. side so if they ever wanted to immigrate or get legal residence, they had a better chance of qualifying. We didn't live all that long in the first house where I was born. My family ran into some hard times for a while, so we moved to my grandmother's house in Juárez. I remember most of my life in Juárez although my memories of my father aren't too vivid. I have vivid memories of my maternal grandparents who helped raise me and whose home we used to live in. I have very fond and adventurous memories of when my grandfather would take me to see certain things in Mexico. Since I was the firstborn, he would take me everywhere. He was a very proud *Mexicano.*

When my parents decided to move to Tijuana, I stayed with my grandmother in Juárez to finish the first grade. Before I started second grade, I went to Tijuana and experienced my first airplane ride by myself. They just put me on a plane and I flew to San Diego airport and my family picked me up there. When we were in Tijuana, my grandmother came to take care of us while our parents worked in San Diego. There was one time period when my grandmother had to go back to Juárez so they had a lady taking care of my younger brother and sister, but my parents would take us to school in the morning. San Diego was interesting because it was the first place in the United States that we lived in. We lived in tenements, with people from many ethnic backgrounds. Many Navy men and their families also lived there because they had a naval base in San Diego. African Americans and *Mexicanos* also lived in our neighborhood. The housing was very run-down with graffiti all over the place. People would write on our house, "Mexicans go home. Go back to Tijuana." We reacted at the moment that something, like the graffiti, took place and then went on with our lives. It wasn't until I started reading about racism and discrimination that I understood what had been happening to my family.

My grandmother went back to Juárez when we moved up here to the Santa Clara Valley. My family did not have any relatives living in the United States. Our relatives stayed in Mexico in places like Juárez, Chihuahua, Veracruz, and Casas Grandes. Once we settled in the U.S. in 1960, we never went back to Mexico until 1969 when I had the opportunity after I graduated from high school. My sister Lily and I took care of us and my younger sister and brother.

### NAVIGATING THROUGH SCHOOL: "IF I HADN'T GONE TO COLLEGE, I DON'T KNOW WHERE I WOULD HAVE ENDED UP"

When we moved to San Diego, I experienced culture shock because even though we had lived along the U.S.-Mexico border in Juárez and Tijuana, we kept to ourselves and didn't really go into San Diego much even though my parents worked on the U.S. side. We'd had exposure to the English language through *Frontero,* the

TV program piped into Juárez. You'd try to figure out what Zorro was saying or what Mickey Mouse was saying so we had some exposure to the English language. When I got into third grade in San Diego, I had to figure it all out. The primary barrier was language, and although we adapted after a while it was hard at first because I was in third grade and was expected to know English. When you're younger, maybe from the first to sixth grade, and come from another country, you pick up the language pretty quickly. You are immersed in the language five days a week and have to do the work and there's another *Mexicanito* or *Mexicanita* helping you get it right. Eventually I became a very good speller and I enjoyed writing. I whizzed through that, but writing, spelling, and reading were tough at first.

My parents, of course, couldn't help me adjust because they didn't know English at all. They always placed importance on education by making sure that we always did our homework and that we got good grades. My father taught me how to play the guitar. I consider this one of the best gifts my father gave me. I went to Castro Elementary School, then to Isaac Newton Graham Junior High School, and then Los Altos High School from 1965 to 1969. My grammar school and high school had a diverse student body, but mostly Mexicans, Anglos, *Chinos*, and *Japoneses* [Chinese and Japanese]. Only a handful of Mexicans attended Los Altos High School. In those days, the school district was named Mountain View-Los Altos Hills High School District. White, upper-middle class kids lived on one side of the town and Mexicans and lower-class white kids on the other side.

When we went to Los Altos High School, we broke ties with our friends who went to Mountain View High School because there was a big rivalry between the two schools. My sister refused to go to Los Altos High School, and she made up a phony address and went to Mountain View because she did not want to deal with being only one of a handful of Mexicans at that high school. When I was going to high school there, the big event was that they decided to bus in three blacks from Ravens High School in East Palo Alto. They thought they were doing something really progressive. Naturally, those three guys and we few Mexicans would always hang around with each other. I made friends with nonminority students too, but I didn't quite fit the mold. We were insulted a lot. Even though I'm fair skinned, my sister is *morena* [dark complexion], and I used to have to back her up when people were calling her names. People would make fun of my accent and my last name. It was our own situation that we were dealing with, and we didn't tell our parents about how we were treated. I just learned to live with it.

I received a good high school education although it didn't give me any direction for the future. I was completely turned off to English during my freshman and sophomore years. I was very alienated from the literature that was being taught. Even though I remained a good speller throughout, I was bored with *Beowulf* and the classic English poetry. It wasn't until my junior year that I regained my interest in English when the class included creative writing. I started writing poetry about what was going on in the 1960s, such as poems about conditions I could relate to like racism. The world of poetry allowed me to express my feelings and my frustrations. I remember my poem "Sky Pilot." I got an A for it. The poem was about pilots bombing Vietnam at the same time that there was poverty in the United States.

Some progressive teachers were having us read Ralph Ellison's *Invisible Man* and a couple of James Baldwin's works. I started to understand the world around me. I looked at myself as a *Mexicano* and Mexican American when I was in high school. One of the authors that really spoke to my specific condition as a *Mexicano* in the United States was Ralph Ellison. I identified with his descriptions of the situations confronting black men. My family and I were experiencing similar problems. Ellison reacted in a very angry, graphic way, and I identified with that as well. I was a prime candidate for the Chicano Movement. By the time I got to San José State, there were other kids like me that had the same experience. Martin Luther King's campaigns provided me exposure to the civil rights issues. Nobody at my school did anything associated with civil rights or social change; it just didn't happen. I felt disconnected from a direct involvement in the civil rights movement. I had heard about the farm workers and the grape boycott, but we were pretty isolated in my high school. I was never really that vocal about my opinions, although when we were asked to write essays or poems in my English classes, I always wrote about social issues. I would write anti–Vietnam war or anti-racist material. I was beginning to understand that Mexicans and blacks shared the experiences of racism, poverty, discrimination, and injustice.

After I graduated from high school, I started working and saved up enough money so that my younger sister and I could take a trip to Mexico. We wanted to go reconnect with our family and relatives who lived in Mexico. We stayed there about a month. When we came back from Mexico, it was during the '60s era and our awareness about being *Mexicanos* had just exploded. Our trip exposed us to a lot of the history and culture of Mexico that we didn't get when we were in school. We experienced a really deep sense of pride because for many years, people had given us the idea that being a Mexican is bad and that we were stupid and lazy. Being a Mexican had a very negative connotation back then. We turned everything around and started talking about our ties to Mexico and our Chicanos, a sense of pride and knowledge in our history. We came back from Mexico with a strong sense of being proud to be *Mexicanos*.

When I got to San José State, things started to crystallize for me regarding the world around me. Going to college was a surprise for me. When we were in high school, there was not that much talk about us going to college. We didn't consider college as an option. Even though I wanted to go to college, I didn't know what I had to do to get admitted. I was really unsure of myself. My parents never really calculated college in terms of their finances for us or gave us a sense of encouragement. A counselor was supposed to meet with students during their junior year and advise them about their goals and give them options for careers. I had a C+/B- G.P.A., and the counselor recommended I join the Air Force or the Army to pick up a skill or a trade. I think I said on my own that I wanted to go to college. At the time, I worked at a warehouse as a shipping clerk, but I had other responsibilities given to me, and I was thinking about studying business management. They told me I wouldn't be able to do that. Other students would talk about applying to this college and that college, and I said, "Well, why am I not applying to college? What's for me in the future?" My mother found out about the EOP program through her *comadre* [friend/neighbor] and that's how I got in college.[2]

My family had no exposure to any programs that existed for *Mexicanos*. The EOP was the result of battles that had already been fought in the 1960s to create programs to help minorities. There wasn't that much community-wide exposure to those programs. I went to the counselor and said, "Look, here is the Educational Opportunity Program. They have special admissions and provide financial aid and I want to go to college." She still said she didn't think I was college material. At that point, I said, "The hell with you." I got letters of recommendation from instructors and from my bosses. I filled out my application, wrote my autobiography, and I was accepted. Going to college changed my outlook on life and opened up all different types of things for me.

I started in September of 1969. I had work-study at that time. It's like a part-time job where the financial aid program at the college would pay your way and you get assigned to work for a nonprofit business. I worked at an elementary school at MACSA when I was going through that program.[3] I was able to go through college with the help of student grants and low-interest loans such as the National Student Defense Loans. My parents never had the resources to pay for my college education. They sometimes loaned me money when things were pretty tight for me, but they were never able to save money specifically for my college education because they just didn't make that kind of money.

I was never in the military, but I had to sign up for the draft when the Vietnam War was going on. I had a friend who had come back in a coffin. I was really against the war, and when the anti-war movement started, I backed it up all the way. A lot a people were going to Canada to avoid the draft, and I had considered that if I got drafted, I'd jam down to Mexico. I was just not going to go. My draft number came up, but since I had a student deferment, I didn't get drafted. If I hadn't gone to college, I don't know where I would have ended up.

## EMERGENT IDENTITY: THE ROLE OF THE CHICANO MOVEMENT

I consider myself a Chicano although I identify with my *Mexicano* background, culture, and experience because that's part of how I was raised. But I call myself a Chicano because of the political consciousness that came with being a Chicano and that I carry through in all my work and will carry through the rest of my life. I would look in the mirror and see a Chicano that doesn't particularly look like a dark-skinned Mexican. I have red hair but that also has historical and cultural experiences of being a Mexican. My family and my community did not see me as different; they considered me a Chicano.

I also say *raza* because for me Chicano and *raza* are synonymous. I heard the term *la raza* before I went to San José State and before I heard "Chicano." The term is also used in Mexico. Chicanos are a specific group of people, but *la raza* is everybody. You don't have to be Chicano to be *la raza*. Nowadays, when the term Chicano is used, people are not sure what it means. I will tell anybody who asks, "Why do you call yourself a Chicano?" I tell them that I still believe in the idea of liberation, which was what all those different forces and elements were trying to promote in the '60s. They were promoting the liberation of our people and our communities from oppression and from racism. Those were vehicles that helped crystallize and mobilize the community's efforts to bring about social change. A lot of these changes that developed were transitory because we really didn't have the power to make them stay in an institutionalized way. The influence and gains that were made back then, particularly in educational institutions and welfare institutions, were the result of all that kind of thinking and demanding social change. I used to look up to and identify with leaders in the movement like Juan Olivérez.[4]

When I first went to San José State in 1969, the EOP program sponsored a summer preparatory program for Chicano freshmen that included discussions and presentations on issues that affected Chicano and *Mexicano* families, including the farm workers. While we had heard about César Chávez and the farm workers in high school, and saw it on TV sometimes, I really didn't get to know it in detail until I got to San José State. We had instructors like Mario García who were teaching us Chicano history.[5] I went through a process of learning about the Chicano *Movimiento* and developing intellectually.

The civil rights movement and the Chicano student movement played an important role in my development. The *Movimiento* at San José State and other local issues in San José really affected me. I recall the walkouts at San José State because I heard about them on the news and saw them on television. The walkout at San José State was primarily a demonstration to show that the university was not addressing the higher education needs for Chicanos. There was a lack of Chicano staff, programs, and curriculum material related to the history, the discoveries, and the cultural aspects of Chicanos in the United States. Chicanos protested and demonstrated to bring attention to that issue. Basically, the educational needs of Chicanos were not being addressed because we had high dropout rates. Then, a couple of months later, I was introduced to a lot of people who were involved in the walkouts at Roosevelt Junior High, but I wasn't aware of them as they happened.

I was not at *Fiesta de las Rosas*, but I was home watching television and then all of a sudden I saw the news about this riot and saw police and people getting beat up like Ernestina García.[6] I saw that on television and said to myself, "Wow, man! This is really awful." *Fiesta de las Rosas* was an annual parade that glamorized the Spanish *conquistadores*. People just rebelled against that image. Chicanos protested because Chicanos and *Mexicanos* were experiencing lots of problems that needed to be focused on instead of a parade. I didn't get the full history of *Fiesta de las Rosas* until I went to San José State because I was in high school when it happened. At the time that it happened, it was just another one of those things that made me say to myself, "Shit's happening." There was a lot of protests all over: the riots, the assassination of Martin Luther King, Robert Kennedy, the student strike in San Francisco, the takeovers at universities by students and the anti-war movement.[7] When I came to San José State, I learned about all these things that had happened.

The anti-war movement had a Chicano bent to it because at that time we became aware that there was a disproportionate amount of Chicanos dying in the Vietnam War. We represented about 8 percent of the population, and about 20 to 25 percent of the dead in Vietnam were Chicanos. We wanted to end the draft and improve the general condition of education for Chicano youth. We had a big program at Spartan Stadium that brought in high school and junior high students from all over to hear speakers talk about education. We wanted to expose them to higher education and teach them about their *Chicanismo*, their culture and their history. This program lasted for a couple of years.[8]

I remember the Vietnam War going back as far as when I was in the eighth grade. It was part of everybody's awareness or consciousness that was growing up in that time. It started impacting me personally when some of my friends were getting drafted and dying over there. Of course there was also the mass media putting out the body count all the time and the debates going on in television. Some students groups at my school tried to organize students and get them to demonstrate against the war. Around 1967, Joan Baez came to the Los Altos High School and there was almost a big riot and students were arrested. I was looking at it from the outside since I wasn't involved, but I was aware of the war, but I was off doing other things. I wasn't involved in that in high school. However, seeing some of my friends die over there and going to their funerals began to have an impact on me. I said to myself, "Hey, what are we fighting for in Vietnam?" The answer was "Nothing!" We were losing the lives of young men and were involved in somebody else's internal conflict. Why should we be over there? My consciousness of the issue and a deeper understanding of the issue didn't come to me until I was in college. I remember hearing the body count on the daily news and seeing the images of people getting shot in the head right there on TV and that little Vietnamese girl running with the napalm on her back. Those things had an impact on me. My reaction was directed towards society as a whole rather than at one leader. At the time, we also had civil rights, and a lot of different things going on at the same time. I also became aware of Reies López Tijerina and his *Alianza* in Nuevo Mexico, which everybody saw as a nationwide issue.[9] I saw all kinds of movements of people trying to make a change.

The Community Alert Patrol (CAP) already existed when I became a student at San José State.[10] CAP developed as a very direct community response to police brutality. People from United People Arriba and some other community groups started CAP. People in the community patrol used cameras and tape recorders to document police arrests. The Chicano community had been experiencing incidents with the San José police as a result of the *Fiesta de las Rosas*. People in East San José saw the police as the enemies of *la raza*. The CAP was a way to combat police brutality. The police brutality that Chicanos saw during the *Fiesta de las Rosas* increased the mistrust between the Chicano community and the local San José police. Incidents of police abuse against the Latino community had been going on for a long time and so the community decided to monitor the police. We had access to shortwave radios so we could monitor police calls. When the police arrived, we would have our tape recorders and our cameras ready to record their action. We would stay there until the police left the scene. Then a reform started to take place in the police department and eventually CAP just started to phase out, but it was still around after I stopped being involved with it.

I was in my sophomore or junior year at San José State when I got elected chair of MEChA. During that time, MEChA at different universities in California joined together and organized statewide conferences. When we attended a conference in Coachella, farm workers were on strike. MEChA was a part of my education and a source of strength. MEChA brought together different students who didn't necessarily have the same point of view of how to approach an issue. MEChA made an effort to make the organization very democratic, and the officers encouraged input from all its members. San José's MEChA participated in the educational pilgrimage to Sacramento. About 1,200 or 1,500 students went on the march. MEChA organized consciousness-raising activities for Chicano students so that they would join us when we had protests. For example, we challenged the *Spartan Daily* when it printed an advertisement for the Spartan Bookstore with a Mexican sitting under a cactus tree with a *sombrero* [hat].[11] The next day all the *Spartan Daily* newspapers were in the fountain. We felt good about organizing this protest. We got back at the student newspaper for printing such an advertisement. We stormed the *Spartan Daily* office and we had people hanging out windows and doors. It was just hundreds of people at the *Spartan Daily* office, making certain demands that had to be met so they would change their ignorance or their attitudes and racism.

We also did a lot of consciousness-raising in the classrooms to challenge the stereotypes that people had of Chicanos. The Chicano students at San José State were very strongly influenced by what was happening in the community itself. We supported many community issues. It wasn't just a student thing; it was students supporting the community. We participated in *La Confederación de la Raza Unida* [The Confederation of United Peoples], United People Arriba, Chicano Priests, the Farm Worker Boycott Committee, and a number of other different community organizations.[12] When I was in MEChA, we tried to connect our students to those issues that were in the community. We tried to develop our militancy by going out to the community besides dealing with issues on campus. We didn't want to isolate ourselves on campus. Not only did we want people to come and learn in the college, we wanted the people in college to go back and help the community. It was great!

There were a number of different people that had identified the low status of Chicanos in higher education throughout the state. Different Chicano groups had walkouts, different kinds of protests, and sit-ins. These protest succeeded in pressuring college administrations to establish special admission programs for Chicanos and other minorities. I probably wouldn't have ended up in college if it had not been for such programs.

MAGS [Mexican American Graduate Studies] was created to offer educational experience to Chicanos and non-Chicanos about the Chicano community, culture, and the Chicano experience. MAGS dealt with community organizing and other different topics. MAGS offered a master's degree for the study of Mexican American issues and culture. After earning their master's degree, Chicanos would get into the community or other colleges with the ability to address issues and create awareness about Chicanos. The School of Social Work at San José State was also established as a result of a lot of pressure on the school. Chicanos recognized that the university was not addressing the needs of Chicano and minority communities. Well-trained social workers were needed at community agencies, at the county level, and at the head of county government level.

When I was a freshman and sophomore, I didn't have too much interaction with the MAGS program because getting a master's degree was something to think about in the future. But we did have interaction with some of the MAGS professors. They provided us with viewpoints that were different from anything that we had ever been exposed to in our education. They were very strongly influential to the development of our consciousness as Chicanos. It was the first time I'd had another *Mexicano* or Chicano as a teacher. I didn't know what was going to happen until he started talking about what we would be studying. Then I said, "Oh, OK. Someone is on our side." It was a United States history course, and that was a great experience with Mario [García] because he helped develop the consciousness of a lot of people.[13] I had direction for things that I felt were important, like social justice. I thought I would be able to achieve that through unity with other Chicanos.

At some point, an ethnic studies class was required for graduation. We didn't see too much backlash from the general student population, although there were some students from the student body government that didn't always want to provide funds for Chicano activities. For example, when we asked for money to do *Semana Chicana*, they would always try to say there wasn't any money around or that they could only give a small amount.[14] Then they would turn around and give funds to some fraternity and all of a sudden there was money for their activities. So you see, Chicano students struggled with the Associated Student Body Government. In most of my classes, I got the feeling that non-Chicanos felt somewhat threatened by Chicanos and blacks because we were demanding our rights. We were protesting for the creation of programs dealing with Chicano history and culture.

While I was at San José State, Chicano, black, and Asian students joined together and formed a Progressive Coalition Party and ran candidates for positions in the student body government. They ran on issues that we all identified with such as fighting racism in the institution, maintaining and establishing an educational curriculum that was sensitive and relevant to the needs of the minority people. I worked with the Progressive Student Coalition on several activities and supported their candidates.

What kept me going through all those struggles was a desire to change society. The organization United People Arriba was working in the community, and I asked myself, "What does that mean? My answer? It means unity. Defend yourself. Promote yourself. Make your own headway and do it in a way that makes an impact for your people." There were debates along the way among Chicano students, but everybody knew which side was which. We knew that we had to overcome social barriers. There was the establishment and the *Raza*. Establishment is the term we used to refer to all the institutions of U.S. society that have the power to exclude your community. We debated about tactics, approaches, and priorities, but we all agreed that we had to change the conditions that our people were facing.

I also worked with the Mexican American Community Services Association (MACSA) when I was at San José State under the college work-study program. MACSA was founded to focus attention to the social, economic, and educational needs of Mexican Americans in the San José community. They had different types of programs, from community advocacy to educational, employment, and training programs. We identified some high schools that we knew had certain issues because some of the students had been telling us about their experiences. I worked with students at San Jose High School and James Lick High School. Some schools were not allowing Chicano students to organize some activities dealing with Chicano issues. We also identified different schools where we wanted to have a forum on the Vietnam War and on racism. We were trying to bring community awareness into the high schools and help them deal with the issues. Some of the issues were basic things like students wanting to become organized and not being able to form an organization. There were certain educational problems such as dealing with a teacher that was racist. We also wanted to provide Chicano students with information about college opportunities. I worked with Chicano high school leaders and helped them focus on their Chicano Student Unions to help make them strong. It was a mixture of a lot of different things. I helped two organizations—the Chicano Student Union and MAYO—organize activities such as giving out information regarding the draft, civil rights, and higher education. The goal was to raise cultural awareness and cultural pride through different types of programs at the high school level. We got thrown out of a couple of high schools when we tried to organize a rally against the draft.

We also organized programs that we wanted the community to come and see, like *Semana Chicana* [Chicano Week] at San José State. We'd put on *teatro folklórico* [folkloric theater], mariachi, and also bring guest speakers like Reies Tijerina, Corky Gonzales, and César Chávez. We wanted to go out into the community and have the community come to the college to participate in the programs. We wanted it to become an educational experience and have the community bring their kids to the college and let them know that we were there and expose them to the types of thing we were trying to do.

While at MACSA, I became the program coordinator of a large art project. I ran all the different levels of activities. I supervised staff and did proposal writing to get money for the project through the arts council. The project was for all the residents in the south San José area. At one time, they also put on the Cinco de Mayo and *Dieciséis de Septiembre* [September 16] parade and program before the G.I. Forum took it over around 1981 or 1982. I was also involved with *La Palabra*, a community newspaper. *La Palabra*, *El Machete*, and *Bronce* were local newspapers. I had a couple of poems and an essay published in *La Palabra* around 1970 or 1971. It was not a widely published magazine, but it was distributed to different community centers and to people who were very active in the San José community.

## *TEATROS*: THE BEGINNINGS

When I started at San José State, the Mexican American Student Confederation was transitioning to MEChA and they decided to form a theatrical group. They said, "Hey, Adrian plays guitar, let's get him over here." I knew a couple of *corridos* [Mexican folk songs], so I started playing in the *teatro*. I took some theater workshops and really liked them. In 1969, some Chicanos founded the *Teatro Urbano* [Urban Theater], the predecessor to *Teatro de la Gente* [People's Theater]. They did an *acto* at our student orientation program and it was just mind-blow-ing.[15] My God! Mexicans, Chicanos were on stage, acting and making people laugh. They were putting on the play *Los Vendidos* [The Sell Outs]. I said to myself, "Wow! This is amazing!" It was this demonstration of these stereotypes and Mexicans making fun of their own stereotypes. In those days, stereotypes of Mexicans were all over the place, including on television. I wasn't seeing positive images of Latinos or Chicanos anywhere.

I didn't see too much mainstream theater, just a couple of theatrical productions at the high school like *The Crucible* and *Anthony and Cleopatra*. The performance of *Los Vendidos* was the first contemporary theater piece that I'd ever seen, and it was right there in the throes of what was going on. I loved it! I have some lifelong friendships that developed with some of the people that performed that day for us. They were talking about politics, history, and social issues. That was when I realized how powerful theater and media of acting and performing were and I decided that I wanted to work with *teatros*.

Artistically speaking, our group didn't really bloom until the mid-1970s. The whole time I was a student at San José State, we had *Teatro de la Gente* and we performed for political rallies, social rallies, fund-raisers, and a lot of other different types of events. We performed at Cinco de Mayo programs throughout the Bay Area. We were pretty much the only group in the Bay Area. A lot of the other colleges invited us to perform at their programs. Then, a couple of us in the group thought about it and said, "If we're really going to do this right, we should study more about theater." So we started majoring in drama and theater. We became alienated because of the emphasis on Western culture in our drama classes. What did we do? We started challenging our professors by speaking up in our classes. We'd talk about Chicano theater and Chicano history. Many of us also talked about black arts. Taking these drama classes provided us with a forum because we chose to interact and enter into intellectual dialogue with non-Chicanos about theater, art, and the impact of it on culture. We talked about how our culture meant one thing and how their culture meant another. For our student projects, we would stage *actos*, our own plays based on issues, mostly political ones, grounded in the Chicano experience.

The drama and art departments at San José State were blown away by our *teatro*, but at the same time didn't know how to relate to us. They wanted us to be a part of their thing, and at the same time they saw how original and dynamic our group was. We took advantage of that. For example, I did my senior thesis on doing the publicity for the International Chicano Theater Festival in 1973. There weren't too many foundations or bases for them to evaluate me on what I'd done because it was the first time something like that had ever happened here. You had to present and support your thesis to a group of professors. My work and those of other Chicanos involved in the *teatros* exposed them to our art. We realized after seeing all these negative images in the media that we had to create our own dramatic images. If we did not have the power to run TV stations, if we did not have the power to make Hollywood films, if we did not have the power to have our people's images on main stage in a theater, then we had to create our own images and make our own mediums to get these images and these stories that not only counteracted the stereotypes, but brought out the positive images. We challenged the stereotypes by creating our own personal images of our people and culture through theater.

I saw *Teatro Urbano* as a foundation for social change. I specifically decided to enter into the drama program even though I was a sociology major. We decided to attack the drama department and along the way picked up professional dramatic and theatrical skills like acting, directing, and writing. I taught method acting to the rest of the Chicano actors because I studied it in the drama department. Had I not studied that, they would not have had that technique and perhaps the work would not be as polished or as dynamic as it became. That was the benefit of having gone through the drama department. I picked up skills that I could then teach because the rest of our membership, actors in the group, even when we got to be full time, were not necessarily all from college. We staged several *actos* in the drama department. We saw the *teatro* as a place where Chicanos could bring about social change by challenging the stereotypes about Chicanos.

*Teatro de la Gente* was started in the spring of 1970. A number of students from San José State and the San José community had been part of *Teatro Urbano* that was directed by Danny Valdez, Luis Valdez's brother. Several people from *Teatro Urbano* decided to participate in a more local theater group since *Teatro Urbano* was touring throughout different parts of California and the country. We felt we needed a group that would still do what *Teatro Urbano* was doing nationally but also focus on local productions and develop a local audience in San José. At the beginning, we performed at various colleges and schools in the area. We organized specific performances in support of the farm workers. We wanted our *teatro* to bring attention to some of their issues such as their boycotts and the strikes. Our first major performance was a rock concert benefiting the farm workers where Joan Baez and a couple of other rock stars from that era were performing. We did our twenty-minute *acto*. The play was called *Dr. Huelgaby*.[16] In the *acto*, a woman wearing a *sarape* [Mexican shawl] bursts into Dr. Huelgaby's office. She's covered with Chicano Movement buttons and shouts, "The movement is dying. The movement is dying." Dr. Huelgaby says, "Let me see," and he asks her certain questions and gives a solution, "You need community organizations. You need militancy." We also made fun of Chicano militants. We satirized our own reality as well, but this *acto* was basically about bringing in new blood to the movement. Dr. Huelgaby comes back on stage and says, "I know how I can help you. I need to give you new blood." This, of course, meant that the movement needed new people and more consciousness-raising. Some actors bring out a big jug of Red Mountain wine, and we'd put a tube into it and feed the woman through the IV. We were feeding her new blood! Chicanos proposed different solutions to keep the movement going, but the only real solution was new blood. We were also trying to communicate that the farm workers needed more support and new blood to keep their movement going.

The purpose of our *teatro* group was to focus on the local community, develop a local audience for *teatro*, and address local problems facing the Chicano community in San José. Our *actos* brought attention to these community struggles. The issues were sometimes broad ones, like the farm workers' struggles, but we gave them our local San José flavor. We focused on what was happening back in those times, such as drug issues and education. We also performed music. We performed "*La Canción del Movimiento Chicano*" [The Song of the Chicano Movement]. A lot of music that was coming out was being composed with lyrics that reflected the social changes that were taking place at that time.

In 1973, we started seeing a lot of different dynamism developing nationwide and encouragement. People would say, "Hey, what you guys are doing as a theater group is great! Keep doing it." So while we were in college, we decided, "All right, let's make it a nonprofit organization." Then we decided, "Well, there is also the Chicano visual artists, poets, and musicians on the campus." We decided to come together as a center, as a nonprofit organization, and started generating the effort to get funding from places that had not funded Chicano arts before. Little by little, within a three- or four-year period, we were able to get funding from a lot of places including the city, state, and federal government.

In 1975, we were finally able to organize the *Centro Cultural de la Gente* [The People's Cultural Center] and became a full-time theater company. The *centro* was located in part of a building in downtown San José. We eventually had to move out and went to Madison Community School and set up there. We were intent on getting more funding from the Fine Arts Commission and Cultural Arts Council that was available but had never gone to Hispanic artists. At the beginning, all our performances were free. Sometimes when we performed at a college, such as San José City College or Ohlone College, they paid us but the performance would be free for the audience. This was the philosophy of *Teatro de la Gente*: being for the people, of the people, and by the people. We did a lot of performances in parks, community centers, and churches.

We started touring nationally around 1975, right after the 1974 Festival de Mexico. We were invited to go back and performed in Morelos, Mexico, during one of their religious festivals. We were there for about two weeks. We packed up our props, went down there, and had a lot of very interesting experiences. Then we said, "OK, we can tour," and we traveled to several festivals. We set up a whole structure for our touring such as networking with universities and communities and distributing our publicity brochures. By this time, our plays were becoming more sophisticated. They developed into full-length dramas instead of just twenty-minute *actos*.

## MIDDLE PERIOD OF *TEATRO DE LA GENTE*:
## "WE DREW FROM DIFFERENT PEOPLE, FROM DIFFERENT PLACES"

Throughout the middle period of the *teatro*, we were a full-time company. Even though I was administrative and artistic director, all the members decided on the major goals and projects. We considered ourselves a collective, and although it seemed that everybody could do everything, it didn't work out that way. You had to have a division of labor. I took on the role of playwriting since that was the main thing I studied in college. We would decide on the type of play that we wanted to do and then do some research on the topic. *Teatro* members would then do improvisations around the theme and then discuss various scenarios. Based on our discussions of the scenarios and the improvisations that the group did, I would then go back and come back with a script. The group would review the script, and we would make additional changes where the group felt we needed them and then it was staged. We went into rehearsals, and I'd look at it from the audience viewpoint, directing the formal staging. But at every step of the way, we'd regroup and evaluate everything we were doing.

I think we accomplished quite a bit as a group from 1976 to about 1979. For about a three- to four-year period, we were a full-time theater company. When we started getting funds, we employed about ten or fifteen people working full time. When we held auditions, we put out word throughout the state to other *teatros* for other individuals who might want to do this type of work full time. In addition, we formally auditioned people who were already in the group to become full-time members.

People would come to audition from other groups such as Fullerton's *Teatro Espiritual de Aztlán* [Spiritual Theater of Aztlán] and *Teatro Urbano* from Los Angeles. There were other people that were part of the group that functioned as a support group. Some were involved in the plays, but not necessarily working full time with the group. All of us were members of the *Centro Cultural de la Gente* that involved visual artists and other non-*teatro* [non-theater] musicians. These musicians were developing Latin fusion: a combination of salsa, salsa rock, and contemporary Chicano/Latino music. An explosion of cultural expression developed in the *Centro Cultural.* Chicano artists started to create posters, graphic works, paintings, musical arrangements, and compositions. As *teatro* staff, we not only did our *teatro* work but also supported the work of other artists. In some instances, we organized joint activities, such as when we toured throughout the Santa Clara Valley schools and had a children's program that involved both *teatro* and music. We called our tour "*Música es Cultura*" [Music Is Culture].

The *teatro* took on different kinds of forms. Some were full-length plays with music. I wrote one on my own, *El Quetzal.* A *quetzal* is the beautiful bird with regal feathers that exists in the Yucatán and Guatemala. If a *quetzal* is put into captivity, it dies. It will not reproduce; it just lies down and dies. *El Quetzal* is a story of a *pinto* [prison inmate] who has been in for eight years and becomes politicized in the prison system. He was a young Chicano who had been set up and framed for a drug bust. The play starts with him being released from prison and going back to the barrio and seeing all the changes that had taken place. He tries to be a community organizer and runs into all these different situations that reinforce the political idea that Chicanos are in prison whether or not they're actually in prison.

I coauthored *El Hombre que se Convirtió en Perro* [The Man Who Became a Dog]. It was about a man who's just getting starting out in life with his wife when he loses his job. He looks for work everywhere but can't find anything. He goes to this one place and the owner says, "You know what? Our watchdog just died. Would you do the job as a watchdog?" He takes the job as a watchdog, and the rest of the play is his reactions and things that are going on while he performs his job as a watchdog. Eventually, there's a strike at the company and this man now works as a watchdog and is face to face with his *compañeros* [comrades]. He finds himself caught in a dilemma and says to himself, "Do I want to be the boss's dog or do I want to be with my *compañeros?*" He remains a dog. He's put in the dog pound and then he escapes. That was our first full-length piece that developed out of a collective artistic process.

I wrote the lyrics for *El Corrido de Juan Endrogado*, a song type of play with a lot of music and rhythm and rhyme in the language. Our *acto La Migra* [The Border Patrol] became one our best-known productions. Manuel Martínez originally scripted this *acto*, and eventually I worked on the piece with him. It became a really collaborative piece. I know that it doesn't seem like we put on many plays during the period between 1975 and 1979. But you need to keep in mind that we were one of three Chicano theater groups in the United States who actually toured. Besides doing local performances, we also toured nationwide and in Mexico. We also did some material from *Teatro Campesino*'s *acto* book. In 1976, we produced *La Cantata de Santa María de Kiki*.

Another project involved doing theater with people who didn't have any theater background at all, but had a lot of life experiences. We worked with them to bring their emotions and experiences to the stage. We used paid actors with experience and people from the Chicano community involved in our productions. It was important to actually have people right off the street, from the canneries, and refugees into doing theater. We felt that was important, and that's why we did *La Cantata*.

We had to research our own barrio language usage and our own barrio characters. Our individual life experiences as Chicanos became the source of our characters because we had only ourselves to study from since nobody had actually written books about Chicano drama or comedy. We had to explore our own sense of drama, our own sense of comedy. I was a big fan of the German playwright Bertolt Brecht who created a particular type of political theater during Nazi Germany. His staging techniques influenced us. We also drew from the experiences of the *Teatro Campesino*. Stanislavsky, the Russian actor and director who is considered the father of modern acting, had a strong influence on all of us. Our acting followed his view of what acting should be like.[17]

We also researched indigenous music from Mexico and popular music from Chile, Argentina, and Bolivia. Our *teatro*'s repertoire included songs from just about every country in Latin America. During the time that we were producing plays, we were also conducting workshops in *teatro* for the community. Sometimes these workshops were organized at the *centro* or were taught as a class or part of a class at junior college or a college. When I think back to how many people have been in *Teatro de la Gente*, although I can't remember everybody, I would say that as many as three hundred or four hundred people were involved in it since it started. The faces changed a lot at the beginning, and then, when we were a full-time group, the group stabilized with a regular crew. It makes me feel really good that so many people have participated because our goal was to really be *Teatro de la Gente*. We really did become that in San José. When we toured throughout the Southwest, we made sure that people from the community became involved in some way with the *teatro*. Our plays related to people's daily experiences as Chicanos or Latinos. I feel real good about that because we realized our goals.

Luis Valdez created TENAZ, a national organization of Chicano theater groups, and it sponsored a Chicano Theater Festival that took place every year until about 1980.[18] His idea was to have an annual festival where *teatro* members could see each other perform, perform in each other's communities, attend workshops, and learn acting and production techniques.

Our group played a significant part in this festival. We developed a play in the winter and toured in the spring. In the summer, we held workshops or did some local performances, and then toured in the fall again with the same play. We repeated this cycle until the next summer, which was generally when the festival took place.

We hosted the festival in 1973 and 1976. When we hosted the festival in San José, about fifty Chicano theater groups from throughout the United States attended. We performed our last production, called *Painting*, at the Montgomery Theater around 1982 when the group no longer had full-time members. We had experienced many changes. Our *teatro* always wanted to expose the audience to plays by Chicanos and allow the artist's work to be produced and performed.

## ON THE ROAD TO CHINA AND CUBA: THE INTERNATIONALIZATION OF THE *TEATRO DE LA GENTE*

As a result of our work with community struggles, such as those of the workers' strike against the Farah Manufacturing Company, the *teatro* met people who were setting up U.S.-China friendship groups. This was in 1973, during a period of time where Nixon had gone to China and the doors had opened for some exchanges with China. The Chinese government, along with local friendship associations, was beginning to take delegations of students, workers, educators, professionals, doctors, and others to China so they could see what the society was like. China had been closed to us for many, many years. The *Teatro de la Gente* was asked to be part of a student delegation, and I was selected as the *teatro's* representative. I went to China in June or July of 1973 when I had just graduated from San José State. Our group consisted of about eighteen or twenty students from various parts of the country.

We traveled to different parts of China such as Canton and then up to Peking. We went to Shanghai and a village near the Korea border. We also went into the interior of the country and visited several rural organizations. Having had some exposure and reading some books on socialism and communism, I had a sense of what a socialist society and organizational structure looked like, but in China I actually saw how it worked. It was a system that seemed to be working well for them. They were able to feed a billion people. Mao was still alive at that time. They were just at the tail end of the Cultural Revolution, a time when China revitalized and reorganized the arts to reflect China's social situation. Our group attended many cultural events including Peking Opera, the ballet, films and art exhibits. We visited a couple of universities with programs that focused on China's ethnic groups because China has a lot of different ethnic populations. They had a university that was dedicated to the cultures of the minority people in that region. Students from different regions of the country studied in their own language and their cultural heritage in addition to learning a trade.

My trip to China had a great impact on me and, as a result, on the rest of the work in the *teatro*. I realized that the *teatro* needed to have a clear idea of where we were going. There was a need for an ideology, a political line, and an analysis of our group's focus. *Teatro* members were deciding what Chicano political groups and organizations to support like CASA—*Centros de Acción Social Autónoma* [Center for Autonomous Social Action].[19] CASA focused on organizing immigrants back in the '70s and throughout the '80s. As a *teatro*, we formed alliances because we believed in some of the causes that were going around. So *nosotros compartimos nuestro trabajo, música y teatro* [we shared our work, music, and theater].

Before I went to China, the *Teatro de la Gente* was floundering a little bit because people were graduating, leaving the college, and going on their own way. There was a core that remained in *Teatro de la Gente*, but it was right before we incorporated as a nonprofit cultural center. While I was in China, I learned about the techniques for collective organizational involvement and leadership. These techniques were particularly interesting to the arts because the *teatro* already used a process of collective creation and so we were able to apply some of the Chinese techniques. We learned how to look at ourselves as a collective in the same way that China's farms and industry were organized. We did not put emphasis on a hierarchy, but rather distributed the organizational, administrative, and creative responsibilities amongst the members of the group. That worked really well for us for a long time, and it was also very efficient. It brought us to a point where we could then say, "We want to incorporate, not just as a *teatro*, but as a cultural center along with other artists."

About a month after I had gotten back from China, we opened up the *centro cultural* with the *teatro* and other artists. We had a gallery for artists and a little performance space for musicians and writers. We were in the middle of campaigning to get funds from the Fine Arts Commission. They had never funded a Chicano group before, and we were in the middle of negotiations. After submitting our proposals, we provided the commission with the rationale for funding us, but we also exercised our political muscle since a minority group had never received any of their funds. Then the FBI came around and said they wanted to know about my trip and what I saw and with whom I talked and who else went on the trip. They just talked to me right there in public, with the people visiting the gallery, looking at the paintings and artwork. I told them, "I really don't have anything to say to you, I don't have to talk to you and I don't need to talk to you," but they just kept prying. I said, "I'm sorry, but I really don't have to talk to you. Excuse me, but I have a program to do." Of course, I didn't answer the questions, because as long as you don't lie to the FBI, you don't have to talk to them. I just told them, "*Adiós*" [good-bye].

When the FBI comes down to your cultural center, you can get scared and people don't want to stay involved. The community is going to be more cautious about what song they sing or what image to put on a painting or what kind of play they are going to do. We were not scared because we knew to some extent what our rights were. I was feeling personally responsible for other people feeling paranoid, because I had gone to China and the FBI had come around because of it. The whole experience was just interesting because we were applying knowledge that we had gained in a way that was benefiting us, and yet the FBI was coming around looking at an ideology that was in conflict with U.S. ideology. We were just trying to do a *teatro* Chicano and contribute to the social justice movements.

About seven or eight years after I visited China, I went to Cuba. My experiences in China were different from those in Cuba. China was more of a mysterious experience because we were going to a country that had been shut off from the world and we knew very little about it. At the time, it was more of an adventurous curiosity and educational experience. When I went to Cuba, it was like, "*¡Órale, somos Latinos!*" [Yeah, hey, we're Latinos]. I felt connected to Cuba. It is only ninety miles away from the Florida coast and its revolutionary ideology survives to this day. This creates a special connection. The Cuban interviewers wanted to know all about how we operated as a theater company. They asked us about the kinds of themes we were developing in our *actos* and plays. They read our scripts and asked us for permission to use them. The Cubans were also interested in how our group made decisions. When I was over there, I staged *Soldado Razo* [Common Soldier] with the other Chicanos who were part of the delegation. The Cubans provided us with props and a theater. We had a lot of publicity, and we performed in front of large audiences. *Soldado Razo* was the *acto* written in the 1970s about the experience of the Chicano in the Vietnam War. The Vietnam War was just about over by that time so the play provided audiences with an understanding of the perspective of Chicanos towards that war. It was a period piece. I directed it and played the character of *La Muerte* [Death]. It was an incredible experience of being able to do our art in Cuba and offer it to the Cuban people and have it appreciated. I brought back the Pan-American consciousness of being connected by cultural links to all of Latin America.

I made three trips to Mexico with the *teatro*. The first one was the *TENAZ Encuentro Internacional* [International Congress] that took place in 1974 in Mexico City and Veracruz. As a result of our participation, we were invited to the Festival de Tlaltenango, which was in Cuernavaca. A couple of years later, we were invited back to perform at some universities in the Mexico City area. Each one of these experiences had its own characteristics and dynamic experiences. When we went to Mexico for the Festival de Tenaz, about five hundred Chicanos who were involved in *teatro* attended. About the same number of *teatristas* [theater performers] from Latin America also attended. We were all together in the common festival, almost a thousand of us, performing in different theaters, in the streets, and ultimately performing in front of the pyramids in Teotihuacán and in El Tajín, Veracruz. For a lot of Chicanos, this was their first experience in Mexico, although some of us had gone down touring a little bit here and there. This experience had a big social, cultural, and political impact on all of us. For a lot of *Mexicanos*, this was the first time they had seen Chicanos en masse and heard and seen our art and culture. Chicanos and *Mexicanos* really did experience an *encuentro*.

The second time we went to Mexico, we were a little bit more isolated because we were part of a community festival in Zacatecas, Mexico, that pays tribute to *La Virgen de Tlaltenango* [the Virgin of Tlaltenango]. They invited us to do *tandas*. *Tandas* are outdoor performances on stages right on the lawns, like a circus tent but not exactly a *carpa* [tent]. It's just a covering over the stage and over the people, *amarrado* [tied] here and there. There were a lot of different performers and different musical and theater groups. It was very interesting because we took two theater pieces there. One was about Mexicans immigrating to the U.S. This was a surreal experience because we were performing a play in Mexico that showed the process of Mexicans going into the United States. That piece was bilingual, but we did another piece that was 90 percent in English, *El Quetzal* [The Quetzal]. So the Mexicans had to understand Chicanos speaking English in the theater piece. Then, on the same day, the Mexicans put on a Spanish/English version of *Waiting for Lefty*, which is a U.S. theater piece.[20]

The first time we were in the festival, we were surrounded by intellectuals, academics, organizers, and political people. When we were at the Festival Tlaltenango, it was *la plebe* [the common people]. It was just the *gente* [people] that lived in the town. One day, it started raining during our performance and the tent started to fall, and we had to poke it up while we're performing so it wouldn't come down on everybody. Those were the conditions we worked under. Our experiences reinforced our belief that we were on the right track in getting our *teatro*'s messages across, no matter what the obstacles might be, like the rain.

## THE CURTAIN COMES DOWN: REFLECTIONS ON THE TEATRO

The *teatro* passed through many phases from its beginnings as a student grassroots community *teatro* to a professional theater group and then returning to being a community-based *teatro* once again but with many more resources. In this way, the productions looked professional even though they were a grassroots theater. We had the technique, ability, and time to train people to perform well on stage. Eventually, it just faded away because I did not have the energy to continue, and the people who were part of that last production really were tied to the production itself, not so much with keeping the group going. We had always wanted to do high-quality *teatro*, whether it was grassroots, community based, professional, or semi-professional. At the end, the resources were no longer there and I had a lack of energy and it just dissipated.

The *Teatro de la Gente* impacted the Chicano community in a lot of different ways. We performed where some kind of social or political conflict, like a picket line, or a university event, such as the Cinco de Mayo celebration, was taking place. We performed and sang our songs. It would be a tremendous spiritual uplifting for people. Everybody was out there trying to feel good about being Chicano. We would be part of that reinforcement. The *teatro* touched people on the consciousness level and at the *corazón* [heart] level. We did something that only a cultural art form can do; you couldn't have done this with newspapers. We helped to rally people and to strengthen them with the issues they were struggling with. I think that the common themes in our *actos* are struggle, unity, and the effort to fight back against injustice. I think that people have definitely been able to understand them because to a great extent we're just reinforcing what's already taking place in Chicano communities and tapping into its *logros* [achievements]. Sometimes people are peripherally related to the issue that's being performed. Either way, they paid a ticket price or went to the rally where this particular *acto* is going to be done because they wanted to find out what was going on. Once we have an audience that is somewhat allied with what you're doing, you reinforce the need to be united and continue to struggle in whatever form it takes. There were ups and downs both in terms of personal relationships and financial hardships, but I have no regrets. I did theater in a period in my life when I had the energy and ability to do it and I'm really glad for what I did. I probably would not be here right now talking to you if I had not been in *teatro* because I don't know where I would be.

## REFLECTIONS/*PENSAMIENTOS*

I was involved in the Chicano student movement, in *teatro* and a community agency. I think all of us who worked in the movement made an impact on youth. We educated youth about the need to resist the Vietnam draft and got them thinking about going to college, working on community issues, having pride in their cultural ancestry and the accomplishments of Chicano people. When we went out into the community, we brought the community into the college, and I think we had a big impact because we would bring thousands of people into the college. During the late '60s and early '70s, in addition to making young people aware of why they should resist the draft, we also organized Chicano communities against the Vietnam War. We went to Los Angeles to participate in the Chicano Moratorium, a large demonstration put on by Chicano anti-war groups. In San Francisco, Chicanos in the art community mobilized artists to attend those demonstrations. There were economic issues in the barrios but not that many solutions. We were trying to do something directly with city hall and places that have power to generate resources and commitment to improving the neighborhood.

The Chicano Movement had its biggest impact on the educational system. Although a lot has changed in the educational system, not enough has been done. We still have a high dropout rate of Chicanos in elementary and high schools, although there are certainly more avenues for Chicanos to get into higher education. The desegregation issue was spearheaded by the Chicano community in the San José Unified School District, and after years of court battle, desegregation was implemented in the early 1980s. There were many more Chicanos going into the teaching profession who thereby created and strengthened programs like bilingual education and others that are relevant to the educational needs of Chicano youth.

I had the opportunity to teach a college theater class that was directly relevant to the culture and issues of the Chicano community. I was able to teach students how to start their own theater groups as an offshoot of my classes. I gave them the knowledge, information, and techniques so that when the class was over, they would still be able to have their own theater group in the community. That worked really well. I started groups in Santa Rosa, Sonoma State College, Salinas, Hartnell, UC Davis, and *Teatro de la Gente* here in San José. That same process took place throughout the state. Chicanos who got their education in college developed technical skills to do theater and establish groups in the various communities. There was something like five or six Chicano theater groups in Los Angeles alone and others in places like Sacramento, the San Joaquin Valley, and Fresno. *Teatros* were able to act out issues on stage that were actually taking place in Chicano communities. Audiences saw Chicanos on stage and identified with them. It helped establish positive role models and strengthen communication within the community.

## THE STRUGGLE CONTINUES

My primary interest in life was doing what I could to maintain and develop cultural arts for the Hispanic community that was socially relevant. I always felt I needed to be doing some kind of work that was in some way or another helping people out socially. It's nice to look back on everything that was done. What we did in the *teatro* and other activities shouldn't be forgotten because it's important to our *gente* [people]. I can't say that I'll never do *teatro* again. I'm interested in going to see plays and I've done some theater work with other companies and the new company *Teatro Visión*,[21] but it is not the great, engrossing, all-encompassing obsession that it once was. I can't really say what changed it for me aside from getting a little older, trying to find out what life is going to be like for the rest of my time here, and just trying to figure out how to maintain my happiness and my *corazón* [heart].

Every one of us needs spiritual faith to know that what we're doing is the right thing. What sustains my hope is feeling that I've been developed by being part of a process and knowing that I am still an actor in that process. We can draw on our belief in family unity and our faith to help us sustain that kind of hope. We have to have faith in the spirit, whatever way you define it. We need to have knowledge of our culture, background, and history. This is important because culture gives you values. Injustices are still occurring, and we need to continue the effort to fight back. The struggle continues and it takes different shapes and forms, but that change is the only constant in the universe.

## NOTES

1. In 1972, workers, mostly Chicanas, at Farah Manufacturing Company in El Paso, Texas, went on strike to protest low wages and unfair labor practices by the company and ended in 1974 when discussions with the company were called off after only two-thirds of workers voted in supported of a union.

2. California established the Educational Opportunity Program (EOP) to provide college students with financial aid and counseling support for minority and low-income students.

3. MACSA stands for the Mexican American Community Services Agency. See interview in this anthology with Esther Medina, a director of MACSA.

4. See interview with student activist Juan Olivérez in this anthology.

5. Mario T. García was a faculty member in the history department.

6. See interview with Ernestina García in this anthology.

7. In late 1968, a lengthy student strike erupted at San Francisco State University. Led by the Third World Liberation Front and supported by SDS and the Black Panthers, students demanded a Black Studies program and an end to the Vietnam War. Students shut down the campus for six months. The chancellor of SF State was S. I. Hayakawa, who went on to become a U.S. senator from California. The strike didn't end until the school acceded to student demands and created an Ethnic Studies Department at an American university.

8. Juan Olivérez helped to organize these programs. See his interview in this anthology.

9. Reies López Tijerina was a Chicano activist leader who founded the Alianza Federal de Mercedes of New Mexico, a land reclamation organization. Tijerina, a fiery orator, played a significant role at many Chicano political conferences until he was arrested in New Mexico and sentenced to prison.

10. See interviews with Ernestina García and Sofía Mendoza in this anthology for additional information on the Community Alert Patrol.

11. The *Spartan Daily* was the San José State University student newspaper.

12. See interviews with Ernestina García and Sofía Mendoza in this anthology.

13. See note 5 for information on Mario T. García.

14. San José State students sponsored *Semana Chicana*, a weeklong series of lectures, cultural events, and workshops.

15. Luis Valdez, founder of the *Teatro Campesino* [The Farm Workers' Theater], defines the "*acto*" as a short, improvised dramatic skit. The "*acto*" is unique in content for it deals exclusively with Chicano themes. Other Chicano theater groups beginning in the early 1960s commonly used it.

16. The title of this *acto* is a play on the name of a popular television show, *Marcus Welby, MD*, which ran from 1969 to 1976.

17. Born in Moscow in 1863, Constantin Stanislavsky had a more profound effect on the process of acting than anyone else in the twentieth century by creating an approach that stressed the psychological and emotional aspects of acting. The Stanislavsky System, or "the method," as it has become known, held that an actor's main responsibility was to be believed rather than recognized or understood.

18. TENAZ—Teatro Nacional de Aztlán. The Fourth Festival de los Teatros Chicanos was held at San José State University on June 15, 1973. The purpose of the festival was to consolidate, reveal, and define contemporary theatrical achievements in the context of Chicanos coming to political and cultural power. The most important result of the festival was the drafting of the "TENAZ Manifesto," which established common goals for all theaters.

19. CASA, founded in 1968 largely through the efforts of Bert Corona, was an organization that set out to increase Chicano political awareness and international solidarity. CASA focused on the plight of undocumented immigrants and working-class concerns. It developed close ties to the general Mexican American community and provided militant leaders for organizing Mexican workers.

20. Clifford Odets's 1934 play, *Waiting for Lefty*, is based on a 1934 strike of unionized New York cab drivers. Its major political message was the advocacy of a communist revolution in America. First staged at the height of the Great Depression, it won rave reviews.

21. *Teatro Visión* is a Chicano theater group and the resident theater company of the Mexican Heritage Plaza of San José.

# 11

# Rigo Chacón

*Rigo Chacón emigrated with his family from the small community of Janos, Chihuahua, Mexico, to the United States and as a child worked in the fields picking fruit. He has spent most of his life in San José. Shortly after attending San José State University, he began his career as a news reporter and South Bay bureau chief for KGO-TV, Channel 7, which lasted for more than twenty-nine years. He is known for pursuing stories that capture the human spirit and for his leadership in community service. A three-time Emmy Award winner and recipient of the Governor's Lifetime Achievement Award, Chacón was honored by* Esquire *magazine as an example of men and women who are changing America. He founded the Abrazos and Books Program, which raises scholarship funds for deserving students. He has also served on the board of directors of the National Hispanic University, as past president of the Community Services Organization, and on the advisory board for Inn Vision, an agency dedicated to helping the homeless.*

## CHILDHOOD MEMORIES

I was born in the small community of Janos in the state of Chihuahua, Mexico, approximately two and a half hours south of the U.S.-Mexico border. Interestingly, I was born on November 12, 1945, *el día del cartero* [mailman's day], and a friend of mine once said maybe that's why I became a messenger. I lived in that community until I was about seven years old. My dad owned a small general store in Janos, and he ran it like many general stores in Mexico or the United States. As the owner of the store, he would give out merchandise on credit and got paid with harvest. In the early 1950s, the weather destroyed the crops and consequently destroyed his business because the people who owed him money could not pay him. We were forced to move to the adjacent town of Asunción that was only a few minutes away.

We went through a lot of hard times, but we never went hungry or lacked proper clothing. I cannot say that we were destitute or severely poverty stricken. My dad owned the general store, but it wasn't that he was well off. The general store was simply his livelihood. My dad was a very generous man and is one of my heroes. One day, for example, when school was about to start, a truck came into town and my dad's brother, *Tío* [Uncle] Chon, started handing out *mochilas* [backpacks] to the children in the town. My brother and I didn't get one, so I asked my uncle why we didn't get one. Uncle Chon responded, "Well, you'll get one at home." I persisted to find out why we wouldn't get one there and eventually learned that my dad had bought them for the town's children. Years later, when somebody asked me how Abrazos and Books [a philanthropic organization founded by Rigo Chacón] started, I said the day of the *mochilas*. Even though I was a child, I remember how inspired I was that day.

Life in Janos was that of a typical little town with dirt streets and no electricity and no running water. We had outhouses and would bathe in the nearby creek or in a big tub. We would heat the water outside with wood and then carry the hot water inside to another tub and bathe. We would get a haircut from someone who was willing to cut our hair. It was a small town with a low-level economy. I think to some degree we realized we were poor because we didn't see big gifts from Santa Claus or anything like that. There were times when we didn't have what we wanted, but my parents were hardworking people so I never lacked for any essentials. I'm very grateful for what they did considering that they had so many children. My parents had seven children in Mexico and two more were born in the United States, so we were nine children total. We crossed to El Paso, Texas, and my dad started working making air conditioning pads for ten cents a pad. Somehow, he managed to feed our family that way. He then worked at a series of different jobs in El Paso and eventually got what was perceived as "the good job." He went to work for American Smelting, which paid well under the circumstances. Now I look back at those days and think maybe that's where he sacrificed himself, because now American Smelting is one of the Superfunds in the United States. Back then, in the late 1950s, there was a U.S. Steel strike—not a full-fledged strike but some kind of slowdown—and there was a layoff because U.S. Steel was a supplier for American Smelting. That layoff forced my dad and the four oldest children to make the trip to California. My sister Hermelinda, who is now the executive director of San José's CET (Center for Employment Training); my sister Hortencia, who is retired from Del Monte cannery; my brother Manuel, who is a retired machinist; and my father and I traveled to California. We came to San José to pick crops while my mom and the little ones stayed back in Canutillo, a small town outside of El Paso. We picked crops that summer of 1959, then we went back to Texas and my dad found odd jobs during the school year. The following summer of 1960, we came back to pick crops again. We picked everything: apricots, cherries, walnuts, and pears. We also picked garlic in Gilroy. We picked pretty much most of the crops that were part of the valley back then.

Our world was almost the same as it had been in Mexico. I didn't see any dramatic difference because everybody spoke Spanish. The kids who were first generation or had been here longer would make fun of our accent but not in a malicious way. We couldn't pronounce the word "girls." If you can't speak English, you can't say the word "girls" because it's a difficult word. But my Anglo friends can't say *parangacutirimicuaro* [no translation: this is a Mexican tongue-twister]. It was okay; I don't remember that as a painful experience. We didn't face any peer discrimination in El Paso and Canutillo among our non-Mexican friends. This was at a time when it was not a Latino world; it was a Mexican world because we were all Mexican kids. Two of my best buddies were rich kids from the farms. I didn't think about discrimination much because we were all the same. Our neighborhood was a Mexican one. It wasn't as we see today where we can move our kids from one neighborhood that is completely different to the next one. Because of the way our world is today, I can take my kids to play in a low-income neighborhood and then I can take them to dinner at the Fairmont. We didn't have that kind of world.

I don't think my upbringing is dramatically different than others. We learned the basics like being honest, being kind to others, helping people when you can, and being courteous. I remember one day that my brother Uriel and I were delivering newspapers in the area of Alum Rock Street and Jackson Street when we were kids. He found a tiny toolbox with a couple of screwdrivers in it at five o'clock in the morning and went to an extreme effort during the day to find out who in the neighborhood had dropped that toolbox. It got to the point where I said, "You're not going to find this person. Why are you looking so hard?" Then he said something that I will never forget: "My dad would look this hard." He was right. My dad would have looked that hard. This is the kind of lesson I learned from my mom and my dad. I have said this time and time again that Abrazos and Books, a project of which I'm very proud, is not my project but a product of my parents.

## PARENTS AS ROLE MODELS

My parents had a tremendous influence on me. My mom was born in New Mexico and left for Mexico as a child during the Great Depression. When things became rough in Asunción and in Janos, Mexico, we started looking northward, not necessarily towards El Paso but more towards Juárez, Mexico [border town with El Paso, Texas]. Eventually things did not work out job-wise in Juárez and we moved to El Paso. At that time, there were seven children plus my mom and dad in our family. I have a lot of respect for my parents for many reasons, but when I think of that specific period of my life, my respect for them skyrockets. Here was a relatively young couple with no job, seven kids, one of them a toddler and one of them an infant, and we walked across the border. At the end of that day, my dad had a job and didn't quit working until he was too old to work.

My dad didn't give up his dream about going back to Mexico until it became impractical for him to even consider it. That dream always stays with someone who comes here as an adult. They want to work, earn some money, and go back to Mexico. If they come here for opportunity, then perhaps they come here with a mind-set to stay. My dad came here for livelihood, for his kids, but with the idea that when things got better we'd go back to Janos, Mexico. He doesn't think that anymore, but for many years the heartbreak of his life was that he never went back. He's past that now [his father died in 2006].

I was born into a home led by two good parents, and my political values were shaped by my experience in society. I had a lot of discussions with my dad when I was a young man, and he and I would disagree politically. But my sense of fairness, my intense desire to want to help others was driven by what my parents taught me. I learned about goal setting from my parents. They were schoolteachers who met on a school campus in the little town of Galiana in Mexico, not too far from Janos. They've always been very inspirational people to me.

I don't know that there has ever been a day when my mom has not prayed the rosary. She's eighty-three and she still does it. Religion was very much a part of our lives. We observed the Holy Days of Obligation that are important in Catholicism, especially in Mexico. There is a picture of my older brother Manuel and me after our First Communion that was taken in front of a *sarape* [Mexican shawl] draped over a clothesline that was the backdrop for our First Communion picture.

To this day, I have always been spiritual. When I got married, one of the first things my wife noticed was that every morning I would sit at the edge of my bed and pray for a few minutes before I started my day. I don't remember a time when I didn't do this. I've been very consistent about being religious in an institutional sense, like going to Mass. There came a time when I didn't go to confession anymore because your mind-set changes, but religion is still a major part of my life. I'm one of those people who will walk into a church for no reason. I'll either go out of my way to go to church or just walk in because I am near one. I'll almost always go out of my way to walk into a church when I have something to be grateful for. When I won my last Emmy Award, I couldn't wait to get to a church.

Most of what has happened to me goes back to my parents. The *dichos* [sayings] that I remember weren't told in the context of conveying a lesson but in the context of day-to-day conversation. Consequently, it was an incidental lesson. Many things were taught by example, like stopping off the side of the road to help somebody fix the tire or getting up early because someone didn't have a car and a way to get to work. When I picked crops here in Santa Clara Valley, my dad was my working partner so I was very lucky. We sang together. We laughed together, and because men will be men, there would be settings where there would be off-color jokes in a farm field. There were never any off-color jokes when I was around because everybody respected my dad.

Both my parents always taught us to be fair. The most resounding message I kept hearing from them was to have sense of fairness to fellow human beings. They wanted us to be fair and honest. When I worked at the *San Jose Mercury News* as a paperboy, I would get the newspapers dropped of at a corner and I would count them before delivering them. If you have three hundred clients, you needed three hundred papers. If you get 299 papers, you have to get to the rack to get one to replace it, and at that time it was the "honor" rack. It wasn't locked up and so you could just grab the newspaper. I would pay for it although I didn't have to because the *Mercury* sure didn't need my money, but in the back of my mind I would hear my mom and dad saying, "Pay for it." The message of honesty and helping others was really driven through to me by my parents.

Since we would spend more daytime hours with my mom, she was the anchor as far as doing everything right when we were with her. She was the spiritual guide, the counselor, the one who would help with homework, the daytime anchor. If we did something wrong, it was never concealed from my dad. We didn't do anything dramatically wrong, but nothing we did that was against the rules was ever concealed from my dad. She was a very strong parent in his absence. His absence was driven by the fact that he had to work, but he was a very strong anchor when he was there. I see my parents pretty much as equals. I recognize the different roles that men and women have in life, but as far as my parents go, I see them as equals having different influences based on the fact that they're different people. For example, my mom was very influential in the fact that I like poetry and my dad was influential in the fact that I like politics, government, and news. I learned from both of them to appreciate the beauty of the language, more so the Spanish language because it's their language, but also the beauty of the English language. I like poetry because my mom would read it to me in Spanish and so she exposed me to poetry in Spanish.

## EDUCATION: AN ALMOST "SHATTERED DREAM"

We were always late returning to school because the prune season ended after the school year started in El Paso. In December 1960, my dad could not find a job in El Paso so he returned with my brother and sister to San Bernardino County, California, to look for work. Then my dad showed up on a Tuesday night and said, "We're moving to California." I thought he had come home to visit, and he actually had come home to get us. He said that we were moving the next day. At that time I thought it was a shattered dream. I already had a lot of goals. I was doing well in school. I had a lot of friends, and I had set the goal of becoming student body president. I was a good student, and I thought that this move was going to be absolutely disastrous for me. I still think of that day as one of the most shocking days of my life. I talked him into allowing me to go to school until noon on the day when we left. We left at one o'clock. We lived in Upland, California, for a little bit and then moved to San José, California. We continued picking crops for the summer and then I went on to school.

I also have vivid memories of school events. One of these was winning a spelling bee in our region in Texas because, as you know, if you speak and write Spanish, you become a good speller in English. I won the spelling bee in my region and went on to compete in the statewide competition. I would have gone on to Washington, D.C., if I had won that one but I didn't. They gave me a word I had never heard before; it was an easy one, but I was still learning English so I couldn't spell it. The word was *tepid*, so every time I hear *tepid* it still scrapes my eardrums. Discrimination is so insidious that when it confronts you as a child, you don't know that it's there, but it happened to me during that spelling bee experience. I was in the sixth grade and there were several of us who were pretty good spellers. Most of us were kids from Mexico who had learned the language: like my friends Joey Arrayal, Evenido López, and Johnny Flores. We were good spellers, and we would spell for days at a time and not lose. The best speller among the non-Spanish speakers was my good friend, Rita White. Nobody could beat Rita White. In the spelling bee contest of 1960, Rita and I were the last two standing. We spelled every day for a period of time after school until somebody would miss the word. Then you would qualify to compete at the University of Texas at El Paso, which was at that time called Texas Western College. The thing about spelling bees is that they give you difficult words, but sometimes they'll throw in an easy one that will catch you off guard. That day Rita misspelled *cemetery*, a relatively easy word. The rules are that the opponent must spell not only that word but also another new one. I did and I won the championship for Canutillo, Texas, and all the little surrounding communities. It was a very special day because despite the large population of Mexicans, nobody with a Spanish surname had ever won that spelling bee. Since it was a little community, word traveled fast that I had won the spelling bee, and by the time I was walking home, people in the town already knew that I had won. *Señoras* [ladies] and *viejitas* [elderly women] were saying, "Rigo, *te felicito*" [Rigo, I congratulate you]. My mom made a special dinner and it was exciting.

I went back to school the next day and my homeroom teacher, Mrs. Outwater, who was Latina but her name was Outwater, said, "I need to talk to you after class." She said, "Mrs. Edwards says that you have to compete again this afternoon." I asked, "Why?" and she said, "Well, I can't really explain it to you but one day, on your own, you'll understand." I am assuming she didn't want to go into detail, and in our culture, especially at that age, we are taught to respect authority, especially a teacher, parental, or elderly authority. I don't know why, but despite that training and background I said, "No." I don't know where I got the courage to refuse, but I said, "No, I won't compete because I already won." She was surprised. I don't know what Mrs. Edwards's reaction was. She was the coordinator of the contest and had been my teacher the previous year and, ironically, was a pretty good teacher. I refused to compete and went home. I told my parents the story, and as they listened my mom got a tear in her eye and my dad said, "You know you won yesterday, Rita knows you won, Mrs. Edwards knows you won, everybody knows you won. So if you compete again and lose, it won't matter because you will forever know that you've won. So you are going to compete. End of subject." I competed and I won and then I misspelled *tepid*. That was my introduction to something so painful.

I recently went to a class reunion in El Paso and I ran into Rita. But it wasn't her doing; it was circumstantial and part of my experience. Generally, my elementary school experience in El Paso was good. I had good teachers. I have a good memory for detail so I remember something I learned from almost every teacher I had. The reason I say the situation with Mrs. Edwards is ironic is because I learned a lot from her. I learned more about fractions and decimals from her then from anybody else. She was such a good teacher. Miss Ortega, my second-grade teacher, taught me how to appreciate verbs; I remember she would say "action verbs." Mrs. Flores, my fourth-grade teacher, taught me how to diagram sentences.

I don't remember much about my first-grade teacher, but that was the time when I couldn't speak English. I remember it more as being frustrating than being painful. I don't remember it being at all like the horror stories you hear about teachers yelling at kids who don't understand them. Other than that, I don't remember anything because I couldn't understand my teacher. I couldn't ask for help because the boy sitting next to me couldn't understand her either because we were all immigrant kids from Juárez. I don't remember, however, it being an unpleasant experience the way I hear some of my friends who say they were yelled at or scorned. I don't remember anything like that. I just remember being frustrated that I couldn't understand her. I also remember they had academic tracking: the blue birds, the yellow birds, and the red birds. I was a blue bird because I guess I wasn't smart enough to be with the reds. Second grade was a good experience. By then I had started to learn a little bit of English and Miss Ortega was a terrific teacher. In fact, when I won my first Emmy Award in 1974, I called Miss Ortega to tell her. She meant that much to me. I had a good educational experience.

Elba Duran was and is a special friend in my life. I haven't seen her in more than twenty years, but she had a significant impact on those of us who were lucky enough to have met her when we were children. She was a classmate of mine for about three years. She demonstrated her leadership in the seventh grade during an incident that happened. One student was punished physically for something minor he did in class. He threw a book from where he was sitting instead of handing the book to another student. He was sent to the office and was consequently punished by being hit with a paddle. Juan had been in a fire as a child so he had sensitive skin, and when he came back we noticed that as a result of being struck by an adult with a piece of wood, his skin had broken. We were traumatized. I'm fifty-eight years old and that was a long time ago, and I'm reacting right now. That must be an indicator as to how traumatized we were about it.

Later that day, either right after school or during recess, Elba Duran gathered a small group of us and she said, "We need to talk about what just happened." She could tell we were angry, sad, and horrified, all at the same time. She basically said, "I haven't seen this much collective intensity, so instead of just leaving it at that, adopt that kind of feeling and make a commitment to get educated." I can't remember what her exact wording was, but that was her message. She was in essence saying, "Take that kind of intensity and apply it towards studying and you'll become what you want to become." She said, "I don't know what you guys are going to become. I'm going to become Dr. Duran." One thing I do remember specifically is that she said, "You'll always know me as Elba, but the world will know me as Dr. Elba Duran." And she did become Dr. Elba Duran.

I am sure I became a newsman because of my dad and Mrs. Phillips. Mrs. Phillips was my seventh-grade history teacher in Canutillo, Texas. She had us read the newspaper every night prior to coming to class. That was a tall order because we couldn't afford the newspaper and our parents didn't subscribe since they couldn't read English. The kids would take turns buying it, and fortunately for us, her class was after lunch and so we had a chance to share the articles and prepare for the class discussion. Mrs. Phillips insisted that you needed to be a student of contemporary history. That experience influenced my wanting to be a newsman. I specifically remember the story in the *Weekly Reader* about Van Cliburn winning the first Tchaikovsky contest in Moscow in 1958. I remember that day because I was so impressed that this eighteen-year-old kid from the United States had won the Tchaikovsky contest in Moscow. In 1960, I also remember when John Kennedy talked about the issue of Catholicism because everybody was making a big issue about him being Catholic. I listened to that clip so much that I know it to this day. He said, "I hope that no American considering the critical issues facing this country will waste his franchise by voting either for me or against me because of my religious affiliation. It is not relevant. I am saying to you that my decisions on every public policy will be my own as an American, as a Democrat, and as a free man." John Kennedy was another one of my heroes.

Another memorable teacher was Ruth Cravath, my speech and debate teacher at San Jose High School. She was one of the best educators that ever set foot in the classroom. I would have been a news reporter even if I had never met Ruth Cravath, but I'm not sure I would have done the job as well. She was so fantastic that I have a scholarship named after her.

Going to San Jose High School was a very strange experience for me because it had the same reputation back then that it has today. I would hear people make negative comments about certain schools in San José: "You don't want to go to San Jose High School. You don't want to go to Overfelt High School. You don't want to go to Silver Creek High School." I used to hear the same stories for the same reasons you hear them today: racial reasons. People still say that a lot of rowdy Mexicans go to school there and there are knife fights and gangs. I heard the same stories in 1962. I went to Samuel Ayer High School, which was a predominately Caucasian school, and I did not exactly have a good experience. I didn't enjoy going to Samuel Ayer High School, although I was a good student and did what I was supposed to do. When we moved away from that attendance area, I found out that I had to go to San Jose High School and was dismayed because I believed all the negative stories I had heard. In fact, I was so dismayed that my first day of sophomore year I went to Samuel Ayer, thinking I would get away with it but I got caught. They sent me away and said I belonged at James Lick High School. I hitchhiked to James Lick where they registered me and sent me to two classes before calling me into the office. They said they had made a mistake and I didn't belong in their attendance area either and that I didn't even belong in their district. They told me I belonged to San José Unified School District, so I took the bus at Capitol and White to Twenty-fourth and walked to San Jose High School. I arrived at one o' clock in the afternoon, just in time to get to Ruth Cravath's last period class. I could have waited until the next day, but I was already on the bus so I thought, "I'll just go to one class." I wasn't going to go back home and tell my mom, "I'm not going to San Jose High." I went reluctantly because there were all these supposedly horrible people there, which wasn't true. This class changed my life.

When I got to San Jose High School, I found out that Ruth Cravath was organizing a serious speech team for perhaps the first time ever at San Jose High. She said, "We're going to become a powerhouse in the Bay Area, and we're going to win speech tournaments in this town, and we're going to put San Jose High School on the map against Bellarmine College Prep in San José, against Lincoln High School in San Francisco, and against Fremont High School in Sunnyvale." She said we were going to beat these teams who were the powerhouses at the time. I started going to speech tournaments where nobody looked like me, but we set out to win and we did. We beat some of the best schools in the Bay Area in public speaking because Ruth Cravath believed in us. Ruth Cravath was the wife of a vice president of Chevron back when it was Standard Oil. She lived in Los Altos Hills and led a comfortable life. Ruth Cravath really had no need to work, but she went back to teaching because the principal was a friend of hers who asked her to come back to teach speech. I ended up in her class, and she could tell that I could get up and speak so she took me under her wing and remained my friend until she died. I was one of the four people who scattered her ashes; that's how close she was to me. The first day I met her she said, "I'm going to make you a speech champion; we're going to win the Bay Area title for San Jose High School," and we did. I've been fortunate in that other people who are close to me in my life have complemented what I've liked.

It was very rewarding when we won speech tournaments that put San Jose High School on the map, especially when we went to the state tournament three years in a row. I just wanted to win. We especially wanted to win against Bellarmine, a private boys Jesuit Catholic college prep school in San José, because nobody could beat them. Bellarmine, Fremont High School in Sunnyvale, and Lincoln High School in San Francisco were the powerhouses in public speaking. You may find this hard to believe, but in many ways I'm a shy person, and winning humbled me. I was a bit embarrassed that I won. In fact, there is a picture that shows that I'm surprised as if I were thinking, "Oh, I won!" However, I wasn't shy while giving my speech. When I saw all those guys get up and speak, I could tell which one was the one I would have to beat. I remember thinking to myself, "Okay, that guy is very good but I can beat him, but it is going to be difficult." There was a guy from Bellarmine who beat my perfect record junior year.[1] He beat me in the last tournament of the year, and I was devastated. He had a perfect record going during his senior year, and I ruined it. Somebody told me he's now a congressman in Ohio.

Running for student body president at San Jose High School had always been a goal of mine. I didn't know where I was going to be student body president, but that's where I ended up in high school and I always wanted to be student body president. What added impetus to this goal was a guy in Samuel Ayer High School. I went to Samuel Ayer, an old high school in Milpitas, during my freshman year. Ron, the student body president, welcomed the freshman class and he said, "There are 463 of you here today. By next year there will be 380 of you. By your junior year there will be 250. By your senior year there will be 190." Although I knew that was true, I didn't like the fact that he was delivering a negative message. He said, "Only one of you will be student body president," and I remember thinking, "You're absolutely right and that's going to be me." It wasn't arrogance that I felt, but it was a recognition that his message was negative and only the last thing he said was positive. I grabbed onto that positive aspect, and by then I had already decided to become student body president.

I decided to run for student body president because there had not been a Mexican president at San Jose High School since 1928 and I decided that that couldn't happen again. When I ran for office, *Mexicanos* [Mexicans] who had never bought a student body card bought one. At that time, the school had what amounted to a poll tax. Students had to own a student body card to vote. It was an exciting and fun time in my life. I ran but it was a coalition of different ethnic groups that got me elected. I have never really made my ethnic background an issue because I have always thought that it speaks for itself.

My parents had a tremendous influence on me regarding education. I liked school a lot, more so than my siblings. It's not that my siblings were not good students because they were, but it was just that I thrived on school. I didn't like college as much as I liked high school and elementary school, but I wanted to do well. I wanted to win the spelling bee. I wanted to be student body president. I wanted to win the speech tournaments. I'll be honest with you, I was driven, especially in high school, by the fact that no *Mexicano* had ever done that. When I heard that no *Mexicano*—we used to say *Mexicano* back then because the terms Latino, Chicano, Hispanic didn't exist—*había ganado el* [had ever won the] spelling bee. I said to myself, "Well, let's change that." I remember having that kind of mind-set, and I was fortunate that I was a good student.

I was still in high school when I was invited to a meeting of MACSA (Mexican American Community Services Agency), which had received a large grant. I was feeling overwhelmed, which speaks to my shyness, when Lino López from MACSA asked me to start what was the equivalent of MACSA at the high school level. Lino, who was a very soft-spoken man, very methodical, just a low-spoken *viejito* [term of endearment for an elderly man] kind of approach, just sat there. He was very effective. He got a lot of questions from others at the meeting because all these people who were sitting at the meeting with Lino were questioning him. They asked him, "Where did you come from? How did you get this money?" It was an educational experience for me. If it was alien to these guys, imagine how alien it was to me because I was a kid. He told me that I could start an arm of MACSA at the high school level and call it whatever I wanted. I came up with a name and he said he liked it. I adopted the name MAYO: Mexican American Youth Organization because *Mayo* [May] is such a significant month.[2] Cinco de Mayo—May 5—is a Mexican holiday that celebrates the victory of Mexican forces against the invading French army in 1862. I asked him what he wanted MAYO to be and he said whatever I wanted it to be. It became a scholarship organization where we raised money for scholarships for kids who couldn't go to San José State University. It wasn't easy to start this organization because it was new and there was a chance it could be misinterpreted by the faculty. I thought it might be considered a separatist group because there had never been such a student group. I was worried that it would be interpreted as that, and maybe that's why I first focused on scholarships. We thought, "Who's going to take issue with that?" I organized a meeting with Lino and the administration so he could explain to them what MACSA was. That meeting worked wonders because the administration saw it coming from a professional who could present his case. Then they saw the benefit in it, so MAYO actually became very successful. We had car washes and other small fund-raising events. We didn't know how to do anything else to raise money. We also organized peer groups to pressure students who could achieve but were not achieving. We would lean hard on them and tell them, "Look, if I'm getting 3.8 grade average and five years ago I couldn't speak English, what are you doing with a 2.1 grade average and you were born here?" The reaction was mixed, but I think some students became college graduates because of that peer pressure. There weren't too many of us who were in student government. MAYO wasn't only at San Jose High. Olga Vasquez from Gilroy High School started her own chapter at Gilroy. Jesse Delgado at San Jose High School was an upperclassman that was helping me. A guy named Toby Solórzano at Gilroy High School and Frank Villa at James Lick High School also started chapters. We just did it. I hope it made a difference. MAYO eventually had chapters throughout the Southwest and then became the Chicano Student Union. One of the first ones began right there at San Jose High School.

## THE CHICANO MOVEMENT AND POLITICS

I graduated from high school in 1965. The Chicano Movement started shortly after that, actually, more in the late 1960s. The Chicano walkout at San José State University's commencement represented a key event in the Chicano Movement. Graduates from San José State don't know the turmoil that must have gone on in the minds and the hearts of the young men and women who decided to walk out of their own college graduation. That had to be a very difficult decision. In most cases, it was the first time in the history of the family that there was a college graduate.

If I had been there and decided to walk out, I think my parents wouldn't have liked it. My dad probably could have understood it, but my mom might have seen it as defiance of authority. I wish I had been there when it happened. There was anger in the community because it was seen as very anti-American and separatist. The community thought, "How dare they insult the integrity of a commencement!"

It wasn't well received by the general public. There were also significant sectors within the Mexican community who didn't agree with the walkout.

Other protests started in 1967 and 1968 and later became more ignited by the death of the newspaper reporter from *La Opinión* in Los Angeles: Rubén Salazar. He was killed during the 1970 Chicano Moratorium, a demonstration in Los Angeles by Chicanos against the war in Vietnam. The protest over the *Fiesta de las Rosas* in San José was one of the key events that happened in the community that angered a lot of people. I think that created a catalyst. The *Fiesta de las Rosas* parade was commemorating part of history that would be considered insulting to today's Mexican American community because it harked back to the Spanish heritage. It formed a catalyst for frustration, anger, and involvement. It coincided with Lyndon Johnson's War on Poverty and the emphasis of getting people involved in community services by providing federal funding sources.

San José changed along with the country. For example, it was during this time that Al Garza became a councilman. It's too bad that he eventually didn't do well, but he opened the door for other appointments. Those were pre-steps to Ron Gonzales becoming the present mayor of San José. This perhaps isn't understood by today's generation because it took place too long ago and these political building blocks are not as visible.

The term "Chicano" is used to refer to a movement, a call for social change: *Chicanismo*. One of the reasons it took me a while to accept it is because I used to see it as a huge collective cop-out to adopt a slang word [Chicano] for a group of people. The reason I saw it as a collective cop-out for a long time was because I think white America has historically denigrated successfully the word "Mexican." That's why you hear people say he's Filipino, he's Italian, he's Portuguese, and he's Mexican American. Mexican is the only one they have to soften with the word "American." Nothing else has to be softened so there's still some perception that the word "Mexican" needs to be uplifted a little bit. When the word "Chicano" was accepted and adopted as the name of a group, I saw that as a cave in and resented it. Italians don't call themselves anything else. The issue is not about us all being American. I'm not talking about that because of course we're all Americans. I'm talking about identifying our ethnicity, and we are the only ones who hyphenate for a comfort zone safety. By using the term "Chicano," I felt we were saying, "Okay, we'll give you a word that makes you feel comfortable because I know 'Mexican' makes you feel uncomfortable." It still does today! I have friends who say Lloyd LaCuesta is Filipino, Vick Lee is Chinese, and Rigo is Mexican American. I think, "Why am I not Mexican?" My parents were never in a setting where it became a discussion. They were two folks with nine kids, working all the time, so they weren't in a setting where it became an issue. They probably reacted against the term like so many other people, but now they fully understand it. I also recognize that there are people who will never say "I am Mexican." Luis Valdez would never say, "I am Mexican" because he says, "I am Chicano" and I understand and respect that. I'm Mexican. It could be argued that in my case there would be an asterisk to it because I am Mexican. I was born in Mexico. But I feel my kids are Mexican—they were born here in San José. They'd say Mexican, but they don't get insulted if somebody calls them Chicano. They're okay with it either way; it's not an issue for them. If I were in Europe, I'd say I'm American, but I have an issue with that, too. I have an issue with Americans calling themselves Americans because Americans are from the Aleutian Islands to the tip of Argentina. There is a national arrogance in the United States who adopted the term "American" for its population. A baby born right now in Buenos Aires is American as we are, but this country doesn't call him American. He's American! He's born in South America. Historically this country decided that the term "American" applies only to people born within the United States. Vicente Fox [Mexican president from 2000–2006] is American.

Protest is an imperative for change and an imperative of democracy although certainly not violent protest. I believe that elections are a form of protest. I was in Mexico City when the Zapatista sympathizers marched from Chiapas to Mexico City. It took days and it started as a couple of hundred people, but by the time they got to Mexico City, there were probably a million people marching from every walk of life. I was staying at a hotel right on Reforma Street and couldn't go anywhere because this march lasted ten hours.[3] All our plans were destroyed because we couldn't move, and there was a man from Cleveland on the same balcony with me who said, "Don't you just hate this?" I said, "No, I actually love it!" He complained that we couldn't do anything, and I said, "Well, think where they're coming from. If they're willing to march with babies in their arms for hundreds of miles, they probably have a better reason than we have for going to dinner to a restaurant. I don't mind it. They can protest all they want. They're not breaking windows, they're not hurting anybody, and it's not a riot. They're delivering a message. They can deliver it all day long. I don't care. I can go to a restaurant when I go back home. Protest is an imperative of democracy."

## COMMUNITY ACTIVISM: "SHIFTING GEARS"

I think my involvement with the Community Service Organization [CSO] was an extension of being involved in high school. I got involved in CSO when I was twenty years old. I had been a very active student. I was student body president and got involved in everything. I was simply shifting gears into an adult involvement when I joined CSO. I became president of CSO in 1968. I was originally hired by CSO as an employee to run an immigration and naturalization project. Then I resigned to take a job in a loan office, and since I was no longer on staff at CSO, I could go back and run as president. By then I knew the organization, so I felt that I could serve some purpose as president.

I became involved with CSO because it was a community organization helping people and it was located in my neighborhood, walking distance from my house. I also knew people who were already involved so I started showing up as a curious volunteer and then eventually I ran for president of the organization. I was president during 1968, and it was interesting because the membership was much older than I was. I went to San Jose High School with a young lady whose grandfather was one of the members of CSO when I was president! So that gives you an idea about the difference of age group among the membership. We helped people with immigration problems and were an information and referral center. I was president at the time of social turmoil. The student protests here at Santa Clara University and San José State were starting to become significant. But CSO wasn't a type of organization that was involved in marches or demonstrations. It was a low-key organization that helped folks and it is still that way today.

The *Confederación de la Raza Unida* was starting to emerge at that time I was involved with CSO.[4] They were a much more activist group than CSO. CSO members just needed somebody to talk to them. These were voiceless people, and that's why I got involved with CSO. My nature was not to be like the people who were organizing the *Confederación de la Raza Unida*. We each served a different role, and occasionally the people in the *Confederación*—friends of Sofía Mendoza and Ernestina García—would let it be known that we were too passive, but it was never antagonistic. The arguments were, "CSO is not going to go protest in front of the mayor's house," which was true because we were different kinds of people, different kinds of organizations.

I think that Sofía Mendoza and Ernestina García became voices that were not only loud, but also eloquent and committed. They made their presence known. So city hall, and I don't necessarily mean just San José City Hall, but city halls in general, started listening to the issues that these folks were bringing to the discussion table.

CSO was more of an information and referral organization and not an activist organization, as I said before. It was there to help people know about health services, their rights as citizens, rental problems, landlord abuse problems, and those kinds of issues. In contrast, the other organizations were talking about issues that needed attention by the city council in legislative terms. At the same time, during the 1960s, people like Reies López Tijerina in New Mexico and Corky Gonzales in Colorado were becoming involved. There was a societal adrenaline that led these leaders and their followers to say to the governmental system, to the educational system, to the institutions, "There are a lot of things that need to change." I wasn't part of that process; I was simply part of CSO. I was just the president of CSO and a person trying to feed a young family. I did what could be done to help people within that framework and raised funds whenever I could for scholarships. I've always wanted to do that because I went to school with so many people who couldn't afford to go to college.

Back then, community organizations like CSO and the *Confederación* played different roles, but we didn't confront each other because of the difference in our roles. To this day, there is mutual respect between Sofía, Ernestina, and myself. It was a great experience to be involved with CSO, but I had to leave because I couldn't afford it. I was a twenty-one-year-old dad with two kids, working and broke, living in a one-bedroom apartment. I had to move on, make a living, and pursue my goal of broadcasting, which I did three years after I left CSO.

When I got involved with CSO, César Chávez had already been gone from CSO for quite a while because he was president in 1952 and I was president in 1968. By the time I heard about César Chávez, I was already a sophomore in high school and he was picketing the Safeway where the Mexican Heritage Plaza is today. My first meeting with Chávez was at the CSO National Convention in Visalia, California. That was a striking moment for me because he was a speaker and at the end of a fast. Imagine, being twenty or twenty-one years old and meeting César Chávez when he is being helped to go to the podium because he can't walk and you're seeing César Chávez for the first time in your life. I was sad but I was just full of admiration. I knew I was standing in front of an American hero. I was honored to be the master of ceremonies at the unveiling of his stamp because I remember the day I saw him and it was an overwhelming moment for me. It wasn't like he walked up; he was carried to the podium. It was quite a moment ,and I don't know if there was anyone there without tears in their eyes because it was pretty impressive. César Chávez was talking about *el campesino* [the farm worker] and the rights of farm workers, delivering the same message for *campesinos* that Samuel Gompers had delivered earlier in the century.

I'm not sure Chávez changed my life so much as added inspiration to my life. Although I had been a farm worker, his impact on me was more of an element of inspiration than a direct impact. When I was a farm worker here, most of the time I ended up working in places where you almost didn't need the United Farm Workers Union because I happened to be lucky and worked for fair employers. I worked for some farmers who were so fair that UFW would never have been needed if every farmer were like that.

## NEWSCASTER: A FIRST

I tell people that Pancho Villa changed my life.[5] When I was at Channel 11 in San José—I was there for two and a half years—I took my boys to Chihuahua, Mexico, during their summer vacation. I was driving by Tenth Street where the Pancho Villa museum and the former home of Mr. and Mrs. Villa are located. I saw soldiers out on the street. You can't be a newsman and walk past a bunch of soldiers without wondering why they're there. I turned around and asked them, "What's going on?" There were too many soldiers there for it to be normal. They said, "No, nothing. We're just the contingent in charge of watching the Pancho Villa museum." I didn't even know the museum was there. I took the boys out of the car and went inside to look at it. It's a fascinating place. His car is there, riddled with bullets from his assassination. I saw this elderly lady sitting there and found out she's Luz Coral, *viuda de* [widow of] Pancho Villa. This took place back in 1973. I started talking to her and I asked her, "If I make arrangements for you to go to San José, California, would you go? I work for a television station and I'd love to do a one-hour interview with you." She said, "Yes, I'll go but I'll never see you again." I asked her why she said that and she said, "Because at least two hundred reporters have told me the same thing from the United States and they've never come back." I told her that I would come back. I made arrangements and that program won an Emmy, which got me the job at Channel 7, which changed my life. That's why I tell people that Pancho Villa changed my life.

I absolutely think that these kinds of chain of events are the power of God, but I also agree with John Kennedy. In John Kennedy's inaugural address, the last thing he said was "Let us go forth to lead the land we love asking His blessing and His help but knowing that here on earth God's work must truly be our own." I think that's true and God gives us the power to do His work, but it has to be our willingness to do it. Certainly the ability is a gift and that was John Kennedy's closing line.

I'm not a shy person professionally but I am shy personally. For example, at high school dances, the guys usually cross the floor to ask the girls to dance. I don't ever remember doing that or striking up a conversation in an elevator. I was shy in all the settings where you find shyness, sometimes even now. But I'm not shy when I'm working or competing. My shyness is probably cultural, going back to Janos. I don't have enough of an education to analyze it, but I think it had something to do with the totality of my background. Perhaps it's the spelling bee episode, but there is definitely something that makes me personally shy. When it comes to being *Mexicano* [Mexican] in a world where *Mexicanos* [Mexicans] have not been usually active or successful, I take it as a challenge. I'll thrive on that not for reasons of defiance or *Mexicanismo* or *Chicanismo*. I just think that we haven't been there and we need and deserve to be there. We're good but with all due respect in so many ways we're better than good. I can speak the language [Spanish] of twenty nations, which many of my friends can't. I can understand the emotions of the people in those twenty nations based on how they express themselves in their native language, which many of my friends can't. I can help somebody who's in a predicament and has a language barrier, which many of my friends can't. When there's a chance to be where we have not been, I say, "Let's go." I say this not in an arrogant or defiant way but in an exciting way, like winning a speech tournament or an Emmy. Several years ago, Channel 7 put up 450 billboards throughout Menlo Park to Gilroy that said something like, "Rigo Chacón is Channel 7 news" with my picture on it. That's another incident where I thought, "There's never been a Mexican on that many billboards." That was my first reaction because that was huge; it had never been done. I wasn't thinking in terms of myself but as a Mexican American. My first reaction was: "Yes! That's a first! That's a first for us!" And if it happens again, it's no longer a first; it becomes accepted, which means we have made some strides. We don't get shocked at seeing African Americans on commercials anymore and that means that they have succeeded.

When I was a child, I was an immigrant farm worker. I identify with this experience and I love that part of my life. That experience taught me many lessons. I have friends today who were my friends back then and some did not do well. I run into homeless people who were fellow farm workers and this breaks my heart. Some of the greatest experiences of my life came from my experiences as a farm worker. The decisions I make today, especially as a newsman, were driven by those experiences. Channel 7 would sometimes give me an assignment about hot weather, for example, when it was about 102 degrees. This is a trite assignment that every television station gives to one of its reporters. Most reporters would go to the Santa Cruz beach, Raging Waters Theme Park, or Great America Theme Park—all the places where people were enjoying the hot weather. I would go to places where people were working outside and were enduring the hot weather because I know what it is to endure the hot weather. My experience as a farm worker gave the television viewer a different perspective about the hot day. The hot day is not running along the beach in Santa Cruz. A hot day is picking crops in Morgan Hill or putting down asphalt on Pierce Avenue in downtown San José or putting tile on a roof in Gilroy. That's a hot day; tossing a beach ball in Santa Cruz is fun. Management actually enjoyed it because it was a different idea. It was something that was unexpected so it worked in their favor.

As a reporter, I wrote my stories accordingly. I never violated the definition of a press pass, despite my strong feelings on a given subject. I don't mean this self-servingly, but because I am a Spanish-speaking immigrant and because I grew up here and because of my life experience, the totality of these elements allowed me to cover a story more fully. Was I a biased messenger? No. I was an unbiased and experienced messenger for the issues and concerns of the San José Latino community. I knew what they were saying because I lived next door to them, grew up with them, worked with them, and arrived from Mexico with them. They were my friends. I covered the student occupation of the president's office at this university [Santa Clara University]; the people who were arrested were friends of mine. I believe I covered this story objectively. Were the students heard in the news reporting? Absolutely they were heard. Was the administration heard? Yes, the administration was heard, also. Were they equally heard in other media outlets? I would say with certainty that they were not, because I could approach them and they knew me and I knew what they were saying. I was part of the generation of on-camera people who were unknowingly among the first part of the Chicano Movement. The fact that my face or the way I speak the English language or the way I pronounce my name or the fact that I was on television was part of the movement. It seemed incidental to me, but it was a part of the movement. I'm not sure I realized that until I got older. I realize it fully now. I'm not saying, "I, Rigo Chacón, made a difference." I'm saying the fact that a Latino who happened to be named Rigo Chacón became part of the most powerful medium in this country was significant and made a difference.

The critics of my television reporting are principally people who take exception to the fact that I say "Rigo Chacón" and use a Spanish pronunciation. They're the bulk of the critics. They criticize how I pronounce my name. I say my name the way my parents say my name. Why should that be criticized? But barring that, it's the only time I make my ethnic background an issue. The way I pronounce my name is not making it an issue. I'm just pronouncing it the way my dad pronounces it. It's not flag waving; that's my name. My name is not Rigo [English pronunciation]. My name is not Chay-con [English pronunciation]. My name is not Rye-go. My name is Rigo. My name is Rigo Chacón [Spanish pronunciation]. If you ask my dad what my name is, this is what he'll say and so that's what I say. It's not a statement; it's my name but people see it as a statement. The television station never came out and said it was a problem. Over the years, I could sense that there were people in management who would prefer that I didn't pronounce my name in Spanish, but nobody ever came out and said it and thank goodness for this because then it would have been a discussion.

I used to get hate mail when I became a news reporter. When I heard my colleague Len Ramírez say, "Rigo has a lot of guts. It took a tremendous amount of courage to be the first Latino in the Bay Area," I thought of how painful the days were when I used to get hate mail. That's why I can now say I recognize that our presence was part of the movement. If my presence generated hate mail, then there was something significant about that presence that bothered people, or moved people to act negatively or positively. I now recognize that the impact of the first minorities who were hired to be on camera was very significant. When I hear Len saying that, I remember that being the first Latino in television news in this area was a painful experience. I have said in an interview that "here is it more than thirty years later and it's still painful." Some of those letters I got were expressions that were pretty offensive and designed to wound the human spirit and did.

They didn't damage me; they just wounded me. I'm a big boy and I can take that. I worry about what happens to the little boy or the little girl who encounters the people who wrote me those letters. What happens to those people? About five years ago, I went to cover what was classified as a tornado in Sunnyvale. A carload of young men drove by and mocked a Spanish accent to me, to my face. I had been a professional television journalist for more than twenty-five years at that point and these young guys were doing that, not hesitating for a second about doing it within five feet of my face. They didn't do me any damage whatsoever. They damaged somebody wherever they were going to. They damaged some child, a young lady because from racism extends sexism and other negativisms that exist in society. I was wounded, but wounds heal. Damage that's more than a wound can't heal, and those people who wrote those hate letters in the early years of my career more than likely went on to do some damage. I think to be racially confronted should be seen for what it is. It should be seen as a challenge, an obstacle that should be used as an opportunity to break it down, to challenge it, to try to undo it. I would say to these people, "Yes, I know you are resisting me simply because of my ethnic background and for no intelligent reason, and that's too bad. I have a goal to accomplish and you're in the way. Please step out of the way." That's the attitude they have to take. That's what we all must do. We just get working and get going at it. In some situations, a lot of people went through experiences that were much more painful than anything I could have gone through. When I say that the reaction from some elements of society when I started in TV prompted pain, that's simply a statement of fact. It did. But it's miniscule when you read history and see what others have gone through.

I'm very fortunate in that a lot of things have happened for me. I'm the father of four sons. And although I interpret the accolades I have shared with you, I recognize that, undeniably, they're still for me. They still make me cry. When I retired from broadcasting, there were thirteen separate events where I was given an award. There comes a time when that overwhelms you as a person; you're humbled and you're grateful. I had a very long career and intense career, yet I never saw anybody get thirteen events after they retired. I am very lucky and there are times when I have to accept that they are recognizing "Rigo." I always, however, see myself as a product of a lot of people. It's not like an athlete; I wasn't born a fast runner. I was born a kid in Janos, Mexico, whose life crossed the paths of a lot of people who helped me. I wasn't born with the ability to do all this. A lot of elements played a part in creating circumstances that worked my way. If you're born to be an athlete, then you have that ability and nobody else gave it to you. Whereas in my case, a lot of people contributed to my abilities and I was lucky to take advantage of them.

## PHILANTHROPIST: ABRAZOS AND BOOKS

Abrazos and Books started from tragedy. My wife had just lost a niece who died within days of being born and so she was at a funeral in the Los Angeles area. I didn't go because I had already made a commitment to speak at a conference at the St. Francis Hotel in San Francisco. I had asked for the next day off to go join my wife in Los Angeles. Although there was really no reason to go to the television station, I thought, "I'm this close, I'll pick up my mail and say 'hi' to my friends that I never get to see since my communication with them is mostly by phone." It was early in the morning, about eight o'clock, and a colleague came up and said, "Did you hear about the earthquake in Mexico City this morning?" I told him I had not, and he said "Apparently, there has been a pretty strong earthquake in Mexico City." This was September 19, 1985. We lamented the fact that there had been an earthquake and went on about our conversations.

Nine o'clock rolled around and the managerial planning meeting for the newscast was going to start. I never got to attend those either, so I decided to sit in on the meeting, and as we were there, a colleague came into the conference room and said vehemently, "Guys, turn on those monitors and put them on Mexican satellite video feed. That is a serious earthquake." So the monitors were turned on and sure enough, it was awful. My news director said to me, "Will you go to Mexico City?" I said, "You know, I'd rather not. Why don't you send someone else?" I didn't want to go because of my personal situation. A few minutes went by and he came back and said, "I'd really rather have you go than anybody else," and since he was not only a boss, but also a friend, I agreed. That decision changed my life.

We got there and saw the worst tragedy I have ever seen. We saw an unusual collective display of tragedy, courage, compassion, and cooperation. We had more stories to tell than the newscast had space to broadcast. At one time, we were fourteen reports ahead of the newscasts because we were always sending in reports and had so many things to tell. As a result, the viewers started sending in donations and they sent in $1.3 million. Much of that money came in checks written to the International Red Cross, and we made sure the funds were used in Mexico. Some of the funds were used to buy home construction equipment, and hundreds of homes were rebuilt because of that. About $250,000 was used to rebuild two elementary schools on the outskirts of Mexico City, in the area of Xochimilco. Those schools were rebuilt and dedicated almost a year later, one week short of the anniversary of the earthquake.

When I was covering that dedication, a young girl got up and thanked the Bay Area for rebuilding her school. Her name was Brenda. Brenda approached the school principal after the program was over, and because Latin America is a very formal culture, the students were all dressed in their Sunday best. It was a special day and all the administrators and teachers wanted to show me the classrooms that had been rebuilt, but as we were walking out, Brenda, this nine-year-old child, approached the principal and asked if she could speak. She was very quickly told no because the assembly had already ended. The reason they weren't back in class was because there were still guests on campus and culturally that would have been the wrong thing to do. When I found out that I was the reason they were not back in class, I said, "Well, I've got to go then." Brenda asked again and was more sternly told, "No, you can't speak." She looked at me and said, "I really want to say something." I don't know what it was in her eyes or in her voice or in her sincerity that told me this child should be allowed to speak. I asked the principal if she could speak and, out of respect, he couldn't tell me no since I was the one who came with the donations that rebuilt the schools. Brenda was allowed to speak and had that not happened, I never would have known the hundreds of students I've met through Abrazos and Books because that moment created Abrazos and Books. Brenda got up, thanked the Bay Area tearfully, eloquently, and succinctly. At that moment I told myself, "What we're doing here is not teaching people how to fish. We're just giving them a fish. We're giving these kids a building, but that's all we're doing. Then we're leaving. We should do something to help them beyond the building that will one day go away anyway." I decided to start a scholarship project and combined that effort with informal fund-raising efforts I already had here and called it Abrazos and Books. Brenda was the inspiration for the idea, and she is now a married adult woman and I was very proud to be in her wedding. She happened to be in the audience when I got my Emmy Award last year. She changed not only my life but also my family's and hundreds of people, potentially thousands if you consider the impact that Abrazos and Books will have on the people who cross their paths in the course of their life. This is a generational change. Brenda will have an impact on people's lives a hundred years from now, all because she wanted to say thank you. And she almost didn't get a chance. And I almost didn't go to Mexico City.

I couldn't do Abrazos and Books without the help of my wife. The reason we called it Abrazos and Books is an emotionally involved process. I knew we wanted the word "books" in it to convey that it had to do with education, but I didn't want to call it the Rigo Chacón Scholarship Program. I wanted to do something that said more than that. Every time we would go to Mexico to visit the families of the students for whom those schools were rebuilt, we would always be greeted by an endless *abrazos* because that's part of the culture. *Abrazos*—the embrace—is part of Latin American culture. One day, driving down the street with my wife in the car, I said, "I've got it! I've got the name for the scholarship." I don't know if it was a subliminal impact that the greetings prompted me to come up with the name or if it was because I knew it would be all-inclusive since we don't discriminate. Abrazos and Books is color-blind because we award scholarships to kids of any ethnic background. The majority that receive the awards happen to be Latinos, but that's because the majority of applicants are Latino. It was an emotional spark that came up within me. When people who don't speak Spanish ask, I tell them what *abrazos* means and I use it as an opportunity to say why it's called Abrazos: we want to embrace all communities.

Since I was an immigrant child I don't want to perpetuate discrimination. Since I'm in charge of Abrazos and Books, then this program won't perpetuate discrimination. If you were to line up the three hundred or so recipients over the years, I always say they look like the United Nations. I now say they would look like Santa Clara County because the county is so diverse. They are beautiful young men and women, and some of them are walking around this city. I think it is a unique opportunity in life to have come up with an idea that I believe is making a change. Our vision, on the surface, is simply a scholarship project, but if you look beyond that, Abrazos and Books does more. For example, we don't eliminate wealthy young men or women from receiving the scholarship. We have gotten applicants from Los Altos Hills, and it is more than likely that young man or woman is affluent. But if that applicant spends summers building homes in Latin America, going to the reservations in the Southwest, volunteering at homeless shelters, doing just incredible things beyond their own comfortable world, then they should be recognized. So we select those kids, too, and some of them give us the money back! But we give them the recognition. Now that teenager from Los Altos High School gets to sit next to a recipient from Overfelt High School, Silver Creek High School, and Mt. Pleasant High School and in some cases they become friends. If it were not for Abrazos and Books, those paths would never cross. Abrazos and Books is much more than a scholarship program. If we get funding, the goal is to have chapters in other parts of the country of Abrazos and Books so that we can duplicate the message. We need to be inclusive. We need to be one. We need to show a national and international *abrazo*.

The reason I haven't brought in other charitable organizations to Abrazos and Books is because I have not found others who are in complete agreement with me on the concept of Abrazos and Books. Almost all those potential contacts from other organizations are involved in efforts that are strictly directed for our own ethnic group: Latinos. The Latino Peace Officers Association has only Latino recipients. I don't criticize their policy because that's their choice. It's just my choice to do it the way Abrazos and Books selects recipients. I applaud what other community organizations do because they're helping a lot of people.

## VALUES: "NOTHING CAN CHANGE SOCIETY AS DRAMATICALLY AS EDUCATION"

Fairness always comes up as uppermost in my mind as a key value. If we were all fair to each other, we'd be better off. That to me is both individually and collectively a very important value. Benito Juárez said, "*El respeto al derecho ajeno es la paz"* [Respect for the rights of others is peace]. That's profound! The respect of other's rights translates to peace. That is pretty simple and doable. Learning, of course, is another important value, which extends to the educational process. Helping others, not necessarily only the less fortunate, is another key value. You can be helpful to somebody who is more fortunate than you are in life and still improve the group, the environment around us. Fairness, knowledge, and a desire to help others are important values to me.

What would I say to young people? I would say something that generations have been saying to young people, and that's simply the importance of education. Nothing can change society as dramatically as education can. Violent uprisings certainly do, but as far as constructive, lasting change, nothing can do it like education. I think that's the reason we have not seen more constructive changes in our community. Somewhere we have failed dramatically in not driving home the point that education is important. We have to identify the reason our kids aren't pursuing higher education the way other groups are pursuing higher education and address it vehemently. As long as we don't do that, a generation from now is going to be where today's generation is and that is heartbreaking to even imagine. Why do we [Latinos] have to have the largest dropout rate in schools? Why don't we have more kids who aspire to attend Princeton, Harvard, MIT, San José State, and Santa Clara University? What are we doing wrong that we're not conveying the importance of education to our kids? And what are we doing wrong that allows our kids to organize within their own ethnic community to organize for violence? What are we doing wrong that allows that? It is sad when you consider that at least in this part of the country, we are the only significant group that has predominately young men hurting or killing each other when conceivably they could have the same great-grandparents. They get up in the morning with the intent to go hurt that person, and as a group and ethnic minority of this country, we are doing something wrong in not defining what causes this behavior. I don't buy all this talk about feeling a lack of inclusiveness and saying it's a lack of family or of being unwanted. I don't buy that because why are we the only ones doing it? We're not the only ones that have broken homes and low incomes. We have loving parents, a beautiful heritage, and tremendous writers and contributors in our history. We have cultures that go back hundreds and hundreds of years that have contributed to the human development so why are we not taking advantage of all that? Why don't we use that as a unifying element in becoming a vibrant, contributing element to this country, to this world, and to our lives?

## NOTES

1. Bellarmine College Preparatory is an all-male, Roman Catholic private secondary school located in San José, California, and it is one of the oldest secondary schools in California.

2. The Mexican American Youth Organization (MAYO) was founded in 1967 in San Antonio, Texas, by José Angel Gutiérrez and other Chicanos. It attracted large numbers of students. The organization's main objectives were to make Chicanos aware of their civil rights and to encourage political activity.

3. Reforma Street is a major street in downtown Mexico City.

4. *Confederación de la Raza Unida* was a grassroots organization. See interviews with Ernestina García and Sofía Mendoza in this anthology.

5. Pancho Villa was one of the Mexican revolutionary leaders during the Mexican Revolution of 1910.

# Mary Andrade

*Mary J. Andrade emigrated from Ecuador to the United States in 1967, after having received her B.A. degree in journalism from the University of Guayaquil. In 1978 she established residence in San José, California, and cofounded with her husband, Franklin, La Oferta, a bilingual Spanish and English weekly newspaper, whose purpose was to highlight the accomplishments and needs of the Hispanic community in San José. In the 1980s, she interviewed and photographed numerous people who worked for many years to improve the social, economic, and political presence of Hispanics in the Bay Area. She has received several awards for her work, including the prestigious Ohtli Award, which was presented in 1999 by the secretary of foreign relations through the Program for Mexican Communities Abroad, for her support as editor of La Oferta to the Mexican citizens and Mexican American residents in San José. Her work has also been recognized by the City of San José and Santa Clara County. As a professional journalist and photographer, she had published several books on the pre-Hispanic tradition of Day of the Dead in Mexico, for which she has received the Silver Quill and Silver Lens awards from the former presidents of Mexico Ernesto Zedillo and Vicente Fox.*

## GROWING UP FEMALE: DREAMING ABOUT JOURNALISM

I always wanted to be a journalist. I grew up in Guayaquil, Ecuador, where the opportunities for working in a newspaper were very scarce.[1] My interest in journalism started when I graduated from high school. I had a teacher who wanted me to study to become a lawyer. She said, "I'll help you to pass all the tests that you have to take before being accepted in the university." I said, "Thank you, but I want to study journalism." And she said that the only people who are journalists, in our city, are the sons of the owners of the newspapers. She said, "You won't have a chance," and I said that's fine, but I still want to be a journalist. I didn't know how I was going to do it, but I knew I had to study four years in the university level.

My mother was a housewife, and my father worked for many years for the government of Ecuador in the custom office of the port of Guayaquil. My father loved to read and had a wild imagination, talking about places. He didn't travel much; in fact, the first time he traveled was when he came to the United States. We also traveled with him to Mexico. He used to read a lot about Europe, about Spain and Italy. He used to tell us this imaginary story of when he was in Spain, and when he went to Italy, and he was so vivid that I think he awakened interests in my sister and me to travel and go into different careers. I went into journalism because I liked to dream about being a journalist. I didn't know how I was going to do it, but all this dreaming of my father—this aspect of his personality—influenced me. And my mother was supportive all the time. They both supported education. I remember both of them telling us that we needed to study: "You need to study, you need to graduate from the university because that is what is going to give you different opportunities and experiences." At that time, when I was a teenager in the 1950s, my father used to tell me that I had to study because "if you marry and you fail in your marriage because your husband is no good or if he dies and you have children, you have to be responsible for your children and the only way you're going to be able to survive is through your education, through what you accomplish through education," and so he pushed me in that direction.

I remember the first year in journalism at the university. We started with sixty students, and as we progressed from one year to the other, from first to second to third to fourth year in journalism, we ended up with eleven students: six women and five men. Some got married; others left because they had to go to work. I worked during the four years that I was studying. Other students went into different careers because at that time there weren't that many opportunities to work in journalism. I remember that one of the students who graduated in journalism had already been working in a newspaper for many years, but wanted to have his diploma in journalism and show that he went to school and learned the career academically. He became like a teacher figure for us, supporting us with his love, his understanding. I remember going into the streets with him to interview children who worked as shoeshine boys on the corners of the downtown area in Guayaquil. He was our mentor.

## CHRONICLE FOR THE COMMUNITY:
## *LA OFERTA* (1978) OF SAN JOSÉ, CALIFORNIA

Twenty to thirty years ago [prior to 1978] there wasn't any newspaper published for the Hispanic community in San José. My husband had been involved since a very young age with newspapers in San Francisco. He worked for several newspapers in the country in the circulation department. One day we were talking about the situation here in San José and because I had graduated from journalism in Guayaquil, Ecuador, my country, I mentioned to him the possibility of starting a publication putting together his expertise and my studies. So we decided to start doing that because at that time the main newspaper was representing the news about Hispanic communities in a very, I'll say, negative aspect. There wasn't too much reporting of issues that were focused on a positive way, such as the contributions that so many people [Hispanics] have made. It was always negative news regarding the Hispanic community. We didn't find positive news regarding the Hispanic community at that time, so I said to him, "Let's start a newspaper that will focus mainly on the contributions of the members of our [Hispanic] communities." We started very humbly. At the beginning it was just a "shopper" newspaper, not full size. It was a small monthly newspaper that started out with eight pages, and then, as we started growing with advertisements, we increased the number of pages and the frequency of the publication.

Our goal was to reach the general Hispanic community. We wanted to bring together merchants and consumers and portray the Hispanic community in a positive way. We knew there were a lot of problems, but it all depends on how you present the news that influences the community. And that was the main reason we put together this paper. We started the publication in our home. That was 1978. Then we moved from the concept of a "shopper" newspaper with very few news stories into a larger publication, and we changed the format to the regular format that we now have. Along the way, we tried also to publish twice a week. My husband was convinced that there was the market in our community to support a biweekly newspaper. And we did it over a period of a year, but it was too much. We didn't have the results that we had expected. We needed advertisements to be able to pay expenses of the second publication during the week. So we went back to a weekly publication until four or five years ago, about 2000, when we started publishing *El Vistazo* for the southern part of the Bay Area. There was a process of growth, and it was subject also to some economic support from the community and advertisements.

As I mentioned earlier, we started publishing in our home. It's funny now, looking back, but it was hard for the family. We used one of our bedrooms as an office. Little by little, we started taking over almost the whole house because after having just one bedroom, we needed more room for the graphic designer to bring in the other type of equipment to use to do the typesetting. It was hard for the family because we didn't have enough room to keep the family activities separated from the business activities. We were there in our house at least four years. Later, we moved to an office space, after that to another place on the East Side of San José, and finally we bought this building, I think it was 1993.

Two or three years later, *El Observador* came into the community.[2] I think that their format was mostly English, but *La Oferta* was more Spanish. Later we tried to strike a balance between English and Spanish articles in the paper because we wanted to target both the English-speaking and the Spanish-speaking communities. We also want to target the general community and the professional community. Those first years, *La Oferta* was mainly a "shopper" newspaper with limited news information. In later years, we started including more information about the Hispanic community and focused more on individuals. We were growing into a different stage of journalism in that respect.

At the beginning, I was more comfortable writing in Spanish. It is my first language. *La Oferta* was published by very few people. My husband dedicated himself to the advertisement and the circulation aspects of the paper, and I dedicated myself to the editorial aspect. Later, when we had the resources, we started hiring freelance people to write articles in English, which is where we are now.

My husband and I have always thought that because we were born in Ecuador that some members of the Mexican and Mexican American community resisted us a bit because we were not Mexican or Mexican American. However, eventually that sense of "You are not Mexican" disappeared. We also had problems with advertisements. There was no conviction that the Hispanic market was one that people wanted to reach, so paid advertisements were a bit harder to get in the first years. We were always behind in that aspect, but we put everything that we could from our own resources to keep going. Later, we had the support of the community, the merchants, the advertisers, and the professionals who placed advertisements in the newspaper. That helped us to keep going because we paid all the expenses of the publication and circulation through the advertisements. The newspaper has always been free to the community during the twenty-five years that we have been publishing *La Oferta*.

We are here to serve a community that needed and needs to be presented in a positive way. We were serving people, and we all share the same needs. It's not just a matter of nationality. We were aware that the majority of the community was Mexican or Mexican American and so we got very involved with the Mexican government and the Mexican Office of Tourism. I ended up doing research there and publishing books. I feel Mexican too in that sense. I was involved with the Mexican government in the beginning through invitations to promote tourism. And from that point, because logically we were addressing a community that was Mexican, we published stories about Mexico because people have the need to read about their country. There are many people who are descendants of Mexicans who have not gone to Mexico and seen the country of their parents. So they like to read our newspaper and what we have written about the different places in Mexico from the tourist point of view. And from that we evolved into reporting on aspects of Mexican culture and traditions. And that's when I became interested in doing and covering the celebration of the Day of the Dead that I've been doing since 1987.[3]

Our Hispanic community in San José is evolving, growing up, becoming aware of its values and becoming aware of its power. I am aware that we're members of a national organization of Hispanic newspapers, and I remember several campaigns for waking up the "sleeping giant" that we were. It took awhile, but we were there, together with other newspapers in the country. We wanted to establish this connection between the Hispanic merchants and all Hispanics to support the businesses of their own community. We serve as a vehicle to do that.

The advertisement aspect has been the responsibility of my husband. Now my two daughters are also involved. The whole family works in the paper. It was my husband and I working as a team. We worked together on this, so maybe I found a lot of strength in him as the editor of the newspaper.

We went from the Spanish content into the English content. We started bringing in newspaper writers, freelancers to write about the community, mostly Mexican American. Yolanda Reynolds wrote a lot of interesting stories with us.[4] She was with us at least for ten and eleven years. So probably she will be able to tell you more about the stories that she wrote for *La Oferta*.

With *La Oferta*, we are trying to be in the center of the community. Privately we have our own ideas about politics, but we do not take a stance on endorsing any candidate or political ideology. As individuals we support some candidates, I support others, but we don't use our newspaper to endorse anyone because I think I belong to the old guard in Ecuador where we try to keep newspapers politically independent. If we endorse one candidate over another, it seems to me that we are unfairly influencing the opinion of our readers. We try not to do that. No, what we do is to present information about the candidates. In the last election for the state assembly candidates to represent district twenty-three in San José, we interviewed the two opposing candidates and published the interviews. We do that kind of journalism here. If political candidates buy advertisements, we publish them, but we do not endorse candidates. Privately, we do, however, endorse candidates and we work on campaigns.

I feel that there is a more educated readership, more aware of the issues, more involved in the community than in the past. I get a lot of telephone calls to cover their Mexican Americans events and issues that they are bringing to the attention of city hall. We gather a lot of information on issues, but we don't have time to cover them all. We don't have the space because we have a specific number of pages that we can publish so we have to select what is more, I won't say important, but more applicable for that issue or more timely. People send us press releases via e-mail, fax. They call me for example and say, "Well, we're having this student demonstration against the cutting of the education budget. I hope you can come and cover the event, or can you send one of your writers?" I guess they contact the media because they need media coverage on their particular issues. Like today we have a writer covering an extensive workshop on the issue of housing. It is happening in the Mexican Cultural Heritage Plaza.[5] They sent me a fax and an e-mail, and they called, saying, "Please come, this is an issue affecting our community; come and cover it." So we send writers. I do not write editorials. I love to write about cultural aspects, tourism, and traditions. That's my forte. We have several people who write editorial pieces. We have people who send editorials from San Francisco, right here in San José, also from Washington, D.C., and also from Los Angeles.

We worked with the Mexican government and with the Office of Tourism. It was easy to get in touch with them, to present the newspaper to them. I remember starting with the Mexican government's Office of Tourism in Los Angeles. Then they sent copies of La Oferta to the secretary of tourism in Mexico City. I guess they reviewed the paper and then they invited me to be part of the group of journalists who travel every year to Acapulco for an international convention. So that's how we established that relationship. The way to keep it going is that every time that we have published an article promoting Mexican tourism, we send a copy to all the offices including Mexico City. So they know we are promoting tourism into the country. That's the way we have kept this relationship going to the point that I know a lot of people in the different offices like the State Office of Tourism. They have supported me on my research of the celebration of

Day of the Dead. We have some writers who send us articles from there [Mexico], sometimes articles about tourism and sometimes politics. We have a person who sent us a lot of information about historical aspects, which have helped us to do some special publications and celebration like the Cinco de Mayo.[5]

## *SOLIDARIDAD*: LEGACY OF THE ELDERS

I started doing this research with one of my teachers of photography at that time at De Anza College. Her name was Shirley Fisher. We put together close to one hundred interviews and photographs of older people who for many years worked for the benefit of the Hispanic community; the majority of them were Mexican or Mexican American, at least 90 percent of them. There were also *Californianos.*[7] It was wonderful to meet these people, to see what they have gone through. What they did was open the way, the road, for their children to have better opportunities in society, to get ahead through education and through politics.

As I mentioned before, I wanted to create a publication that showcased the accomplishments of the people of the Hispanic community. We did that through different projects. *Solidaridad* [Solidarity] was one of these projects that lasted from three to four years. The project was successful because we focused on profiles of elderly people who had already, for many years, been working to benefit some segment of the Mexican American community. I wanted to honor them for their age and their contributions. Sometimes we focus too much on younger people, the ones who are starting, but we forget that everything we are accomplishing now is largely due to the efforts of our elders. And sometimes we don't pay attention to the older people and their contribution, and I wanted to do that through these journalistic articles published *in La Oferta.*

Shirley and I started publishing their stories in English and Spanish. She would write the interview in English, and I would write it in Spanish. We would put it together with the notes she had taken with mine to make it almost similar in the translation and publish it in two pages of the paper, one page in English followed by another page in Spanish. Shirley Fisher received credit for the English version; I received credit for Spanish.

## WOMEN ORGANIZING WOMEN

Besides being involved in the *Solidaridad* project, I started working with an organization, the *Concilio of Hispanic Women* [Hispanic Women's Council].[8] The Hispanic Women's Council put together programs to benefit Hispanic women.

The organization, I think, is not functioning any longer, but it went on for, I guess, three to four more years. I went to the first meetings but left because the work here in the office producing the newspaper is very, very demanding. So I decided to do what I can do the best. I was asked to join the organization by Carmen Johnson, who founded it. She was an educator and involved with the educational aspects of the community. After the inauguration of the organization, she focused on serving a specific group of students. I remember the first conference because I was part of that. It was probably 1988 or 1989. And every participant was a professional woman. They had their own jobs that demanded more time. At that time, our newspaper office was located on Alum Rock and just across the street from the East Side Senior Citizens Center where Carmen Johnson was the director of that center. So that's why we were in close communication. I used to just cross the street and go to the meetings. The first opening conference covered different aspects. At that time, the city of San José was developing technologically, so there were several professionals involved in that field who gave workshops. Also, there were teachers giving workshops on education. Professional women served as mentors to young women. Being a woman to me means power.

## RECLAIMING MEXICAN CULTURE

In 1987, I began doing the research on the celebration of Day of the Dead because many of our readers were Mexican and Mexican American. So I decided to go to Mexico and do reporting on the celebration in the state of Michoacán. When I went there, I loved what I saw, what I learned. I decided to write an article and mount an exhibit with the photographs I took in that celebration. And the following year as the time of the celebration of the Day of the Dead approached, I wanted to visit other places, learn about how they celebrated the Day of the Dead in other states in Mexico. So I went to Oaxaca and started collecting information until 1998.

I have published six books on the Day of the Dead tradition plus one more on the celebration of Christmas in Oaxaca. As a writer, as a person involved in and with the community, I saw there was nothing written, nothing published on that subject. From the trips that I have taken to Mexico and from the conferences on tourism I have attended, I have learned that some beautiful traditions in Mexico have not been covered or researched. So I decided to concentrate on this tradition of Day of the Dead in Mexico. At the beginning, I was publishing these articles in the paper, but later started collecting so much information and photographs that I decided to publish them in book form.

It was hard for me to find a publisher for my book because they said that it wasn't a good subject, although it was nicely presented. They were afraid that if they printed 30,000 copies they wouldn't sell them all. So my manuscript was rejected by large publishers. So I said to my husband, "I have all this information and would love to publish it as a book, can we do it?" And he responded, "Yes, let's do it." Because of the expenses involved we decided to publish a book series but first focusing on one state at a time. So that's the way I started publishing this series *Through the Eyes of the Soul: Day of the Dead in Mexico*.[9] In 1998, I published the book about Michoacán. The following year, I published my research on Oaxaca, after that Mexico City, and then the state of Morelos, later Puebla. I also wrote a book for children. My son-in-law who is a teacher did the illustrations for that book. There are now seven books in the series. At the present time, I'm working on the research that I did last year, last November [2004], in the sierra in Michoacán, an area where the celebration is beautiful. Last year, I went and I covered the sierra, the highlands where these communities are located and where the celebration is completely different.

We have a large Hispanic population in the United States, and my books bring the traditions that are celebrated in many countries in Latin America. Unfortunately, there's not much written about it. There are no books, for example, on the celebration of Day of the Dead in Guatemala or in Ecuador, Perú, and Bolívia. But it's celebrated there too. I want to reach a larger readership, and I'm selling the books all over this country and in Mexico.

Mexicans in Mexico view *La Oferta* as a very serious newspaper, a very committed newspaper. They respect it. Let me mention two examples. The first one is when we went last year to Michoacán, to the highlands to do the research on the celebration of Day of the Dead. The Office of Tourism created an itinerary to show us other aspects of the culture of that state. They took us to different small towns to show us beautiful chapels of the sixteenth century with paintings they call *tesonados*, paintings on the ceilings. It was a beautiful experience seeing this part of the history of that area, religious and cultural history in the ceilings of ancient churches. I decided to write about these churches, these chapels. I wrote a series of three articles about each town and took many photographs of the people who were there and everything involved in these communities. I sent the newspapers to the Office of Tourism in Michoacán and Morelia.

The message that I would want young Mexican Americans to get from my books is to go back to their roots, to their culture. Latin American culture, like Mexican culture, is so rich and it has so much to give to the world. For example, I interviewed a young man who is involved in *La Casa la Cultura* in Michoacán and he said that the Day of the Dead is a beautiful tradition that can teach many other cultures about our philosophy, but also about the way we see life. People think that death, for example, is the end and they don't want to talk about it. When we are suffering from pain of losing someone, we try to suppress that pain. We try to forget about that person because we don't want to face the suffering of that loss. But in Mexico people let those feelings come out, but in a beautiful way, which is celebrating their life. And that is what I have learned and that's what I see every year that I go there and that's what I try to put into my books. I write in Spanish, and I get somebody to do the translation into English. When the translation is done, I'll review to make sure it reflects my feelings I express in Spanish.

Eventually I would like to set up a publishing house to publish other kinds of books. In fact, I did another book here and this is like the project of *Solidaridad*. We have a writer here at *La Oferta*, her names is Guadalupe C. Bellavance. For several years she has kept a column called *Perfil de los Nuestros* where she has interviewed younger people,[10] Hispanic women and men, including students, who are very involved in the community, in different fields. We published fifty interview-type biographies in the newspaper first, and after that we put together these interviews and published them as a book.

## REFLECTIONS ON THE MEXICAN AMERICAN COMMUNITY

I remember when San José was not divided into many ethnic groups and the largest group was Hispanic, and continues to be Hispanic. The Asian group was very small in the late 1970s. Now, Hispanics and Asians make up the majority in this area. Politically we Hispanics are very active. I know that the Asian community is starting to feel the need to be involved politically in city affairs. I know that they are increasingly involved in education boards. It's a growth that we have seen, and that is crucial because each group needs to be represented.

I see MAPA [Mexican American Political Association] and La Raza Lawyers as very involved politically.[11] I'm seeing young people, students, getting involved in politics. There is a group of students, I think it's in Redwood City, who is organizing a big demonstration for the Cinco de Mayo in support of the driver's license for undocumented people. I see that happening for the first time this year, 2005. This group of students has been going through different parts of the state, like in a caravan, calling attention to issues that are affecting the community and their education. So they're getting very involved.

I would like *La Oferta* to be remembered as an independent newspaper. We take pride in that. As a newspaper that made a big contribution to the community in many aspects. We try to do our best and I think that we are doing it. But readers will have to give their opinion, I guess. We [*La Oferta*] use the ethnic label Hispanic and Latino but in general [we use the term] Hispanic. I don't see anything against *la raza* or Chicano because there is a segment of the population that has particular needs to be identified like that. But no, we at *La Oferta* haven't used these ethnic labels.

The major issues in San José are generally the issues of labor, the issues of education, the need of recognizing people who made contributions to this country through their work and who are being denied many rights. I think as a community we need to get together and make changes to improve the communities. Unfortunately because of politics at the present time, many of those accomplishments are not recognized and our needs are not met. We all need to work together in different aspects, supporting each other as individuals supporting organizations and *La Oferta* supporting their causes. Information is very important. I think that the newspapers and television stations and radio stations that are serving the Hispanic community are all doing a very important job and that eventually will give us Hispanics more power.

I don't see conflict among ethnic groups. I think that initially there were worries about the Asian community's economic power. But I don't see conflict. In fact, I see that we can work together and create that power, that together it will be better directed into accomplishing good results. For example, there is an organization, New California Media, here in Northern California.[12] Their main office is in San Francisco, and it has combined all the ethnic media and it is becoming a very powerful organization because it has recognized the power that small and medium-size publications have in their own community. I'm talking about Indian, Vietnamese, Japanese, Chinese, Spanish newspapers. So the power is here; we have it.

We [*La Oferta*] can lead by providing information to the Hispanic community. The mission of the media is to inform and educate. And when you educate you are leading.

I've been so involved with the Mexican people here. I'm very involved with Mexico and people in Mexico. I have traveled so much there that I feel Mexico is like my second country or my third country. I always say that I have three nationalities: I'm Ecuadorian because of my birth and because I grew up there; I am an American citizen because of the many, many years that I have lived here, where I made my life, have my family, and my children were born here. And I'm Mexican because of all that I'm doing there in Mexico, the hospitality that I have felt, and the support that I have received from Mexican people in doing my work.

## MY LIFE/MY COMMUNITY

The values that guided me through my life are the need to communicate, the need to share information, and the need to learn because this has been a long process of learning and we learn everyday. I learn from information that the writers bring to us every week. I learn from what the people tell me through their e-mails, their telephone calls. For me, it is a world of learning from everybody. American society gives me freedom, the freedom to be myself and the freedom to express my opinion; I value that very much. I would like to define the American Dream as people coming together from many different countries and dreaming about what they can do and about what they can give.

The dreams of the Latino community are to grow and to be part of the larger society, but at the same time keeping and valuing their own culture. That's very important for everybody because we can and we need to become part of this larger society. But as individuals we need to keep our own identity and that is something that is very personal, but it's there. I feel proud and I feel happy to be here in the United States, but I'm also proud of being born in Ecuador and I'm proud to be able to go back and forth from Mexico and enjoy the friendship of the people that I know there: to enjoy the opportunity to learn about their culture and to bring that to other people here and be part of this big community.

Sometimes anti-immigrant feeling in the United States is very subtle and sometimes you see it. It can touch us on the state level. You see it through the politics that go on in Sacramento. And sometimes everything is calm, but these calm times change, like seasons, and we have difficult times, and life goes on, but in general the opportunities are here and we have the power to take advantage of them. No one can isolate us; that's impossible. That's impossible.

I think that Hispanics are growing in the Republican Party. I've seen more information coming into the Hispanic newspapers from the Republican Party, so they're reaching out to Hispanics more. I think that they are trying to reach everybody. But when you see that, well, this is private, personal. You see what's going on right now.[13] I think that people are starting to think about changing political parties; that's what happened with my husband and my daughter, but again, it all depends on what's going on in Washington and in the world.

I can say that I owe a lot to the newspaper because, as I mentioned before, I have been able to learn a lot, to grow, and it has given me the opportunity to do many things that in another field I probably could not have had, to explore, to travel.

I tried to do my best and in everything, like in my writing, I would like to be remembered as a good writer and I'm trying to be a good one. I don't know if I'll ever get to that point, but I'm practicing. The general message that I have for young Latinos and Latinas is the same message that my father used to give me. Education is the door that will open so many opportunities to you. He's [her father] always present with me, and this is the same message that I have given to my daughters and hopefully to my grandson about education. We have the obligation to reach a higher level. And my daughters need to reach higher than us, and my grandson needs to reach higher but, more importantly, to be a good citizen, a person with compassion and willing to help others.

If I had the opportunity to write an editorial, which would be targeted, to the young Latino population, I would tell them that I'll be leaving with a lot of gratitude for the community that has supported us for so many years in our job, in our desire to help them to grow at the same time that we grew with them. And I would tell them that, again, to look for inspiration and role models in their teachers, in their friends and to accept that they have a commitment, with their own community and with their own society, to give the best they can do in their life for their self, for their family, and for the community.

## NOTES

1. Even though Mary Andrade is not Mexican American, we decided to include her in this anthology because of her identification with and invaluable contribution to San José's Mexican American community.

2. *El Observador* is another Spanish-language newspaper in San José, California.

3. The Day of the Dead (*Día de los Muertos*) is a Latin American celebration that takes place on November 1. People visit the graves of their family and friends, bringing flowers and food to celebrate their lives. Celebrants believe that the souls of the dead return and are all around them. Families remember the departed by telling stories about them.

4. Yolanda Reynolds worked as an educator and freelance writer for *La Oferta*. See her interview in this anthology.

5. San José's Mexican Cultural Heritage Plaza is a focal point for the community, providing a general venue for artistic, musical, and theatrical activities.

6. The holiday of Cinco De Mayo [The Fifth of May] commemorates the victory of the Mexicans over the French army at the Battle of Puebla in 1862. Celebrating Cinco de Mayo has become increasingly popular along the U.S.-Mexico border and in parts of the U.S. that have a high population of people with a Mexican heritage. In these areas the holiday is a celebration of Mexican culture, of food, music, beverage, and customs unique to Mexico.

7. *Californianos* is a term used by some to identify themselves as members of families that can trace their cultural heritage to eighteenth-century California. In 1968, a small group of descendants of Spanish Alta Californians formed *Los Californianos* in anticipation of the bicentennial year of the discovery of San Francisco Bay in 1769 by the expedition led by Don Gaspar de Portolá. *Los Californianos* was created for the purpose of preserving the heritage of the early Hispanic Californians in Alta California by conducting research on genealogy and civil, religious, military, social, and cultural activities in Alta California in order to provide an accurate and authentic oral, written, and pictorial interpretation of the history of Spanish and Mexican Alta California.

8. The Hispanic Women's Council was an organization founded in the late 1980s by a group of Hispanic women in San José, California, to address issues of specific concern for Hispanic women.

9. Mary Andrade's book series is titled *Through the Eyes of the Soul: Day of the Dead* and is published by La Oferta Review Newspaper. This series includes volumes on the Mexican states of Michoacán, Mexico City, Mixquic, Morelos, Oaxaca, Puebla, Tlaxcala, San Luis Potosí, and Hidalgo.

10. Guadalupe Camelo Bellavance, *Perfil de los Nuestros* (San José, CA: La Oferta Review, 2003).

11. The Mexican American Political Association was founded in Fresno, California, in 1960 and has been and is dedicated to the constitutional and democratic principles of political freedom and representation for Mexican, Chicano, and Latino people in the United States of America. La Raza Lawyers of Santa Clara County is an unincorporated association of Chicano and Latino attorneys that are dedicated to promoting diversity in the both the bench and bar of the greater Silicon Valley. They support and encourage law students with mentorship programs and scholarships and attempt to represent the Latino community in the legal profession.

12. The ethnic media in California is emerging as a powerful and important new force in American journalism. These media organizations have joined together as New California Media (NCM), a statewide consortium of more than six hundred ethnic news organizations founded in 1996 by Pacific News Service. NCM promotes ethnic media by strengthening the editorial and economic viability of this increasingly influential segment of America's communications industry.

13. Andrade is referring to the 2004 presidential race.

# V

# RELIGION AND COMMUNITY

# Sal Álvarez

*Sal Álvarez, son of Mexican immigrants, was born in Santa Maria, California. He grew up in San José and graduated from James Lick High School in 1958 and San José State University in 1963 with a B.S. in sociology. After working for San José Social Services as a case worker, he attended the University of California at Berkeley where he received his master's degree in community organization. He was commissioned a deacon in the Archdiocese of San José and was hired as the executive director of the U.S. Catholic Conference of Bishops for Spanish Speakers, representing the western region. He entered the Ph.D. program at UC Berkeley and began teaching as an associate professor in sociology at San José State University, where he founded the community-based School of Social Work. In 1975 he joined the UFW as a researcher and later worked for César Chávez as a lobbyist in Sacramento and Washington, D.C. During this time he formed the "Padres," an organization of Latino Catholic priests who were committed to meeting the needs of Latinos within the Church. Currently, he is the director of the Institute for Non-Violence, Office of Human Relations, Santa Clara County, a community organization that provides training on peace building, conflict resolution, mediation, and negotiations for civil rights and human rights advocates. He serves with the National Farm Workers Ministry; as legislative representative to the United Farm Workers of America, AFL-CIO; and as vice president of the Dolores Huerta Foundation.*

## PARENTS/CHILDHOOD

My mother was a farm worker who emigrated to the U.S. from Sonora, Mexico. Her father was part of the Mexican Revolution of 1910, so in some ways I'd say that

I came from refugees that needed to cross over the U.S.-Mexican border. My maternal grandfather worked on the border, and his wife, my grandmother, was part Indian and part Russian. So I have *mestizo* [Spanish and Indian] blood but Russian heritage, too. My dad was born in Juárez, Mexico, where his family had a big *rancho* [ranch] that was broken up because of the Mexican Revolution. He, his father, and his siblings came through Arizona and worked in the mines for a while. So I come from a family of miners. Then they came up to Santa Maria, California, to do farm work and that's where my parents met.

My dad only went up to the eighth grade, just like César Chávez and my mother to the tenth grade. In those days, when they went to school, they saw signs, "Mexicans and dogs not allowed." This was in California, not Texas. We're talking about San José, where there had been a lynching of Mexicans in downtown San José at St. James Park.[1] My mother learned enough English so she could write it. *Se quedaba calladita* [she kept quiet] but she learned what she could until she dropped out of school. My dad, whom I consider an intellectual, is eighty-eight years old and writes perfect Spanish, a lot better than I do! He's a self-taught man, like César Chávez. He would read something like ten books at one time. He was what Octavio Romano would call the "intellectual *campesino*" [farm worker].[2] *El campesino intellectual.* He was very bright and very intelligent.

My father was in a WWII veterans' group called Clifford Rodriguez Post 809. It was a Mexican American veterans' group. He talked about the war and how fortunate he felt that he didn't have to land in Japan. He thought, "Oh, my God, why did the U.S. drop the atomic bomb on Hiroshima and Nagasaki? How could anybody do what President Truman did?" We had conversations about that dilemma, and part of me felt that what happened there was unconscionable. He came back like many of the WWII veterans with G.I. benefits. He never went to college like a lot of others did, but he came back with world experience. During my high school years, my dad worked for the railroads, but he could not and would not be promoted beyond being a clerk because of ethnic inequality. The Italians had the next rank because there was an ethnic ladder and nobody crossed over that ladder. My dad worked as a clerk for thirty-two years.

I was born in a central coast area of Santa Maria, California. My mother gave birth to me while my dad was working in Fresno, driving a tractor from six o'-clock at night to six o'clock in the morning. When I was born at the county hospital, my mother was horrified that I had a twisted leg. I had a cast on several hours after being born. Because in Santa Maria they didn't have crippled children's services, my parents decided to move to San José so I could go to the county hospital. During those early days, we used to travel up Highway 101 in a Model T Ford. When they came to San José in 1940, World War II was already part of our family history. Three families lived in one house on Albert Street, and I went to Washington Elementary School, the barrio school. I remember growing up with my grandparents, uncles, and aunts. We all lived close to each other in this neighborhood. It wasn't as though my parents had friends. With an immigrant family that I grew up with, the close-knit family relations were there. We were raised on rice and beans. My dad worked as a clerk, and my brothers and I worked in the fields. What the three of us boys made in the summer helped a lot in terms of family income. We picked pears, prunes, and apricots.

On Sundays, we would go to Sacred Heart Church, where the pastor was an Italian priest. I made my First Communion there. I felt welcomed in the neighborhood. When we went to Washington Elementary, I got myself expelled from the third grade. I never got in trouble again after that, but my mother had a big fight with my father over whether he was going to buy a Model T car or move us to East San José, out of the barrio. She felt that the three of us boys were going to have a hard time surviving without getting ourselves into more trouble. So they bought an acre and a quarter in East San José. At the time, there was nothing but orchards in East San José. They bought a cow and a horse. I had thirty rabbits and about sixty pigeons. We used to walk from White Road all the way to Five Wounds Church, which is now a Portuguese church.

## I'M A *POCHO*[3]: NAVIGATING CONFLICTING IDENTITIES

I'm part of the Chicano or Mexican American generation that was told by their immigrant parents, "Do not speak Spanish." They said that because they wanted us to do well in school. When we went to see my grandparents, we'd say, "*¿Como está, Abuela?*" [How are you, Grandma?] That was all we could say! Years later, when César Chávez asked me to translate something, I said, "César, I'm a *pocho*; I never learned that much Spanish." He laughed. Once, at school, they had a Cinco de Mayo celebration and there were some Mexican kids in the school who spoke Spanish, but I didn't. So I decided to wear a Mexican sombrero. All the Mexican students made fun of me because how dare I wear a Mexican sombrero when I didn't know or speak any Spanish. So when I went into James Lick High School in 1954, I signed up for Spanish class. The first day of class, the Spanish teacher pointed at me and says, "Sal Álvarez , you're in here. Can you speak some Spanish for us?" I was embarrassed and said, "I don't speak Spanish, but I can understand it." There were three to four Mexican theaters in downtown at San José at that time and my parents always took us on Wednesday nights to see Maria Félix, Miguel Aceves Mejía, and all the old-timers. So I understood some Spanish. But I walked out of the classroom and never took another Spanish class.

I went to high school with Luis Valdez, who had come from Delano. Luis and I met in our freshman year and he was freshman class president. During our junior year, we were all invited to a party, but my mother *nos castigó* [grounded us] so I couldn't go. I went anyway and there was beer at the party and guess what? The juvenile authorities rounded up about thirty or forty students who landed in juvenile hall. The story came out in our student paper with the headline, "Luis Valdez entertains the kids in juvenile home as a ventriloquist."

I decided to run for sophomore class president against Luis Valdez. I beat him by one vote! In high school I was sophomore, junior, and senior class president. I took up a leadership role, like my brother Ed. What's frightening about what happened to me in high school is that because of a lot of my insecurities, I never considered myself smart like my brother Edward or my brother Raúl. The fact that we took leadership positions in schools helped us despite the fact that there was no Mexican ethnic representation in teaching at elementary school or high school. We never saw an image of a Mexican American teacher. Luis Valdez and I competed for the only Mexican American scholarship in Santa Clara County. We had to compete with five other high schools for one $250 scholarship. It was given by the Mexican government, and Luis actually went back years later and thanked them for it. Luis and I both won it that year. They'd never given it to two people. So he had $100 and I had $100 and we used it to go to San José State University.

When I went to San José State, I connected with the Newman Club.[4] It took me five years to graduate and I was on probation most of the time. I was a history major and then I became a sociology major. But what happened at San José State is very interesting because I got to be in a leadership role at the Newman Center. Eventually I ended up with a National Cardinal Newman Award. I was president there for three years. We used to pack the place with about four hundred students that listened to the lectures.

## RELIGION AND SOCIAL CHANGE:
## "WE ARE PART OF THE CHURCH TOO"

Because I was born crippled, I attended summer school with other crippled children. I had a number of operations, and my last one was when I was a junior in high school. I experienced what it was like to be left in a hospital and my family said, "Well, we'll see you tomorrow. Or we'll see you in a couple of days." That was very hard for me. I never saw any Mexican American nurses or doctors. I look back now and say, "Wow, there was nobody in the church. There's nobody in the schools. There's nobody in the health care system." My Chicano experience, growing up without any role models, led to a lot of my insecurities and feelings of inferiority. When the Chicano Movement was born in the 1960s, it helped those of us that were raised in that environment to fight even harder for Chicano teachers, professors, priests, and doctors. It was a period of time that also turned me to the Church and my faith. I had an image of a white Christ, but I had an image of a brown *Virgen*. I think about my dad and the importance of that image of Juan Diego, and of César Chávez carrying the *Virgen* in the front of the marches all the time. What a powerful experience that was for me.

In the summer, my uncle got me a job stacking cans in boxcars. But then I had the opportunity to go to Stanford Newman Center to take a course on the Gospel of John, and I joined Amigos.[5] I ended up going to Mexico with a small group in an old bus to work in a small village in Michoacán. That's when I started learning Spanish, in Mexico in 1961. We started with a small group, and the organization grew to six thousand around the country from mostly Catholic universities. I had the experience of breaking away from my family and getting away from home for the first time, since I never went away to school. Going to Mexico was my *grito de independencia* [cry for independence]. I was able to have some freedom, and I loved working with the poor. Mostly the seminarians were in the first group that went, and they would talk all the time about how they were going to enter the seminary and become priests. I found that as a Mexican American, I wasn't wanted at the seminary. I too wanted to become a priest, but because Spaniards in the seminaries of California did not think Mexican Americans spoke correct Spanish, we were spit out, literally, as we tried to explore it. I never felt I had a chance to go into the seminary to become a priest.

But during the time that I was going to high school and college, the Second Vatican Council reversed everything.[6] No longer were there Latin Masses and no longer were the priests saying Mass with their backs to the congregants. We were allowed to have Spanish Masses, whereas before there was no Spanish allowed and no *Virgen de Guadalupe* allowed in the churches. Vatican II was a welcome revolution in the Church for César Chávez and the rest of us. I remember coming here to Santa Clara University when the students were picketing and there was no *Virgen de Guadalupe* in this church. I brought the *Virgen de Guadalupe* statue. The Chicano students were actually having a sit-in in the chapel. So there's a story about what happened here at Santa Clara University that changed the climate on the campus.

I worked with Blanca Alvarado to demand that churches in San José have statues of the *Virgen de Guadalupe*.[7] We would say, "We want *la Virgen* in the church." And if they wouldn't give it to us, we would write to the Vatican. Ron Gonzales's father once told us to write and we did. "We wrote a fifteen-page letter to the Vatican complaining about the racism in the church. We demanded to have the *Virgen* inside our church."[8] But it wasn't easy. The Italian and Irish families had the white Virgin, and I don't want to take anything away from them, but we had to step up and say, "We're part of the Church, too." A lot of us Mexican Americans started reading about Vatican II and we would say to ourselves, "So the laity has as many rights as priests and religious people."

Then when I was twenty-one and in college, my barber convinced me that I should go on a *cursillo*. I said, "What's a *cursillo*?" It originated in Spain. It's a short course on Christianity, and it was a life-changing experience for me. César did his *cursillo*, at about the same time that I did, and we went to the San Joaquin Valley. The story goes that César *se hincó* [knelt down] and said, "I am going to give my life to the farm workers." This is a different story than the one Richard Chávez tells of when he and César were picking apricots in Evergreen when César told his brother, "Someone has to do something about these conditions. How can you make a living; how can you support a family picking apricots at this pay?" Fast forward to 1963 when César *se está hincando* [is kneeling down], saying, "I am going to commit my life to the farm workers."

I got my strength when I go up in the morning by walking to church, going to Mass, praying, and going to school every day. I look back now at going to Sacred Heart and it's very vivid in my memory. On Good Fridays, for the Stations of the Cross, César and everybody from the barrio would be at Guadalupe Church. Father McDonald had this long telephone pole in the shape of a cross that took eighty men to carry and he'd be in front of a jeep. It's one thing to have the image of Jesus carrying the cross. This projected vividly for the farm workers' movement and the pilgrimages that bearing the cross together, we could do it. Together we could carry and lift up that cross.

I was able to go to Guadalupe Church and a Portuguese church, but I never saw any Mexican American priests or even a priest that was doing community outreach. If somebody asked me if I were interested in working with the Church, I'd say, "Yeah, I'd be interested," but that's as far as it went. There was no demonstration on the part of the Church to reach out to Mexican American priests. Later, when I became the national director for Hispanic priests and religious brothers and deacons, there were only three hundred Mexican American priests in the country. I know how hard it's been for that small group of Mexican American priests to survive in a Church where they felt they weren't wanted. But again, we changed that. That's part of my history, how Father Flores became Archbishop Flores and how we went from no bishops to twenty-eight bishops in the country.[9]

There was a part of *La Causa*—the Chicano Movement—that was trying to make changes in the Church, struggling to maintain ties to it and not give up on it. When I interviewed César during his twenty-four-day fast, he wrote on a piece of paper that is now published in *El Grito*, "The church is a powerful institution. We don't want charity. We don't want food baskets. We want the economic and spiritual power of the church to help the farm workers and to help the Mexican American community, to help poor people around the world." That's a powerful statement.

I found a place in the Newman Center, and at Sacred Heart Church and St. John Vianney's Church but was still able to relate to the Guadalupe Church experience, that Catholic *mestizo* part of it. I felt comfortable in both the English dominant church and also the Mexican *mestizo* church. When I was asked to enter in the deaconate, I said, "Get out of here. I wouldn't do that!" My dad said, "*¡No, para qué quiero un hijo que tiene faldas!*" [What do I want a son who wears skirts for?] His experience in the Church in San Diego and other cities was that Mexicans, like him, were not welcomed in Catholic churches. When he was in the Army, he went to a Catholic church and they said "No, no, no, no, the church is on the other side of town for you." I grew up in a family where it wasn't so much that they were anti-clergy. They just did not feel welcomed by the Church hierarchy. That was their experience. It had nothing to do with his faith.

In 1975, I entered the deaconate program on a bet that I wouldn't get accepted. This is now my twenty-seventh year as a deacon. I've gone all over the world. I've baptized our first granddaughter in Ireland; I've read the gospel at the high altar of St. Peter's. I've worked with the Apostolic delegate, and I've been a mediator between the Vatican and the gay community. Part of my life experience is that I've been at that level. So I thought, "What are you afraid of, Sal?" I don't know what God has in mind for me for the rest of my life, but I do know that I've been very blessed to have been raised in San José and had all the experiences that I have had.

However, I still have that basic insecurity that I don't belong. I'm clergy and I go to the priest on weekly study days, but part of me feels that I don't belong. That was ingrained in me, sort of like when I became a professor, "I don't belong here." I belonged, but I didn't belong. You know? I try to explain to people that for Chicanos, that basic insecurity that we carried about not having a sense of belonging to the institutions. Are we betraying the community by becoming a professor? Are we betraying the community by getting ordained? Because it's sort of like you cross over and you're on the side that you've been fighting all the time. It's been hard.

My life has presented a dilemma. Do I become part of the establishment? Now I'm asked, "Will you be the chaplain of La Raza Roundtable?"[10] I'm the chaplain of the California LULAC. People say, "There's a spiritual part of you that comes through." My wife has a way of putting it. She says, "That's where God wants you. That's where you're going to be. God didn't want you to stay a university professor. He wanted you helping César Chávez and Dolores Huerta. It was meant to be." She calls this "synchronicity." My wife prays over me. She's more spiritual than I am. She says, "Sal, breathe in God's healing energy and His spirit. Breathe out your anxieties and your fears." That's part of my tradition. I would watch César kneel before his mother who would give the Sign of the Cross and eventually I would do the same. His one hundred-year-old mother was always *persinándolo* [giving him her blessing]. That's the way I was raised.

## UNIVERSITY TEACHING

When I graduated from San José State in 1963, my dad said, "Don't go to Mexico. Work and help your people here." Herman Gallegos was the only person I knew who had a master's degree in social work. He had worked in the probation department and was also in the Community Service Organization with César. He said, "Go to work there," and I did, but I didn't like it. I worked at juvenile hall for six months and I felt locked in. Police would come in with Chicano kids and so then I said, "I'm going to work in another place." Another friend said, "Come to the social welfare office" and so I became a social worker. Then the board of supervisors said, "Well, OK, get all your clients who are on welfare and get them on the bus to work in the fields." So I used my leadership skills that I had learned in high school and college and started a union, the first local 535 here in town. I chaired the organizing committee and the union and then for some reason they didn't want me in town anymore so they got me a mental health scholarship. I went to Berkeley and got my master's degree in 1965. This was the same year César started the strike and even though I was at Berkeley, I met Chávez for the first time.

In 1966, I met Octavio Romano while working on my master's program at Berkeley. We didn't know how to identify the Chicano students on campus so Octavio and Juan Huerta, who is now general counsel of the Smithsonian, and I, along with some others, came up with the idea of having a "moldy enchilada" day. We put a sign on the table at Sproul Hall that read, "Get your moldy enchilada right here." Chicanos would come over and sign up. That's how we started *Quinto Sol*.[11] Octavio started giving a lot of speeches about stereotypes at the Mexican American youth organizations and the MEChA student groups. He finally wrote it and published that speech about stereotypes.[12]

We had a problem with UC Berkeley because there were very few of us Chicano students. We said, "Let's complain to the United States Civil Rights Commission." We got them to come and have a hearing at UC Berkeley. We met with the staff and said, "How many Chicanos do you have on your staff at the national office of Civil Rights Commission?" They said, "None." I ended up testifying against the Civil Rights Commission; the very same investigating body didn't have any Mexican Americans. Then I left Berkeley and taught at San José State for four years. I was thirty years old and one of the youngest professors in California when I started teaching as an associate professor of social welfare in their graduate program. When the students had a sit-in at Tower Hall at San José State, the president called me up and said, "Hey, I need you to come down and see if you can settle this problem with the students." I said, "What can I do for you? You can start a graduate school of social work." He hired me as a consultant and said, "What do you need?" I said, "Well, I've gone to a school of social work at Berkeley and there are very few Chicano or Chicana social workers. So let's start one." We sent somebody to New York to get the accreditation body lined up and we started organizing and we brought the faculty aboard.

The mission was to help build community development. In the early days of that school of social welfare, students helped Chicano parents organize. They taught the parents how to go to school board meetings and build community organizations. There was a lot of excitement and a lot of change going on in those days. Sofía Mendoza was part of that whole movement.[13] The lesson we learned from that was that in establishing a graduate program, whether it be MAGS [the Mexican American Graduate Study program] or the School of Social Work, the university was not going to solve problems for school districts and important community issues that needed to be confronted. The university was part of the establishment.

I was sanctioned by the university and not allowed to teach for a year because they wanted a different direction for the school of social work. I was given a little room and money for some interns. I left after that and taught at UC Santa Cruz for another four years until César called me, and that's when I left the teaching world. Of course it wasn't easy for me to leave. Had my dissertation been accepted, I probably would have stayed.

## THE CHICANO MOVEMENT, SOCIAL CHANGE,
## AND THE CATHOLIC CHURCH

I was asked by Herman Gallegos and Monsignor Roger Mahony to take on a job at the capitol.[14] I was hired to be the consultant to the bishops on the West Coast, although I had had very little experience at that level. César was on strike so I'd talk to him and say, "César, I'm representing the Catholic Conference. What can we do for you?" He'd say, "I need a priest." So I negotiated with Mark Davis from the Franciscans and he got a priest, but the growers said, "No. Get rid of the priest." Dolores Huerta led a group of farm worker women into Bishop Manning's office in Fresno and asked, "Why did you take our priest away from the farm workers? We're not going to leave until we get an answer." Bishop Manning said, "I'm going to go now and pray." Two hours later, he came back and said, "I've been praying to the Holy Spirit." Dolores and the women said, "We are the Holy Spirit incarnate. We are the poor!" He thought about it and agreed.

I always dreamed about representing the farm workers in Washington, D.C., and I realized that dream when César assigned me to go work on the immigration fight for legalization for farm workers. I met Claude Pepper, the most powerful person in the House of Representatives, and I sat with Peter Rodino, who led the hearings on Nixon's impeachment.[15] They'd say, "Reverend, what can I do for you?" So many doors opened. People asked me, "How is it that 1.4 million farm workers got legalized in 1986?" Dolores Huerta asked me, "How did you get entry to all those places that nobody could get entry before?" And I said, "Dolores, I don't know." When I first started lobbying, I'd lie to Dolores. She'd send me to talk to a senator, and I said, "Oh yeah, I talked to the senator." I was lying through my teeth. She could tell from the tone of my voice that I was lying, so she'd ask, "Well, who did you talk to and what did they say?" I said, "Well, I didn't actually talk to the senator. I talked to staffers." Then, she told me, "See that senator? He just went in the men's bathroom. Go and get him. I can't go in there." That's how I learned to lobby. I'd walk in and say, "I'm Sal Álvarez, I'm representing the United Farm Workers and we'd like to know what your position is on this particular bill." Then I would report back to César. César taught me this: "I don't want to hear all the good stuff from you, Sal. I just want to know what problems you're having. I can't help you do your job unless you tell me what the problems are. If you don't ask me for help, I can't help you." Those are two lessons that I've carried on for years and years now. I'm not afraid to go right up to the president of Mexico, or wherever I need to go. I learned not to be afraid because farm workers deserve the best representation they can possibly have.

I went back to Washington, D.C., and to San Antonio and I was also able to make some great inroads with the bishop of Stockton. I said to him, "Bishop, we need an office for the Spanish-speaking people here. We need to organize some leadership and organize a Catholic Council for them." He said, "Well, do it." So I hired someone from New York to work part time in Stockton. I showed him how to do it and he gathered three hundred people. The offices for the Spanish speaking and the bishop's offices that I opened up were modeled after the Catholic Councils for the Spanish speaking that had been set up in Mission District. This organization served as an advocacy group.

Chicanos were demanding more representation and were madder than hell because the Church in the valley was siding with the growers. In San José and Los Angeles, the Chicano Movement raised the question: "What is this? What kind of church do we belong to?" There were a lot of demands made on the Church, and we started meeting with the Apostolic delegate from the Vatican, who was starting to get complaints from Chicanos about bishops. At the same time, Father Patrick Flores started *Los Padres* in San Antonio.[16] He eventually became archbishop but not without nearly one million postcards going to the Vatican asking for it. Chicanos learned to lobby inside the Church.

I would attend the National Conference of Catholic Bishops and be a Chicano lobbyist inside the Church. I saw how one could bring about change if you were on the inside and if you had a key position. César saw me in that role and asked me to help him in his cause. Those relationships that I established at that time have lasted twenty-five years. When the decision was being made as to whom would be the archbishop and the new cardinal of Los Angeles, Monsignor Roger Mahony asked me and others for help. He said, "I want Chicano support to become the archbishop and cardinal of Los Angeles." The *Los Padres* organization supported him because Monsignor Mahony had emerged as being appointed Auxiliary Bishop and then Bishop of Stockton. Governor Jerry Brown appointed him to chair the Agricultural Labor Relations Board in 1975.[17]

## CÉSAR CHÁVEZ AND THE CHICANO MOVEMENT: A SPIRITUAL JOURNEY

César and I believed in the importance of meditation. César practiced yoga; he got up at four o'clock in the morning and at six o'clock we would have conversations about what it was like to draw from a spiritual experience. He once told me, "Sal, with all the problems that I've had, I get migraine headaches and the only way that I can see my way through all of this is by reaching out to Gandhi

and to St. Francis." He read everything he could about Gandhi and the importance of fasting. How was it that St. Francis could levitate? People would find his
body up on a tree. I've always been drawn to that. In 1986, César assigned me to
go to Washington, D.C., and I would get up in the morning, go to St. Matthews's
Church, light a candle, and focus on St. Francis. César and I also related as *cur-
sillistas* [short Catholic course takers]. He taught me how to get in touch with my
energy centers. He would use breathing techniques and meditation to re-energize
himself. We had that in common. He could meditate and he could relate to the
experiences of Teresa de Avila, John of the Cross, and Gandhi.[18] He knew that in
order to get through what he had to get through, he had to draw himself in. I
said, "César, teach me." I became a confidante of him in that sense. César wanted
to develop a religious order, and we talked about what it would be like to be able
to establish one. One time, I went to Rome to investigate this and when I came
back and I told him, "Well, César, it's up to the local bishop," and he said, "Oh,
wow. The local bishop. It's not going to happen here, right?"

César needed support from the Catholic bishops, and my role was to inform
them of the truth. I'd say, "No, I'm sorry. That's not what's going on; we need this
to happen." César would tell people, "I need Sal out there because he knows what
he's doing in terms of the Church." When they sent me to Washington, D.C., to
lobby in 1986 and in 1996, they knew that I could relate to the Catholic Conference, the American Jewish Committee, and to the National Council of Churches.
I could go into the AFL-CIO and sit at the table with ninety *gabachos* [whites]
from around the country and be the UFW representative. César hired lobbyists
who ran for office and then left the union. He knew that I was not going to do
that to him. We had a close relationship. It was spiritual, sacred. I don't know how
he understood it. Having grown up where there were no Mexican teachers, no
Mexican principals, and no Chicanos at all and then seeing what César and the
rest of us were able to do when we banded together was very inspiring.

There was a lot of tension in the union because there were all different kinds
of groups with their own views on how to help the union. When César negotiated a contract, they'd call César a betrayer and that he sold out to the movement.
They'd say, "How could you negotiate contracts like that?" Sometimes large numbers of people would leave the union. One time, six hundred left because they
thought César had turned his back on the farm worker movement because they
saw it as being socialistic. They didn't see it from our perspective. How did he respond? Having gone to Berkeley and working in social welfare administration,
one of the things that I became very aware of is organizational development.

César struggled with that. When the Church helped the union get the grape contract, twenty thousand workers came to the union. I was doing doctoral field-
work at Berkeley at the time, and I went to Delano in the back of my pickup with
my wife and our two kids. I found out that the union did not have the infrastructure to handle twenty thousand members. Having paid their dues, farm
workers would come up from the Coachella Valley with their little membership
card. They'd get to Delano and there'd be another card. How do you handle
twenty thousand cards? It was an unmanageable kind of situation. César had to
leave. He couldn't do administration because he had to go lead the fight against
the Teamsters who went into Salinas. He was not able to develop a good management structure. In 1972, three thousand of us ended up going to jail. We lost
the contracts. Part of César's tension was, "OK, how do I turn myself from being
a movement leader to an administrator? And then how do I get people in the
movement who came in to fight help me administer the contracts through contract administration and negotiation?" It's one thing to come in and organize,
and it's another thing to teach people how to run a union organization. The people who didn't want to be involved with running a union organization or ad-
ministering contracts left the union. And César said, "*Adiós!*"

The *Los Angeles Times* ran some articles that criticized César. They claimed
that he was not into organizing farm workers anymore. That criticism was not
valid because what César actually said was, "Hold it. Don't have any more elections. We have to train negotiators to negotiate the contracts." César set up a
school for negotiators. The criticism by those on the outside, including the *LA
Times,* was that he had stopped organizing farm workers, when in fact he was
building an infrastructure for an organization to grow. I was his special assistant
at the time. I knew management theory and that an organization did require certain kinds of things to happen. He knew that I understood when he said, "I'm
bringing in a cost accounting administrator to set up the finance department and
reorganize other aspects of the union." He would tell me, "I send all these orders
out to all the field directors. They don't listen! They don't want to do what they
need to do." He was asking himself, "How do I move people from a movement to
running an organization?"

This type of tension always existed. At the same time he knew that *La Causa*, the
farm worker movement, demanded a lot of time to go out there and be with the
people, which took him away from again running the organization. As a successor,
César picked Arty Rodriguez, who went to graduate school for social welfare in
Michigan and is an administrator. That's who he [César] trained; somebody who

had gone to a major graduate school and knew something about organizational development theory and how to manage.

I would be driving in the car with César and say, "Well, César, Archbishop Sanchez called you a dictator." He'd say, "He did? Well, who told him I was a dictator?" I'm not going to name names, but there were people in the union that would say, "Yeah, he was a dictator." The people wanted him to continue organizing and really disagreed with him and how he was running the organization. They wanted to be out there organizing farm workers to win elections where they couldn't get contracts. César would tell them, "I have a bunch of bishops out there who want to do their own thing and organize the way they wanted to organize." He had a constant battle over that. That was part of who César Chávez was and the way he was grounded. He used his spirituality to try and bring unity to the organization that was having a series of problems. One of these problems was some Filipinos not wanting to be in a Mexican union, and some Mexicans not wanting to be in a Filipino union. He went to the garage and said, "I'm not going to be your leader. I'm going to go on a fast." By the time Bobby Kennedy came to see Chávez, the Filipinos and Mexicans were begging him to stop and saying that they were going to work together. It was out of that first fast that he moved us from being a Mexican union to telling everybody in the world that this was not about *la raza*. He rejected that concept of just *la raza*, saying that the farm worker movement had to be inclusive and that there had to be a lot of diversity in that respect.

I tell young people whether they're Filipinos or Asians or Mexicans or whatever color, "Think about spending some time, giving up part of your life to volunteer to a good cause." The other side of the coin was that a lot of us burned out. César was a driven person and he never took vacations. Dolores Huerta was the same. The only way Dolores would ever allow herself to take any kind of vacation or time for herself would be if she'd get sick. Even to this day, she has a hard time taking time off. I've had to learn to balance my life differently. When I left teaching at UC Santa Cruz, I promised my wife that I would volunteer for only three years. She supported the family for twelve years. There's no question that I crashed and burned. I got into a deep hole and the dark night of the soul. That too was a very spiritual experience. What am I going to do with myself now that I'm not connected to the farm worker movement in that sense? I saw Dolores go through it in 1988 after she got hit with the baton in San Francisco. She got extremely depressed. I think she started asking herself, "What am I going to do with my life?"[19] I would go to her home and offer a communion service and just try to help her.

## FROM THE MOVEMENT TO A MEDIATOR

I have been part of a number of peace delegations around the world. I was invited be part of the Hispanic delegation, with the Jewish American committee to Israel to study the Israeli-Palestinian conflict. After visiting the Lebanese border, Golan Heights, Beersheba, and other parts, I came back to the United States saying, "Hey, the Palestinians are like us. They're the ones who are the hotel workers and they're the ones who are doing the farm labor." By the way, I met a lot of Spanish-speaking Jewish people from Latin America in Israel.

I also direct the Institute for Non-Violence where I teach conflict resolution, mediation, and negotiations. I've become an expert negotiator and mediator. I mediated between the Vatican and the gay community in San Francisco. The gay community comes to the first meeting and puts a box of condoms right in front of the archdiocese. I settled that dispute by getting the Pope to agree to come to the Mission District. The gay community said, "Well, the Hispanics are the ones that are doing the worst against gays." So we came out with a study showing that wasn't true at all and that got them to back off, and we got a settlement.

I went with a delegation to the archdiocese in Guatemala. I learned the importance of the UN's Human Rights Commission and the impact it had in Guatemala. I also went to El Salvador and saw what it is like for people to know that the clergy were targeted. I had the opportunity to go to Australia and study the land grant movement, where the Aboriginals were getting back their land. I went to Manila and actually did some training at one of the Jesuit universities, with people who were working on Muslim-Christian disputes. I also participated in the Stanford Forgiveness Project, which involved bringing people together for three summers, who were from Northern Ireland and who were both Catholic and Protestant. The Forgiveness Project involved getting Catholics who had family members murdered by Protestants and Protestants who had had family members murdered by Catholics to come into the same room and begin to dialogue. At the beginning of the session we'd start them with tai chi laughing, with a tai chi instructor. They were learning the importance of doing tai chi breathing and getting tensions out before you even start the dialogue.

I went down to Chiapas, Mexico, and worked with Bishop Samuel Ruiz when I was the national director of *Padres*. I asked him, "What can I do for you, Bishop?" I was part of a Mass that was celebrated in four languages. When I got back I went to Congress and asked the Foreign Affairs Committee members whom I knew to aid Chiapas. I also traveled to Ethiopia as part of a church delegation and saw all the poverty. I learned about the African Union of States. I traveled to Uganda, then listened to the Sudanese talk about their suffering. I saw the AIDS projects in Tanzania. I also went into South Africa and dialogued with South Africans about the Chicano experience and the apartheid kind of system that we live in today.

Chávez was taking on the burden of being the leader of the farm worker movement and people were drawn to that. I was drawn to that, and as a result, I left university teaching. In order to get out of oppression and repression, we have to create that movement and work hard in organizing people to do that. This is what I am doing as the vice president of the Dolores Huerta Foundation. We're organizing poor people and bringing in students from Stanford and other universities to help them organize. We're connecting the students and saying, "It's not about us helping you. It's about us doing this together." That's very powerful in terms of people knowing that *uno merece la ayuda de los que están educados* [one deserves the help of people who have an education]. We're continuing to bridge that gap.

**LESSONS LEARNED**

I see today that a lot of young Chicanos are being left behind. When you look at who's succeeding in the world today in terms of the Chicano community, it's the young Chicanas and that's wonderful. The woman's movement has helped Chicanas enormously. The woman's movement has really helped to free the Chicana from many cultural shackles.

I believe that there needs to be a man's movement that talks about having healthy relationships. That's what I do. I go into the National Hispanic University and train the boys and girls in conflict resolution skills. I help empower them so that they can see that they can do needs-based negotiations, instead of power-based negotiations. Part of the struggle in the Chicano community today is about reaching or getting Chicanas and Chicanos to teach and help each other. The guys need help, but they don't know how to ask for help and they think how are they going to ask for help from a girl? "Oh, my God!" It ought to be all right and that should be a wonderful thing. There shouldn't be that inability to ask for help.

I'd like to take credit for what I've done, but I can't. I think about my mom and the credit goes to her, to my dad and my grandmother. They prayed in front of me, and when there was real distraught and crisis in our family, we'd gather to pray. When people got killed in the union and were murdered in the field, César would call us to organize a Mass and we prayed and fasted. That's part of my life. I'm grateful to my grandmother who taught me how to pray and to my mother and my father. I am also grateful to my wife, Sylvia, whom I met here at Santa Clara University when I came to give a talk. She had wanted to become a nun and I had already thought about becoming a priest. She came from a very poor family when we got married. She's been the love of my life. She does an enormous amount of "dream" work, like Dolores Huerta. I have learned so much from her. For example, in the first part of our marriage, I didn't like arts and my counselor says, "Now isn't it possible that God gave your wife gifts that He didn't give you, so that you could learn? Why don't you let her be your higher power?" So I allowed her to teach me. I am so glad I did.

## NOTES

1. The 1933 kidnapping and murder of Brooke Hart resulted in mob violence in San José. About 10,000 residents (approximately one-sixth of the city's population at the time) stormed the jail and lynched Thomas Harold Thurmond and John "Jack" Holmes, who had confessed to the killing. The case drew international attention to San José for the kidnapping, lynching, and for the praise that Governor James Rolph directed to those who participated. It is also notable as the last public lynching in California's history. Álvarez , like some other Mexicans and Mexican Americans, recall this incident but identify the men who were lynched as Mexicans. Such a discrepancy is an excellent example of how oral history accounts reveal a "reinvention" of actual historical events. In this case, the account by the interviewee may be revealing the historical and contemporary tension between the Mexican population and the Anglo population in the city. In his history of San José, Stephen J. Pitti found similar discrepancies in other accounts by Mexicans in their recollection of this lynching. See Stephen J. Pitti, *The Devil in Silicon Valley* (Princeton, NJ: Princeton University Press, 2003),104.

2. Octavio Romano, anthropologist, taught at the University of California at Berkeley and is considered one of the most influential intellectuals of the 1960s Chicano Movement. He founded the journal *El Grito*, one of the first Chicano journals.

3. *Pocho*, literally short or small, is often pejoratively applied by Mexican nationals to American-born Mexicans, who have adopted Anglo American customs or who do not speak Spanish or code-switch.

4. The Newman Club, named after John Henry Cardinal Newman, is a Catholic student organization that seeks to promote the spiritual growth and community service responsibility of its members through religious practices and educational forums.

5. Amigos, founded in 1965, is a nonprofit organization that builds partnerships to empower young leaders, advance community development, and strengthen

multicultural understanding in the Americas. Each summer, volunteers work on community development and public health projects in more than half a dozen countries including Costa Rica, Dominican Republic, Honduras, Mexico, Nicaragua, Panama, and Paraguay. Projects are carried out in collaboration with international development organizations, local government agencies, youth counterparts, and community leaders.

6. The Second Ecumenical Council of the Vatican, or Vatican II, was an Ecumenical Council of the Catholic Church opened under Pope John XXIII in 1962 and closed under Pope Paul VI in 1965.

7. See interview with Blanca Alvarado in this anthology.

8. See interview with Ron Gonzales in this anthology.

9. In 1970, Father Patrick Flores became the first Mexican American and second U.S. Latino to be appointed a bishop in the Roman Catholic Church. As a parish priest and later as bishop of El Paso, Texas, Father Flores addressed the social problems facing his Chicano community such as lack of jobs, education, and housing. Father Flores became archbishop of San Antonio in 1979.

10. See interview with Victor Garza in this anthology. Garza is the founder of La Raza Roundtable, a Mexican American political action group in San José, California.

11. Quinto Sol Publications was an organization founded by a group of Mexican American writers, including Octavio Romano, at Berkeley, California, in 1967. Its most important contribution to the Chicano Movement was is publication of *El Grito*, an outstanding Chicano literary and cultural journal. The name, Quinto Sol, refers to Aztec mythology's reference to the people of the Fifth Sun, who, according to legend, were destined to perish as a result of a major world disaster.

12. See Octavio Romano, "The Anthropology and Sociology of the Mexican Americans: The Distortion of Mexican-American History," *Voices: Readings from El Grito*, edited by Octavio Romano (Berkeley, CA: Quinto Sol Books, 1973).

13. See interview with Sofía Mendoza in this anthology.

14. Herman Gallegos has played an important role in the struggle for human rights. He served as president of the Community Services Organization (CSO), a group that helped spawn the work of César E. Chávez and Dolores Huerta. He also helped create the National Concilio of La Raza (NCLR) in the 1960s. Mahony later became Cardinal of the Los Angeles Archdiocese.

15. Claude Denson Pepper was an American politician of the Democratic Party, and a spokesman for liberalism and the elderly. He represented Florida in the U.S. Senate

from 1936 until 1951 and in the U.S. House of Representatives from 1963 until 1989. Peter Rodino was the Democratic U.S. congressman from New Jersey from 1949 to 1989. Rodino rose to prominence as the chairman of the House Judiciary Committee, where he was chair of the impeachment hearings that led to the resignation of President Richard Nixon. Rodino was generally known as a liberal and a proponent of civil rights legislation and immigration reform. Rodino sponsored the 1986 Immigration Reform and Control Act that granted amnesty to more than three million illegal immigrants. The measure had included a provision for a national identification system that, after intense political debate, was dropped from the bill.

16. PADRES stands for *Padres Asociados para Derechos Religiosos, Eductivos y Sociales* [Association of Priests for Religious, Education and Social Rights]. The organization was founded in San Antonio, Texas, in 1968 and grew into a national organization.

17. In 1975, Mahony became bishop of Fresno and, in 1985, was appointed Archbishop of Los Angeles, the first native Angelino to hold the office. Mahony was made a Cardinal by Pope John Paul II on June 28, 1991. During 2006, Cardinal Mahony spoke out against anti-immigrant sentiments in the United States and Congress.

18. St. Teresa de Avila (1515–1582) was a Spanish nun and mystic. St. John of the Cross (1542–1591) was a Spanish mystic and poet.

19. In 1988, Dolores Huerta participated in a peaceful demonstration against the policies of then presidential candidate George Bush. Protesters stood outside the Sir Francis Drake Hotel on Union Square in San Francisco, and Huerta was severely beaten by police officers. She suffered two broken ribs and a ruptured spleen. In order to save her life, she had to undergo emergency surgery but she lost her spleen. The brutal assault was captured on video by a local television station, and the evidence helped Dolores Huerta win the largest lawsuit against the police and the city. Huerta used the $825,000 to benefit farm workers.

# Sister Gloria Loya, PBVM

*Sister Gloria Loya, PBVM was born to immigrant Mexican parents in El Cerrito, California. She attended Presentation High School in Berkeley and San José State University. At the age of twenty-two, she entered the religious order of the Sisters of the Presentation of the Blessed Virgin Mary (PBVM). During her novice year in the order, she visited migrant labor camps in Salinas and provided services to migrant workers and their children. In the early 1980s, she became actively involved with Hispanic ministry as codirector of El Centro Pastoral. In this capacity she worked tirelessly in ministering to Latinos and on developing Hispanic Catholic leadership in the individual parishes and the overall diocese in San José. Currently she teaches theology at the Jesuit School of Theology at Berkeley's Graduate Theological Union.*

## PARENTS: LEGACY OF LOVE, FAITH, UNITY, STRENGTH, AND HARD WORK

My mother is from Jalisco, Mexico, a place called La Chona. We still have family there, and my childhood was going back and forth to see the family, the Quezadas. We're still very close to the family in Mexico. My mother's sisters and brothers are now in the Bay Area. My father was from Casas Grandes in Chihuahua, but they moved up to El Paso and Juárez during the Mexican Revolution. Our grandfather had a store in a ranch and consequently was killed by Pancho Villa's people. The family story is that my *abuelita* [grandmother], María de Jesús Loya, was a young widow, still carrying my father and she was told, "You'd better get out of town because they'll come for you as well as your daughters." They say she left in the middle of the night in a buckboard and headed for Juárez. She had brothers in El Paso and decided that she needed to start a life for her children.

My mother, María Nicolasa, and Manuel Enrique, my father, met around this part of California [the Bay Area], working in the canneries. They came up here in the '30s when they were teenagers and felt very happy to have work during the Depression, when many Americans didn't have work. Both families worked in the canneries of Sunnyvale and Santa Clara. Then they would go up as far as Sacramento, following seasonal crops. My parents got to know each other through these old Mexican families who knew each other, and worked together, that kind of thing. They were married in 1940.

My father managed to go to school, and his mother, oddly enough, bought some property over in El Cerrito, which we still own. It was a little ranch that she put together with her children. It's amazing because to this day, we've got a couple of acres up there. My dad graduated from Richmond High School and wanted to go to the university. However, he was told he should go and work in a *fábrica* [factory] because he was Mexican. He always told this story, not to make us feel sorry for him, but because he longed for an education. It is something deep in our family and in my spirit, to really see what a privilege it was to be able to be educated.

My mother had to leave school after the eighth grade because her father became very ill. So the three eldest children had to work because they had to help take care of the family. Both of my parents began to work at a very, very young age. They have told us many stories of the joy and the sorrow of what it meant to be fourteen years old and be forced to say you were eighteen because it was the only way to get a job. My mother talks about when she, my *nina* [godmother] Josefina, and my Tía María would get jobs in the canneries. They would be ready to go and they would say, "We need thirty women." And my *tías* [aunts] would say, "We're ready!" They always had this sense of pride, "We're ready." That's the way they were. I have an abundance of great stories of the family, both living and dead, and of how they managed to go forward.

My *abuelita* [grandmother] died young and so my mother and my *tías* took care of the rest. And like so many other families, they stayed together. My mom is ninety-two and she still has her head on straight. It amazes me!

I carry my parents' sense of living in this country but of not losing who we are as *Mexicanos*. It's interesting because I always thought my father was the tough one. But then I realized my mother was so tough in her own way. She really was the leader of the family, even though it looked like my father was. It's quite amazing when I think about these things. I don't see stereotypes of Latinos in our family! After my parents got married, my *abuelita* gave them some of the land in El Cerrito. They built the house in which I now live. It's a magnificent house, up on a hill, with a tremendous view. They were developing their marriage as they built the house, so it's got so much love in it. It's a house of many memories, of fiestas, of family gatherings where we danced downstairs. I said to my brother, "I'm so glad that after my dad died we kept this home." There are many, many memories of my parents and extended family.

The family struggled. My mother has always said that a large family has many more blessings and also more sorrows. My *abuelita* was the head of the family, no question about it. Then when she died, my father became the head. You could just tell because everybody came to him when they needed something. I think that his leadership captured me in my psyche of what it means to lead a family and to be able to see ahead, even when things are difficult. I attribute to my parents a lot of qualities that I have been able to develop. My dad had that kind of wisdom that you can't get in books! He had that wisdom and confidence. I see that in my mom as well. She's starting to forget some things now and I find that painful because I love her dearly, but at ninety-two, it's OK to forget some things! Last week, she said to me, "*Hija* [daughter], we've had a lot of things happening in our family, but our religion, our faith, has really kept us together." That's probably why faith is very important to me as well. Not a phony kind of faith, but a lived faith, which is what I saw in my parents and my whole family. I would say that's the *tierra*, the soil, in which I grew up, which has been a tremendous gift.

## A REFLECTIVE STUDENT IN A PROTECTIVE LEARNING ENVIRONMENT
Before moving to the El Cerrito area, we lived in East Oakland, where mostly Mexicans and blacks lived. I first went to school there as a little kid and I loved school very, very much. When we moved out to El Cerrito, I wondered where all the *Mexicanos* were! It was just different. The first memories I have of people speaking negatively about *Mexicanos* was in El Cerrito. It was very deep in my mind that we were a loving Mexican family, but I would hear little kids in school say negative things about Mexicans. I would say, "Mom, why did they say we're dirty Mexicans?" I couldn't understand it. My mother would say, "They don't know what they're doing. They're ignorant. And you have to keep living and these are just words that they're saying." But it really penetrated my thoughts. It's the first time I had the sense of wondering, "Why are these people doing this?" But I loved school itself. I went to public school up to the eighth grade and then

I went to Presentation High School in Berkeley. I had never been around nuns and schools before that. We went to catechism, which I hated, because it meant Saturday morning we couldn't watch cartoons. But we had a lot of fun, innocent times in high school. The young women in my class were of different cultures: Irish, Italian, Mexican. I really loved those years and I loved learning to study in a serious way. But I also loved my social life. For example, we would go out and learn how to drive a car. We struggled and learned. I learned to love the sisters as well. There was an attraction there although I had not thought about religious life at all as a kid. We had events to help the poor and the sisters had missions in Chiapas, Mexico. Something touched me about what I wanted to do. I thought there was something else I could do with my life besides go to school and get married, which were very important things to me. High school was a very important time in the sense of getting to know the sisters. We were sixteen or seventeen, and we'd sit there [and say], "We think we're losing our faith, Sister." We didn't know what we were talking about. Little did we know when we got in college what it really meant to be challenged and lose your faith! It was a time of being secure even in high school.

I began to think, "What else am I going to do with my life? Is this what it's all about?" Being a wife and mother was something very important in my family, so when I thought of religious life, I thought, "Oh, that doesn't sound like something I was taught about." Those things were in the back of my mind. Living in the East Bay, I was also beginning to see the student movement and the César Chávez movement in the '60s in Berkeley. Those things were like shadows, and later on, they really got to me as I went on to college. I really enjoyed my high school years and treasure them very much. Catholic girls' school was a very protective place. I was prepared intellectually, but I wasn't prepared to deal with the chaos that came with the '60s. Some of the sisters would talk about that in a course supposedly called "Family Living" where we really raised a lot of questions. It was a good forum, sort of like early group therapy. There were probably a more homogenous group of kids. We didn't have kids that were from broken families, like today. It was very different. It was a more protective environment because of the culture of the time, because it was a Catholic girls' school and probably because of my family.

I was the rebellious one, not my brother. I would talk back. My brother never did! I would say to him, "How come you had to be that way? You never say anything wrong!" Like most teenagers at that time, I wanted more freedom. My parents were very *Mexicano* in a lot of things. Even though my brother was three years younger than I, I had to come home at twelve o'clock from a date, but he could stay out until one o'clock in the morning. I always thought that was very weird. I said, "Why is that?" My parents said, "*Mija*, you have to understand." I'd say, "I don't understand." I was starting to question life, authority, and even my own faith. Part of my rebellion was that I didn't even know my own questions at the time. When I got out of school, I wasn't sure what I was going to do with my life. That's when the real onslaught came of questioning what was going on in my own life, in a more serious way. I remember struggling with, "Oh, I wished it could be so simple." The questions were becoming more difficult in society.

## ENTERING THE NOVITIATE: A DIFFICULT BUT RIGHT DECISION

I had raised the question with my parents about going to religious life when I was a senior, which was a complete bomb to the family. There was no question about it. That was very powerful and very difficult. It was a time when young people were getting into the Peace Corps, and frankly it wasn't so unusual to enter a religious life or a seminary. That choice was very, very painful to me and to my parents. They thought I needed psychiatric care or something. They'd say, "What's wrong with you? You don't want to get married and have children?" I thought, "Well, if this is such a good idea, why is it so divisive in our family?" That was very hard for me. So then I decided that I would go on to a community college and work to get a feel for what people do when they're working, rather than go away to school. That way my parents might see that I'm committed to them but I have to figure out what I have to do.

My mother had a very difficult time dealing with this emotionally. I don't think it was because I wasn't going to have children. At that time religious life meant you left your family and went away to enclosure. My family's fear was not so much that I wouldn't have children but that they would lose me. That whole notion was very difficult for them.

I really hated work. It was so boring. I was a clerk in an insurance company. I felt like there was no feeding of my mind, although I would go to school. Finally at twenty-one I said to my parents, "I think I really have to do this religious life thing because I've got to get it out of my system." I went to Europe with a friend of mine for the summer, and when we got back, my parents met me in New York. I was going to enter the religious community in September and this was in August. My parents said, "*Hija*, we know you want to do this but we would like to go with you back to Europe to continue . . ." They were presenting me with the apple. "Oh, my God! I'd love to go back to Europe," I said. "But, Mom and Dad,

I have to go [to the convent]. I have to try this." There we were in JFK Airport trying to make a decision about my life! I came back but it was not easy. My parents were upset and said, "Well, we're not going to be there for you when you go." I know that was very hard for them. I kept thinking, "Well, if God is God, why is this such a difficult thing for all of us if this is the right thing?" It was a real struggle. I wasn't sure. The sisters in this community and my friends knew I was struggling, but we all felt I should try this. I could become an educated Chicana and go off and make money or I could say, "This is my community." God was saying, "What are you going to do?" That was a challenge to me.

The day that I entered the convent, my parents were so upset you'd have thought it was my funeral. But of all the things, my father took me shopping a couple of days before I entered. He took me to lunch and I looked across the table and my father had tears in his eyes. He said, "*Hija*, you know whatever you have to do." It was quite interesting and I still think about the fact that my father was the one that reached out to me, even more so than my mother did. I always thought of God's blessing through my dad. The day that I entered, they invited me into their bedroom and had me kneel down and they gave me their blessing. It was very touching for them and for me because none of us really knew why this had to be! It was really a faith thing for me and for them. I knelt down and they both blessed me and I knew that it would be OK. I just knew that we were together, that this was hard, but God is in this somewhere. I think back today, not in a sad way, but just one of those moments that you know God is working here, that there's something bigger than what I could understand.

### PARTICIPANT IN THE CIVIL RIGHTS MOVEMENT:
### IN SOLIDARITY WITH THE POOR

I realized how wise my parents were because I didn't enter until I was twenty-two, which meant that I entered after the Second Vatican Council. Thank God that this community and many others took the Vatican Council's new direction of renewing itself in the modern world very seriously. Women religious took that very seriously because women religious really were in cloister up to that point. I don't know how they did it. They would leave the convent, go to school or work in the hospital, and have to go back to the convent. Many of them could not be at their own parents' funerals. That's probably the kind of stuff my parents didn't want me to suffer through. When I entered, we were lucky. We were in the process of renewal, which meant I could go home and visit my family. We didn't have enclosure. There was so much openness. The families were much more a part of the "formation" as novices.

They were part of the novitiate family and it wasn't a separation. I thought my parents were very wise. If I had entered when I wanted to, I probably would have been like so many others and left early because priests and sisters entered when they were sixteen, eighteen years old. They'd never really had a chance to work or to go to school or to date. I realized after that how fortunate I was.

But when I entered, it was also chaos in terms of Vietnam and the farm workers. I lived three years in Los Gatos because our novitiate was at Presentation Center on Bear Creek Road. I have lots of warm memories of being a novice up there! We were going to San José State University while we were novices so there was a whole Chicano Movement going on as well. It was about increasing scholarships for minority students and supporting the farm workers' cause for justice. We were jazzed up about those issues. It was a whole new life where young Chicanos were standing up and being proud of whom they were and what they believed in. What struck me was that this self-awareness and ethnic pride did not begin in Mexico, but it began with us here in this country. It gave us a sense of who we were here, that we had a voice. This movement also gave us studies in Chicano history and stimulated Chicanos to write creatively and things like that. I like that Chicano spirit—all of us together striving for social justice. But the Chicano Movement was really fueled mostly by students.

I remember when Martin Luther King Jr. and Robert Kennedy were shot. We were at San José State and we were coming out of class and they were throwing tear gas at us! They published a large picture of this event in the *San Jose Mercury News* and there were three of us nuns in it. We were novices and thought, "Oh, God! It looks like we were in the demonstration! We're going to be thrown out now for sure." We said to the novice director, "We were just standing there and they were throwing the tear gas!" That was very real. When Martin Luther King Jr. was killed, we went to a memorial service at San José State and the Black Panthers got up and said they were going to be killing everybody. There was just so much chaos and violence. But we knew that this was our generation and what we were studying about God had to affect this world. It was a really important time to be formed.

Interestingly enough, while we were studying up there, we would go out to work in different ministries. The first place they assigned me was in the migrant labor camps in Gilroy. I grew up in a middle-class Mexican American family, knowing that our roots were poor but I'd never really been in a migrant camp, not like this. It was amazing. I was in Morgan Hill and Gilroy and loved it. The people were tremendous. They were so wonderful, just to go down to visit them, to listen, to be in there with the kids. We'd come home filthy from the children grabbing onto our skirts and it was so hot. But it was an experience that I'll never forget.

It also was the time of César Chávez. Immediately there was a connection for me, to know that in our own Latino community we had leadership that was rising up. Right out of Sal Si Puedes in East San José.[1] I was very much in tune to it and was out there in the demonstrations as well. My parents were very proud of me. But it was not easy. In Coachella, priests and sisters were getting banged up.[2] Before we would demonstrate, we would fast and pray so that we were disciplined to go out. This was not just fun and games. The first time I went to see César, I'm saying to myself, "Where is he?" Here's this guy sitting on the corner, quietly watching, until he gets up and I realize, "Oh, my God! That's him!" His humility and spirituality, along with that of Dolores Huerta, were very Gandhian. I was really connecting with what I was studying and with the possibility of being a sister that could be with the people in some way. Back then we were basically a community of teachers. I went into teaching in San José at St. John Vianney and at a high school in San José. I think that was my real formation, no question about it. I can't talk about school without saying, "Is this making sense? My education can't just be for me because there are too many memories of my father, saying it's for the community." Therefore, I think it's a treasure to work with our students and kick them a little in the butt to get their education!

I saw the humanity and the goodness of people who were living in migrant labor camps, but I also saw poverty and the moral problems that they faced. When you've got ten people living in one room, there are lots of difficult issues. However, I also could say that I saw my people and myself right there. That really was a challenge, to know that we're all one. With César Chávez and the struggle, I saw how much faith and justice were wedded together. I saw, "This is who I am. This is where I came from. But look at the nobility in that poverty. Look at the humanity and at God in that poverty." It drew me to reflect and to want to be more spiritual and prayerful. A good thing about the novitiate was learning to pray in silence. The noise and distractions are within you sometimes, but the cry of the poor saying, "We are human. We must get out of this" is in your being.

I was also watching and hearing stories of what some of the *patrones* [bosses] would do. I know lots of women and men working in the electronics industry, in the so-called wonderful Silicon Valley, who have cancer because of the pesticides. My choice became more and more that I wanted to serve, and that if I was going to continue with religious life, I didn't want to just go work with the wealthy. Being with migrant workers made me feel I had to be with our people. To this day,

I will go out to workshops. I went to Reno last year to do workshops and it reminded me of Gilroy. The people who are working in casinos and in the mines
are scared to death right now because of immigration. I keep feeling that pull to
do what I can, to be there and take time to learn. Those images are very powerful to me, along with the work of César Chávez and Dolores Huerta. I had the
opportunity to interview her a few years ago for an article I had done about how
to love the *patrón*. She said, "We had to learn what it meant to not hate the other
one that is oppressing." That's so Gandhian and so Jesus Christ. I'd say to myself,
"Can I really do that?" This is where I get my theology. Dolores has talked about
how difficult but how important it is to be able to say, "The other also needs to
be treated like a human being. Otherwise, this is what happens. We're all in the
rat race. We're all hating each other." That nonviolent, deeply spiritual value is
what I try to keep working at.

Another encounter with *patrones* was when I was asked to go up to Sonoma,
where migrant workers were looking for a place to live. The people that own the
wineries said, "Oh, they're only going to be here for a while. Why do we have to
worry about where they live?" I can't answer their question fully, but I feel I have
to be with the people to keep remembering who I am. When we do workshops,
we do it to give them a better sense of who they are and what they can do to empower themselves. The times in the migrant camps remind me that these are my
people and I want to be a part of this. I know a lot of people say "empowering
the poor," but I think they're empowering me! We're not empowering anybody.
People can do it, but we're walking with them in solidarity.

When you're with a *pueblo* [community of common people], you're with the
people. You're not just there by yourself. Now as then, even the immigration picketing we did here in San Francisco, they are young families. This is the future.
Other people say, "More immigration laws. Don't let them in!" We look at it as
something positive and you feel the energy of the movement. There's prayer;
there's *fiesta* [celebration]. I felt that way in the beginning, and I feel it now when
I go to these pickets. But it can also be a dangerous place. I feel like the people
have their leadership. We have a public voice. We're united. It's not just *Mexicano*,
Chicano. It's *Salvadoreño, Nicaraguense*, all of us. That's an exciting way to look
at our future. But I'll be happier when a just immigration law is passed.

## PASTORAL WORK: FAITH THROUGH THE PROMOTION OF JUSTICE

The church of San José was very much the people's parish, the Latino community. We used to work with them a lot. It was not easy sometimes because they

were frustrated and angry. There would be meetings of *agentes de pastoral* [pastoral workers or agents] trying to plan for what we needed, like workshops. But at the same place there would be maybe one hundred people from El Salvador, people from both sides of the civil war, sitting right before you. Religion becomes very realistic at what I call spiritualizing, because there's pain and the need for reconciliation.

Working in ministry throughout the West, I feel the Anglo is poor in family and spirituality, although they might be wealthy in money. Maybe our people don't have all the economic necessities yet, but we're wealthy in our values, like our families, faith, and the possibility of education. At our school we do a summer program in Spanish because so many of our kids can't get into a university yet they're hungering to learn. They have the capacity, but they haven't gone through the system here. To get as far as possible in education is important for their future, not to make money, but to better themselves as people. The spiritual realm is key in that it brings that richness in us in this materialistic world.

I must say, for those of us who are Catholic and Protestant, I know what the difficulties are with our Church as an institution. As a woman in the Church, I know it very well. I love my Church and I can't just walk out of it, but I can help it to be better from inside. In those spiritual traditions, there is an ethic that is very important when we work for justice. When we stand together as Catholics and Protestants for the immigrant and we can stand with our bishops and our leaders, it's very potent and very powerful. César Chávez saw that. Ana María Isasi-Díaz, a wonderful Cuban American feminist, says, "*En la lucha*" [in the struggle]. We should join "la lucha." I really do think that taking responsibility and the struggle for justice is really important, especially now in regards to immigration.

I teach a class on ministry, and I use a book called *Reconciliation* that goes back to César Chávez. How can we reconcile? I don't mean in a phony, superficial way. There are women who have been abused, and Father says, "You have to forgive." Well, forget it! But when it's appropriate, when a person's ready, it's about how the victim can become empowered to even forgive the others. Dolores Huerta spoke of that in my interview with her. It's something I still struggle with but that's what she said. With César and Gandhi, it's a stronger force than being violent. I call that God's grace. I have to be in touch with these things or I'll lose my own soul.

## BETWEEN TWO WORLDS: RICHNESS AND TENSION
The Latino community is more organic in its nature, in its faith, in its way of being. Celebrations and *fiestas* are all part of spirituality as far as I'm concerned.

The North American Church is more organized. For example, when you walk into a parish and you want to baptize your child, first they'll tell you how many classes you have to go to. That's why I think the Jehovah's Witnesses are attracting so many of the Catholics. We Catholics first give the rules and then say, "Come to the community," and by then it's too late. There are some difficult things, no question about it. People who work in the ministry in the Latino community are always in two worlds. This is also true of the Mexican American. We're always in two worlds. Virgil Elizondo, one of my great friends and a great theologian, says this.[3] This is our role as a mestizo people, which we call borderlands theology. We're always between two worlds and there's a richness there. It's rich that I can read Cervantes and I can read Shakespeare. Or I can go to a Mass in English and I can go to a Mass in Spanish. But when it comes down to it, there's a lot of tension between the two. There's no question about it.

I do think there is much to be done for those who are bilingual and bicultural. We can bridge some of this, but we have a long way to go. I don't think we, the Latino community, have power in the Church. I have a cousin, Rich García, who is an auxiliary bishop in Sacramento. The fact that he is auxiliary and not ordinary means he doesn't have any real place. We have a wonderful Mexican American bishop in Los Angeles, but he doesn't have his own diocese. So we have the people, but our leadership sometimes is not recognized. So this is very difficult because I have love for the Church. But I learned in the Vatican Council that through our baptism, we have as much power as anyone else. We have a voice and we need to participate in it. The easy way is to leave the Church, but the hard way is to stay in there. We have to raise our voices and say, "That's important to me."

The Church is a hierarchy. I must say that while I was in San José, Bishop Pierre DuMaine was very helpful to us. He knew Spanish well, so he spoke directly to the people and we didn't have to be his interpreters. It's important that we have people in the Church who understand the faith and culture. I find it troublesome that people who are in formation and are going to work in California don't have to learn Spanish. It's difficult but they don't care even though this is the biggest community. Part of the problem is not understanding and not accepting the fact that the Church is no longer Euro-American. The good thing is that there are more people working in the churches than when I began. On the other hand, I must admit, structurally we have the Centro Pastoral. We had a place that was in the barrio, next door to Our Lady of Guadalupe Church. The people saw that and knew we were representing the diocese in the barrio. The people knew that we were part of them.

## "WE ARE THE CHURCH"

I was brought up a cradle Catholic, but I also know it's my spiritual home. It's very Protestant to change your religion with the wind. But I say, "We cannot just be changing our religion like you change your shoes. We have to have more depth." Now if you're really called to move out of that faith, that's one thing. But it's almost like a fad in our country to say, "Well, I left them." Yeah, you left them, but I found that when it comes to real problems, they come back. They say, "*Hermana, dicen que no existe la Virgen de Guadalupe*" [Sister, they say the Virgin of Guadalupe does not exist]. I say to my Protestant cohorts, "You've got to respect the spirituality of the people." There are a lot of good things happening within the faith community, Protestant and Catholic. We have a long way to go, but that's the place that will help us struggle for justice and immigration. If we're going to be individualistic about our religion and God, okay, that's very nice. But if you belong to a community of faith, it gives you the possibility of putting it in the public forum where you have a public voice.

Now when I work in the Latino community, it's usually with people who are going to be leaders in catechetical offices. I say to them, "You have the power but you have to understand how the American Church works as an organization. It's like going to a university. You have to know how it works. Otherwise you're never going to get through the pearly gates." I say, "You have the leadership. You have the ability. You have the gifts." But on the other hand, you can't just be crying about this. You cannot go to the bishop and think he's like Santa Claus: "*Necesitamos, necesitamos*" [We need this, we need that]. No.

When Pierre DuMaine came to San José, we gathered all the leaders and said, "This is who we are. This is what we have to offer. We're here. We're ready. We're ready to work with you. But we are also equal. We're partners. We have to be partners with the Church because we are the Church."[4] The Christian, Catholic, and Protestant Church has a tradition that can give us guidance for the struggle for justice. Cardinal Mahony standing up for immigration is powerful. When we stand up for the right things, this is a very powerful body of Christ. When we stand up as Latinos, we have a lot to give to this Church. I don't think we should back off and say, "*No nos quieren*" [They don't want us]. The church of San José was built on the shoulders of many others, like Ron Burke and Antonio Soto, who all started before us. These guys used to go out to the migrant camps with a mission band, and they started retreats and they started the *movimientos* [movements] like *Movimiento Familiar Cristiano, Encuentros Conjugales* [marriage retreats], and all that.

There's so much that is possible and it has to go forward. I think some people may not be able to do it, but the real leaders will. We are the Church. We are the greatest number. If there's going to be a life-like church and a vibrant church of San José, the Latino community must be a part of it. This is also the age of lay leadership, such as lay ecclesial ministry. People that are prepared must rise up. I see lots of *luces* [lights], but I also see *sombra* [darkness]. *Sombra y luz* [darkness and light], but we cannot get so lost in the *sombra* that you don't see the *luz*. There are real issues, such as raising new leaders for the Church and giving resources so that our people can have their meetings. We're far better off now. When I was there, the only Hispanic pastor was at Our Lady of Guadalupe. Then we had guys like Tony McGuire and Matteo Sheedy who were very good with our people and were Latino in spirit.

There are a lot of areas we still have to grow. I don't know if I should say this publicly but of course I believe that women should be ordained. This is a touchy issue and we're not supposed to talk about it, but it will come. It will come because we'll have women that are ready to do this, because we need them. We've had women doing ministry in the Latino community from the time of the Indians. Who was the *partera* [midwife]? She was the one who was with the *moribundos* [the dying], both blessing and baptizing. Who was in charge of funerals? We've done this, but now it needs official recognition and imposition of hands and oils over the head, the way that ecclesial commitment is to men and women. These things will change too, but we have to work hard and not lose our way. It means a lot of prayer and bringing our spirituality with us as we struggle so we know which way to go.

## EL CENTRO PASTORAL CHANGED LIVES

In the '50s the whole Pastoral Hispano started in San José with people like Tony Soto and Reynaldo Flores, who were Franciscans. There were a number of them who gathered together and called themselves the Mission Band. They went out to do workshops and visit the migrant camps and started the *movimientos*, as I mentioned earlier. In the '70s, Tony McGuire, Rich Garcia, and Sister Sandy Price of Notre Dame de Namur began the Centro Pastoral. It was a pastoral place for the people. At the time, we were part of the archdiocese of San Francisco and it was so far to come up for meetings. One good thing about being so far away from the archdiocese was that we had a lot of creativity. We paid a dollar a month to use the old building at Notre Dame High School. People could come in for whatever their needs were. We would do information, referrals, family counseling, and retreats. We also organized our *encuentros* in that building. It became a center for the folks to know if they needed something, we were there, and that we were representing the bishop in the diocese. It's ironic because women cannot be ordained in the Church, but if you scratch the surface in many places, lay women and sisters do the work of any pastor or priest. Maybe not saying Mass, but you really do hear confessions.

I always had this question in me about why the places for our people and the poor are crappy. Our people don't need a Hilton Hotel, but they deserve dignity by the places they're in. That bothered Ana María Pineda and myself, so we found the house next door to Our Lady of Guadalupe Church, which is now used for religious education.[5] We talked to Pierre Dumaine and we said, "We'd like to use that because it's more like a home and we could fix it up." Ana and I had a big joke because the owner was this big Anglo guy who owned all this property over on the East Side. We were trying to get him to deal with us to use this place. He always had these big plants so I'd always call him Señor Perchera [*percha* is a piece of timber to support anything]. "Oh, God! Here comes Señor Perchera; he's probably going to throw us out again." I always think you've got to have a sense of humor because sometimes it's just beyond what you can imagine.

In 1985, Alviso experienced a big flood. I went and there were two hundred people standing by the center's [Centro Pastoral] door in desperation, not knowing what to do. It became a place where people knew that they could come and we would try to help them out. It was pastoral, the work of *evangelización* [evangelization] and culture. Every step of the way, issues of justice were with us, whether it was the people of Alviso, immigration, or abuse in a family. It was a good and safe place for the Latino community. It was wonderful being next door to Our Lady of Guadalupe Church. When we left, it went back to Our Lady of Guadalupe and it's now used as their catechetical center. We had all of our documents and archives in the garage, and I've often thought, "God only knows whatever happened to it" so I'm glad you're asking about it.

One of the things that we were very concerned about was our *memoria* [memory]. There's a young woman now working in the diocese who happened to be my student at Berkeley, and I said, "You have to know that a lot happened before." They have to know the Latino community has had leadership and a voice. It's not just starting now. We became a diocese in 1981 and continued to use the Centro but also tried to be present at the diocesan offices because they wanted to have us there. It was good because it meant we would have a voice at the table for the diocese where they're making decisions. I really must say I appreciated that Pierre

Dumaine understood the Latino community so well. Apparently when he was in the seminary, a good friend of his was Mexican American and he would often visit their home. That's where he learned Spanish and about the Latino family. He was very attentive. We would say, "Pierre, you really need to talk to the people about this" and he would. It was really good for the people to know they could talk directly to their bishop. We were in between two cultures, being with the people and coming up to the diocese. There was an advantage for the Centro to have its own team, when there were six of us. We had Ricardo Ponce, a social worker, his wife, a couple of sisters, and a young person. We were like a real *equipo* [team], what we call *equipo ecclesial* [ecclesial team], where it was laity and religious and the priest together. It was a nice balance for the people.

We had about fifty parishes in the San José Diocese, and about twenty-five of them had a Spanish Mass and a number of Latino people. We would try to be in touch with those pastors to be a resource for the Hispanic community and to do workshops. Ana María would help with the catechetical so there would be a bilingual aspect to that as well. Our basic task was training leaders. We started the *Instituto Hispano* [Hispanic Institute]. Every Wednesday night for a year or two, we selected various pieces of Scripture that they could understand and they really loved that. But our work was always from the context of our culture, not just from the Bible. It was more about what the Scriptures say to us as Latinos. "If Jesus is from Galilee, the back roads of Israel at that time, and comes to the big city, Jerusalem, he's laughed at because he had an accent." We tried to put it into a context that related to their reality.

We'd have marriage encounters and I would see these big Chicano guys with tattoos up and down their faces and their heads. Somehow they would come to the *encuentro* and I'd see some of these guys break down, change their lives. When we did *encuentros*, we would have four couples and a sister and priest work with them. We weren't therapists, but the whole process was one of memory, and some of the couples on the team were people who also had experienced abuse in their families or drugs or alcohol. But they changed their lives. They were the ones who talked to the couples that would come on the retreat.

The programs were very moving. It was mostly formation of leaders so that they could become leaders in their parishes, which was very challenging. We would make up the curriculum. There was a pedagogy we were making up because we knew it had to be culture and faith and there weren't a lot of materials. We would go to the seminary and make videos. We had Father Fausto López from Guatemala, who was a wonderful theologian.

## AGENT OF CHANGE WITHIN THE CHURCH:
## "IN TENSION THERE IS GROWTH"

It was not unusual to have a struggle to have a Mass in Spanish. They would agree to a Mass in Spanish, but it was always at an odd hour. They'd say, "Well, then you have it at two o'clock in the afternoon. Because then the other Masses will be over." I remember that's why it was such a pride in the community that the people built Our Lady of Guadalupe Church with their hands. That was part of the struggle. The Catholic Church in the U.S. used to have what they called "national churches." At the turn of the 1900s, the Irish or the Italians would have their own priests, sisters, and parishes along with their own language. In the '70s those "national churches" began to go down the tubes. The U.S. bishops didn't want that. It sounds so romantic, but they wanted the Latino community to be part of the larger parish. Well, that's very nice, but it's not so easy to do. It was a struggle in many cases to have a Mass in Spanish. There were many places where the people would have to struggle and show that there were enough of them to do it. That's where our people really showed their leadership and that the Mass meant so much to them. And that's all they were asking. That's why the Centro Pastoral was put together, because there were no more national churches. San José was a young diocese, therefore Anglos and Latinos were thrown together in the same parish, and we had to start to work that out.

There was a certain town in the diocese where the data clearly showed that it was 75 percent Latino. I said, "Don't you think you should have a Spanish Mass here, Father?" He replied, "Oh, we don't have any Latinos," and I'd say, "But the census says . . ." This is why the *agentes de pastoral,* the ministers, have to understand and be prepared. Not everyone in the Anglo Church is racist. You can't just go in there crying about it. I might cry later, but meanwhile I'm going to be ready with my data to say, "This is really what it says here." The Church understands that kind of honest dialogue.

As I mentioned earlier, I remember some of the student movements at San José State in the early '80s. They were cutting back student scholarships, and we would go with our young people to picket. So we were out there with them because it was so important to support them. San José has always been rich in leadership from the various agencies, along with parish people. The Chicano Movement was very important to me as a Chicana. There was a lot of stuff going on with the various community groups. We would definitely go help and support San José State and other public places. We paid a lot of attention to that, especially at the educational level. It was great that we always had strong agencies in

San José. There were so many I don't even remember them all. We were miles away from thinking that a place like the Mexican Heritage Plaza could be possible. Who would have ever thought something like that could rise up at that time? The whole East Side was like the Sal Si Puedes neighborhood. The streets around Our Lady of Guadalupe weren't even paved. It really was like a little town. We'd stay in contact with agencies because it was very important to us not to be a little entity, but to be in touch.

I gained a sense of distinct identity that incorporates my Mexican roots, but also incorporates who I am up here in the United States. I can be both of those. Otherwise I'm going to be always warring one against myself, whether it's the *Indio*, the American, or whoever. I don't know how many *Indios* [indigenous] or Europeans were in my past. Who knows?

That's part of knowing your identity as a Chicana. It was so exciting to see our women. I belonged to *Las Hermanas* [The Sisters], and oh boy, we were all mad at something! There were sparks flying, and it was a good thing. *Las Hermanas* started as a national organization for women religious. We knew the Chicanas in each group, so we formed a group where we would meet every year. We supported the farm workers and in fact were a great support to the Mexican American Cultural Center in Texas. I did a year there, which was a wonderful experience, getting into my Texas roots. That's when I began to do some theological serious thinking. At MACC, the Mexican American Cultural Center, Virgil Elizondo had gone to the East Asian, Manila Pastoral Institute and began to piece together Asian culture and faith and see what the Asians were doing. He said, "Well, why can't we do this with Mexican Americans?" In more contemporary times, I would say he is one of the first Mexican American theologians. It was the first time I ever met a Hispanic theologian. I said, "A theologian that's Hispanic? My God! They're always European!" That was very exciting because we had the experience of the Latino from all over the U.S. Although it was called the Mexican American Cultural Center, we had some Puerto Ricans and *Cubanas* [Cuban women] and men and women were coming together. As a religious organization, it was a fun place because we could let down our hair. The Texans would have Texas barbecue every Wednesday night. They would be dancing *norteñas*, and it was just a lot of fun.

But it was also a serious place where there was heated debate about the Church and racism. I really got in touch with the Texas experience with racism. It opened up to me some things that I remembered when we used to go to El Paso. I was seven years old and we were going to get breakfast in El Paso, and I remember reading the sign that said, "Mexicans and dogs not allowed." The sisters and priests would also talk about suffering in racism. In Californian, racism is here, but it's subtle. Terrible, but subtle. In Texas it was, "String them up and kill them." The sisters really suffered because they came from communities that were European. I didn't experience a lot of that in my religious community because I entered the convent after the Vatican Council. MACC was a place to let out your anger but also a place to see the possibility of a new theology. I thought, "So what does this mean? We can develop a theology that comes from our people." In a broader sense, it means borderlands theology. The Puerto Ricans and the Cubans say "theology of exile." Virgil was a catalyst in the development of a new theology. He would speak of borderlands theology, mestizo theology, and the elements of that. It was certainly borne out of our Lady of Guadalupe and our practices and so on. Theology is a heated place, but it was really heated there, and that was part of the Chicano Movement as well.

It's still part of being in between the organic and the organizational. The theologian David Tracy says, "The tension is in the middle," and that's very true.[6] But then David Tracy says, "In the tension is the growth." The difference between fundamentalist Christians and Catholics and Protestants is that our faith in religion isn't just "Alleluia, *Gloria a Dios*" [Glory to God]. I wish it would be that simple. It's doing the hard work and being in the tension. I do know that if I'm in a particular group, I will always be myself and no one is going to take that away. However, there are times I will talk about some things in a particular group that I won't with others, even in my own community.

I belong to a community called Guadalupe Community. We're all Latinas and we're all bilingual. I need that community for sustenance and where I can let down my hair. That's where you get support, prayer, and challenge. That's probably where we talk most. I have to be prudent in the public world because I want people to hear what we have to say. But I'm not going to water it down. It's a fine line you have to walk, to say something as a Chicana feminist. For example, I won't use the word "feminist" in front of my little old sisters because they'd probably fall off their wheelchairs because they don't understand the difference between feminist and feminine. But I get it in there whenever I can. In fact we have a book coming out called *The Handbook on Latina/o Theology*. It's edited by Edwin Aponte and Miguel de la Torre, who are both Protestants.[7] The article I have in it is titled "Four Perspectives on Latina Feminist Theology." In this article I'm trying to address four different feminist perspectives that I see in the United State. Chicanas are in most of them, except for the first one, which is more of a fundamentalist approach. I'll find out what people's reactions are. In that forum I can put it out there and see if am I totally off the mark. Then I can learn something, which is what theology is about.

My sisters might be bored with some of this, but my small community loves it. But I also know my sisters love me and I love them too. We're all from different cultures, but our foundation was Irish. When I went to Ireland, I thought, "Oh, God, this is acculturation for me in the reverse!" But then I found that the real Irish are not so different from Latinos in their family, their *fiesta*, and their suffering. But I have found that many Irish Americans don't know their culture anymore. They don't even know what St. Patrick's Day is, which worries me, as does the celebration of the Cinco de Mayo. Do we really know what that is or is it just time to go drink? I hope I am who I am everywhere. But not everybody wants to hear all the things that give me passion, and as a religious I need to learn to listen. One of the courses that I teach is pastoral counseling, and we talk about listening to other cultures.

## "THE LADY OF GUADALUPE IS THE HEART OF OUR ETHICS"

Our Lady of Guadalupe is the heart of our ethics. It is not just a logical construct in a systematic way, an American way. If you look at Guadalupe, it opens up many different levels. One is ethics, in the sense that she informed Juan Diego to be a leader and build a new *templo* [temple] in the Americas. This is more than folklore to me. It's not an apparition; it's what we would call a theophany. A real thing happened and it has potency because I believe God's grace is in that. It's a collective story that has remained in the community for five hundred years, not just as a figment of somebody's imagination. People say, "Well, the *españoles* [Spaniards] put her there." I'm passionate about this and I've read that the *españoles* would have been too afraid to give the Indians anything that had to do with their Indian traditions. Our Lady of Guadalupe also represents the feminist face of God. This opens up to us a new way of looking at our faith, which definitely is not European. It's a perspective we need in the Americas for everyone, not just for the Latino community. It's a point of view like the one expressed in the *Popol Vuh*, which is that God is both mother and father of the earth.[8] It's a much more holistic story.

I always say to my students, "The *abuelitas* [grandmothers] are the theologians of our Latino community because they were keepers of our collective memory. Pay attention. They are a walking memory. We need to thank God for this kind of oral history project that will hopefully preserve some of our memories before we all forget and the *abuelitas* are gone." My mother's family came from Mexico during the persecution of the Church, so they carry stories in which practicing your faith meant death. They say that people from Jalisco are more Christian than the Pope! I told my mom, "Now come on. Calm down!" But I would say they're very different from the Chihuahuans, like my father. My mother will talk about how they hid the priests and the sisters in their homes. The Eucharist was a privilege for them and they had it in the home. It was such a clandestine situation. I don't think we can separate our stories from our faith. The stories are wonderful, and they tell us who we are. I would certainly put Guadalupe as number one. I remember getting up at five in the morning to go give flowers in my First Communion dress. I didn't remember exactly what the whole story was about, but I remember there was *pan dulce* [sweet bread] and chocolate afterwards and it was a lot of fun! But then I realized, "My God, this depth . . ." In the Latino community, our faith flows from aesthetics. I think the Anglo suffers because they so often have such a rational, logical approach. I think the story of Guadalupe says as much or more as St. Thomas of Aquinas and his wonderful books.

## "WE STILL HAVE A LOT TO DO"

I feel the diocese has grown a lot although there is a lot more to do. I am concerned about the lack of Latino kids in Catholic schools. Only 9 percent of them attend Catholic schools, which isn't very many. I know that if Latino kids go to Catholic schools, they learn. The topic of education is troublesome to me, and I don't know what will happen. The middle-class kids can't go to Catholic schools because it's just too expensive. But we have to look at endowments and those kinds of things because we have an obligation. We can't just let ourselves off the hook. We still have a lot to do.

Are we going to have more lay leaders? The diocese at San José now has the *Escuela de Ministerios* [Ministry School] and they have a whole track in Spanish. I have taught in it and it's good. I'd like to see some of those young people go to the university. I think we have to keep pushing for the next level, especially for the young adults. They can do it. I'm very interested in seeing if there's ever going to be an affiliation with Santa Clara University or the University of San Francisco. I know they were talking about it and it would be quite interesting.

The cultural part is always a challenge and intriguing and gets me passionate. It's faithful, it's a struggle, and it's sexy. I'm talking about sexuality in the larger sense that faith is sexuality. Life is sexuality. But we've reduced it so much in our culture, which is too bad. It's embodiment. Talking about life and engaging with my students and my community gets me passionate. I find some *viejitas* [old ladies] over here who are ninety years old and have taught for sixty or seventy years. They have built the community without a lot of support. These are women in the Church, and they are not just Latinas. The Church was built on the backs of women, but unfortunately they still need to be recognized for what they've done. I look at the women religious who have built the schools in this country with nothing and living out of cloister. I think, "Wow, that's really something." There's a wonderful Filipino Baptist theologian at the GTU and he says, "You can't just put your culture on a pedestal like it's the only thing." That's one thing I've learned from my Chicana days. But as you grow up, you have to go through thinking that your culture is the only one alive and it's on a pedestal. Learning about various pieces of who we are and different cultures is very exciting to me because we have so much in common.

I think the voice and place of women in the Church is still a struggle. Yes, she's accepted more. Yes, I think that we have women who are probably doing more than some priests but are not being recognized for it. But it shouldn't be that way. We should start recognizing women too, officially. I think that the Holy Spirit is bigger than all this and it's going to happen. It may not happen in my lifetime, but I think it will happen. There's still patriarchy and that's very, very painful. I'm not saying all of them are like that, but it's still structured that way. But I also say that some of the sisters and the rest of us can act in the same way too. It's not only in the priesthood. I love having women at the theological table because we have to bring these issues out, even though we're not supposed to talk about them. We're faithful, but we also have to be faithful to truth. Intellectual truth is absolutely important. But I don't think we should just be *gritonas* [loudmouths] without doing our homework. Truth is truth and has to continue to be brought out. It's how you do it. I can bring the truth out more in writing, in teaching, and, when it's appropriate, in the picket line. I try to be loyal and faithful to my church. It's painful to think about some of the things the Church has done and not done. But at the same time I believe we are the Church. No one can kick us out. We are it. I look at the religious giants like Teresa de Avila and Sor Juana Inés who lived with tragedy.[9] But look at what they did and said. They really spoke out. We must too.

## NOTES

1. Sal Si Puedes [Get Out if You Can] was an economically poor neighborhood in East San José where César Chávez and his family lived.

2. In 1969, César Chávez organized a march from Indio, California, to Coachella, California, to protest the practice by growers of hiring undocumented workers from Mexico as strikebreakers during the Grape Strike. The march lasted nine days. Thousands joined the marchers along the way including celebrities, politicians, and hundreds of farm workers. For more on this march, see Richard Griswold Del Castillo and Richard A. Garcia, *César Chávez: A Triumph of Spirit* (Norman: University of Oklahoma Press, 1995).

3. Virgil Elizondo, a well-known theologian, pastor, and popular speaker. Author of *Galilean Journey: The Mexican American Promise* (Maryknoll, NY: Orbis Books, 1983); Virgilio P. Elizondo and Timothy M. Matovina, *Mestizo Worship: A Pastoral Approach to Liturgical Ministry* (Collegeville, MN: Liturgical Press, 1998).

4. Bishop Roland Pierre DuMaine was named by Pope John Paul II to be the first bishop of the new Diocese of San José, where he was installed officially on March 18, 1981. He retired in 1999.

5. Sister Ana María Pineda is currently a faculty member in the Religious Studies Department at Santa Clara University.

6. David Tracy is the Andrew Thomas Greeley and Grace McNichols Greeley Distinguished Service Professor of Catholic Studies and Professor of Theology and the Philosophy of Religion in the University of Chicago Divinity School. He is the author of *The Analogical Imagination: Christian Theology and the Culture of Pluralism* (New York: Crossroad, 1981).

7. Edwin Aponte and Miguel de la Torre, ed., *The Handbook on Latina/o Theology* (St. Louis, MO: Chalice Press, 2006).

8. *Popol Vuh is* the book of scripture of the *Quiché*, a kingdom of the postclassic Maya civilization in highland Guatemala.

9. Saint Teresa de Avila (1515–1582) was a Spanish Carmelite nun and mystic who was a leading figure in the Counter-Reformation. Sor Juana Inés de la Cruz (1651–1695) was an important colonial Mexican intellectual and literary figure who fought for women's rights.

# Index

# About the Authors

Francisco Jiménez is Fay Boyle Professor in the Department of Modern Languages and Literatures at Santa Clara University. He received his B.A. from SCU and Ph.D. from Columbia University under a Woodrow Wilson Fellowship. He has published and edited several books, including *Poverty and Social Justice: Critical Perspectives*, *The Identification and Analysis of Chicano Literature*, and *Los episodios nacionales de Victoriano Salado Alvarez*. His autobiographical books *The Circuit* and *Breaking Through* have received several national literary awards. He was selected the 2002 U.S. Professor of the Year by CASE and the Carnegie Foundation for the Advancement of Teaching.

Alma M. García is professor of sociology at Santa Clara University. She received her Ph.D. from Harvard University. Her publications include *Narratives of Second Generation Mexican American Women*, *The Mexican Americans*, and *Chicana Feminist Thought: The Basic Historical Writings*. Her 1989 article, "The Development of Chicana Feminist Discourse, 1970–1980," has been published in fifteen anthologies and was named one of the fifty "Classic Articles on Race and Gender" by the Memphis Center for Research on Women. Her current research project is on Latina day laborers in Silicon Valley.

Richard A. Garcia is professor of history at California State University, East Bay. An intellectual cultural historian, he is author of *The Rise of the Middle Class, San*

*Antonio 1929–1941* (1991); coauthor of *Cesar Chavez: Triumph of Spirit* (1995) with Richard Griswold Del Castillo and *Notable Latino Americans* (1997) with Matt S. Meier and Conchita Franco Serri; and coeditor of *Race and Ethnicity* (2000) with Alma M. Garcia. His latest article is "Religion as Language, Church as Culture: Changing Chicano Historiography," published in *Reviews in American History*.

CPSIA information can be obtained
at www.ICGtesting.com
Printed in the USA
FSHW020014020821
83737FS